GW00992296

OIL AND EMPIRE

OIL AND EMPIRE

British Policy and Mesopotamian Oil 1900–1920

MARIAN KENT

THE LONDON SCHOOL OF ECONOMICS
AND POLITICAL SCIENCE

First published 1976 by
THE MACMILLAN PRESS LTD
London and Basingstoke
Associated companies in New York
Dublin Melbourne Johannesburg and Madras

SBN 333 15451 7

Printed in Great Britain by
Cox & Wyman Ltd
London, Fakenham and Reading

To my parents

Contents

List of Plates

(*between pages 82 and 83*)

Preface

This volume is the first product of researches in which I have been engaged for a number of years and in which my aims have been to examine the efforts of British governments to obtain and safeguard oil supplies for the armed forces and the economy, and to assess how such efforts contributed towards evolving a national oil policy and affected foreign policy.

My research began when I worked in the University of London on a doctoral dissertation. The present book is based on my work of that time. I have examined the years from 1900 to 1920; that is, I have included the crucial period when oil became a major source of energy for the British economy in general and the armed forces in particular, and I have included the catalytic period of the First World War.

During this period the main hope for increasing the quantity and security of Britain's oil was seen to lie chiefly in the two areas of strong British influence, Persia and Mesopotamia. The Persian monopoly was secured as early as 1914. I have therefore devoted my attention in this book almost entirely to Mesopotamia, although where Persian oil affected oil policy development, as in the 1912–14 period, account has been taken of that as well. The fundamental policy aims laid down for Persian oil in that period were adhered to for Mesopotamian oil from 1912 to 1920, even though the methods of achieving them developed differently.

The development and pursuit of oil policies in the first two decades of the century laid clear lines for government and diplomacy to follow. Further development and extension of policy during the next two decades, up to the beginning of the Second World War, will be treated in succeeding volumes.

Although a good deal has been written on oil and foreign policy and on Middle East oil itself, much of what has been written has necessarily suffered from lack of information and lack of accuracy. The major documentary sources have only recently become available, under the thirty-year rule of access to British official records, and I have found this material vast and invaluable. In addition, some material in the possession of oil companies had not been accessible until it was made available to me. The great wealth of detailed information on which I was thus able to draw has therefore at last made possible a detailed examination of the subject.

In the course of my work I have had the assistance of many institutions and individuals, to whom I owe thanks. For documentary material made available to me I want to thank the following: the Public Record Office, the India Office Library and the former Ministry of Power, for official British Government records and private papers; the British Museum, for the Balfour papers; the Foreign Office Library, for the Arthur Nicolson papers, since placed in the Public Record Office; the Bodleian Library and the Librarian of New College, Oxford, for the Milner papers; the Birmingham University Library for the Austen Chamberlain papers; the Cambridge University Library for the Hardinge papers; the Librarian of St Antony's College, Oxford, for microfilms of the papers of Sir Mark Sykes and of Captain William Yale; Mr A. Pearsall and the National Maritime Museum, Greenwich, for the Sir W. Graham Greene papers; Mr A. J. P. Taylor and the Beaverbrook Library for the Lloyd George papers; and the London Library for the A. T. Wilson papers.

I wish also to thank Mr W. C. B. Tunstall for permission to use the Julian Corbett papers, and Mr B. Sherman for facilitating this; the late Colonel Robert Henriques for obtaining permission for me to use the Bearsted papers, and his kind hospitality to me while I used them; Mr Mark Bonham Carter for permission to use the Asquith papers, deposited in the Bodleian Library; the Institute of Petroleum Library and the Library of the Shell International Petroleum Company Ltd, London, for allowing me access to their resources.

The Shell International Petroleum Company Ltd and the Bataafse Internationale Petroleum Maatschappij NV, The Hague, are owed particular thanks, for allowing me to use their archives, and so too is Miss Daphne Griffin, who arranged access to these.

I have had kind advice and assistance from Professor M. S. Anderson of the London School of Economics; Miss Elizabeth Monroe of St Antony's College, Oxford; Professor Bernard Lewis, of the School of Oriental and African Studies; Brigadier S. H. Longrigg, D. Litt.; Sir Reader Bullard; Mr J. Collard; Dr Lawrence Lockhart; Dr Rose Louise Greaves; and Dr Yukka Nevakivi. I owe particular thanks to Professor W. N. Medlicott, formerly of the London School of Economics.

For their invaluable help with photographic and other research, cartography and typing I should like to thank Miss Ann Hoffman, Mr Graham Willoughby, Miss Eva Takacs and Miss Maria Giuffre.

The research for this volume was made possible by awards from the University of London and the Central Research Fund. The publishers and I gratefully acknowledge the generous financial assistance given by the Flinders University of South Australia and the Isobel Thornley Bequest of the University of London, without which this book could not have been published; and I want to thank the Publications Committee of the London School of Economics for their practical assistance.

M.K.

NOTE ON SPELLING

The spellings adopted here for names of persons and localities are those commonly occurring in official British Government correspondence of the time. A number of names that are not to be found in official correspondence have been spelt according to common English usage.

Part I
The Background

1 Introductory

By the beginning of the twentieth century, European interests had already acquired important economic and political influence in the Ottoman Empire. The empire was vast in size, sprawling over the Near and Middle East from the Balkans to North Africa and the Arabian peninsula. The cost of administering so large an empire and subduing its dissident parts was never successfully met by what appeared to European observers to be a corrupt and inefficient bureaucracy led by capricious and extravagant rulers. The empire had sunk more and more into debt to British and other European financiers. A large proportion of the national revenues was pledged to the foreign-organised Ottoman Public Debt Administration, in order to service old debts and stand surety for the raising of new revenue, which was then, as likely as not, used for military adventures.[1] Although possessing great and largely untapped mineral, and therefore industrial, potential, the empire lacked the financial resources and technical expertise with which to develop its natural wealth and organise its own services. European investors could provide both, and concessions for a great variety of undertakings were easily obtained in return for loans and advances to the government, and *baksheesh* (gratuities) to its members.[2] Even the Young Turk revolution of 1908–9, which removed Sultan Abdul Hamid and reimposed the old constitution, achieved little in the way of reforming and modernising the empire, and 'degenerated into a kind of military oligarchy', which ended with the defeat of the Ottoman Empire in 1918 amid 'failure, bitterness, and disappointment'.[3]

The European governments were themselves deeply involved in the fortunes of the Ottoman Empire. The ostensible reason for this involvement was to provide support for the interests of their nationals.[4] European residents in Turkey were protected by the capitulations, treaties ensuring them extra-territorial rights, and European traders and investors were assisted also by low Turkish customs duties, which could be raised only with the consent of their governments. Basically, however, each of the European powers wished to obtain as strong an influence as possible in an empire that appeared to be on the point of collapse and fragmentation, and was geographically of vital strategic importance in the world. To Russia, the Ottoman Empire was an obstacle blocking her southwards expansion and preventing her from having free access to the Mediterranean. Similarly, her expansionist ambitions were to some extent frustrated by Britain's influence in Persia. France had obtained a strong position in Turkish finance and railways and was particularly interested in securing predominance in Syria and in the North African provinces of the empire. Italy also was fishing in troubled waters, and sought territory and concessions in parts of Anatolia and areas south of the Mediterranean. Germany had since the late nineteenth century, when she took up her large railway-construction concessions, been rapidly overtaking Britain's previously paramount influence in Anatolia and the Asiatic Turkish provinces. With the Baghdad railway her main instrument, she intended to open up the Near and Middle East to German economic exploitation and political influence, check British predominance in the Persian Gulf and beyond, and open the way to the heart of the British Empire, India. These same reasons in reverse motivated British Government policy in Asiatic Turkey, as will be shown in the next chapter. If British interests were maintained and strengthened, on land in Turkey's Asiatic provinces and in neighbouring Persia, and at sea by control of the Suez Canal and the Persian Gulf, then it was considered that the British Empire would be safe against both Russian and German threats.

Such specific strategic and general economic considerations were not the only reasons why Britain was vitally interested in this area. Oil had become important, and an area of such promising oil potential as the Middle East would have attracted attention for this reason alone.

In the early years of this century oil, as its uses multiplied and its propellant qualities were increasingly utilised, was gradually coming to achieve a more important position in the British economy.[5] Further, one of the British Admiralty's most vital concerns in the years immediately preceding the First World War was to obtain and secure a satisfactory supply of fuel for the Navy. The coming of Churchill to the Admiralty in October 1911, and his close association with Admiral Fisher, who had long prophesied war against the growing strength of the German navy, heightened this preoccupation. Britain was, albeit somewhat belatedly, joining the revolution in marine engines and their fuel. Oil had many advantages over coal as a fuel, and, on a weight-for-weight basis, provided more power, used less space, and was considerably cleaner and easier to handle than coal was.

However, at this time virtually all Britain's oil came from the USA and Russia, with much smaller amounts coming from the Dutch East Indies and Roumania, Mexico superseding Roumania only from about 1913 onwards. With the exception of Mexico, all these countries were outside Britain's control; indeed, the world's largest oil concerns were of American, Russian and Dutch nationality.[6] In addition, these were years of steadily rising oil prices. The possibility of obtaining oil from sources and companies amenable to British control was therefore attractive to the British Government, and as a a result Mesopotamia and Persia acquired even wider significance than the strategic and commercial considerations already indicated would suggest. In these areas companies, backed by their governments, were scrambling for concessions, and British companies could hope to obtain them only if they had at least the tacit support of their government.

A number of British Government departments were involved in giving such support to British nationals. These included the Foreign Office, which up to about 1916 effectively framed British policy towards Middle East oil concessions as an adjunct to wider political considerations. From about 1912, however, the Admiralty came very much to the fore in formulating policy for this area. The Admiralty stated its oil needs, which were to be met extensively from Middle East resources, and the Foreign Office was left to translate Admiralty demands into foreign policy. So far the Admiralty had largely relied on buying its oil from commercial companies. Its oil purchasing policy was in the process of changing, and through Middle East oil it sought to attain security of supply as well as stability of price. In translating Admiralty demands into foreign policy the Foreign Office was obliged to consult increasingly in that area. From about 1913 onwards the Board of Trade was called in to provide expert advice on the more commercial and technical aspects of the oil concession negotiations in which the Foreign Office found itself increasingly involved. The extensive involvement of British Government departments makes it clear that the Government did all in its power to help British concession hunters in the Ottoman Empire and in Persia, and it is this theme that will be developed in succeeding chapters.[7]

Up to the early years of the war the framing of policy remained the preserve of the Foreign Office. This meant, during the Foreign Secretaryship of Sir Edward Grey, that it was effectively in the hands of his permanent officials. It was after Grey left the Foreign Office in 1916 that the framing of policy was taken over by other bodies, notably the War Cabinet (strongly influenced by the War Office), and later the Petroleum Executive. Between 1918 and 1920 even the Prime Minister, Lloyd George, from time to time usurped this power.[8] Nevertheless, British foreign policy concerning concessions in the Ottoman Empire was basically consistent throughout the period. This policy was that the interests of British nationals in the Ottoman Empire, as in any other foreign country, must be upheld and 'fair play' ensured. However, due to the additional factor of the great strategic importance of Mesopotamia, their interests would, if necessary, be supported extremely strongly, even to the extent of issuing ultimata and taking retaliatory action against the Ottoman Government. The Foreign Office normally accorded equal support to all British nationals with equal claims and acceptable backgrounds, though to avoid diplomatic embarrassment it would encourage rivals to come to terms with each other.

In one important respect, however, this general attitude did not hold with regard to the question of the Mesopotamian oil concession. One British claimant, William Knox D'Arcy, became the British Government's protégé, on the ostensible grounds that he had been first in the field. In fact there was an important reason for this patronage. D'Arcy had already established in neighbouring Persia the oil concern that came to be Britain's major economic undertaking in that country. Some preferential treatment was therefore due to him, and, as he pointed out increasingly frequently from about 1912 onwards, this was essential in order to preserve intact his Persian enterprise.

If D'Arcy was to be favoured by the British Government then this had to be at the expense of his rivals, the chief of which was Shell.[9] D'Arcy's Anglo-Persian Oil Company was clearly a purely British company, but Shell, after 1907, was 60 per cent owned by the Royal Dutch Petroleum Company. Furthermore, Holland and, therefore, its international companies were subject to strong German influence. Shell was consequently viewed with suspicion in its dealings with the British Government, the more so as it was part of a large and expanding combine suspected by the Government of attempting to form a world-wide cartel.[10]

Seeking to answer these problems led directly to attempts to evolve a British oil policy. There were two major steps in this evolution. The first was the Government's decision to buy a majority shareholding in D'Arcy's Anglo-Persian Oil Company. The Government's agreement and long-term contract with the company was concluded, the public was told, to help ensure adequate and reliable oil supplies for the Navy in time of war or peace. When war broke out almost immediately afterwards, this hope was shown in the short term to be illusory. Apart from supplying the local British Expeditionary Force and a small amount to the Royal Navy, Persian oil production was still minimal by the end of the war. Total output was less than 2 per cent of United States output,[11] and Britain obtained more than 80 per cent of her oil requirements from the USA.[12]

The exigencies of war led to the second major stage in the evolution of British oil policy. By the middle of the war, loss of tankers had left Britain extremely short of oil.[13] In addition, it had by then been discovered that oil was valuable not only for propelling ships, lorries and aeroplanes, but also on account of the fact that some varieties contain a significant proportion of toluol, a basic constituent of explosives. It was therefore essential to create an efficient machinery for the planning and co-ordination of oil supplies. Out of the wartime arrangements grew the Petroleum Executive and its offshoot, the Petroleum Imperial Policy Committee.[14] While the executive was to carry out oil policy and co-ordinate oil affairs, the committee was empowered to investigate the oil needs of the British Empire and to formulate an oil policy for dealing with them.

The bases on which it was stated that oil policy would be formed were those same British interests as have already been described, but with one important addition. Central to the formulation of oil policy was Britain's imperial position in the world and her strategic requirements. These would be upheld essentially through the British Government-controlled Anglo-Persian Oil Company and British control over the Mesopotamian oilfields. The potential of these oilfields was held to justify such a policy. The innovation in its execution was to be that, instead of attempting to avert the danger of a Shell stranglehold on Britain's oil supplies by avoiding close contact with that company and seeking to exclude it from Mesopotamia, the Government would now attempt to obtain control over the group, first by trying to neutralise the company's foreign component by submerging it under British control, and, second, where that did not succeed, by bringing the company and as much as possible of the Royal Dutch–Shell group under British control. It was hoped that in this way the British Government would be able to obtain control over even wider sources of oil supplies.

This development shows how far British oil policy had evolved within two decades. Initially the British Government would do no more than give its support to a particular concession seeker, in this case D'Arcy. Eventually, however, the Government thought in terms of gaining a controlling interest in a minor oil company operating in the Middle East, and of either forcing one of the world's major oil combines to merge with it or at least encouraging the combine to come under British Government control. Although in the event neither result came to pass, such developments were characteristic of the initial stages in the evolution of Britain's oil policy.

2 British Policy and Interests in Mesopotamia to 1920

Since the Mesopotamia oil negotiations could be isolated neither from Britain's general oil policy nor from her international dealings with other great powers, it is worth inquiring how they fitted into Britain's general Mesopotamian aims and preoccupations during these years. General international interest in the Ottoman Empire has already been indicated. But how were more specifically Mesopotamian interests occupying Britain during these years?

The basic aims of Britain's policy towards Mesopotamia between 1900 and 1914 changed little, despite the varied background against which they had to be pursued. Britain's basic aims were, first and foremost, the maintenance of her paramount influence in Mesopotamia, the Persian Gulf and beyond, and, second, the upholding of her special commercial interests in Mesopotamia. These two aims could be secured during this period only by achieving the further aim of maintaining Turkey's (and thus her empire's) territorial integrity, and that required that peace between the great powers continue. In short, strategic, commercial, and balance-of-power considerations were basic components of the British Government's attitude towards the Mesopotamian region of the Ottoman Empire.[1]

The background against which these aims were pursued was complex and changing. Basic to everything was the relationship between the British and Turkish Governments, and that was to fluctuate according to the Turkish regime in power. The Turkish side of the relationship was represented first by Abdul Hamid and his government, then by the Young Turk regime (whose initial attitude to the British later changed somewhat), and, finally, by the enemy Turkish Government of the First World War. Relations between the two sides were influenced also by the machinations and manipulations of the great powers as they competed for favour and, thus, for political and economic influence in Turkey's affairs. The climax – or *dénouement* – of this competitiveness came in the events of the First World War and the ensuing peace settlement with Turkey. The chief diplomatic question involving Britain's strategic, political and commercial interests in Mesopotamia was the negotiations over the Baghdad railway. Associated with, or parallel to, these negotiations were a number of others, over which, and as part of a general settling up of disputed matters in the pre-First World War setting, Britain and other powers tried to reach bilateral agreement with the Turkish Government.

Finally, all these negotiations took place within the conceptual framework of British Government thinking about Turkey. On the one hand, Britain saw herself as the morally upright, great imperial power, defending her own world interests while at the same time acting as international arbiter and conscience. On the other, the power she was dealing with appeared, except at the time of the Young Turk revolution, when transient and illusory hopes were raised, to be politically and morally decayed. Further, it was on the brink of disintegrating should not the international balance of power be maintained and the wolves restrained from tearing apart their prey.

In general, the British Government's relations with the Turkish Government were far from good in the period up to 1914. In the years before the Young Turk revolution the British Government found itself in a difficult situation largely through its moralistic tendency to urge Abdul Hamid to institute reforms in his realms, against his wishes, help to persecuted minorities being the main object of British representations, and in upholding, on occasions, the non-Turkish side to a dispute. At the same time the British Government, like any major European government, was keen to secure economic and political concessions within the Ottoman Empire, concessions dependent on the goodwill of the Sultan. Small wonder that Germany – seen by the Foreign Office and its diplomatic servants as unscrupulous and amoral – was able, in the competitive climate encouraged by the Sultan, to garner many rich fruits, in the form of economic concessions and political influence with the Sultan and his government, while British diplomacy had fewer and harder-won successes.[2]

The Young Turk revolution of mid-1908 seemed to both public opinion and government in Britain the great chance for Turkey's political and economic regeneration. The Sultan was deposed, the 1876 constitution was reimposed, and the prospects for Turkish reform and British investment seemed bright. The Foreign Office had telegraphed warmest congratulations to the new Turkish regime and instructed the British Embassy in Constantinople to do all it could to help the Turks. But the revolution lost both its pace and its initial reforming zeal, and the superior diplomatic influence that Britain had so recently acquired gradually slipped away again as Britain appeared to the Turks to resume her 'unco-operative' and moralistic former role. Germany was thus able to resume her own former role of best friend to the Turks.

During the pre-war years the British Government's hopes in Mesopotamia were unavoidably influenced by the negotiations over the Berlin–Baghdad railway. This railway was being constructed under an agreement of 1903 between the Turkish Government and the Baghdad

Railway Company, whereby the company's existing railway-concession rights were confirmed and extended, with permission being given for extension of the line, to the Persian frontier, the Mediterranean and the Persian Gulf, and for port construction, at Baghdad, Basra and the terminal point on the Persian Gulf. In addition, the company by means of, among other things, guaranteed payments per kilometre by the Turkish Government received preferential treatment to help with funds for construction and rolling stock, customs exemption for imported essential goods and tax exemption on the company's entire property and revenue for the whole period of the concession, and extensive mining, quarrying, forestry, and water rights along the railway's route, as well as a number of commercial concessions.

The railway thus represented a firmly held German concession, and was likely to be completed and operating within the foreseeable future. Once this happened British interests in Mesopotamia would be threatened far more than by any other railway in Anatolia. The Baghdad railway was to pass through a region long dominated by British Indian trade, passing important Shiah religious shrines visited each year by increasing thousands of British Indian subjects. The railway company's navigation rights on the Tigris river and its port rights at Baghdad and Basra threatened the long-held British monopoly of the Euphrates and Tigris Steam Navigation Company, while its mining rights, as will be seen in later chapters, were to create considerable difficulties for British oil hopes in the Mosul and Baghdad provinces. Apart from its threatened competition with British transport interests, through provision of a much more direct route to India, the railway was seen by Britain as a strategic threat. Britain had long held supremacy on the shores and waters of the Persian Gulf, where the *Pax Britannica* had, over the last hundred years, greatly reduced piracy, slaving, and tribal feuding. If the small existing German interests were supplemented by completion of a direct German railway, Britain's paramountcy in the Gulf region, which she saw as essential for the defence of her empire, would undoubtedly be threatened and possibly superseded, while at the same time British prestige would be sadly reduced.[3] Thus the implications of the Baghdad railway for British interests in Mesopotamia were great. Important considerations of prestige, strategy and commerce were at stake, and it is a measure of the reality and importance of Britain's and Germany's interests that in the years just prior to the First World War those countries undertook long negotiations jointly and with the Turkish Government to reach an accommodation.

By the middle of 1913 agreement had been reached on the Baghdad railway and also on a number of associated matters,[4] which, taken together, give a substantial picture of the diversity of British interests. The compromise arrangement reached regarding the railway was that two British directors would sit on its board, that the terminus would be at Basra – nearly 100 miles upstream from the Persian Gulf – and that any railway beyond Basra to the Gulf must have prior agreement from, and be on conditions acceptable to, the British Government. British interests were guaranteed equality of treatment on all railways in Asiatic Turkey, while the sole remaining British railway in the region, the Smyrna–Aidin railway, received permission to increase its mileage by over 50 per cent on a concession prolonged till 1999.

On river navigation, an Anglo-Turkish navigation commission was established for the Turkish-owned Shatt el Arab, the outlet to the Persian Gulf from the junction of the Tigris and Euphrates rivers. With British assistance, the commission was to ensure that this key waterway would be better conserved than previously and be open to all nations (although in 1912, for instance, 217 of the 240 ocean-going ships that entered it were in fact British).[5] British shipping was given formal predominance on the Euphrates and Tigris rivers, where British ships had held a virtual monopoly for over 200 years, and British participation in the ports company set up to construct port facilities at Baghdad and Basra was assured.[6]

The agreements helped consolidate Britain's authority in other important ways as well. One of the agreements signed was the Turco-Persian Frontier Protocol of November 1913. This provided for definite frontier demarcation by an international commission. Apart from its local importance, in seeking to end endemic frontier feuds, the definition of the frontier, and particularly of its southern half, was of special importance to Britain's Mesopotamian interests. For one thing, in an annex to the protocol the border running through the oil-bearing territory worked by the Anglo-Persian Oil Company under its concession from the Persian Government was settled in such a way that the company lost nothing.[7] In addition, British interests were served by the fact that the Turks were persuaded to recognise and define the special position and rights of the officially Persian, though in fact virtually independent, Sheikh of Mohammerah, with whom Britain had close treaty relations. His territories straddled the Shatt el Arab and he had long held much *de facto* power over shipping and commerce in both Persian and Turkish territories.[8] Britain had already secured influence in Koweit, and her agreement of 23 January 1899 with the Sheikh, supplemented by the secret agreement of 15 October 1907 securing British control over the Sheikh's land, was designed specifically to prevent the Baghdad railway from reaching the shores of the Persian Gulf except under conditions agreeable to Britain.[9] In other words, by the end of 1913 Britain controlled the only suitable outlet for the railway on the Persian Gulf, she controlled river access and egress between the Gulf and Basra, and she had secured participation in port construction at Baghdad and at the upstream railway terminus of Basra. Other agreements made at this time and bearing on Britain's interests in Mesopotamia included such general matters as Turkey's agreement to review and possibly reduce light dues levied upon shipping, her agreement to submit to arbitration a large number of pecuniary claims, and her agreement to regularise and confirm the legal position of British institutions – medical, religious and educational – in Turkey. The Mesopotamian oil negotiations and 1914 agreement are, of course, the outstanding example of a specific economic concession, and this is treated at length in succeeding chapters.

It might well be asked what induced the Turks to allow so many foreign favours at this time – since Britain was after all only one of the suppliant great powers, and not the favourite at that. The answer is that Turkey was subjected to great pressure from the other negotiators of parallel agreements, and that she had pressing needs of her own that needed great-power consent to be fulfilled. Fiscal concessions were to her the most important, since in her chronic economic need – increased, in the years immediately prior to the First World War, by the Balkan Wars – she could not raise extra revenue without great-power consent. The bargaining lever used constantly by the British and German Governments in their negotiations with Turkey was their threatened refusal to allow her to increase her customs duties from 11 to 15 per cent *ad valorem.* This she was eventually permitted to do, and in addition she obtained various other fiscal relaxations. Britain did not, however, allow her to abolish the capitulations system – that had to wait for unilateral action in the First World War.

One question long in the minds of European politicians and equally in the minds of the Turks, particularly in the years immediately prior to the First World War, was that of the fragmentation of the Ottoman Empire. Britain's policy in this period was to reiterate its belief in the territorial integrity of Asiatic Turkey. This, after all, was a necessity if Britain's basic aims were to be upheld. British prestige, and Britain's need to maintain her strategic hold on the Persian Gulf and protect her other interests in Mesopotamia were all seen to be dependent on a Turkish Mesopotamia. Given that, and the continuance of the existing weak and reasonably co-operative Turkish rule, Britain could retain her sphere of influence unaffected. However, should a general partition of Turkey's empire occur, Britain, though she would claim Mesopotamia, could not guarantee that she would get it – except in the case of victory in war, which is what eventually happened. In 1910 the Foreign Office officially informed the Turkish Government that 'The policy of Great Britain in Mesopotamia is directed towards the maintenance of the *status quo*, His Majesty's Government emphatically disclaim any designs of territorial aggrandisement in those regions and they are prepared to furnish the Ottoman Government with the most binding assurances to this effect.'[10] This was no mere piece of window dressing. It was in Britain's best interests to maintain Turkey's territorial integrity. In the period between August and November 1914, between the outbreak of the war in Europe and Turkey's entering it on the side of Britain's enemies, Sir Edward Grey repeatedly offered Turkey Britain's guarantee of upholding her territorial integrity.[11] This was done somewhat frantically to be sure, as a bait to induce Turkey not to enter the war, but it was only after Turkey had entered the war on the wrong side and Britain was being pressured by her own allies that, as will be seen in a later chapter, Britain changed her policy.

Britain had of course a great many other interests and aims in the Ottoman Empire. These ranged from electricity, dockyard, arsenal, and banking concessions in Constantinople, to training the Turkish Navy and providing a British appointee as customs adviser. But Mesopotamia and the Persian Gulf were the key to what really mattered to Britain. Commercial interests, prestige, and maintenance of Turkish territorial integrity all played a part in British official calculations, but in basic analysis what mattered above all else was strategy. The Mesopotamia–Persian Gulf region was a crucial region for British strategical thinking, which underlay not only the complicated Mesopotamian oil negotiations, but also all significant British Government involvement in Turkish affairs.

During the war British policy evolved, not surprisingly, somewhat differently. Britain was involved in fighting in the Middle East for a variety of reasons. These included the need to protect her routes to India and her interests in Egypt and Mesopotamia, to open up the Dardanelles for supplies to Russia (one of Britain's allies) and, once that campaign was failing, to conduct a successful Mesopotamian campaign, so to regain face in the eyes of her Moslem subjects in India, who had already been stirred up against their British overlord through a call to religious war by the Turks. But the war situation meant that Britain had to integrate strategic objectives with practical considerations. It was wartime pragmatism that more than anything else led Britain to abandon her former concern for Turkish territorial integrity, to agree to Russian claims for Turkish territory and then to join in the paper division of the Ottoman Empire with France and, later, other allies. Britain's concern remained with Mesopotamia, for which, as for Palestine, she was subsequently to receive the mandate. But under the Sykes–Picot Agreement, the chief wartime Anglo-French partition plan, part of Mosul – the supposed oil-rich part of Mesopotamia – was granted to France, not Britain. This indicates that Britain was influenced more by non-economic than by economic factors, when it came to defining her own requirements.

At the end of the war, however, the allied victors were faced with an awkward situation in the Middle East. In the pressure of war, apparently conflicting promises had been made to Arab, Jew, and European ally respectively, and these promises now had to be met and reconciled.

Britain had realised almost immediately the Sykes–Picot Agreement was made that the territorial boundaries it defined were a mistake. This was partly because with Russia's withdrawal from the war and the agreement, the need for a buffer against her was gone; but by the end of the war, British policy makers realised also that in giving up to France the one area where Britain might have had unlimited oil potential under her own control was a serious error, made worse by France using it as a lever to further her own territorial ambitions with regard to Syria. The whole process of adjustment took some eighteen months, ending with the conference of San Remo in April 1920. By this time British desiderata and policy had been worked out, through prolonged interdepartmental discussion, and, with the armed-services leadership still dominant in Britain's councils, strategic motives were again supreme. Even gaining control of Mesopotamian oil supplies was, as we shall see in later chapters, part of general strategic and defence planning; marketing of the oil had value only to the commercial oil companies and, in a way, to the Mesopotamian administration, which looked to oil royalties to help cover some of its costs. In terms of *foreign* policy, marketing profits were not a consideration.

In general, therefore, British foreign policy towards Mesopotamia provided a fairly consistent pattern against which British oil policy could evolve. Throughout the period in question, this policy sought to secure recognition of Britain's paramount position, whether in the capacity of adviser or of mandatory guardian, in Mesopotamian affairs, and sought to uphold British individuals' commercial and other interests in the area, so long as they did not conflict with basic political considerations. Above all, it sought all these things in the interests of the British Empire at large, to which this region was a key.

3 Early Rivalries for the Mesopotamian Oil Concession 1900–12

Early interest in oil seepages – The Ottoman Government and the procedure for obtaining concessions – The Anatolian and Baghdad railway companies' concessions – D'Arcy's interest in obtaining a Mesopotamian oil concession, and British diplomatic support for him – Analysis of the German interests' position under the 1904 agreement – Renewal of British negotiations, 1906–7 – Other competitors – Opinions on D'Arcy's claims – The Young Turk revolution and its effect on D'Arcy's negotiations – The effect of German pressure on the Ottoman Government – Competition from Shell – Frederick Lane's scheme – The Eastern Petroleum Syndicate – The Euxine and Marmora British Development Syndicate – German and British Government opposition to the Chester and Glasgow schemes – D'Arcy's scheme 1911–12 – Summary of chapter

In Mesopotamia, as in Persia, certain areas had for thousands of years been known to contain oil springs and seepages, but, apart from primitive local uses, there was no developed industry.[1] European interest in the possibility of exploiting Mesopotamian oil commercially had been manifested since the last quarter of the nineteenth century. Individuals and expeditions visited the area, and even before the turn of the century numerous reports had been made on its oil potential. As early as 1871 a German expedition reported favourably on the prospects,[2] while in the 1890s several reports were made,[3] either to the home governments or to learned societies, or, as in the case of C. S. Gulbenkian,[4] to the Turkish Government. The Ottoman administration was thus forced to become aware of this possible rich source of of revenue,[5] and at the suggestion of Agop Pasha, Director of the Privy Purse, Sultan Abdul Hamid issued firmans in 1888 and 1898 (renewed in 1902) that placed the revenue of the oil properties of the Mosul and Baghdad vilayets (provinces) under the control of the Sultan's Civil List. Thenceforth any negotiations for oil concessions in these areas had to be conducted directly with the Civil List authorities. Legal rights to any concession could be obtained by a concession seeker only through an official contract, an imperial firman, or by a *permis de recherche*.

Permis were initially given for one year, and, if by the end of that time the Ministry of Mines was satisfied with the nature of the preliminary exploration completed, it would extend the period for another year. If during this extra period further exploration or work was carried out and the minister was satisfied with the ability and resources of the concessionaire, he might grant the applicant a firman of concession.[6]

The first foreign concession that concerned Mesopotamian oil was obtained in 1888 by the Anatolian Railway Company, an operating company financially organised and controlled by the Deutsche Bank.[7] It was to build and operate a railway continuing the Haidar Pasha–Ismid railway from Ismid to Angora, and the concession provided also for the possibility that the line might eventually be continued to the Persian Gulf. At the same time the company obtained from the Turkish Government a promise of preferential treatment with regard to mining rights. This was confirmed in the Baghdad Railway Convention of 1903,[8] which permitted the continuation of the railway line from Konia to the Persian Gulf and included definite mineral and oil exploitation rights, applicable to a twenty-kilometre strip on either side of the proposed line. That oil was recognised as being an important aspect of the concession is clear. In 1900 Sir Nicholas O'Conor, the British Ambassador in Constantinople[9] wrote of the scheme, 'Discoveries of bitumen and naphtha would greatly increase the productiveness of the line.'[10] The German viewpoint was expressed plainly by Dr Paul Rohrbach, who in 1902 wrote a pamphlet on the Baghdad railway and the related political and economic considerations.[11] Among the latter he included the petroleum springs in the Kirkuk area, commenting,

> . . . we ought to attach the greatest importance to the circumstance that the Baghdad Railway will pass close to the petroleum districts. The only thing to be feared is that foreign gold and foreign speculators should succeed in securing a preferential right in the exploitation of Mesopotamian naphtha before any effective German initiative has been taken.

German initiative was taken. Article 22 of the 1903 Baghdad Railway Convention gave the Germans a preferential – though not a monopolistic – right over oil along the line,[12] and the following year, in July 1904, the Anatolian Railway Company, acting for the Deutsche Bank, signed a contract with the Civil List authorities.[13] Article 1 of this contract gave the company a one-year option to undertake preliminary investigations – '*les études préliminaires* (*sondages et autre*)' – for oil in the Mosul and Baghdad vilayets. At the end of the year the complete results and their cost had to be reported to the Civil List, and the Ottoman Government undertook that if the company then applied to work the deposits it would conclude with it a special convention, granting a forty-year concession (Article 2). If after completing the preliminary study, the company declined to exploit the deposits, the Civil List could dispose of them to others without the company's having the right to claim any expenses or indemnity; but, should the exploitation convention not be concluded for any other reason, the Civil List undertook to repay the company with interest at 5 per cent per annum the expenses of the preliminary study, while the company would retain a right to receive preference in any future tenders submitted on terms equal to those offered by any other person or company who might wish to obtain the concession for exploitation (Article 6). This contract was of particular importance for the Mesopotamian oil scramble, for much of the ensuing negotiations and international discussion hinged on the question of whether or not it had been fulfilled.

The years 1904 to 1912 saw the development of interest in Mesopotamian oil, chiefly among British, German and American concerns, and during this period they established the bases of their claims. The practice of sending out 'scientific' or 'archaelogical' missions, conveniently studying what were also the best known oil areas,[14] became supplemented and finally openly replaced by strong diplomatic intervention at Constantinople on behalf of the various would-be concessionaires.

British interests in Mesopotamian oil were represented primarily by William Knox D'Arcy.[15] After obtaining the neighbouring Persian oil concession in 1901, he sent his representative, Alfred Marriott, to Constantinople to seek one for Mesopotamia,[16] for even at that stage it was realised that the Mesopotamian and Persian oil springs and seepages were probably part of similar oil-bearing geological strata. Marriott was unsuccessful and was replaced in 1903 by H. E. Nichols.[17] During these early years the British Foreign Office was informed of D'Arcy's interest in the concession and was inclined to regard it favourably. This is shown by the fact that in March 1904 D'Arcy's efforts had interested the Foreign Secretary, the Marquess of Lansdowne, sufficiently for him to instruct O'Conor at Constantinople to pass on to Nichols certain information respecting the Mesopotamian oil deposits.[18] By mid-September O'Conor was reporting rumours of the Anatolian Railway Company's 'concession' for the Mosul and Baghdad vilayets, but, when the Embassy approached Nichols to suggest that perhaps the time had come when it might usefully intervene at the Porte on D'Arcy's behalf, the offer was not accepted.[19] Nichols said he was at present actively negotiating with the Palace and was still optimistic about the outcome; diplomatic intervention was more likely to complicate and retard than to hasten a favourable solution. This was an unfortunate miscalculation for the D'Arcy interests, for some weeks later the existence of the German contract became known and verified,[20] and in the meantime the D'Arcy group had decided that it was not worthwhile pursuing the concession. Their reasons for not continuing to negotiate with the Turks were given later[21] as want of good faith among their partisans at the Palace, the difficulty of finding in London the large amount of capital required to cover the initial expenses of forming an Ottoman-registered company, and the predisposition of the Sultan to give the concession to the Germans anyway. At the same time, in August 1905, the Germans' railway and petroleum survey expedition returned after seven months to Constantinople and, as the British Embassy reported, it appeared to be well satisfied with the results obtained.[22] In November the Embassy further reported that the Germans had successfully renewed for another year their 1904 agreement with the Civil List.[23]

This, though believed by the British Government of the time and since then generally accepted by historians, was not the case.[24] In fact, the Germans and English saw the events of these years differently from each other, and to date very little has been known about either view. Both interpretations need to be presented, because each of the two main rivals relied on its own version of events as a guide to action. To a large degree, their respective activities, in competition and later in co-operation, were based on misconception of each other's position and on bluff about their own.

The real facts about the German position from mid-1905 can be established substantially from the original correspondence exchanged between the Turkish Civil List Ministry and the board of the Anatolian Railway Company.[25] On 8 August 1905 (letter 1) the Minister of the Civil List, Ohannès Effendi Sakisian, wrote to the Anatolian Railway Company pointing out that the year's term permitted by the 1904 contract had expired and asking the company to remit the results of its investigations. The company replied on 4 September (letter 2) that it had now heard from its exploration mission. As the geological samples had only just arrived in Europe and would require careful analysis, it requested the Turkish Government to extend the original time limit of one year, by a further ten to twelve months. The Minister of the Civil List responded on 22 October (letter 3) simply by requesting forthwith the company's geological report and a statement of exploration expenses incurred.

It seems very strange indeed that the company did not apply for an extension of the time limit earlier. It would have known well in advance that the deadline probably could not be met; it had waited six months after signing the 1904 agreement before sending out its exploration mission; and it did not ask for the extension until after the Turks had themselves written, after the expiration of the time limit. The Turks, it seems, in merely reiterating their request, were not prepared to give credence to the company's protestations about difficulties.

However, whether they were particularly patient, or dilatory or, more probably, in too weak a position *vis-à-vis* the Germans or their rivals, the Turks waited seven months before again pressing for the report. Then on 26 July 1906, almost a year after having initially asked the company for information, the Minister of the Civil List wrote again (letter 4), 'urgently requesting' a 'categorical reply'. This letter also went unanswered, and a fortnight later, on 9 August (letter 5) its message was repeated. In addition, the Minister pointed out that the company had already exceeded by thirteen months the time limit for making available to the Civil List the results of its exploratory work, and that for close on a year the Civil List had heard nothing from the company. The Minister referred to paragraph 6 of the 1904 convention, which stipulated that the concession for exploiting the oil area in question could be granted to others if the company did not wish to take it up. The company was therefore asked to send immediately the documents requested and inform the Civil List formally whether it intended to take up the concession.

The company at long last made its reply a fortnight later, on 22 August (letter 6), submitting its commission's report and a blanket statement of expenses incurred (340,000 francs). In the remainder of the letter the company could not have been more equivocal. Though it had been given one year, which it could spend on exploration, to make up its mind whether it wished to take up the concession for exploiting the region commercially, it did not say whether it had done so, but instead opened up a completely new discussion, stating that, although the results obtained by its exploration party had not been very encouraging, the company was nevertheless prepared to continue exploration by drilling. This would be expensive but was necessary to show definitively whether the fields warranted commercial exploitation; drilling would, however, not be proceeded with unless a new agreement were concluded between itself and the Civil List. In other words, the company wanted a new and 'mutually acceptable' contract before it would continue with its assessment of the oilfields' commercial potential, a matter that should have been settled under the previous contract.

Two months later, on 24 October (letter 7), the Minister wrote again to the company. He pointed out that the exploration report that had been submitted by the company with its last letter had been returned immediately for translation from German into Turkish and French, and that at the same time the company had been requested to submit the draft of a new convention. Nothing had been heard from the company.

Another month went by, and on 26 November (letter 8), the Minister yet again reminded the company that the Civil List had still received no answer whatsoever to its two urgent requests. When the translated report and the fifteen-article draft convention were received, they served only to add fuel to the fire. On 26 January 1907 (letter 9) the Minister wrote formally to the company that since exploration by drilling had been one of the company's undertakings under the 1904 convention and neither this nor the one-year time limit for completing the work had been observed, and, further, that since the company's recently submitted draft convention did not accord with the terms of its 1904 precursor, the Civil List declared that the 1904 convention had been broken.

This letter, at least, brought a swift reply. On 9 February 1907 (letter 10) the company denied that the 1904 convention contained such undertakings as were stated by the Civil List, and therefore 'categorically rejected' them. Apart from stressing the great expenses it had incurred, the company assured the Civil List that it had done 'more than could reasonably and scientifically be done', and stated that the company's rights therefore remained in full force.

The specific points raised by the Minister of the Civil List were not in fact discussed in this letter. These points were (a) that during the original one-year period the company had not done any drilling, drilling being held by the Turks to have been a condition of the original contract; and (b) that the original time limit had to date already been exceeded by eighteen months.

Were these points valid? The 1904 contract was undoubtedly quite clear about the one-year time limit, and, indeed, the Turks had never formally answered the company's application for a one-year's extension. Even if it could be argued that this extension had been granted by default, it had again been exceeded by six months, and that without a further request for more time having been made.

On the question of drilling, the 1904 convention was indeed extremely loosely worded. On the one hand, it could be held, that under the convention drilling was merely recommended and not made a condition (if indeed the phrase '*sondages et autres*' went so far as to mean 'drilling' at all). On the other, the company had undertaken by the contract to complete its investigations within one year, and to state whether it wished to take up a concession for exploitation. In its own letters it had admitted that, even one and a half years after the expiration of the time limit, it had still not sufficient preliminary studies, and that drilling was necessary to enable it to make its final assessment of the commercial viability of the oil sources. In that case, why had it not done so either during its permitted year or directly after?

On 4 March, in its reply (letter 11) to the company's communication, this was exactly the stand taken by the Turkish Government. The Turks reiterated that the original exploration period, of one year, had been exceeded by one and a half times. Further, the Turks stated explicitly that drilling was agreed on as 'obviously the method most likely to contribute to the establishment of the extent of the oil sources in question', and this the company had not done. Finally, the company had drawn up a totally unacceptable draft convention. Under the circumstances the Turkish Minister informed the company that 'there is absolutely nothing further that can be added to this matter', implying that the Civil List regarded itself free to act as it pleased.

The Turks had, in fact, already been quietly sounding out the British rivals of the German company. After having been becalmed for a few months in early 1906, British interests had begun to feel more hopeful again. In March 1906 the Foreign Office received pleasing news from O'Conor.[26] The Ambassador reported that he had heard recently that the Palace, needing an advance of £T50,000, had instructed the Civil List to invite the Germans to take up their option at that price. The Germans (O'Conor thought), convinced that their position was absolutely secure and that they could afford to defer taking any action until their railway plans were further advanced, and having also (thought Nichols) some difficulty in finding the full amount of the money, formally rejected the Civil List's proposal. This was taken by the Turks as a refusal by the Germans to exercise their preference rights, and an Imperial irade (literally, 'wish') ordered the Civil List to offer the concession on similar terms to any other reputable group. The Civil List accordingly began negotiations with an English firm in Constantinople, Messrs Gilchrist and Walker, who were looking after the D'Arcy group's interests. After three months' negotiations with the Civil List the British interests felt they were on the point of success.

As in most negotiations with the Turks, however, such hopes were overoptimistic, and a year later the situation was little different. In February 1907 Nichols called on the Ambassador. Messrs Gilchrist and Walker were trying to induce D'Arcy and the Burmah Oil Company[27] to provide the funds necessary for securing the concession, but these two, having between them already sunk £350,000 in Persia, so far without return, were anxious for reasonable security. The Civil List asked £T30,000 for 'preliminary expenses', and a deposit of £T50,000 as 'caution money', to be returned to the concessionaires if, after exploration, the oilfields did not appear profitable. Nichols therefore asked if the Embassy would support D'Arcy in securing the return of the caution money should the need arise. O'Conor agreed, and gave the Foreign Office his opinion that

> . . . there is every ground for believing that this concession, especially as Mesopotamia is developed by the extension of railway communications and irrigation works, will prove exceedingly valuable, and . . . the creation of such important British interests in that country will greatly enhance our influence and general position.[28]

The year 1907 showed also that other groups were becoming increasingly interested in the Mesopotamian oil concession. Among these were a Belgian group and a British group, the latter including Messrs J. W.

Whittall, a British firm of merchants in Constantinople, and H. F. B. Lynch, of the Euphrates and Tigris Steam Navigation Company.[29] The Foreign Office took care to inform D'Arcy of their existence,[30] but there was one competitor of whom neither D'Arcy nor the Foreign Office was yet aware. That same year the Shell Transport and Trading Company, newly combined with the Royal Dutch Company,[31] opened a Constantinople office, which, under Gulbenkian's direction, kept a careful eye on Mesopotamian oil claims.[32] Between March and June, members of the House of Commons asked the Foreign Secretary, Sir Edward Grey a number of questions about the relative legal status of the D'Arcy and German claims, while various other interested individuals proffered their opinions. Sir Adam Block, British President of the Ottoman Public Debt Administration, thought that the only practical solution to the two rival claims was combination.[33] Not only did he think the German opposition too strong, but in addition he believed that the Sultan had no wish to give the concession to anyone else, and that in any case the 1904 contract was too cleverly drawn up for the German claim to be completely disregarded. As early as April that year, O'Conor described the state of the D'Arcy negotiations succinctly when he wrote to Hardinge that 'Nichols is still hammering away at the Mesopotamian oilfields negotiations, but as he is on the point of closing something goes wrong and the Civil List slip out'.[34] In his opinion Nichols's only chance was 'to sweep the board by offering terms far beyond the greed of avarice', while at the same time refusing to pay a penny until the agreement was signed. By October he was so dissatisfied with Nichols's lack of progress that he half threatened to take the matter himself to the Sultan; it was only Nichols, who wanted to wait till he was in a stronger position, who persuaded him not to do so.[35]

In July 1908 the Young Turk revolution occurred and the 1876 constitution was reimposed.[36] All negotiations with the Sultan had to be suspended, and, by a decree of September 1908, confirmed in May 1909, control of the petroleum fields was transferred from the Civil List to the Ministry of Finance, to which all claims had to be resubmitted.[37] In November 1908 D'Arcy wrote to Hardinge asking for diplomatic support to help Nichols gain the concession, the grant of which he now thought likely.[38] Hardinge considered that D'Arcy was 'a man of substance, both physically and financially, and deserves encouragement'; consequently Gerard Lowther, the new Ambassador at Constantinople, was told to continue the Embassy's support of Nichols. No further progress could be made until the Turkish situation had cleared, and this at least meant waiting till the deposition of Sultan Abdul Hamid in April 1909,[39] but in June 1909 the Grand Vizir (then Hussein Hilmi Pasha) informed Lowther that the Council of Ministers had 'formally decided to give the concession' to the D'Arcy group.[40]

All was not to be so simple. At one moment the negotiations would seem to be proceeding smoothly, while at another a series of obstacles would appear.[41] First the Turks tried to reserve for government purposes certain wells (*gisements*) in the area covered by the concession, but strong D'Arcy group opposition modified this reservation into a stipulation that oil from certain wells should be sold to the Government at cost price. Then, when the D'Arcy group's proposals were all but agreed, the Minister of Finance, doubtless because of parliamentary pressure, suddenly informed Nichols that there would have to be a three-months' delay, for it was necessary first to publish the offer, in order to make sure that there was no one who would tender for the concession on terms more favourable to the Turkish Government. The group refused this proposal absolutely. Next the Turks proposed that they would not publish the D'Arcy offer, but merely put the concession up for the highest bid. Lowther thought that they had been prompted to do this 'partly by a not very serious offer made to them by an apparently not very serious Roumanian firm[42], but more especially by the fear of the responsibility for granting any concession whatever, lest it should be commented on unfavourably and to their disadvantage in the Parliament'. Finally, when the Ambassador discussed the subject with the Grand Vizir at the end of August, he was told that the Turkish Government would take no further action in the matter until the question of railway concessions had been settled.[43] A week later the Ambassador made a further effort, hinting (on the Foreign Office's suggestion) that unless this and other concessions were granted to British interests the British Government would not look favourably on the Turkish request for a 4 per cent increase in its customs duties; but this was of no avail.[44]

The Turks' attitude towards the D'Arcy group was undoubtedly influenced by renewed pressure from the Germans. On 19 June 1909 Huguenin, the Director-General of the Anatolian Railway Company, wrote to the Turkish Finance Minister, Rifaat Bey, officially reminding the Turkish Government of his company's oil 'rights'. In response to the Minister's reply of 8 July, which declared firmly that the company's lost rights could not be resurrected, the company issued a formal protest on 4 August. It threatened that if within fifteen days the Government did not recognise the company's claims, the company intended to take action in the courts to secure recognition of its rights and to claim all damages and costs. This threat apparently did not worry the Turks overmuch, and, hardly surprisingly, nothing further happened on either side. The Germans had taken the legally correct step in case of future need, by not allowing their 'claim' to lapse by default; they had now to wait for more propitious times before pressing their suit, and had also to acquire other avenues for doing so.

One cannot escape the conclusion that the Germans were well aware of the weakness of their claim, and might even to a great extent have lost interest in pressing it. As private correspondence between the

Constantinople and Berlin offices of the German railway companies shows, privately the Germans spoke quite frankly among themselves about the weakness of their case. One letter admits, 'Legally our rights to the petroleum wells are very weak . . ..'[45] This might explain the company's extreme dilatoriness in its dealings with the Turkish Civil List, and its lackadaisical approach to clinching the agreement. As for the Turks, the Civil List was prepared to overlook irregularities in the German company's behaviour so long as no other suitors were in the offing. As soon as a serious rival to the German company appeared – that is, Nichols – the Turks stirred themselves. The intentions of the German company then became of immediate concern, and, if it suited the Civil List, the company could be thrown to the wolves. German claims could then be denied, and possibly more favourable offers by an English group be given prior consideration.

The question of the railway concessions was to occupy the Turks and vex the British and German oil supplicants for several years, but during this time there was little the latter could do except watch, wait and protest. Meanwhile, in 1909, further competition appeared, the main contender being the Shell interests.[46] At the end of July Sir Marcus Samuel, Chairman of the Shell Transport and Trading Company, wrote to the Foreign Secretary that his group sought the Baghdad and Mosul oil concession and requested HM Government's support in obtaining it.[47] The Foreign Office replied that for a number of years it had been supporting the D'Arcy group, whose negotiations appeared to be on the point of completion. If it supported any other applicant it must be assured the company would be preponderantly British. Extremely reluctant even to grant an interview to the chairman of the company, Sir Marcus Samuel, the Foreign Office obviously did not consider the Royal Dutch–Shell combine as mainly British, since, after all, in any undertaking the Royal–Dutch held 60 per cent of the shares and Shell only 40 per cent. This point D'Arcy, when informed of Shell's interest in Mesopotamia, did not hesitate to underline, stating also that he had 'not the least desire to be associated with them in this business'.[48]

A further aspect of Shell's interest in Turkish oil displeased the Foreign Office. In September an associate of both Royal Dutch–Shell and Rothschild (Paris) oil interests and of Gulbenkian, Mr Frederick Lane,[49] presented to the Foreign Office a scheme for a comprehensive petroleum company in Turkey; this company's activities would include exploration, production, importation and marketing over the whole empire.[50] The concessionaires would pay the Turkish Government £300,000 per year and give it a share in the profits, and the Turkish Government would be able to raise a loan on the security of the revenue. Lane said that the prospect of being able to raise this loan was attractive to the Turks, who had all but accepted his proposition; but that now, prompted by the Germans, who themselves sought to establish such a company they required him to have his government's support. He indicated to the Foreign Office his reluctance to combine with D'Arcy, saying that the latter wished to obtain the concession merely to resell it, but that his (Lane's) associates intended to work it themselves.[51] The Foreign Office was strongly opposed in principle to what it saw as 'a huge international combine for the control of the petroleum markets of Turkey and the world', and consequently Lane's scheme did not gain its support.[52] In any case, its success seemed problematical, if only because of the conflict of interests involved. By Lane's own account to the Foreign Office he was associated with the Royal Dutch–Shell and with the Paris Rothschilds, and he warned the Foreign Office of the intrigues of the Deutsche Bank. Yet a letter from Arthur von Gwinner and Karl Helfferich (managing directors of the Deutsche Bank, and president and director respectively of the Anatolian and Baghdad railway companies) to Constantinople some months later showed not only that the Deutsche Bank was itself seeking an alliance in this with the Paris Rothschilds (and the Ottoman Bank), but that Lane had asked the Deutsche Bank to join in his own group's scheme. This scheme, however, the Deutsche Bank considered, 'was framed with insufficient knowledge and is quite unworkable'[53] while, to make quite sure that it would be so, the bank protested against it to the Turks.[54]

However, the Royal Dutch–Shell interests had at this time a further iron in the fire. On 26 November 1908 the Eastern Petroleum Syndicate had been incorporated, having developed out of the early efforts of Lt.-Col. Henry Picot and H. F. B. Lynch MP, and now it was joining those seeking the Mesopotamian oil concession.[55] The substantial businessmen numbered among its subscribers included members of the boards of Shell and the Royal Dutch, and an effort was made to formalise an agreement establishing close co-operation between the syndicate and the Anglo-Saxon Petroleum Company, a Royal Dutch–Shell subsidiary; the syndicate was to obtain the concession and then hand it on to the latter company. But the prepared draft agreement was never signed, due to disagreement over the degree of closeness necessary in the working arrangement, and the parties went their separate ways.

A further British interest in Mesopotamian oil during 1909 was that of R. L. Harmsworth, MP, who wrote to the Foreign Office late in August asking for diplomatic support in obtaining the concession.[56] The Foreign Office pointed out the competition of the D'Arcy group, and its own past support for that group, although promising to give Harmsworth 'the usual support' should the concession be put up to tender. But Harmsworth was unwilling to tender and the Foreign Office advised him, as it had Shell, to come to terms with D'Arcy. While Harmsworth was willing to do this, D'Arcy demurred. He tried to suggest that the other's financial standing was poor and that he was not genuinely interested in working the concession – with neither of which points the Foreign Office agreed – and Harmsworth declared his intention of continuing 'to pursue this matter to the utmost of my ability and resources'. However, until this intention materialised as 'a group of reliable English financiers', the Foreign Office found it had to follow D'Arcy's line after all, and declined to be of assistance to Harmsworth.

Nevertheless, it was the railway schemes that most troubled and delayed the would-be oil concessionaires. The most important of these schemes were American.[57] Mr Bruce Glasgow represented the Anglo–American firm of J. G. White and Co. and first applied for a railway concession in July 1909. Already, in March 1908, Admiral Colby M. Chester had applied to Sultan Abdul Hamid for a concession for a line from Aleppo to Alexandretta;[58] in August 1909 he renewed his application to the Turkish Government, but this time for a much larger concession. His syndicate was represented by his two sons, Commander Arthur Chester (who became its Constantinople agent) and Colby M. Chester Jr., and by their brother-in-law, C. Arthur Moore Jr.[59] These two American interests competed for virtually the same lines,[60] which were to run eastwards from Sivas, via Harput, Arghana, Diarbekir, Mosul and Kirkuk, to Suleimanyia, with branch lines to the Black Sea port of Samsun, to Youmourtalik on the Mediterranean (via Aleppo), and to Lake Van (via Bitlis).[61] Besides permitting the construction of railway lines, the concessions were to provide for the concessionary company to exploit all minerals, including oil, within a twenty-kilometre strip on each side of the line. The option period was sixteen months, during which time no other party might make similar studies or be given mining rights either in the forty-kilometre zone or in the petroliferous districts of the vilayets of Van, Bitlis and Mosul. Many Turks were genuinely interested, both for military and economic reasons, in increasing railway construction in their country, but this interest was so interwoven with their desire to raise money, their suspicion of foreigners (though this applied least of all to the Americans, who as yet had no vested economic interests in Turkey), their new-found national pride, and their natural tendency to play off rival groups against each other in order to obtain the best possible terms, that progress was slow. However, by autumn 1909 the competition between the two groups had resulted in the effective elimination of the Glasgow group – although for some time afterwards it was still trying to win support in London.[62] The project was taken up again in May 1911 by a group represented by the Earl of Denbigh (of the Rio Tinto Company Ltd), who wished to make it predominantly British. For some months he corresponded with the Foreign Office, seeking its support, but the scheme came to nothing.[63]

The Glasgow scheme had effectively been removed from the running by the better terms offered by the Chester group. These included, in particular, proposals for a wider-gauge railway and for only a ten-kilometre mining strip on each side of it.[64] The Chester group was also more impressively backed. Glasgow had received diplomatic assistance from the American Embassy in Constantinople, but, in addition to this, Chester had strong commercial backing and the support of the State Department.[65] Between 1909 and 1911 the group made several attempts at reaching an agreement with the Turks. By early March 1910 a detailed preliminary agreement had been signed with the Minister of Public Works, and the company had deposited £T20,000 'caution money' in a Constantinople bank; but by late June the Turkish parliament had adjourned without discussing the project.[66] The company's shareholders became generally very pessimistic, and their doubts were reinforced when in October the company's railway construction engineer, James W. Colt, completed a survey of the proposed route and reached not particularly encouraging conclusions.[67] Nevertheless, after being prodded by the State Department, the company decided to try again: negotiations with the Turks were resumed and continued slowly into 1911. By mid-May the Grand Vizir (then Ibrahim Hakki Pasha) had signed the project and it was before parliament, but on 1 June parliament voted to postpone considering it until next session.[68] The company was now very pessimistic and internally divided; consequently in October it decided to withdraw its financial deposit, a decision that caused embarrassment and consternation in the US State Department and its Constantinople embassy no less than among the group's Turkish supporters; its opponents were of course highly delighted. By that time the scheme was virtually dead.[69] A further attempt to gain the concession was made during 1912–14 by Admiral Chester, but was foredoomed; the State Department lost its enthusiasm, while the British and German opposition had revived.

There had also been a British group interested in railway building in Turkey: the Euxine and Marmora British Development Syndicate Ltd.[70] This group approached the Foreign Office in late September 1909 to ask for its help in gaining a concession. The lines it proposed[71] were more purely north Anatolian than the American projects and they carried sole mining rights to a fifteen-kilometre strip on each side of the line. The group was financially sound and composed of 'gentlemen' (a distinction that nevertheless did not seem to influence the Turks), and consequently the Foreign Office was strongly tempted to support them. The only difficulty was the Russian monopoly rights in the Black Sea Basin, these stemming from the Russo-Turkish Agreement of 1900. Turkey hoped to obtain Russia's abandonment of these rights, but the hope proved chimerical. The Foreign Office had to tell the syndicate that it could receive support only outside the Russian sphere, and suggested that the group form an international syndicate to seek the rest of the concession.

While the American railway schemes were preoccupying the Turks, the British and German oil interests were forced to mark time. They did not merely look on passively, however, and their (especially the German) opposition to the Chester scheme contributed largely to its failure.[72] Besides seeing the scheme as competition for oil rights, the Germans saw it also as the spread of undesirable foreign competition in general, and as a threat to their present and potential Baghdad railway rights in particular; as one way of disquieting the Turks about the project, they carefully fostered the rumour that the Standard Oil Company, the great oil bogey, was behind it.[73] The British Government, when in 1910 the American Government asked it to support the project (which would also, of course, open up the project to British finance), stated it could not do so, being already committed to supporting the schemes of British nationals, though it would not oppose the American scheme just because the latter was not British. The Foreign Secretary told his Ambassador at Constantinople, 'I do not think it is necessary for us to oppose it', and Lowther agreed.[74] Nevertheless, the British Embassy in Constantinople did not hesitate to point out frequently to the Turks the various disadvantages of the scheme, particularly in comparison with the advantages offered by the D'Arcy scheme. Lowther reported that Nichols also was 'doing his best to achieve the destruction of the Chester scheme'.[75] The Foreign Office reasoned that, even if the Chester project were successful, Chester could not obtain the concession for all oil areas in the Mosul vilayet (the Baghdad vilayet was not included). There would still be room left for D'Arcy, although obviously the alignment would be so drawn as 'to take the pearl out of the oyster'.[76] In April 1910, when it seemed that the scheme, with modifications that would more closely affect his oil interests, might go through the Turkish parliament, D'Arcy asked the Embassy to protest strongly against the introduction of any such modifications, and at the same time applied for a concession for the part of the Mosul vilayet that was not included in the Chester scheme, and for the sole right to build and work pipelines in the vilayet.[77] This was a very astute move, for D'Arcy was certain that at the end of the sixteen months to be granted to the Chester group for it to decide whether to accept or refuse the option, the promoters would refuse it and the whole area would therefore fall within the scope of his own concession. Furthermore, a monopoly in pipeline construction was a most effective means of preventing production 'unsympathetic' to the monopolist: there was no use in obtaining a concession to produce oil that could not be transported to its markets.[78] Similarly, D'Arcy had not been worried by the Glasgow scheme: even if the Glasgow syndicate were granted the concessions it sought, D'Arcy thought he would be able to buy out any oil interests it might be able to secure. Both D'Arcy and the Foreign Office in fact regarded Glasgow as a 'shady character', and, at D'Arcy's suggestion, the Foreign Office asked the British Ambassador to tell the Turkish Minister of Public Works that the syndicate was thought to be unsound.[79]

With the demise of the Chester scheme slowly but plainly approaching, and the comparative success of French and German railway interests, Lowther suggested, in August 1911, that D'Arcy's negotiations be revived.[80] The Foreign Office agreed, but nothing came of this suggestion. By the end of the year Lowther was complaining that the D'Arcy group seemed to have lost interest in the concession, for its agent, Nichols, was not there to press its claims. This opinion the group denied, saying that Nichols had been back in London for the last few months only because there seemed no prospect of further progress in the meantime. This unpropitious state of affairs was partly due to the political situation in Constantinople and the belatedly renewed efforts of the Chester group, together with the Turks' apparent uncertainty about whether to offer oil concessions for the Baghdad and Mosul vilayets separately, together, or only in conjunction with railway construction. When Nichols called at the Foreign Office on 3 January 1912, he said he did not think the moment opportune for pressing for the concession, although his group was 'more than ever anxious' to get it.[81] Within a month the Ambassador was reluctantly forced to agree with the D'Arcy group's assessment of the situation. Only the Foreign Office seemed actively concerned in pressing the D'Arcy claims at this time, Grey telling Lowther that 'there is reason to fear that continued inaction by H.M. Embassy may produce in the mind of the Turkish Government an erroneous impression that H.M. Government are indifferent on the subject'.[82] But in the middle of April the Ambassador reiterated his pessimism about the prospects,[83] the Foreign Secretary seemed to be convinced and there the matter rested.

By the middle of 1912 the Mesopotamian oil concession was still no nearer the grasp of any of the parties vying for it. The railway schemes, particularly the American Chester project, had succeeded only in confusing and delaying oil-concession negotiations, giving the Turks scope for exercising their considerable talents for evasion and procrastination. Nevertheless, the basis of the German and British claims had been laid down, and the fact that at this time both Turks and British declared the German contract lapsed was not materially to affect the eventual outcome (two years later) of the Anglo-German competition.[84] The Germans themselves, in their private 'Cospoli' correspondence, admitted quite frankly to each other that their claims were at best shaky, even non-existent, but this did not influence their public stand on their 'right' to the concession. As for the British claim. even the Foreign Office and the D'Arcy group could not honestly pretend that the D'Arcy claim was by any means firm. Each was well aware that the group did not really have any strictly legal rights, only a moral claim by virtue of the long negotiations and verbal assurances of the pre-Chester days.[85] The general attitude of the Foreign Office towards rival British applicants for the concession was that it must be genuinely impartial towards them,[86] although, in attempting to avoid diplomatic embarrassment, it would encourage them to combine, always pointing out to latecomers that for some years it had supported the D'Arcy group, who had long been on the point of obtaining the concession. Conversely, it kept the D'Arcy group informed of rival approaches and continually reminded the Ambassador to maintain his strong support of the group in his dealings with the Porte. The stage was thus set for the struggle of the next two years, the central and most important period in the twenty-five year long international scramble for the Mesopotamian oil concession.

Part II

Examination of the British Government's Involvement in the Mesopotamian Oil Concession Negotiations, 1912-14

4 The Anglo-German Rivalry Intensifies, 1912–13

Preview of chapter – The British Government learns of the Turkish Petroleum Company (TPC) – Greenway puts forward the D'Arcy interests views on the TPC and on the importance of the Mesopotamian oil concession to Britain – The FO's opinion on the two groups – Babington Smith gives the TPC's reaction to Greenway's views – Meeting of Greenway and Babington Smith – Establishment of the Government's position regarding the two groups – Question of a British Government subsidy to the Anglo-Persian Oil Company (APOC), and proposals for using oil on the Indian State Railways – FO reactions – India Office reaction – Admiralty reaction – FO modifies its position and puts pressure on the APOC – FO diplomatic support for the APOC – The Royal Commission on Fuel and Engines, 1912–13 – The British Government's prejudice against Shell – The significance of current oil price rises – The Admiralty's gradual change of front – Cabinet views – Admiralty statement of policy in the House of Commons – The Admiralty Persian Oil Commission, 1913–14 – Details of the British Government–APOC agreement – Views on the strength of the German position in Constantinople – The British Government increases its support of the APOC – The leverage possessed by the Government as a result of Turkey's wish to increase its customs duties by 4 per cent – Fears of the oilfields' being auctioned – The Grand Vizir's difficult position in this respect – The FO's views – The TPC's publicly and privately stated views on the strength of its position – Greenway's and the FO's views – Ambassador Lowther's efforts in Constantinople, and his attitude – Amalgamation of the two rivals first seriously put forward – Summary of chapter

I ESTABLISHING POSITIONS

After two years in which American competition and Turkish dilatoriness had prevented the D'Arcy group's claims for the Mesopotamian concession from making any progress, matters started to move again. The next phase from the latter part of 1912 until mid-1913, saw the development of a much fiercer competition between British and German interests and the emergence of a number of complex problems associated with this competition. The rivalry hardened partly because of the respective governments' increased support for their nationals, and partly because of the allied problem of general commercial competition. The

Anglo-Persian Oil Company was faced with strong pressure from its rival, Shell, to take over its interests. This affected the future of both the Persian and the Mesopotamian oilfields, involving imperial and naval arguments. The only alternative, the Anglo-Persian decided, was to obtain from the British Government far more substantial backing than it had had previously, and during this six-month period it argued its case and presented various means for solving it. It was eventually successful, but meanwhile it had found that the Mesopotamian concession, the obtaining of which was one of the company's chief reasons for resisting the Shell pressure to amalgamate, could not be gained without the two companies coming to terms. So strong was the German diplomatic pressure brought to bear on the Turkish Government, and so difficult and frustrating the process of negotiating with that government, that the Anglo-Persian interests found that, while one type of amalgamation had been averted, another had become a necessity. This period displayed also the differing and evolving attitudes of the government departments concerned, and demonstrated that it was not always the real situation, but rather what that situation was thought to be, that influenced ideas and motivated actions.

In August 1912 the British Government received with a jolt the news that the chief competition for the Mesopotamian concession had come much nearer home. The Constantinople Embassy informed the Foreign Office that Hugo Baring, the acting manager of the National Bank of Turkey, had told them, quite openly, that his bank was seeking, jointly with the Deutsche Bank, an oil concession in the Mosul and neighbouring vilayets.[1] Baring was so unsecretive about this that the Embassy assumed that Sir Henry Babington Smith, the bank's president, must have been keeping the Foreign Office informed of the negotiations. The documentation shows that this clearly was not so[2] and the department asked Sir Henry for details of the new group.[3] He described the company, designated the Turkish Petroleum Company, as including the National Bank of Turkey 'and the English group associated with it' (providing half of the capital), the Asiatic Petroleum Company and its group,[4] and the Deutsche Bank (each providing a quarter of the capital). The company's aim was to explore for petroleum any part of European or Asiatic Turkey in which it seemed likely it might be found. The Deutsche Bank was to make over to the new company the petroleum rights owned by itself and the Anatolian and Baghdad railway companies.[5] Sir Henry hoped that if, in the course of its negotiations, the company should find it necessary to ask for support from His Majesty's Government, the Government would agree to give this. Having initially reacted with nervousness, mixed with wistful hopes at the grandiose and seemingly largely British character of this scheme, the Foreigh Office sought comment on it from Charles Greenway, managing director of the Anglo–Persian

Oil Company and spokesman for the D'Arcy and Anglo–Persian interests.[6]

Obliged to speak firmly against such potentially strong opposition, Greenway presented the case of the D'Arcy interests in considerable detail.[7] Not only did his group seek the Mesopotamian concession for its own sake, having long received British diplomatic support in doing so, but in addition the concession was seen as vital to the company's Persian concession. This latter enterprise, Greenway pointed out, had been undertaken by the company only because of the insistence of the Admiralty.[8] The Anglo-Persian Oil Company already faced strong competition from the Shell interests, the latter pressing it with financial inducements to merge – something his own company had always rejected, largely on patriotic grounds. Now, as a 'flank attack', Shell was endeavouring to obtain the Mesopotamian concession. If the rival group of which Shell was a member gained this concession, then, declared Greenway, through it Shell would start a price war in the Middle East market and force the Anglo-Persian to merge with it that way. Thereafter, he declared, Shell would force up the price of oil, opening up this potentially large source of supply only gradually. If the Anglo-Persian interests, which already had the Persian concession, obtained the Mesopotamian one as well, then, Greenway argued, the Royal Navy would benefit immensely, by a much larger source of supply being in British hands. Thus, in order to preserve the Anglo-Persian Oil Company intact, as a purely British concern providing cheap oil for the Navy and supporting imperial interests in an area vital for the Indian Empire, the rival group must be prevented from obtaining the Mesopotamian concession. To allow foreign interests, which were *ipso facto* unreliable in times of national stress,[9] to become established next door to the young Persian oil industry, purely British in control and sentiments,[10] would be tantamount to aiding the potential destruction of British naval supremacy.

There was yet a third possible course of action, the combination of the D'Arcy group and the Turkish Petroleum Company. When the Foreign Office tentatively put this possibility to Greenway it received the reply that such an amalgamation could be contemplated only if arranged in such a way that combined British interests would have at least a half-share in the concern. In addition the Anglo-Persian interests must manage and control the joint company and a British-appointed chairman must have the casting vote. Any lesser participation would again simply amount to absorption by Shell. The latter's strong financial backing and marketing facilities would be at the disposal of its associates in the Turkish Petroleum Company and it would thereby naturally come to manage and control the new company. Thus, concluded Greenway, Shell would attain its aim of obtaining a vast monopoly in oil supply and marketing.

This was an involved and somewhat exaggerated argument, but it was not without some validity, as the Foreign Office saw. The latter was in a very difficult position as regards the competition: it was not anxious to see large monopolies established, whether by Shell or the Anglo-Persian, but, if such a monopoly were established, one controlled by the Anglo-Persian was certainly a less unattractive prospect than one controlled by Shell, since the former was at least wholly British. To the Foreign Office there seemed to be only two possible alternatives: either His Majesty's Government must oppose the Turkish Petroleum Company and persuade the Turks to give the concession to the D'Arcy group, or the National Bank of Turkey must be persuaded, as the condition of British diplomatic support, to throw over the Shell group and go in with the Anglo-Persian alone. Charles Marling, Counsellor to the Constantinople Embassy, was asked about the likelihood of the Porte granting the concession to the Turkish Petroleum Company.[11] He replied that the new group's prospects of gaining the concession were fairly good, though to him 'This financial alliance with German interests . . . [was] . . . most disquieting', and he suggested that 'the only possible issue seems to me to throw Cassel over . . . [for] . . . his bank has a disagreeable political flavour through its relations with the Committee [of Union and Progress]'. The Foreign Office similarly sought the Admiralty's views, suggesting that it would be unwise for the British Government to encourage any project for a fusion of the competing groups.[12] The Admiralty agreed and proposed that the whole subject be discussed at an interdepartmental conference.[13]

Greenway's arguments, which were adopted by the Foreign Office, were explained to Sir Henry Babington Smith on 28 September. The Foreign Secretary regretted that, under the circumstances, His Majesty's Government could not support the group.[14] Sir Henry replied that he quite understood the Government's reluctance to allow foreign interests to control the oil supply, but that his group had gone so far in its engagements with its associates that it could not now draw back. He insisted that ever since his negotiations had started, eighteen months before, he had not failed to inform the Ambassador at Constantinople of his syndicate's composition and aims, and thought, therefore, with some sense of grievance, that the Government might have told his associates sooner that it was unable to support them. He pointed out the predominantly British interests they represented and prophesied that an enterprise such as his was far more likely to be successful, both in negotiations with the Ottoman Government and in its actual working, if placed, as his group was, on an international basis. Finally he inquired whether his syndicate might expect to receive the British Government's support, should it be needed, in relation to the exploration and working of oilfields in parts of the Ottoman Empire other than the vilayets of Baghdad and Mosul. The reaction of the Foreign Office to Babington

Smith's censure was that it was entirely unmerited, for there was no documentary evidence at all, either in the Foreign Office or in the Constantinople Embassy files, of his project, which obviously had come as a complete surprise.[15] In regard to his provisional application for support outside the Mosul and Baghdad vilayets, the Foreign Office could only note, 'we should presumably observe a neutral attitude between any two, or more, *British* applicants'.

When Greenway was told of the reply made by the Foreign Office to Babington Smith's request for support he was greatly pleased and hoped that the Embassy would continue to press his group's claims.[16] Sir Edward Grey, unwilling to alienate his department's financial protégé in Turkey without making a strong effort to achieve a harmonious solution to the difficulty, persuaded Babington Smith to meet Greenway. The interview did not change the banker's mind, however, for he firmly rejected any idea of dissociating his group from Shell. He also declined as impracticable Greenway's suggested solution of the problem. This was for the National Bank to participate in a syndicate composed of two-thirds D'Arcy interests and one-third others, the concession being divided so that Mosul and Baghdad would go to the British group, and the rest of European and Asiatic Turkey to the European group[17] But there was one most important outcome of this otherwise abortive meeting. Greenway sent the Foreign Office copies of some highly secret correspondence that had passed between the Asiatic Petroleum Company and the Anglo-Persian Oil Company, and that confirmed the opinion the Foreign Office held of the Shell group's intentions. As the Assistant Under-Secretary, Sir Louis Mallett, concluded,

> It is clear . . . that the Shell group are aiming at the extinction of the . . . [Anglo-Persian Oil Company] . . . as a competitor – one of their objects being to control the price of liquid fuel for the British Navy . . . I think we should go every length in supporting the independence of the Anglo-Persian Oil Company and subsidise them if necessary. On commercial grounds alone we should be seriously criticised for assisting in the formation of such a gigantic and powerful ring – and those are the grounds on which I would base my opposition.[18]

The Foreign Secretary, and the Permanent Under-Secretary, Sir Arthur Nicolson, agreed with Mallet, and henceforth the Foreign Office's policy was to 'continue to endeavour to obtain the Mosul and Baghdad oilfields for the Anglo-Persian Oil Company and if we eventually fail His Majesty's Government must consider the question of subsidising the Anglo–Persian Oil Company to prevent absorption into the Trust'. This last alternative was not mentioned to Greenway, and, given the situation in Turkey at the time, nothing could be done beyond 'warning Lowther to keep a look out'.[19]

II THE BRITISH GOVERNMENT'S FINANCIAL INVOLVEMENT WITH THE ANGLO-PERSIAN OIL COMPANY

The question of a subsidy was first proposed by the Anglo-Persian Oil Company at the end of September, and came as an unexpected new twist to the situation.[20] It was regarded with some unease by both the Admiralty and the Foreign Office, who saw it as raising far broader issues of the relations between the Government and commercial companies. The Foreign Office quickly recovered from the momentary shock and accepted the likelihood that such a measure would have to be adopted; the Admiralty proved far harder to convince. Greenway argued that to obtain only the Mesopotamian concession would not save his company from the threat of absorption by Shell.[21] Large Government contracts for fuel supplies were necessary, and indeed were already being discussed with the Admiralty. But in order to increase the company's maximum output of refined fuel oil from 75,000 tons per year to the likely Admiralty requirement from the company of about 500,000 tons per year, £2 million was required for capital development. The company did not have such a sum available. It was young and had spent its available capital on initial exploration and setting up plant; as a result of the lack of further funds and sufficient markets, production was restricted and the company could not yet pay dividends.[22] Consequently, to improve its own situation – but mainly, the company insisted, as a means of ensuring a reliable, British-controlled fuel supply for the Navy, and thereby protecting British imperial interests – the Government should give the company substantial forward contracts and an annual subsidy. Over the following months various schemes for giving this financial support were put forward by the company and discussed with the Admiralty. In the main the proposals were for an annual Government subsidy of £100,000 payable over a number of years, preferably in the form of an advance payment on the contract. In return the Admiralty would receive cheaper oil.

In its efforts to win Parliamentary support and to induce the Admiralty to take on a partner to share the responsibility for oil supplies, the company, again invoking imperial interests, introduced a further factor into the argument. The suggestion that the Indian State Railways become oil-powered, using Persian oil purchased from the Anglo-Persian Oil Company on a long-term contract, had been made by the company as early as March 1912 and recommended by the Admiralty to India.[23] The company argued that not only would it have a greater inducement to expand production if it were assured of two large Government contracts – i.e. the Admiralty, and the Government of India – but that the use of oil fuel on Indian State Railways would in itself be a positive boon to that country's economy. In cost, the company contended, Persian oil would have no difficulty in competing with cheap Indian coal. Now, towards the end of 1912, the company perceived that an Indian contract would have an additional advantage. The Government of India could have the privilege of assisting the financial arrangement between the company and the British Government by guaranteeing a percentage, say 4 per cent, on the capital of £2 million required for the company's development. This would amount to only £88,000 annually for a period of about thirty to thirty-five years and could be set off against some proportion of the company's profits. In short the company argued that it was in India's interests that the Anglo-Persian Oil Company should remain independent, as regards both territory and control, and that it was therefore in the Admiralty's interest to persuade the Indian Government to agree and thereby lighten the Admiralty's burden of risk.

These arguments set off a train of negotiations between the company and the Admiralty. At the same time they were very relevant to the question of the Mesopotamian concession. As Alwyn Parker, who was closely involved in the Anglo-Turkish negotiations, noted:

> If the above desiderata, viz a Government subsidy and preferential rights in Mesopotamia, were not secured to the Anglo-Persian Oil Company then the financial inducements to come to an alliance with the Shell Transport Company would be so overwhelming that the directors, in duty to their shareholders, would have no alternative.[24]

The whole question of the Mesopotamian oil concession was clearly assuming a considerable, and previously unforeseen, importance to the British Government. A number of separate Government departments were now becoming involved, the Foreign Office, the Admiralty, the India Office, and later also the Board of Trade and the Treasury. Each of these departments had its own sphere of activity, which influenced its view of the problem; and not least among the problems raised by the Mesopotamian oil issue was the problem of reconciling these different points of view into a coherent government policy.

The Foreign Office tried hard to encourage the other departments to follow its own approach to the problem. Already deeply committed on political grounds to supporting the Anglo-Persian Oil Company interests in their efforts to obtain the Mesopotamian concession, the Foreign Office therefore readily accepted the concomitant, that the company needed financial support from the Government. The department wrote to the Admiralty on 15 November requesting their lordships' precise views and pointing out that Sir Edward Grey could not

> Overlook the possibility that the National Bank of Turkey, which will no doubt play an important part in the financial arrangements

necessary in Turkey on the conclusion of peace, may, as a condition of a loan, attempt to secure a monopoly in the petroliferous districts of Mosul and Baghdad – a consummation which might seriously affect the independence of the Anglo-Persian Oil Company, since it would enable the Shell Transport Company to cut prices.[25]

On the morning of Wednesday 20 November, representatives of the Admiralty, India Office and Board of Trade went to the Foreign Office for the proposed interdepartmental conference 'to discuss the question of oilfields in Mesopotamia and Persia'.[26] Despite the stress laid by the Foreign Office representatives on the great political risk involved in an extension of German influence in Mesopotamia. that department could not be satisfied with the outcome of the conference. This was simply that, while the Admiralty recognised the naval advantage of having a ready supply of good quality oil in the Persian Gulf, the Navy's Director of Contracts, Sir Frederick Black, was not prepared, as a commercial proposition, to grant the Anglo-Persian a subsidy. The Foreign Secretary at once requested a detailed account of the Admiralty's views, pointing out somewhat heavily, that

> Sir Edward Grey is unaware . . . if the Admiralty are desirous of negotiating with the Company or if they are indifferent whether or no it is absorbed into the Shell Corporation . . . [indeed,] . . . if there are not sufficient public grounds on which to give the Anglo-Persian Oil Company more than diplomatic support the Foreign Office cannot urge them to hold out against the advantageous invitations to throw in their lot with the Shell combine.[27]

The Foreign Office similarly tried to persuade the India Office to consider the problem favourably. Irritated by the fact that the other departments did not seem to approach the matter from the political viewpoint,[28] Mallet wrote to the India Office on 9 December requesting the opinion of the Secretary of State for India, Lord Crewe:

> As you are aware, on repeated occasions during the last fifty years the Government of India and successive Secretaries of State for India have drawn attention to the paramount importance of maintaining our existing influence on the shores of the Persian Gulf; and emphasis has been laid upon the fact that our political position is largely the result of our commercial predominance.
>
> Sir Edward Grey cannot but apprehend that our position both commercial and political will be seriously jeopardised if the most important British concession in Persia, the Anglo-Persian Oil Company, is allowed to pass under foreign control by absorption in the Shell Company.[29]

The India Office admitted the basis of this argument but continued to maintain the same extremely discouraging attitude, which it held to throughout the negotiations. It felt that applying this argument to the Anglo-Persian Oil Company's request for financial support was irrelevant,[30] and it remained quite uninfluenced even after personal visits from D'Arcy, Greenway and Admiral Fisher.[31] Both the India Office and the Government of India were indeed centrally involved in the problem of the maintenance and defence of the Indian empire, but the India Office refused to see any imperial significance either in Shell's obtaining the Mesopotamian oil concession or in its taking over the Anglo-Persian. The India Office did not in any case, believe that Government financial support for the Anglo-Persian could prevent it from coming to an arrangement with Shell whenever it wished, nor that that event would change existing oil-market circumstances. Nor did it feel that such a possibility need necessarily be condemned. Considering this 'an evasive answer', the Foreign Office attempted to persuade the India Office to change it, but in vain.[32] Lord Crewe recommended only 'that all possible support which is not of an exceptional character should be afforded to the Company' and thought that 'the vital interests of India are sufficiently safeguarded so long as the British sphere [in Persia] remains intact and British power is supreme at sea and controls the entrance to the Gulf'. Any preventive action outside the British sphere belonged rather to the Foreign Office, and thus the India Office neatly passed back the initiative.[33]

The Admiralty took six weeks to reply to the Foreign Office's urgent request for its opinion, and its reply, on 28 December, was hardly encouraging.[34] Their lordships certainly approved of the diplomatic support given to the Anglo-Persian Company's representatives in Constantinople and advised that 'all legitimate influence' be used 'to prevent if possible the foreign acquisition of control of the Persian oil-fields via Mesopotamia'. But the commercial, political and military objections outweighed the possible naval advantages of financially supporting the Anglo-Persian Oil Company. While intending to consider the Anglo-Persian's tenders for contracts as favourably as possible, the Admiralty could not neglect other available sources of supply. The Admiralty did not feel able to take up, nor to recommend the Government of India to embark on, 'a policy of finding £2 million capital for a British Company operating in territory which although presumably largely subject to British influence, is nevertheless foreign territory'. The main reasons for this rejection were that,

> Although the proposition is that such an advance shall be repaid, it would depend upon the success of the Company both in finding its supplies and in maintaining its markets against very powerful commercial rivals whether the money would be repaid, and the

> Government would be obliged to appoint representatives to sit upon the board of a commercial company engaged in a business subject to much speculative risk.

Indeed, continued the Admiralty, it rejected this policy on naval, political and military grounds – militarily, because of the obligations of military and naval protection, and the possibility that intervention might be entailed. All these arguments are particularly noteworthy in view of the complete *volte face* of the Admiralty by May 1914.[35] Pointing out the formidable competition from cheap Indian coal on some Indian railways, the Admiralty said that if the Persian oil products could not be adopted on their merits for India (merits that the Admiralty had earlier pressed the Government of India to establish)[36] then, for the Admiralty to invite the Indian Government to take up the question of a subsidy, 'would be practically asking for a subsidy from India to the Company indirectly for the benefit of Imperial services'. This analysis was quite valid and was admitted by the company, although the latter insisted that the subsidy would be repayable.[37] (The objection was not raised again, however, when barely six months later the Admiralty wanted to persuade the Government of India to provide just such a subsidy.[38]) Finally the Admiralty, while regretting, like the India Office, the general tendency to a greater monopoly in the oil-fuel market, felt that if it were to subsidise this particular commercial company it might be called on to do the same for others. It was 'at present very difficult to say concerning any oil field however important . . . whether it is likely to stand in any absolutely pre-eminent or exclusive position from the Admiralty point of view'[39] – an argument that again was to be modified within six months.

The Foreign Office was convinced by the Admiralty's naval argument but was still disappointed, as it felt that other considerations were equally important.[40] Alwyn Parker noted that he was 'not sure that the "political considerations" which "might justify more exceptional measures" have not arisen'. The attitudes of the Admiralty and India Office did, however, have the effect of encouraging the Foreign Office to question its hitherto uncritical acceptance of the Anglo-Persian Oil Company's arguments. Mallet wrote,

> I do not like the attitude of the Anglo–Persian Oil Company who have hitherto posed as being ultra-imperialist. Mr. Greenway first comes to me and hints that, if the Shell obtain the Mesopotamian oil-fields it will be difficult for the Anglo-Persian Oil Company to resist coming to an agreement with them – unless the Admiralty can give them a contract. I did not at that time understand that an agreement meant more than an understanding as to the sale price of oil. Greenway now threatens complete absorption with the Shell unless

the Admiralty give him a contract and the question of the Mesopotamian oilfields seems to have dropped out entirely . . .

Consequently, when Greenway called at the Foreign Office on 9 January 1913, he was questioned closely.[41] Having manoeuvred him into admitting that the Admiralty's unwillingness to subsidise the Anglo-Persian made it practically inevitable that the Company would have to join Shell, Mallet then commented that, in such a case, the Foreign Office need not instruct its Ambassador at Constantinople to support the company's syndicate in obtaining the Mesopotamian concession. This produced the required reaction from Greenway. Mallet informed the Foreign Secretary that 'My object was to get him to admit that even if the Shell obtain the Mesopotamian agreement, a marketing agreement would be the limit of their [i.e. the Anglo-Persian's] compliance.' Mallet reminded Greenway of his company's professions of imperialism and of the support the British Government had hitherto given it, bringing the response from Greenway that he personally would strongly oppose merging with Shell. Mallet concluded to the Foreign Secretary, 'I think that we should be able to induce the Syndicate, if we exercise sufficient pressure, not to go beyond this.'

The company, however, still had more to say. Not only did Greenway point out that Shell was also negotiating with Lord Cowdray for control of the Mexican oilfields, the other important independent British Navy oil supply, but he could demonstrate both his good faith and his strong position by bringing to the notice of the Admiralty and Foreign Office the German Government's application to the Anglo-Persian for a quotation for oil supplies, with a view to making a long-term contract.[42] These two developments disturbed the Foreign Office, yet it could do nothing; and the Admiralty and India Office were adamant. In this dialogue with the company, however, the Foreign Office did have the last word. Mallet wrote to Greenway early in February repeating that the Foreign Secretary

> . . . hopes strongly . . . that your Company will not find it necessary to combine with the Shell.
>
> The support which His Majesty's Government have given your Company in the past, both in obtaining their concession in Persia and in other ways, was given on the understanding that the enterprise would remain British and that it would be a matter of great surprise and regret if your Company made any arrangement whereby a syndicate predominantly foreign got control of their interests in that country. *In such a contingency your Company could not of course hope to get from His Majesty's Government the same support as in the past.*[43]

One thing that had been recognised at the November conference was that if the Mesopotamian oilfields were to be secured for the Anglo-Persian Oil Company then it would be necessary to exercise great pressure and hold out strong inducements at Constantinople. The Foreign Office had already realised the potent propaganda value of the loan offered to the Turks by the Germans and the National Bank to help Turkey overcome her financial difficulties, then so drastically increased by her involvement in the Balkan wars.[44] At the beginning of December the Foreign Office suggested to the Anglo-Persian that offering a loan to the Turkish Government 'might facilitate matters' with regard to the Mesopotamian concession. But the company replied that at present it found this impracticable on any security that the Turks were then in a position to offer. It hoped, nevertheless, 'that the friendly support of His Majesty's Government which the Turkish Government will no doubt desire in the present political situation, will, in itself, be a sufficient inducement to ensure a favourable consideration of the proposed representation'.[45] The Foreign Office obediently complied and on 6 December instructed Lowther to resume that strong diplomatic support of the Anglo-Persian Oil Company that Mallet had described to the Admiralty only a few days previously as 'useless [alone] in preserving the independence of the Anglo-Persian Oil Company'.[46]

The Ambassador was even more pessimistic than Mallet about the Anglo-Persian's chances of obtaining the concession. The Turks were hedging, and Gabriel Effendi, the Minister of Foreign Affairs, was saying he knew nothing about the promises to give D'Arcy the concession. In a letter to a colleague, R. P. Maxwell, Lowther wrote:

> As a matter of fact I do not believe that D'Arcy['s group] have a leg to stand on and that the Germans have their rights legally assured . . . The mere fact that the Cabinet Council took in 1909 a decision in favour of Mr. D'Arcy is mere waste paper and if D'Arcy's do not take the trouble to come out here and work their business the impression is naturally created that they do not care about it . . . If His Majesty's Government attach so much importance to the concession being given to D'Arcy I must have very much stronger instructions, but as long as I am only to frame my protests on rights I am afraid I shall be done for. I am pretty sure D'Arcy['s group] have none and their Agent Mr. Nichol[*sic*] who has been here for an age is quite useless.[47]

This suggestion Lowther also made officially to the Foreign Office on 22 December, and it was duly repeated to the oil company.[48] It caused a month of anxious consultation between the company, the Foreign Office and the India Office, but eventually the suggestion of the Commercial Attaché at Constantinople, Ernest Weakley, prevailed and

H. Stock was made agent in Constantinople while Nichols was retained in London.[49] The remainder of Lowther's private letter to Maxwell caused further repercussions at the Foreign Office. It was answered personally by the Foreign Secretary,[50] who contradicted the Ambassador, saying that he himself was 'advised that upon the documents we possess there is no reason to assume that the Germans have a secure title to an option' and he instructed Lowther to write immediately to the Turkish Government, pressing D'Arcy's claims[51]. If Lowther thought the D'Arcy group's agent dilatory, the Foreign Office obviously thought the same of him, for Mallet had noted, 'I agree that D'Arcy must take more trouble about the concession himself, if he wants us to help him, but unless this Embassy acts with more conviction we shall certainly find that the concession has been given to others.'[52] The Foreign Office questioned Lowther carefully on the reasons for his attitude. These seemed to be based largely on his belief that the German rights under the 1904 convention had never lapsed. He was convinced on this point by Edwin Whittall, the local agent and one of the directors of the Turkish Petroleum Company, who had spoken with Weakley on 27 December.[53] The Foreign Office remained unimpressed by the Ambassador's reports of these conversations. Parker described Lowther's efforts to explain his position as 'moving in a vicious circle', while Mallet was provoked to comment tartly that 'it looks as if the Embassy were too much occupied to give attention to the matter'. Thus justified, the Foreign Office could continue to uphold its policy of supporting D'Arcy.

As the interest of the Foreign Office in the Anglo-Persian Oil Company and the future of the Mesopotamian concession was entirely political, it is understandable that the department was annoyed at the apparent lack of political awareness and excessive parsimony of the India Office and Admiralty. Yet the Admiralty was giving some attention to the problem of Persian oil and its own relationship with the company. In July 1912 a royal commission was set up by Churchill, First Lord of the Admiralty, to study the problems involved in the use of oil fuel and the internal combustion engine.[54] It began its hearings in September, with the purpose of investigating the sources, prices, storage and function of oil. In the process of so doing, it was to provide the Anglo-Persian with one of the strongest pillars of its request for special Admiralty support.[55]

The commission's investigations brought evidence from, among others, Sir Marcus Samuel and Henri Deterding, on behalf of the Royal Dutch–Shell group, and from Greenway, on behalf of the Anglo-Persian Oil Company. Greenway's evidence, given before the commission on 19 November, repeated in full all his arguments in favour of a large Admiralty contract for Persian oil, on the basis of substantial financial support, and described Shell's pressure on the Anglo-Persian to amalgamate. The evidence of Deterding and Samuel, on the other hand, was concerned with demonstrating the political reliability of their group and the unjust Admiralty prejudice against Shell.[56] This prejudice undoubtedly existed. The combine being based on 60 per cent Royal Dutch shares and 40 per cent Shell, it was undeniable that the foreign element was more powerful, a point underlined by the group's strong German connections. Also, though its sources of supply were vast in extent, stretching from the Dutch East Indies to Roumania and Russia, none of these producing areas was British or could be subject to considerable British influence, while many of them were vulnerable to enemy attack. The case for Shell,[57] on the other hand, was that its sources of supply were so diffuse that, if one were attacked, replacement supplies could be obtained from another, and that if the British Navy could not keep the seas open then *no* company's goods were safe, whereas, assuming safe passage, contracts were absolute and enforceable. Samuel and Deterding pointed out that neither of their companies could be bought out by outside, foreign interests.[58] Further, Shell and the Anglo-Saxon Petroleum Company were registered in London, domiciled in London, and their boards were composed mainly of British directors, all of whom were ardent British patriots.[59] Concerning the Mesopotamian concession, Samuel pointed out that the only reason why Shell had joined with the German interests was that,

> as the Government opposed us quite plainly and openly and supported the Company Promoter [i.e. D'Arcy] we had to take the German Bank into it. Fortunately we succeeded in keeping it [the Turkish Petroleum Company] British as far as possible to do so, because the National Bank of Turkey, with Sir Henry Babington Smith as Chairman, took 50 per cent . . . and [therefore] we were able to keep the Germans down to 25 per cent.[60]

On the question of contracts, the findings of the Royal Commission gave great assistance to the Anglo-Persian's case. The commission, subsequently supported by a large and complex report by the War Staff,[61] was in favour of the Admiralty adopting, so far as possible, a policy of forward contracts, rather than annual contracts, for oil fuel (the latter having been hitherto the only type).[62] The Anglo-Persian was only too anxious to make large forward contracts, but the Royal Dutch–Shell and the rest of the oil trade (except the Mexican Eagle Oil Company), while eager to make large contracts, thought long-term contracts uneconomic in view of the constantly rising price of oil.[63] The Anglo-Persian Oil Company's case to the Admiralty was practically won when the commission proposed fifteen- to twenty-year contracts, and advance payments, for all Persian oil offered at the company's suggested price, which it considered very fair.

Closely allied to the question of forward contracts was the evidence of the steady rise in fuel oil prices quoted on the London market: between January 1911 and June 1913 they more than doubled, from 37s. 6d. to 77s. 6d. a ton.[64] The reason for this great rise was mainly excessive freight charges, though this was in itself part of the general effects of market forces on a commodity for which demand exceeded supply. Churchill, however, as First Lord of the Admiralty, chose to interpret the continually rising prices erroneously, as evidence of secret price-rigging by the great oil interests.[65] This was, besides, a reason that his Cabinet colleagues, Parliament and the general public would more easily accept.[66]

From February to May, Greenway and the Admiralty continued their negotiations. These were chiefly concerned with the financial guarantees requested by the company, and methods for reducing to the minimum the financial risk to be incurred by the Admiralty.[67] In February, while the Royal Commission and War Staff investigations were still in progress, and the Foreign Office was testing the validity of the company's arguments, the Admiralty was still uncommitted in its attitude towards the company and reiterating its 'inability to entertain' the proposal for a straightforward subsidy. But the Royal Commission and War Staff findings and the company's own persuasive arguments, particularly as regards price, were having their effect. The Indian Railways question demonstrates perfectly the gradual change of front by the Admiralty. Although in March 1912 the Admiralty had recommended the Indian Government to consider using oil on some of its railways, in December of that year it had also categorically rejected the plea from both the company and the Foreign Office to persuade India to consider the question of a financial guarantee to the Anglo-Persian.[68] In February 1913 the company argued that, since the tests and trials it had persuaded the Indian Government Railways Board to undertake would take some time, and their results 'could only demonstrate the superior advantages of oil', the question ought therefore to be judged immediately on imperial, naval grounds alone.[69] The War Staff report also recommended Indian Government support. The Admiralty was thus persuaded of the theoretical desirability of such assistance.[70] In May it was requesting the Indian Government's views, though stressing that this was without any obligation as to policy.[71] By mid-June, however, drastically changing its tune, the Admiralty was urging India to act jointly and swiftly with the Anglo-Persian Oil Company on the matter of the proposed contract, and underlining the reciprocal advantages of such an arrangement.[72] Its attempt to bludgeon India was based, somewhat unconvincingly, on the India Office's reply to the Admiralty's query. This reply, sent a *month* previously, had in any case been completely misinterpreted by the Admiralty, for India's attitude had not changed at all.[73] A number of additional and not very subtle arguments were employed by the company and taken up by the Admiralty, but, to the latter's frustration, did not impress the India Office.[74]

The Cabinet also rejected this scheme, although its members had by then been convinced – by the Admiralty – of 'the vital necessity to the Navy of a continuous and independent supply of oil in the future', and agreed that this should be achieved by the Government's acquiring 'a controlling interest in trustworthy sources of supply, both at home and abroad'.[75] This policy was set out in Churchill's important Cabinet memorandum of 16 June.[76] The memorandum declared the Admiralty's intention of accepting the Royal Commission's, the War Staff's and the Anglo-Persian Oil Company's recommendations regarding Persian oil, and stated, significantly, as one of its governing principles, the intention 'to frustrate as effectively as possible, by keeping alive independent competitive sources of supply, the formation of a universal oil monopoly and thus to safeguard the Admiralty from becoming dependent on any single combination'. On 17 July Churchill presented the Admiralty's new oil policy to the House of Commons.[77] He made it clear that the Admiralty was going into the oil business itself in order to ensure adequate and reasonably priced supplies for its fleet. To do this it was embarking on a policy of forward contracts with as many firms, and covering as many areas, as possible. Churchill did not however, mention, that only Persia and Mexico had offered such contracts. Nor did he mention that, since the Indian Government was not prepared to co-operate with the Admiralty in a financial guarantee to the Anglo-Persian, the Admiralty had decided to buy a controlling interest in the company. All that remained now was to arrange the finer details of the contract and agreement with the Anglo-Persian and to satisfy the Cabinet and Treasury and educate the public by a predictably favourable report from an Admiralty commission to be sent out to examine the Persian oilfields.

These two aims were to be achieved within less than a year. The Admiralty commission of experts, headed by Rear-Admiral Sir Edmond Slade, remained three months in Persia, from late October 1913 until late January 1914, examining the geology of the oilfields and the Anglo-Persian Oil Company's equipment and proceedings.[78] Its report declared the company's concession to be extremely valuable and, with proper development, to be capable of supplying most of the Royal Navy's needs for a long time.[79] In order to ensure such proper development and safeguard Admiralty supplies, however, the commission strongly urged the Government to obtain some control over the company's general policy.

The Cabinet was thus finally persuaded of the Government's need to participate in the Anglo-Persian Oil Company. Accordingly the Admiralty, the Treasury and the company proceeded with their negotiations on the basis that the Government would find the necessary capital of £2·2 million in return for a 51 per cent shareholding in the company.[80] The agreement eventually concluded was in two parts. One part was the supply contract between the Admiralty and the company. By making this a separate arrangement the Admiralty could maintain its usual secrecy of contracts and disguise details of the actual price of the oil.[81] The second part was the agreement between the company and the Government for the latter's participation in the company. Its financial participation apart, the Government was to have two *ex-officio* members on the board of the company, to supervise general company policy but not interfere in its commercial administration.[82] The agreement was signed on 20 May and presented to Parliament as a White Paper on 17 June 1914. Churchill had prepared the ground three months before, in his speech on the Navy estimates for 1914–15. He spoke then, and again in June, of the advantages of oil power and the difficulties of obtaining oil at a good price.[83] Now he went further and attacked the prices of Shell and the policies of its Jewish directorate.[84] After a fierce debate the bill was passed and on 10 August it received the royal assent.[85]

III TURNING THE MESOPOTAMIAN 'FLANK ATTACK'

The Anglo-Persian Oil Company might well have felt delighted at its success in so radically converting the Admiralty's attitude towards it. The Admiralty was not only giving the company financial support: it was also modifying its whole oil contract policy. Even by mid-1913 the company's commercial future was virtually assured, and the great fear of the company's self-avowed imperialists – that the Anglo-Persian would be absorbed by Shell – was also averted. But what of the question that had precipitated consideration of all these other issues, the 'flank attack' by the Shell combine in Mesopotamia? That remained to be turned.

Turning the Mesopotamian 'flank attack' was to be no easy matter. In Constantinople the pressure of the German–Shell combination was clearly being increased, and consequently communications were passing almost daily between the Constantinople Embassy, the Foreign Office and the Anglo-Persian Oil Company. Lowther and Stock reported that several factors strengthened the German group's position.[86] The Committee of Union and Progress had always shown a leaning towards Germany. Now two of its influential members were on the managing board of the National Bank of Turkey, and the Deutsche Bank–Anatolian Railway Company combine had helped the present Turkish Cabinet with financial assistance at a critical moment. Moreover, the sympathy recently shown in England towards the Balkan allies was interpreted in Constantinople as showing England to be anti-Turk. On 17 February Greenway told the Foreign Office that Whittall, on behalf of the Turkish Petroleum Company, had made a definite application to the Ministry of Mines for the Mesopotamian concession, basing his syndicate's application on the Anatolian Railway Company's rights of 1904 which had been transferred to it.[87] Several of the Ministry's senior officials had been promised 'satisfactory remuneration' if the attempt succeeded, which the D'Arcy group feared would happen sooner or later. Next day Alwyn Parker met Greenway and Stock and discussed what steps to take.[88] Greenway asked that the Ambassador might be instructed to give Stock his most energetic support, and to seek a private interview between Stock and the Grand Vizir. He wished, too, that a memorandum supporting his application be sent to the Turkish Ambassador in London, Tewfik Pasha. At the same time Hakki Pasha, in London for the Baghdad Railway and other negotiations, should be told of the British Government's wish that D'Arcy be granted the concession, as promised. All this was done,[89] not without some fears by the Foreign Office that it might be in vain. The Foreign Office had heard that Babington Smith was visiting Constantinople early in March, and it feared that he might successfully obtain the concession.

Lowther saw the Grand Vizir on 24 February[90] 'and spoke to him very seriously about the importance we attached to the promises of the Porte being carried out in favour of the D'Arcy group'. Mahmud Shevket agreed to look into the matter, of which he said he knew nothing, and promised to speak to the Minister of Mines. On 27 February he saw Stock as well. On 1 March Stock had a preliminary interview, which he thought went satisfactorily enough with the Minister of Mines.[91] At the same time Djemal Bey told him of a very large loan of £T 5·5 million offered by a rival. This, Stock felt sure, was a bluff, although one clearly indicating that the concession would not be granted to anyone who did not have a substantial advance to offer. The Anglo-Persian had in fact set aside £T50,000 (a sum Stock considered too small) as an outright payment and was prepared also to arrange a separate loan.[92] There was evidently no difficulty over the principle of financial lubrication, although, Stock wrote to the company, 'Officially, of course, neither the Ambassador nor the Foreign Office must know of any such arrangement.'

Lowther's communications with the Grand Vizir were becoming fairly regular. At the end of February the Ambassador sent a formal note pleading the D'Arcy group's case, and, early in March, and again on 10 March, Lowther had interviews with him.[93] None of his approaches earned particularly helpful replies, for the Vizir maintained that no record could be found of D'Arcy's 1909 application and that in any case the transfer of the Civil List properties to the Turkish Ministry of Finance would have rendered the concession null and void. The Vizir also spoke of another 'English group' competing for the concession but this subsequently turned out to be the Turkish Petroleum Company. Lowther himself became rather discouraged. He pointed out to the Foreign Office that, in contrast to Greenway's dogmatic assertion that the Grand Vizir had made 'promises' to the Embassy in 1909,[94] he personally had no recollection whatsoever of any direct promises made either to himself or to Marling, for Hilmi Pasha had told him only that the Council of Ministers had 'practically decided' to grant D'Arcy the concession. Lowther declared that he had expressed the opinion then that perhaps Nichols was being 'over-sanguine'.[95] In his remarks about himself, at least, Lowther was not strictly accurate, for he had telegraphed the Foreign Office in July 1909 plainly reporting the Council's 'formal decision' on the matter.[96] True, he subsequently modified his opinion, in view of Turkish prevarication during the following few weeks,[97] but, though, as he said in his later telegram, the Turkish decision had after all 'proved not to be final', he had certainly regarded it as a 'formal' one at the time.

The Foreign Office, having checked only carelessly on the Ambassador's 1909 correspondence, was inclined to accept Lowther's revised views.[98] It did not however, feel, that it was necessary, or even possible, to modify the wording of a memorandum that had been delivered to Hakki Pasha on 18 March. This memorandum had, indeed, been Lowther's own suggestion.[99] He had pointed out to the Foreign Office that the only real leverage Britain possessed to counteract the Germans' strong efforts was the 4 per cent increase in Turkish customs duties, and the other matters that Hakki Pasha was currently and unofficially discussing with the British Government in London. The memorandum described the recent negotiations on D'Arcy's behalf and asserted that 'His Majesty's Government feel confident that the Ottoman Government will recognise his claim, and His Majesty's Principal Secretary of State for Foreign Affairs trusts that Hakki Pasha will recommend it strongly to the favourable consideration of the Porte'. In reply Hakki Pasha told the Foreign Office that he had telegraphed Constantinople and advised the Grand Vizir to exercise great caution.[100]

British pressure on Hakki Pasha was certainly required, for in the meantime yet a further development regarding the Mesopotamian concession had arisen to disturb the British oil interests. The Minister of Mines had suddenly informed Stock of his intention of putting the oilfields up to auction,[101] a course not provided for in the mining regulations, though still fairly common practice. The Anglo-Persian interests were manifestly unable to compete with the rival combine in this respect; the Embassy and the Foreign Office were unanimously opposed to it, and the Ambassador was given permission to protest against any such action.[102] When Stock saw the Minister subsequently, he still found the other's tone and delaying tactics most depressing and was perturbed by the Minister's continued determination to auction the concession.[103]

In response to an urgent request from the Anglo-Persian Oil Company,[104] the Ambassador had in late March two further interviews with the Grand Vizir.[105] These showed more positively Mahmud Shevket's difficult position with regard to the Germans. He made it plain to Lowther that he dreaded conflict between the two embassies, since this would place the Turkish Government in a most embarrassing situation. He pointed out, moreover, that even if the concession were given to D'Arcy the most valuable oil districts would in any case fall to the German group, by virtue of the Baghdad railway concession. Indeed, he stated that there existed a contract, made since the Ministry of Finance had taken over from the Civil List responsibility for the petroleum fields, between the Ministry and 'the German Company', and that, if this contract were not adhered to, the German company would undoubtedly bring a successful action against the Turkish Government. But, the Vizir added, his government was as anxious as the competing groups were for a settlement of the matter, and thus it seemed to him that the only solution was an amalgamation of the two groups. The Foreign Office realised that 'the Grand Vizir is obviously (and naturally) much afraid of the Germans'[106] but did not think much of his suggestion. The Foreign Secretary telegraphed the Ambassador on 28 March to tell the Grand Vizir that

> Our object is to maintain the independence of the Anglo-Persian Oil Company in order to keep competition alive with the Shell Company. Amalgamation of the various interests would not therefore suit us at all, nor would it be to the general interest in view of the great importance of oil in the future.[107]

The Foreign Office expected that 'the most . . . we shall effect at present is to prevent the concession from being given to anyone, either Shell or Anglo-Persian, and this will be sufficient for present purposes'.

Despite its heartfelt and apposite complaint that 'the situation becomes daily more confused',[108] the Foreign Office was not especially alarmed. The mysterious contract mentioned by the Grand Vizir could, on Whittall's own admission, be nothing but the German protest of 1909. Whittall had called on the Ambassador in the middle of March in an effort to try and avoid the inevitable diplomatic friction that would be entailed by a continued competition between the two embassies, since this would probably end in neither group obtaining the concession.[109] This friction, Whittall thought, could be greatly, if not entirely, avoided if the National Bank were to desist from seeking the German Embassy's support, and for this to happen it would be necessary for the two groups to combine under the aegis of Britain. He contrasted the strength of his syndicate's position with the very problematical chances of D'Arcy obtaining the concession – an attitude that the Ambassador thought might be genuine or might be mere bluff, though he inclined more to the latter view.

Although, as Lowther pointed out to the Foreign Secretary, Whittall was 'a very earnest and convinced advocate of a fusion of British and German interests, it would seem that the case he was presenting was indeed bluff. Whittall stated, for instance, that the National Bank 'had no doubts as to the Anatolian Railway Company's rights under the 1904 agreement'. That this simply was not the case can be seen from the Turkish Petroleum Company's own files on the subject.[110] Babington Smith himself wrote to a member of Shell on 18 December 1912 that 'it is quite true that the wording of article 20 of the Anatolian Railway Company's Concession is somewhat vague, and of this we have of course been aware all along.'[111] The Constantinople lawyer Count Leon Ostrorog,[112] who was consulted for an opinion, held similar views, as was shown by his letter of 17 January 1913 to Babington Smith:

> The situation of the Anatolian Railway Company is not what I should call a 'strong case'. The exploration work was not done and the reports not rendered within the time allowed, and even if this is more or less covered by the tacit acquiescence of the Civil List a much more unfavourable thing is that the drilling incontestably called for (Article 1, July 1904) was not done except under a new agreement . . . undoubtedly also the Civil List has the right to say that the Draft Convention presented does not accord with the original principles.[113]

Whatever the reason, Whittall's private memorandum makes no mention of the issue of the validity of the 1904 contract, while the remarks of the German correspondents in the 'Cospoli' correspondence have already been noted.[114]

The Turkish Petroleum Company, moreover, was not making good progress in its own negotiations with the Turkish Government. Its application for *permis de recherche* covering the area from Mosul to Takrit, based on the rights included in the Anatolian and Baghdad railway conventions, was, in fact, after long delay to be turned down by the Turks. The reason given by the Turkish Government, in August 1913, was that 'since these petroleum sources had been conceded to the Civil List before the existence of the Baghdad Railway Company, *permis* could not be given, either to the Railway Company or to anyone else'. In view of the continued Turkish–British negotiations up to and after that time, and the fact that the Turkish Government had long before already infringed this declared policy by granting *permis* in the area to Turkish subjects, the Turkish Petroleum Company was clearly not as strong a contender for a Mesopotamian oil concession as it would have liked its rival and the British Government to believe.[115]

Even in its hope of bluffing its rival and the British Government about the strength of its position, the Turkish Petroleum Company was not particularly successful. Foreign Office minutes declared that 'It is . . . our object to minimise the rights acquired by the National Bank as far as possible', and it was felt that Lowther's information was 'rather encouraging than otherwise', indicating that 'we should redouble our efforts'.[116] These views were supported by Greenway, who, when consulted, thought Lowther's interview with Whittall indicated 'that the German group are *not* now so confident as they pretend'.[117] He declared that the latter's 'supposed claims' to the concession were invalid and might be ignored, and thought Whittall's statement that the D'Arcy group would be unable to work the oilfields even if granted them 'an absurdity' that assumed an unlikely 'supineness to their own interests by the Turkish Government'. Finally, he pointed out that Article 22 of the Baghdad Railway Convention laid down that the mining rights it granted did not constitute a privilege or a monopoly ('. . . *sans que cela constitue pour lui un privilège ou un monopole*'), the very point that Babington Smith and his Shell correspondent had privately agreed about.[118] The Foreign Office was very impressed by Greenway's long and detailed letter, and on 21 April told Lowther that it felt there was 'considerable force in the arguments advanced by the company', and that he was to use them in continuing strongly to support Stock.

The Ambassador (though, interestingly, not his two main aides, Marling and Weakley) agreed that some of Greenway's arguments seemed 'very convincing'.[119] This was especially cheering to him as, after a meeting with the Grand Vizir on 14 April, he had been inclined to believe in the existence of the mysterious German contract.[120] Mahmud Shevket Pasha had then assured him that there definitely was such a contract, and told him that if the Turkish Government, knowing of its existence, had nevertheless said that the Germans had forfeited their rights, this line had been adopted merely to induce the Germans to increase their offer, and the English group had been deceived. Now, on Lowther's attempting to extract from him more information about the contract,[121] the bubble burst. The Grand Vizir immediately qualified his earlier statements – so lamely, that it was obviously just another, rather unsubtle attempt to induce the British group to favour the idea of amalgamation with its rivals.[122] However, a further, far more significant incentive had been held out to the Ambassador at these interviews. If the British would agree to amalgamate, the Grand Vizir was prepared to see that the preponderant share in such a combine should be British, and he begged the Ambassador to lay this proposition before the Foreign Office.

This was an important consideration and it was heightened by the fact that Stock had learnt from his 'contact' in the Ministry of Mines that the whole question of the petroleum fields was being examined by a special, highly secret committee sitting at the Ministry.[123] On its meeting, the Minister of Mines had shown himself anxious to settle the matter as rapidly as possible, by auctioning all known petroleum deposits in the empire – unless prevented by the Grand Vizir. This in itself was not worrying, since it was clear that, because of German and British diplomatic pressure, the Grand Vizir would continue to block any such move. Nevertheless, the message of the Vizir's prevarications and the Minister's intractability was plain. On 25 April Lowther wrote to the Foreign Office stating his opinion

> that the negotiations on behalf of D'Arcy have now reached a point not far from deadlock and I am apprehensive lest the pressure which may be exerted in favour of rival groups by ourselves and the Germans may result in determining the Government not to give exclusive rights to either group.[124]

Outsiders might be allowed in instead. Consequently Lowther suggested two alternatives to the continuation of the rivalry. Amalgamation, with the requisite safeguards, now seemed a possibility, and Stock had assured him that this solution would most likely satisfy D'Arcy. The other suggestion was for partition of the area, with certain exclusive rights to each of the two groups. The Germans could take the Mosul vilayet and D'Arcy Baghdad; half a territory was better than none at all.[125]

Sir Arthur Nicolson apart, partition did not appeal at all to Lowther's Foreign Office colleagues.[126] One of them noted that

> Even if the Germans could be got to accept it (which is doubtful, as if they have any rights at all, they have them over both vilayets) we do not know that Mosul is not much more petroliferous than Baghdad and that the British group would therefore not be making a bad bargain. Besides the sphere system is objectionable in itself. British control of the whole would be far better.

This could be most nearly achieved by means of amalgamation, and the Foreign Office at last came to realise that, 'As this question develops, amalgamation, if it can be secured with British control, seems more and more indicated as the proposed solution.' Greenway was asked (a) whether, if British control could be secured, as suggested by the Grand Vizir, Grey could tell Lowther that 'the objections raised by His Majesty's Government against the scheme would be diminished', and (b) in the event of amalgamation being agreed on, what steps could be taken 'to secure and ensure the maintenance of British control of the enterprise'.[127] Greenway replied that his board felt that if their company were assured majority control of the new undertaking then they would not be against an amalgamation. However, he stipulated that, for his company to attain the necessary degree of control, it should have no less than a 60 per cent share in the proposed new company, plus sole control of its technical and commercial working.[128] At Greenway's meeting with Babington Smith some months before,[129] the latter had stated, just as emphatically, that in the first place the Turkish Petroleum Company certainly could not give the D'Arcy group a majority participation (the most it would consider being a 25 per cent share, and, secondly, that if, as would doubtless be the case, Shell asked for the technical and commercial control of the new company, the National Bank and Deutsche Bank would have to support Shell's claim. It seemed, therefore, extremely unlikely that the Turkish Petroleum Company would agree to any arrangement whereby the D'Arcy group would have overall control of the new company. The D'Arcy group's stipulations were also those of the Board of Trade. When asked for its opinion of what further action the Foreign Office could take to secure the concession for the D'Arcy group, the Board of Trade replied through its Permanent Secretary, Sir Hubert Llewellyn Smith, that nothing further could be done. Any proposal for amalgamation was objectionable unless provisions such as those stipulated by the Anglo-Persian Oil Company could be secured.[130]

The situation seemed even less hopeful when, in the middle of May, a despatch arrived from Lowther describing a further meeting, on 5 May, with the Grand Vizir.[131] When the Ambassador had reminded Mahmud Shevket of his earlier declaration that, in the event of an amalgamation between the British and German groups, he would be prepared to secure for British capital the preponderant share in the new combine, the other replied that he had not meant that the British should have the major share of the capital but simply that there should be a British majority on the board of administration. Lowther coolly returned that all this was premature anyway, as His Majesty's Government was not in favour of amalgamation. In some despair, the Ambassador wrote to the Foreign Office that

> The impression left by this conversation with the Grand Vizir is that he has not studied the question in detail, and is, moreover, not disposed to enter into a discussion concerning the validity of the German rights . . . Mahmoud has again shifted his ground, and has now modified his first statement to me about British participation in the Anglo-German combine he advocated and, in view of his last statement, to the effect that the matter has now become a purely political one, I fear we have for the moment come to a deadlock.

He had heard, further, that a draft contract was being secretly drawn up at the Ministry of Mines, seeming to indicate 'that the Grand Vizir intends taking some definite course in the matter'. In the present circumstances this could point only to the favouring either of the German group or of outsiders. This despatch convinced the Foreign Office that something must be done urgently. On 23 May a note was sent to Hakki Pasha again threatening to withhold British approval to the proposed Turkish customs increase, unless the Ottoman Government made 'without delay arrangements concerning the Mesopotamian oilwells, which will ensure British control and meet with their [i.e. H.M. Government's] approval in matters of detail'.[132] At the same time the Foreign Office realised that stronger efforts must be made to break the deadlock with the Turkish Petroleum Company and present a united front to the Turks, on the theory that if the competition could not be beaten then it must be neutralised. The first step must be to have a full interdepartmental conference, both to discuss the matter and to bring Greenway and Babington Smith together in an effort to discover what the chances of a successful arrangement being effected were.[133] This conference was held on Thursday 5 June at the Board of Trade, and the discussions that took place there were to initiate a new phase in the search for a solution to the question of the Mesopotamian oil concession.

By May 1913, then, the negotiations for the concession had reached stalemate. Amalgamation, though always a possibility, had been rejected by the Foreign Office ever since the proposal was first discussed, in September 1912. Now it seemed to be the only way whereby negotiations could be carried on fruitfully. Neither the D'Arcy group nor the Turkish Petroleum Company had rejected amalgamation outright, but each demanded a controlling share in the capital, management, and technical working of the proposed new company. Agreement, particularly in the eyes of the D'Arcy group, seemed impossible. The Turkish Petroleum Company was far more interested than its rival was in achieving a combination. This was not because it felt its claim to the concession to be any weaker than its rival's – indeed it was obviously capable of exerting great pressure on the Turkish Government, particularly by the lever of finance; but it wanted, and needed, British as well as German support. The question of the validity of the conflicting claims was no clearer, but what was clear was that this was not a particularly important consideration to the Turks. The Turkish Government's attitude had been far from satisfactory: dilatory, prevaricating, vacillating between one group and the other, and between the British and German Embassies, its sheer confusion had been mitigated only by its desperate need for funds. This made negotiations difficult and gave foreigners little reason to expect co-operation and efficiency even if amalgamation were achieved. Moreover, the two competing groups showed no indication of present or future mutual trust. But at least the Anglo-Persian Oil Company could negotiate from a far stronger position. Its basic vulnerability to powerful competition had been skilfully turned into an advantage. Once a small, struggling company, it now had an assured commercial future. Not only did it now have its government's diplomatic support, but also, by becoming so closely involved with the fuel policy it had helped to formulate, it would have far stronger support on political grounds as well.[134] It had failed to draw Indian Government interests into this orbit and the Board of Trade was as yet hardly involved at all; yet, in the next phase of the negotiations over the Mesopotamian oil concession, the Board of Trade was to be centrally involved. This phase in the negotiations was to be the crucial one. The game of economic power politics was to become harder, pressure from outside competitors to become stronger, and the British (as also the German) Government was to identify itself more pointedly with its protégé and to put the strongest pressure on the Turks to grant it the concession. At the same time the two governments worked hard to assist the two rivals to come to some agreement about amalgamation. Each government's deepest hope might still be that its protégé would gain the Mesopotamian oil concession for itself, but it became increasingly clear to both that a united front might well be needed to clinch the bargain.

5 Coming to an Agreement: Analysis of Amalgamation Negotiations, 1913–14

Preview of chapter – Amalgamation conference of 5 June 1913, and the resulting meeting of the groups involved – Board of Trade suggestion – FO suggestion – Reasons behind the FO's attitude – Further outside competition: 'Baron' de Ward – The National Bank of Turkey's indictment of the FO – FO reply – The Bank's attitude on the oil concession – The FO becomes increasingly firm towards the Shell interest and increasingly co-operates with the German Government – MacLeod's (Shell's) proposals, and the British Government's cool reaction to them – The Board of Trade's requirements regarding the proposed amalgamation – The Admiralty's views – The APOC's views and schemes – The German Government finally refuses the British Government's request to exclude the Shell interests from the amalgamation – The FO's objectives in return – FO negotiations with the National Bank – The British Government's negotiations with and pressure on the Turkish Government – Further competition in Constantinople – Amalgamation conference at the Board of Trade, 21 October 1913 – The National Bank anxious for a decision – The FO modifies its attitude to the Shell interests – Negotiations between the Board of Trade and the Deutsche Bank – The Government's high-handed treatment of the APOC and the Shell interests – Their reactions – Gulbenkian's shareholding in the TPC revealed – The FO's upset reaction – Gulbenkian's views – APOC – German discussions on the terms of amalgamation – The Board of Trade seeks to press the APOC for a final decision – The resulting FO ultimatum, and the APOC's reply – Gulbenkian's position and the deterioration of FO – National Bank relations – FO snubs to Gulbenkian – Competition in Constantinople of the Central Mining and Investment Corporation's group – The FO increases its pressure on the Turkish Government – British–German Government negotiations for a purely Anglo-German oil group – Deterding's bitter complaints of his treatment from the FO induces Churchill (Admiralty) to insist on better FO treatment of the Shell interests – FO's views – The National Bank's revised amalgamation scheme concerning Gulbenkian – German and Board of Trade approval – Deterding's threat of legal action against the Crown – The resulting meeting, clearing up misunderstandings – Signing of the Foreign Office Agreement, 19 March 1914 – Analysis of agreement – Summary of chapter

I JUNE 1913: SIGNIFICANCE OF THE NATIONAL BANK'S POSITION

Against such a background of uncertainty, the amalgamation negotiations between the two main contenders for the Mesopotamian concession should have been speedy and determined. Instead, the conference of 5 June did no more than initiate ten months of bargaining over the terms of amalgamation. Broadly, the issues involved concerned the proportion of share capital each group was to have and, accordingly, its representation on the board of the new company. The size of the groups' individual shareholdings was closely connected with the question of national allegiance, particularly the question of British predominance which was sought also through control of commercial policy and the marketing of the company's products. Stipulations concerning the latter varied from territorial division of the concession to allocation by type of product, while the percentage of the total quantity of oil produced to be reserved to the respective governments was regarded as a national consideration.

The conference was held at the Board of Trade and was attended by representatives of that department, the Admiralty and the Foreign Office, together with Sir Henry Babington Smith and Mr Greenway.[1] The departmental delegates stressed the advisability of the two rival groups combining, and the probability that if they did not do so the concession would be granted by the Turks either to no one or to a third party. Both Babington Smith and Greenway saw the force of this argument, but, despite a long discussion, could not find any mutually acceptable basis for combination. Greenway made it quite plain that his group attached most importance to securing for the Anglo-Persian Oil Company the marketing of the products; otherwise he and his colleagues feared this would be done by its rival the Anglo-Saxon, which would use it to try to force the Anglo-Persian into its own orbit. If, by a preliminary agreement, his own company could be assured of the marketing, it would accept a 33⅓ per cent share in the proposed joint company: if not, it must insist on a controlling shareholding. Babington Smith, for his part, proposed that his group should have a 75 per cent share in the new company, leaving 25 per cent to Greenway's group. He would allow no arrangement whatever to be made concerning marketing until the new company was actually producing, at which stage it must take whatever course seemed to serve its interests best. The only thing that was agreed was that the two men would discuss the matter between themselves, in the light of various suggestions put forward at the conference. This happened on 10 June, by which time each had consulted his colleagues; but this resulted only in both sides maintaining the same stance as at the conference and, predictably, no progress was made.[2] Babington Smith wrote formally to the Board of Trade stating that, unless that department had any further suggestions to make, the negotiations must be considered at an end. His group did not consider marketing engagements made an unknown number of years before an unknown quantity and quality of oil was found a commendable commercial proposition, while Greenway's exposition of the Anglo-Persian Oil Company's attitude made no impression on it. What the Anglo-Persian required was, first, an undertaking from the National Bank that it would identify itself with and support the D'Arcy group in the control and management of the business, and, secondly, that the D'Arcy group and National Bank should between them hold no less than 60 per cent of the capital, having at least three-fifths of the representation on the board. In reporting on his abortive meeting with Babington Smith, Greenway repeated his usual remarks about 'the dominant foreign member' (Shell) of the Turkish Petroleum Company, whose 'object . . . is one of attack on the Anglo-Persian Oil Company', and asked that while the British Government continued to press the D'Arcy group's suit at Constantinople the Turks should be told that the National Bank could not be regarded as British. The Foreign Office, not surprisingly, did not consider this reasonable.[3] These conditions were modified somewhat in further correspondence between Greenway and the Board of Trade.[4] The Board of Trade suggested an arrangement whereby the capital in the new company would be apportioned equally, and output approximately equally, between the two groups, with some allocation of markets. Greenway accepted the suggestion in principle and made some detailed proposals as to its application, chiefly that the D'Arcy group must have the marketing of all the fuel oil, while the Turkish Petroleum Company could market the benzine. The marketing of other products would be divided territorially between the two groups. Sir Hubert Llewellyn Smith put these proposals to Sir Henry Babington Smith on 18 June, with a strong plea for accommodation.[5] It was in vain. The Turkish Petroleum Company could not accept either suggestion and concluded, 'In any case, as there is a third party in the field, we consider ourselves free to do anything that seems likely to protect our interests in the matter.' Consequently, on 20 June the Board of Trade informed the Anglo-Persian Oil Company that 'In the circumstances the Board are of opinion that no useful purpose would be served by further efforts on their part to bring about an agreement between the two groups . . . and have informed the Secretary of State for Foreign Affairs accordingly.'[6]

The Foreign Office was not prepared to accept failure so soon. Mallet wrote to the Board of Trade next day, saying that

> Sir Edward Grey is so much impressed by the importance of reaching an agreement that he considers a further effort in this direction

should be made, and *he would be prepared to bring such pressure as may be possible to bear on the representatives of the National Bank group to agree to the following compromise* if the Board of Trade consider that it would adequately secure British control.[7]

The Foreign Office suggested that the British share of the capital should total 52 per cent, the Anglo-Persian having 'about 34 per cent' and the National Bank 'about 17 per cent'. Of the remainder, the Deutsche Bank should have 25 per cent and the Anglo-Saxon 23 per cent. Grey would also urge Greenway's latest proposals. The Board of Trade thought that such an arrangement could secure the interests of the Anglo-Persian Oil Company only if the National Bank gave a binding assurance of co-operation in matters important to British interests (and, to the British Government, marketing was a 'British interest') or if a marketing agreement were concluded in advance in a form incapable of modification without the British Government's consent. The share proportions favoured by the Board were: Anglo-Persian 35 per cent National Bank 25 per cent, Deutsche Bank 25 per cent, Anglo-Saxon 15 per cent. Accordingly the Foreign Office put this latter course before Babington Smith.[8]

What contributed to the Foreign Office belief that the National Bank had 'behaved in a very unpatriotic manner' over this matter, and convinced it that it should 'bring great pressure to bear upon them so as to induce them to come to a proper working agreement with Mr. Greenway',[9] was the complicated background to these negotiations. In the first place, the Turkish Petroleum Company, despite its avowed wish to combine with the D'Arcy group, was obviously increasing its pressure on the Turks in an attempt to gain the concession for itself. On 3 June the British Ambassador in Constantinople telegraphed that the Grand Vizir, under pressure from the Germans and notwithstanding the Minister of Mines' disagreement, had informed the Ministry that he thought the concession should be given to the Germans.[10] This news was confirmed by Greenway.[11] In reply the Foreign Office told Lowther of a note it had sent Hakki Pasha on 23 May,[12] and instructed the Ambassador to hand a similar note to Mahmud Shevket Pasha and the Minister of Foreign Affairs.[13] Foreign Office anxiety was hardly allayed on hearing that an important German newspaper, the *Frankfurter Zeitung*, had stated that in return for the concession one of the Rothschild banks (probably the Paris house, which was closely associated with the Shell Company) had offered the Turkish Government some £500,000 as an advance on the profits the Government would derive from the concession.[14] Hakki Pasha himself, when in mid-June he discussed with Alwyn Parker the respective rights of the D'Arcy group and the Turkish Petroleum Company, came out strongly for the latter,[15] leading Parker to conclude that 'It seems absolutely necessary that the two groups come to terms if there is to be a settlement.' Lowther had by now completely reversed his earlier belief in the superiority of the German claim,[16] a necessary conversion if the British were to have any practical impact on what seemed to be the hardening of the general Turkish attitude.

The anxiety of the Foreign Office was increased by a further complicating factor, that of additional competition. Babington Smith had himself plainly told the British Government that competition from a 'third party' must make the group he represented protect its own interests. This 'party' was generally recognised to be 'Baron' Thomas de Ward, and his numerous visits to the Ministry of Mines and proffered advance of £500,000 in exchange for the concession were all reported to the Foreign Office by de Ward's own group, and by Greenway, Babington Smith and Lowther.[17] As a result of this additional threat to British interests, the Foreign Office protested to Hakki Pasha and the Grand Vizir. The Grand Vizir denied having made any promises to de Ward,[18] but, in view of its experience of Turkish promises, the British Government was not greatly comforted. Marling, in Constantinople, suggested – with reference to the current subsidy/contract negotiations between the Anglo-Persian Oil Company and the Admiralty, and open hints from the Turkish Government that an advance of £500,000 would settle the case in D'Arcy's favour – that the British Government might privately guarantee to D'Arcy, against Turkish bonds, the interest on any advance he might make to the Turkish Government.[19] In reply the Foreign Secretary told Marling that Hakki Pasha had already reported that, pending the amalgamation negotiations, he had strongly advised the Ottoman Government to delay taking any steps regarding the oil concession. The request that he ensure this was repeated to Hakki Pasha on 7 July, with special reference to the National Bank group. Grey told Marling that if the Turkish Petroleum Company proved obdurate his last proposition would be examined, but the Foreign Office was really anxious to reconcile the German and British interests, something that was possible only through the agency of the National Bank.[20]

The ambiguity of the National Bank's standpoint was a further factor contributing to Foreign Office disquiet. On 11 June that department received a bombshell. Sir Henry Babington Smith wrote the Foreign Secretary a long and aggrieved indictment of the British Government's attitude towards his bank.[21] He pointed out that it had been established in Turkey with strong Foreign Office encouragement, and that he had been urged by the British Government to become its president. The British Government's intention, in so doing, was to uphold British prestige, influence and trade in the Ottoman Empire, through schemes of industrial and public works and the utilisation and development of the country's natural resources. Achieving success in such matters naturally depended partly on the course of events in Turkey, and these in any case now left the situation extremely doubtful. He continued,

> But there is another condition which is essential to the successful working of the Bank: I mean the confidence and support of the British Government. The circumstances attending the foundation of the Bank gave us every reason to believe that we should possess this, but to our great regret, this expectation has not been fully realised.

He gave a number of examples of the Government's lack of support, including the Mesopotamian oil concession question. Concerning the latter he insisted that his group was British-controlled, that it had indeed kept the British Embassy in Constantinople informed of its intentions, and that it had been given no reason to suppose that the attitude of the Foreign Office would be unfavourable. At the last moment, however, it had been informed that the British Government's support was already promised to another group. The Foreign Office had suggested a combination between the two groups, but while negotiations were proceeding the whole influence of the British Embassy had been employed against his group and in favour of the other, and he had heard that statements were freely made that the National Bank's group was regarded by the Foreign Office and the Embassy not only as largely non-British, but, in addition, as hostile to British interests. The cumulative effect of all these grievances, Sir Henry wrote, was that his bank had unwillingly been forced to conclude that

> our conception of the position which the Bank was intended to occupy in relation to the British Government and its economic policy in Turkey is widely different from the position which has in fact been assigned to it . . . [and therefore] . . . We propose, at the first suitable opportunity, to relieve ourselves of a task which we cannot . . . satisfactorily perform.

The Foreign Office was carefully conciliatory in its brief written reply.[22] Sir Edward Grey declared that he would regret it if the bank ceased operations in Turkey, and he mentioned that the Board of Trade was still communicating with Greenway in trying to reach a compromise over Mesopotamian oil. Inside the Foreign Office, Babington Smith's description of the setting up of the National Bank was seen as 'entirely correct', and the possibility that the bank and Sir Henry might retire from Turkey was viewed with genuine concern, but his charges were nevertheless denied.[23] Lowther, in Constantinople, denied, as emphatically as Babington Smith asserted, that the two of them had discussed before the end of July 1912 the intentions of the National Bank's group with regard to Mesopotamian oil.[24] Mallet, however, seemed ready to keep an open mind on this particular question. The

Foreign Office finally concluded that if the bank did not consider the economic opportunities in Turkey sufficient, in all fairness it should not be put under any pressure to stay there. Parker discussed the whole matter with Babington Smith on 14 June.[25] He learnt then the important additional fact that the bank, partly because of its association with other firms, did not wish to abandon its claims to the Mesopotamian concession, whatever might be the fate of the bank itself. The bank's decision to withdraw from all other activities in Turkey was confirmed definitely in a letter from Babington Smith on 27 June.[26]

The wish to withdraw from all financial involvement in Turkey, yet not from the oil concession negotiations, was demonstrably untenable and indeed only unsteadily maintained. This was shown when Babington Smith called at the Foreign Office on 7 July to give his reply to the Government's amalgamation proposition of the previous week.[27] He told Mallet that the furthest his group could go was to give the British Government first refusal of all fuel oil for export. He said also that the Anglo-Saxon refused to take anything less than a 25 per cent share in the proposed company, and that the shares must therefore stand at 25 per cent each. If this were not acceptable to the British Government then the National Bank would withdraw altogether, leaving the Deutsche Bank and the Anglo-Saxon free to take what action they liked. Both of these wanted to press ahead but were being hampered in their efforts by the National Bank. However, Babington Smith reiterated that, even if his bank withdrew, it still would not go over to the D'Arcy group.

This reply was not acceptable to the British Government and, indeed, led to a significant hardening in the attitude of the Foreign Office. On the one hand, the Office realised that negotiating with a Turkish Petroleum Company composed purely of Deutsche Bank and Anglo-Saxon Petroleum Company interests would mean negotiating with a far stronger Anglo-Saxon Company meriting a larger rather than a smaller share in the proposed new company. This was something the Government, with its abhorrence of monopolies in general and its dislike of Shell in particular, would not welcome.[28] On the other hand, it was necessary to reach a settlement with the German Government on the urgent questions currently being discussed with the Turkish Government. Thus the Foreign Office became even less compromising towards the Anglo-Saxon while becoming more favourably disposed towards the German Government. The next few months were to show plainly the attitudes of all the groups involved.

II JULY–SEPTEMBER 1913: THE ATTEMPTED SINKING OF SHELL

Direct negotiations between the British and German Governments over the Mesopotamian oil concession really began at the start of July 1913. During a meeting on 2 July concerning the Baghdad railway,

Kühlmann, Counsellor (and sometimes Chargé d'Affairs)) at the German Embassy in London, told Alwyn Parker his Government was very anxious to settle the oil question.[29] The year before, it had induced Gwinner to moderate the German interests' claims and to negotiate with an English group, but now the German interests found that they had become involved with an English group that did not enjoy the support of the British Government. Parker replied that this was because of the Dutch oil company associated with that group; besides, H.M. Government was committed to supporting the Anglo-Persian Oil Company, and, unless the latter could be adequately represented in the proposed new company, no settlement seemed possible. Parker and Kühlmann agreed that this much should be hinted to Gwinner, and it seemed that such a hint would be well received.[30]

This meeting was followed up ten days later by an official letter from the Foreign Office to the German Government[31] stating that Sir Edward Grey concurred in Kühlmann's suggestion of direct discussions between the two governments on the question of the oil concession. Within a few days, Gwinner, in order to facilitate agreement, had offered to give up one of the Deutsche Bank's shares in the proposed new combine, thus giving 51 per cent to the National Bank and D'Arcy group as against 49 per cent to the others.[32] To the British Government, however, this proposal did not affect the situation at all. What did help matters forward was a further discussion between Kühlmann and Parker, on 16 July.[33] This frank conversation showed that the respective positions of the British and German Governments were very close, especially in regard to the Anglo-Saxon Petroleum Company. Parker asked that the Deutsche Bank should not commit itself any further to the Turkish Petroleum Company until there had been more discussion between the British and German Governments. Kühlmann agreed to pass on this request. He was, in any case, sure that the German Government did not wish to favour or establish monopolies in oil, and thought, personally, that provided adequate arrangements were made for supplying his government with a fair share of oil fuel and other products, it would have no objection to the Anglo-Persian Oil Company having technical control of the Mesopotamian concession. He even suggested that, if the National Bank did withdraw from the Turkish Petroleum Company, the Anglo-Persian could have 50 per cent of the whole – a point that pleased Parker, who had already decided that the Anglo-Saxon must be threatened with opposition from the British Government if in these circumstances it would not agree to adequate participation for the Anglo-Persian interests.[34] When Parker asked outright whether the Germans had any particular affection for the Anglo–Saxon Petroleum Company, Kühlmann replied 'no', and said that Gwinner was 'most anxious to be accommodating in the matter'.

The intentions of the two parties were quite clear. It would suit both the German and British Governments to have the Shell interests (and, from the point of view of the Germans, possibly also the National Bank) out of the way; this was the declaration of intent to which the conversations and correspondence of the past few days had all been pointing. That the Germans understood the view of the Foreign Office is quite clear from the letter the German Ambassador, Lichnowsky, sent to his government the same day.[35]

The British Government's views on Shell were displayed plainly, over the next few weeks, in correspondence with the company and between various Government departments. First, the Foreign Office tried to secure the British position in Constantinople. On 17 July Parker told Hakki Pasha that, in the light of British and German Government discussions, it was most important that the Ottoman Government should in the meantime not commit itself further regarding the Mesopotamian concession.[36] To Parker's disquiet, Hakki Pasha could do no more than point to his country's urgent need of funds, the National Bank's advance of £T500,000, and Babington Smith's presence that week in Paris. A week later, Parker, Sir Hubert Llewellyn Smith (for the Board of Trade) and Sir Frederick Black (for the Admiralty) met at the Board of Trade, to try to find a definite set of terms to offer the Germans.[37] Their discussions were much preoccupied with the position of the Anglo-Saxon in the proposed new company, and with a lengthy correspondence with Sir Reginald MacLeod, a director of Shell, who now entered the lists as one of its spokesmen.[38] MacLeod's proposals envisaged the four participants in the proposed new company having the following shareholdings: Deutsche Bank 24 per cent, National Bank of Turkey 25½ per cent, D'Arcy group 25½ per cent, and Shell and the Royal Dutch jointly having 25 per cent (10 and 15 per cent respectively). Each of the four groups would have two directors, but the Shell director could, if so desired, be subject to confirmation by the British Government. Thus British interests would have a 61 per cent shareholding and a majority of two on the board. The British Admiralty should be secured the purchase right to all liquid fuel available for export; this would be marketed by the Anglo-Persian, and Shell would market the company's other products, together with only a small amount of crude oil. MacLeod stressed that Shell could not understand the British Government's attitude towards it and wanted this attitude clearly defined. He asserted the British character of his company and, contrasting it with the Anglo-Persian, stressed its financial stability and the commercial strength of its diffuse connections.[39]

MacLeod's proposition, depending as it did on the disputed point of whether Shell was to be regarded as 'British' or 'foreign', was not well received. Moreover, his differentiation between Shell, as 'British', and the Anglo-Saxon, as 'foreign', did nothing to strengthen his case. Llewellyn Smith, for the Board of Trade, feared that 'These informal conversations may develop into "negotiations" and we are at the same time contemplating a possible arrangement with Germany, one of the conditions of which would be to squeeze out MacLeod's Company altogether!' Llewellyn Smith wished the Foreign Office to avoid further involvement with MacLeod, for he foresaw that

> our regard for MacLeod as an old official colleague may betray us into some momentary forgetfulness of the fact *that he now represents a very powerful foreign combination with which it is quite impossible to discuss frankly the strategical needs of the Empire.*[40]

The Admiralty agreed that it was 'not desirable to allow the Anglo-Saxon to pose as a principal in this matter', Sir Francis Hopwood, Additional Civil Lord at the Admiralty, declaring MacLeod's scheme of directors to be 'absolutely illusory and one-sided' and his marketing scheme 'a specious paper promise'.[41] Like the Foreign Office, the Admiralty foresaw that if the National Bank did drop out of the Turkish Petroleum Company the Anglo-Saxon would thereby be in a much stronger bargaining position, and concluded that

> In these circumstances it seems to us that support to D'Arcy should be steadily continued till a reasonable agreement is in sight. That negotiations should be directed to securing that at least half of the directors shall represent British interests who might reasonably be expected to work together; that the main lines of control of the working of the oilfield and of marketing shall be settled, if practicable, by agreement beforehand.

Mallet had queried whether 'the line which you wish us to take is to be stiff with MacLeod, the aim being rather to get both the "Shell" and the National Bank out of the business and to induce the Deutsche Bank to come to an agreement with the Anglo-Persian whereby the latter would obtain control'.[42] Sir Francis thought that the Deutsche Bank's opinions on such a line ought to be obtained, but in effect he counselled patience and circumspection. In any case, the National Bank's intentions should be ascertained first.

The Foreign Office found it somewhat difficult to remain patient. As it pointed out to the Admiralty,[43] both Germans and Turks were anxious to know the British Government's wishes, while the moment was, from a diplomatic point of view, unusually opportune for negotiations. These, however, the Foreign Office could not embark upon, as it was still unaware of the other departments' conditions. Yet the Foreign Office was, by nature, circumspect, and saw that there would be some advantage in not cutting out MacLeod's company altogether, partly because of the rights it had derived from the Baghdad Railway Company, and partly because 'to exclude a company which commands such large supplies might possibly have regrettable effects from a naval point of view'. The department thought also that there might already exist some agreement binding the Anglo-Saxon Company and the Deutsche Bank together,[44] and that the Turkish Government would prefer, and indeed, might insist on, the admission of the Anglo-Saxon into the proposed new company. The Foreign Office was indifferent as to whether the National Bank would eventually stay in or leave the proposed combine, although on balance it felt that the Bank's presence there might be advantageous for British interests. Even the Government's own protégé, the Anglo-Persian Oil Company, could not be too blindly followed, for, as Mallet explained to Hopwood,

> Our first object is, I suppose, to protect British Government interests as distinct from those of the Anglo-Persian Company; if, in every respect the interests of the British Government do not go so far as the interests of the Anglo-Persian Oil Company's, then the Anglo-Persian Oil Company must be urged to moderate its claims.

Although the Foreign Office understood that the Admiralty, in view of its current contract negotiations with the Anglo-Persian Oil Company,[45] was anxious for as much delay as possible in the amalgamation negotiations, it was still keen to receive from the Board of Trade and the Admiralty a statement of the maximum and minimum requirements for the new company. If it did not have such information, the Office could not reasonably expect the German group to show its hand. Consequently Mallet wrote, rather plaintively, to the other two departments, trying to extract such a statement of their terms. Meanwhile MacLeod received the recommended cool and non-committal replies from the various departments, each of which, to his undoubted frustration, referred him to its fellows.[46]

The maximum requirements of the Board of Trade were simple: the award of the Mesopotamian concession to the D'Arcy group.[47] However, the Board realised that this did not appear practicable and so stated its minimum requirements, for which it declared, certain essential British interests must be kept in mind:

> 1. The desire of the Admiralty to secure supplies of fuel oil from the Mesopotamian oil-fields, with the minimum risk that supply may fail them in time of war or strained relations.
>
> 2. The desire of the Admiralty for other reasons to preserve the independence of the Anglo-Persian Oil Company . . .[48]
>
> 3. The general desire of H.M. Government to support British

> enterprise, and in particular the obligation of the Foreign Office to fulfil any promise of support given by them to Mr D'Arcy and his assignees.

The Board of Trade based its suggested scheme on certain assumptions. These were: (a) that any agreement arrived at must be acceptable to Germany; (b) that both Germany and Turkey would insist on a proportion of the oil fuel produced (c) that both the National Bank and the Anglo-Saxon Petroleum Company would stay in the combination; (d) that, for political reasons, the Foreign Office urgently required an arrangement, but could not officially ascertain in advance the state of relations between the members of the Turkish Petroleum Company; and (e) that HM Government was prepared to put pressure on the National Bank to undertake that, in time of strained relations, it would act in accordance with vital British interests.

Having made these assumptions, the Board proposed its scheme for amalgamation of the two rival groups. The British interests – that is, the Anglo-Persian Oil Company and the National Bank – should have clearly the larger share of the new company's capital, for example 52 per cent, of which the Anglo-Persian must have at least 27 per cent. All the directors nominated by these two groups must be British subjects approved by HM Government, and they must give an undertaking of loyalty to Britain in the event of war or strained relations. The British groups, moreover, must undertake not to transfer any part of their interests without HM Government's approval. Concerning marketing, an agreement must be firmly concluded prior to the formation of the new company, and this should provide the Anglo-Persian Oil Company with 50 per cent of the marketing of each type of product, with exclusive rights to supply the British Government and to market in Asiatic Turkey, Persia, India, Ceylon, Australasia and South Africa and on the east coast of Africa. The remainder was to be marketed by the Anglo–Saxon, with exclusive rights to supply the German and Turkish Governments and the Baghdad Railway Company, and to market in Europe and the rest of the non-specified areas of the world. A binding undertaking must be given that, in prospecting, mining and manufacture, and in staff selection, the Anglo-Persian would be treated on an absolutely equal footing with the Anglo-Saxon. Finally, the British Government was to have an option to purchase up to 50 per cent of the total fuel oil produced, the German Government to purchase up to 40 per cent, and the Turkish up to 10 per cent – the Baghdad Railway Company's requirements being included in either of the latter two governments' shares.

In putting forward this scheme the Board of Trade knew that its proposal regarding the share of the new company's capital to be allotted to the Anglo-Persian was not likely to satisfy Greenway.

None the less, the scheme seemed to the Board to be the only realistic solution, and it did confer certain very substantial benefits on Greenway's company in other ways. The scheme secured the company's existing markets against invasion and ensured equal treatment with the Anglo-Saxon Company as regards mining and prospecting in Mesopotamia. Concerning MacLeod's offer of one Shell director, to be a British subject approved by HM Government, the Board felt that this condition should not be imposed but, rather, accepted if kept open.

The Admiralty quite agreed with the Board of Trade's terms[49] and placed most emphasis on the requirements that the Anglo-Persian and the National Bank give assurances of loyalty to HM Government, and that the Anglo-Persian be assured adequate participation on the board of directors and in the prospecting, mining, production and marketing of the oil. This was to be secured by an unbreakable agreement.

That the Board's scheme did not go as far as the Anglo-Persian itself would wish was evident from propositions put forward by Greenway two days later.[50] Greenway listed four different schemes, based on the number and combination of the members in the new company. Fundamentally, the Anglo-Persian required a 52 per cent shareholding for itself, leaving 48 per cent for the others. The Anglo–Persian was to choose half the board of directors, while the chairman, who would have a casting vote, was to be nominated either by the company or by the British Government. Marketing was to be controlled by the Anglo-Persian, although the Deutsche Bank might bespeak 50 per cent of all oil fuel produced. If the National Bank remained in the proposed new company the Anglo–Persian would accept a joint holding with it of 60 per cent (of which two-thirds must belong to the Anglo-Persian) and would allow the National Bank a voice in electing part of the British side of the directorate. If Shell were to be a member the Anglo-Persian would permit it to market up to 50 per cent of all petroleum by-products, except in those areas defined by the Board of Trade.

The inclusion of Shell in the new company came last in Greenway's order of preference, which was hardly surprising in view of his and the Government's opinions of that company, In mid-August the Government was still hoping that the Deutsche Bank might be able to detach itself from both Shell and the National Bank and come to an agreement with the Anglo-Persian alone,[51] and it suggested as much to Hakki Pasha.[52] In contrast to his caution of only a month before, Hakki Pasha was now not against the idea, but Kühlmann's hopes of Gwinner's compliance turned out to be premature. On 20 August Kühlmann told Parker that he had heard from Gwinner, and that, although the latter had no marked preference for Shell, he feared it would be impossible to free himself from his contractual obligations to that Company.[53] Further, under clause 36A of the Turkish Petroleum Company's articles of association, it was laid down that, if one of the three parties withdrew, its shares must be offered first to the other two parties. If therefore, either the Deutsche Bank or the National Bank withdrew, the holding of the Anglo-Saxon would be increased. Parker argued that not only was the validity of the Turkish Petroleum Company's rights disputed, but that, in the absence of an agreement acceptable to both Britain and Germany, there would be no satisfactory settlement and much undesirable ill feeling. He was not pressing for the exclusion of Shell, but wanted to prevent that company from dominating the situation; it could hardly persist in its claims under any agreement with Gwinner if such persistence paralysed the new company. This was the position of vantage, he thought, from which Gwinner could persuade Shell to accept reasonable terms. Both the British and German Governments were 'anxious to avoid dealing with this question in a contentious spirit and to reach an acceptable arrangement for the future rather than to waste time on an examination of the past', but, if satisfactory terms could not be arranged, the British Government was determined to continue supporting D'Arcy alone. Parker told Kühlmann of his government's principal objectives in any arrangement, and that he thought a 60 per cent share for the Anglo-Persian would be insisted on; but he declared that it would be difficult to make progress towards any agreement 'until the Shell Company came to a proper sense of its own weak position in Mesopotamia'.

This meeting greatly helped the two governments understand each other's views and realise that their respective protégés must make serious efforts to come to terms.[54] It convinced the Board of Trade that its own scheme of 8 August offered the best prospects for reaching a solution acceptable to all parties.[55] The scheme depended, however, largely on the National Bank's participation in the combine as a British concern supporting British national interests, and accordingly the Foreign Office had now to ascertain whether the National Bank would indeed be willing to adopt such a role and to give an undertaking to that effect.[56] Parker wrote privately to Babington Smith on 5 September, detailing the Board's propositions. He underlined their present tentative and non-committal nature, together with the fact that they were far from likely to satisfy the Anglo-Persian Oil Company, and, thus, unlikely to be accepted at all by Greenway except under Government pressure. But Parker's hopes were disappointed. Babington Smith called at the Foreign Office a few days later[57] and told Parker that the National Bank found the conditions impossible and would accordingly prefer to withdraw altogether. In confidence he told the other his reasons. These, broadly speaking, were the hampering nature of the proposed restrictions and the predominant position assigned to the Anglo-Persian Oil Company. In the first place, Babington Smith declared, 'the National Bank was not enamoured of the methods of the Anglo-Persian Oil Company, or its parent company, the Burmah Oil

Company, or of Mr D'Arcy'. (Parker noted that he, personally, had heard similar criticism from 'independent and reliable sources'.) Secondly, Babington Smith said, it was almost impossible to accept any firm marketing agreement when in some years the conditions of marketing might have changed entirely. Thirdly, he did not consider it practical for the proposed new company to employ the Anglo-Persian Company's officials to such an extent as that company wished. These views he confirmed by letter on 12 September.[58]

Despite his earlier hopes, Babington Smith now said that the National Bank's withdrawal must take the form laid down by the statutes of the Turkish Petroleum Company, that of offering its shares first to the Deutsche Bank and Anglo-Saxon before offering them to outsiders. It would theoretically be possible to liquidate the Turkish Petroleum Company, since this required only a three-quarters majority and the Deutsche Bank would not object, but the National Bank was reluctant to force this solution on an unwilling Anglo-Saxon Company, because participation in the Turkish Petroleum Company had debarred the Anglo-Saxon from being able to undertake any independent action in Mesopotamia over the past two years. The banker declared his unwillingness to attend a conference at the Board of Trade on 15 September to discuss the matter further, but, following Parker's warm and friendly insistence, finally agreed to come.[59]

At this conference the Board of Trade and Foreign Office representatives expanded on their scheme. They suggested that the National Bank might be rendered independent of close ties to any other group, with the Anglo-Persian having a smaller share in the control of the proposed new company than the amount of capital it provided would appear to warrant. Babington Smith agreed to put these suggestions before his colleagues[60] and to refrain from taking any decisive step towards withdrawal until the middle of the following month, when, the holiday season over, everyone would be back in London and able to discuss matters more satisfactorily.

During this time other aspects of the Mesopotamian oil question did not remain dormant. The British Government continued its general negotiations with Turkey, the first agreement to come out of these discussions having been signed by the two governments on 29 July. In his covering letter to Tewfik Pasha, the Turkish Ambassador, Grey was able to say pointedly that he felt 'confident that the Ottoman Government will use their best endeavours to secure . . . a satisfactory arrangement in regard to the Mesopotamian oil concession . . .', to which HM Government attached 'very great importance';[61] and, later in these negotiations, the Foreign Office did not hesitate to point out to the Turkish Government that, regarding the proposed Turkish petroleum-importing monopoly, 'HM Government are especially concerned in this proposal, on account of the negotiations now proceeding with regard to the Mesopotamian oil concession, and their decision must depend on, and will be largely influenced by, the settlement reached in respect of that concession.'[62] The Anglo-Persian Oil Company had already furnished Hakki Pasha, at his request, with full particulars on the oil question,[63] while on 4 September the Foreign Office had written to Kühlmann urging speed in settling the matter.[64]

A speedy conclusion was least to be expected in such complicated international negotiations. In any event, as the India Office phrased it, 'Other, and independent, eagles have gathered about the carcase . . .'[65] The pertinacious Baron de Ward apart, these 'eagles' appeared to have been of Russian and American descent. Both the Russian Ambassador, on behalf of some Russian capitalists, and the American Embassy, on behalf of Rockefeller (and possibly, indirectly of Admiral Chester) had made inquiries in Constantinople of the Ministry of Mines, Rockefeller offering an advance of 10 million francs for the concession.[66] On 10 October Babington Smith complained to the Foreign Office that he had been 'positively informed' that even while the amalgamation negotiations were taking place HM Government was strongly pressing for the Mesopotamian concession to be granted the D'Arcy group. This was denied by both the Embassy and the Foreign Office. What apparently caused Babington Smith's apprehensions were efforts by D'Arcy's agent, Stock, to obtain an option on a local man's *permis de recherche*.[67] The comic side to this little flurry, not realised by either the Foreign Office or the Turkish Petroleum Company, was that Stock was trying for an option that the Turkish Petroleum Company had been offered, had rejected, and had contested on grounds of its validity, at about the same time. Moreover, during September and October the Turkish Petroleum Company's concern with the British Government's proper deportment did not prevent one of the companies concerned in the Turkish Petroleum Company, the Anglo-Saxon, from making plans for sending its own geologists out to Mesopotamia.

III OCTOBER 1913–MARCH 1914: GOVERNMENTS VERSUS COMPANIES AND THE GULBENKIAN CRISIS

The amalgamation negotiations were resumed in mid-October. A further conference at the Board of Trade, on 21 October, brought a rejection by the Turkish Petroleum Company of the proposals the Government had put forward at the previous conference.[68] Babington Smith repeated that his bank definitely intended to withdraw from Turkey and to offer to the Deutsche Bank and the Anglo-Saxon the additional 50 per cent holding in the Turkish Petroleum Company, while the Foreign Office reiterated its request for the bank not to withdraw from the Turkish Petroleum Company until a settlement had been formally arranged. The question of the manner in which the bank was to leave the company now seemed the essential matter to settle. The

Foreign Office could not – and indeed, did not particularly wish to – press the bank to continue functioning if it were so unhappy about its economic prospects in Turkey; but until the Government could find some means of compensating for this prospective loss of British influence in Turkey, and, more immediately, ensure a satisfactory outcome to the oil concession negotiations, it did not wish for the bank's disappearance.[69] Clearly a compromise had to be found quickly. Pursuing this aim, Llewellyn Smith made an important suggestion: that the National Bank's interest in the Turkish Petroleum Company should indeed be ceded to the Deutsche Bank and Anglo-Saxon Company and that *then* the Turkish Petroleum Company and the Anglo-Persian Oil Company should form a third company, in which they would have equal holdings. To it would be transferred all the Mesopotamian rights and claims at issue. The D'Arcy group would thus have only half the capital and control, although Llewellyn Smith did admit that the group might insist on a preliminary marketing agreement or on special arrangements concerning the chairman. Babington Smith could not, however, be budged on the question of marketing, and pointed out that the fact that the Anglo-Persian was already marketing through the Anglo-Saxon showed its professions of fear to be a fabrication. In any case, even in the hypothetical event of a price war waged by the Anglo-Saxon, it was obvious that Mesopotamian supplies would play little part. The conference finally decided that further detailed discussion was useless until the views of the Deutsche Bank and Anglo-Saxon Oil Company had been obtained on the manner of disposing of the National Bank's holding.

One outcome of the conference was that Babington Smith agreed to the suggestion that he should visit Gwinner and press him to a settlement that would either give the Anglo-Persian the whole of the National Bank's share outright or follow the lines indicated by Llewellyn Smith. Parker saw Kühlmann the following day to ask that the German Government should press Gwinner to comply.[70] Kühlmann passed on the request the same day,[71] and two days later Gwinner, having been approached by the German Government, gave his reply.[72] In his letter Gwinner recognised the advantage of establishing a joint company under English law (oil exploitation could not be financed under the existing Bourse law in Germany), but confirmed the National Bank's views, that the bank must transfer its shares to its partners before negotiations could begin with the Anglo-Persian Oil Company.

This latter view Babington Smith himself reported to the Foreign Office in late October and again in early November.[73] His tone was not encouraging. Although his bank professed itself anxious to do everything possible to meet the wishes of the Foreign Office, it could not, in fairness both to itself and its partners, agree to make the offer to the latter of its shareholding in the Turkish Petroleum Company conditional upon the satisfactory conclusion of negotiations with D'Arcy.

It was by now evident to the Foreign Office that Babington Smith and his associates were becoming extremely tired of the prolonged delay in reaching a settlement. Worried, the Assistant Under-Secretary, Sir Eyre Crowe, sent to the Board of Trade on 10 November suggesting a conference between Deterding, Babington Smith and representatives of the Foreign Office and Board of Trade.[74] He explained that Sir Edward Grey was 'for political reasons anxious that a settlement of this difficult question should, if possible, be reached by consent'. Crowe pointed out that the oil concession was the one matter outstanding between Britain and Germany in Turkey for which a compromise was not in sight, and, though it might be possible for a time to block the granting of the concession to German interests, it appeared unlikely that it could be obtained exclusively for D'Arcy. If the granting of the concession were blocked by the diplomatic action of the British Government, not only would D'Arcy receive no advantage, but in addition much friction would result. Indeed, the Foreign Office did not think it even feasible to continue supporting an arrangement whereby the Anglo-Persian Oil Company would have undisputed control of the proposed combine. It was clear that this possible change of course was being weighed seriously by the Foreign Office, for Crowe mentioned in this letter the Foreign Secretary's suggestion of a possible alternative solution. This was based on an arrangement whereby Gwinner would receive 25 per cent of the share capital and Deterding and D'Arcy 75 per cent between them in approximately equal proportions, or, if that proved unacceptable, each of the three parties would receive one-third of the share-capital. This apparent capitulation by the Foreign Office was received very poorly by the Board of Trade,[75] but interdepartmental amity was preserved by the timely intervention of a fresh factor in the negotiations.

On 13 November Kühlmann told the Foreign Office that Herr Emil Stauss, Gwinner's partner and adviser in oil affairs, was in Britain,[76] and suggested that perhaps someone from the Board of Trade or Foreign Office should meet Stauss for an informal discussion. Llewellyn Smith saw Stauss the very next day,[77] Kühlmann having already outlined the latter's terms to the British Government. These were that the D'Arcy group would be allowed a 50 per cent share in the proposed combine, with 25 per cent each for the Deutsche Bank and the Anglo-Saxon (the extra 1 per cent that the Germans had earlier offered the National Bank would not be offered to D'Arcy since that would mean permanent subordination to the latter). The first chairman of the new company should be nominated by the D'Arcy group, which, Stauss personally believed, would always control this appointment. In addition, he would agree that the British Government should have an option on up to, say, 40 per cent of the fuel oil to be exported by the new company, and Llewellyn Smith thought that there would be no British objection to a similar arrangement for the German Government. Stauss even agreed that a fair proportion – say, 50 per cent – of the higher employees of the new company who were not Ottoman subjects should be British subjects nominated by the Anglo-Persian, should the necessary candidates be forthcoming. When Sir Hubert explained to Stauss the Anglo-Persian Company's fear that the new company might use its position to undersell it in its own markets and thus drive it into submission or amalgamation, Stauss dismissed the notion; not only would this be impossible if the Anglo-Persian held a 50 per cent share in the new combine, but also the Deutsche Bank would never support any such policy. This appeared to be highly satisfactory to all the parties. In order that the three groups should shortly communicate directly, Stauss agreed to speak to Deterding, while the Board of Trade would speak to the D'Arcy group.

If the two government interests were thus in close rapport, this could not be said of the Anglo-Persian and Shell. On one point, at least, their complaints were identical and certainly seemed to some extent justified. Now that the British Government had come so near to general agreement with the German Government over Turkish affairs, its anxiety to conclude the oil negotiations led it to adopt an extremely high-handed manner towards the participants, who, however, were as concerned about their own private interests as the two governments were about theirs. On 27 November the Anglo-Persian Company – D'Arcy group's representatives attended a conference at the Board of Trade, together with Sir Frederick Black from the Admiralty.[78] Here the company's representatives showed great dissatisfaction with the proposed agreement, repeating their fears of a hostile combination against their interests by the Shell and Deutsche Bank members of the new company. This, however, they were assured, would not be likely. When, further, they wished to go into the question of geographical division of interests in the new company, they met with the new Government line that to discuss any arrangements outside that already reached with the Germans would be utterly impracticable. All the Government really wanted to know was whether the D'Arcy group did or did not wish to be the British nominee in this matter, on the terms agreed with the Germans.

The Government pointed out certain conditions that must be included in the terms of amalgamation and that it would expect the group to fulfil. One of these conditions was the retention, by the British and German Governments, of options on export fuel oil. The Government also stipulated that, of the non-Turkish higher employees of the new company, 50 per cent should be British. Furthermore, in time of war or strained international relations. the British directors would be required to follow their government's guidance as regards imperial defence. Most interesting, however, were the remaining conditions, which provided for the fears that rivals of Anglo-Persian Oil Company had expressed with regard to that company's financial stability and the genuineness of its commercial intentions. These conditions stipulated that all the necessary capital for the new group must be subscribed by the D'Arcy group (and HM Government must be satisfied that the voting power would remain British), that 'promotion profits' must not be made out of the company formed to work the Mesopotamian oil-fields, and that the British group must undertake to work the fields energetically.

Extremely dissatisfied with the conference, the Anglo-Persian Oil Company's representatives met Stauss and, separately, Sir Francis Hopwood, Additional Civil Lord of the Admiralty, in an endeavour to secure a stronger position in the new company. They attempted to persuade Stauss by declaring that if neither the Deutsche Bank nor the Anglo-Saxon Company would give up a part of its holding, the Anglo-Persian would not enter an arrangement and the British Government would be likely to 'block' the grant of any oil concession at all in Mesopotamia.[79] The Germans, having already seen eye to eye with HM Government, were not impressed by this.[80] Nor was Hopwood, who told the Board of Trade that the D'Arcy representatives

> all came to see me on Friday afternoon and were very huffy about it. I took the opportunity of pointing out to them that, if they continued in their present attitude, it might result in their being left out altogether, and that, if they were, they could not with any justice blame British diplomacy.[81]

The Anglo-Saxon interests were similarly displeased with the arrangement. They had even more cause, for, though they could only suspect it, the Board of Trade and the Foreign Office were still interested in cutting them out of the new company altogether. Only the Admiralty supported them, and that on purely pragmatic grounds. When the Board of Trade asked Hopwood whether the Admiralty would object if any means could be found 'by which the Anglo-Saxon Company could be eliminated', he replied, 'We lead a very stormy life in our interviews with the "Shell". I always try to keep on good terms with them myself, because I feel we want their stuff.' The Admiralty, Hopwood pointed out, would not wish to risk an entire break with Shell, for the British Navy could not as yet be independent of the company.

Deterding's fulminations at this time were partly due to this suspicion of the British Government's intentions, and partly also objections to the contents of the proposed agreement, which had been arranged by the two governments without consultation with him and now set peremptorily before him.[82] Deterding was upset, in the first place, to hear of Stauss's meeting with Sir Hubert Llewellyn Smith, whom he had himself been trying to see for months. This he regarded, incorrectly, as an intentional personal insult, but he was correct in supposing that the Board of Trade was far better disposed towards the Germans and the Deutsche Bank than towards the Anglo-Saxon. When, on 18 November, Deterding finally met Llewellyn Smith,[83] the main objection he made to the proposed scheme was that he thought it would better the German position quite unnecessarily. In the present Turkish Petroleum Company the Germans had only a 25 per cent interest; but in the proposed new company the German Government was being given a claim, which it did not possess and could not have obtained in the Turkish Petroleum Company, to a considerable proportion of oil fuel produced for export. The Board of Trade's view on this was that, even so, it was 'a necessary part of the "deal" which we hope to bring off' – in other words, not an isolated transaction, but part of the general settling-up of affairs in Mesopotamia. Deterding said he thought that the Admiralty greatly exaggerated the importance of the Mesopotamian field as a source of fuel oil, certainly for the next decade, and that he therefore considered unnecessary many of the Government's provisions regarding division of fuel and percentages of staff. He also showed great reluctance to accept the withdrawal of the National Bank and urged its retention in the new combination. Deterding was in fact, clearly alarmed at the prospect of being deprived of the commercial profits to be derived from marketing the oil, and of losing his sponsor, the National Bank. Emphasising his group's willingness to meet the wishes of HM Government in every way necessary to safeguard *genuine* 'British interests', Deterding said that none the less, he did not think these interests necessarily synonymous with those of the Anglo-Persian Oil Company. He stressed that his own group at least would have nothing to do with the 'Stock Exchange transactions' and 'large promoters' profits' with which he associated the Anglo-Persian Oil Company. He also clearly doubted the D'Arcy group's ability to find its share of the required capital. Deterding was most unhappy at the fact that the new company was to be limited in its sphere of operations to Mosul and Baghdad, and he declared his concern at the possibility of future competition between individual members of the new company for concessions in other parts of Mesopotamia. The Turkish Petroleum Company's claim covered the whole of Mesopotamia, while the British Government reserved to itself freedom of action in supporting British interests outside Mosul and Baghdad.[84] Finally, Deterding urged – in vain – what he had long been urging as the only sensible way of settling the problem and of preventing relations from deteriorating further: a round-table conference of the participants, to be held in the presence of British Government representatives.

The Board of Trade answered Deterding's objections but would not budge on the proposed agreement.[85] It agreed with most of his comments, but declared that, subject to the D'Arcy group's ability to satisfy the Board about the means by which it proposed to raise the necessary capital, and to demonstrate its *bona fide* desire and intention to develop the oilfields, the Board still considered the present scheme the most satisfactory that could be hoped for. Thus, the Board reiterated that a round-table conference to question the basis of the agreement was out of the question, although it conceded that, if the scheme were accepted in principle, discussions to settle points of detail could be arranged. Deterding was not satisfied,[86] particularly on the question of the German share of the exportable fuel oil, for this was a major consideration to a company, such as his, with large marketing interests. But, despite his efforts, he could make no impression on the Board of Trade.

As a final argument against the inadequacy of the memorandum outlining the proposed arrangement for the new Mesopotamian company, Deterding told the Board of Trade on 24 November that the National Bank of Turkey would not be able to dispose of its 50 per cent share in the Turkish Petroleum Company so easily as the Government seemed to think. A 30 per cent share of the Bank's holding belonged to outside interests, and no arrangements had been made as to its disposal.[87] This news was confirmed by Stauss, who named C. S. Gulbenkian as the owner of this large holding.[88] The Board took this unexpected revelation very calmly – Llewellyn Smith regarded it as 'primarily a matter of internal concern for the consideration of the parties by which . . . [the Turkish Petroleum Company] . . . is constituted'.[89]

The reaction of the Foreign Office was very different from that of the Board of Trade. Over lunch on 28 November (arranged expressly, thought Parker, to impart this information) Babington Smith told Parker that the National Bank, in agreeing to cede its interests in the Turkish Petroleum Company to the Deutsche Bank and the Anglo-Saxon Company, had been obliged to explain to its partners that it would do so only on the understanding that the interests of Mr. Gulbenkian, 'who had been the first mover in all this petroleum business', were protected.[90] Babington Smith admitted that this holding was 30 per cent of the National Bank's holding, or 15 per cent of the whole concern, but he stressed that Gulbenkian held no voting rights and was to receive only the profits from his shares. The Foreign Office thought that the bank had behaved very badly in not informing it about this matter sooner, and on 4 December Sir Eyre Crowe wrote very sharply to Babington Smith.[91] He complained that

> The prospects of a settlement with the Germans appeared, if not decidedly hopeful, at all events improved . . . but now, owing,

Sir Edward feels, to the rather inexplicable silence of the National Bank on a very material point, these prospects appear to have been illusory.

The Foreign Secretary demanded a full written statement of the facts about Gulbenkian's shares, which factor 'must inevitably influence His Majesty's Government in determining their attitude in respect of their recognition of the title of the Turkish Petroleum Company'. The Foreign Office was particularly anxious because Hakki Pasha, extremely apprehensive at the prospect of further delay in the intergovernmental negotiations, had given Parker the same news on 1 December. Hakki Pasha added confidentially that he understood that Gulbenkian had already made over his shares to Shell, and that the National Bank was thus not a free agent in the matter; in fact, he thought, the bank might face an action brought by Shell or Gulbenkian for an illegal transfer of part of the holding.[92]

Five days after Crowe's letter, Babington Smith gave what the Foreign Office considered 'a very lame reply.'[93] Babington Smith pointed out that when he first wrote to the Foreign Office in August 1912 he had stated that half the capital of the Turkish Petroleum Company would be held by the National Bank of Turkey *and the English group associated with it.*[94] This group consisted of Gulbenkian and the banker, Sir Ernest Cassel, each of whom held a 15 per cent share. But he assured the Government that it need not worry about these sub-participations, for Cassel's shares were personal and would be dealt with in the same way as the National Bank's, while Gulbenkian could not exercise any voting powers or, so long as the bank remained in the Turkish Petroleum Company, offer his shares to any interests other than the bank without the latter's consent. He stated further that Gulbenkian denied that any of his shares had in any way already been transferred to Shell interests. This was of course, Babington Smith realised, no protection against anything Gulbenkian might do, or intend to do, in the future, but he believed that the Foreign Office would find Gulbenkian ready to do what he could to facilitate an arrangement, if it were pressed upon him, and that he might even, for example, agree to reduce the amount of his participation. Babington Smith added, finally, that he thought the situation would be simplified if the National Bank carried out at once its intention of transferring its own and its group's shares to the Deutsche Bank and Anglo-Saxon, making the necessary reservation regarding Gulbenkian's shares; it would then remain for the Turkish Petroleum Company, as then constituted, to come to terms, if possible, with D'Arcy's group.

The very next day Hakki Pasha told Parker confidentially[95] that Gulbenkian had just visited him and explained he was in no way committed to Shell regarding his holding and was quite prepared to allow the Anglo-Persian the voting power carried by his shares – a surprise, as so far it had been assumed that his shares carried no voting power. Moreover, he would also agree to the Anglo-Persian having the chairmanship of the new company. He would do all this despite the fact that he was not at all happy at the idea of associating himself with D'Arcy or his companies. But in forming such an association Gulbenkian hoped he would enjoy a measure of protection from HM Government, for he was a British subject and 'of some substance' (he was prepared to put £150,000 of his own into the new company). Finally, Gulbenkian would be pleased to call at the Foreign Office should an interview with him be desired.

Certain questions arise at this point. First, if it were true, as his colleagues asserted, that Gulbenkian's shares carried no voting rights, how could he be prepared 'to allow the Anglo-Persian the voting power carried by his shares'? If it were not true, his colleagues were wilfully deceiving the British Government. If it were true, all that Gulbenkian could in fact do if he did not want a change of patron from the National Bank to the Anglo-Persian was to be obstructive. So long as the change did not threaten to or actually take away his residual, profit-making rights to 15 per cent of the Turkish Petroleum Company's shares, he could not prevent it, as indeed he appeared to recognise. If, however, these rights were threatened or damaged, he would be able to take legal action.

The second point worth considering is that of his relationship with Shell. If there were, as Gulbenkian asserted, no formal arrangement with Shell to transfer his shares to that company, there certainly had been, to use his own words, a 'friendly arrangement' between him and Deterding.[96] By this arrangement, Deterding, in return for 'protecting' Gulbenkian's interests,

> got two-thirds of the business and I got one-third, so that although you have a 25 per cent participation in the Turkish Petroleum Company, by my action in placing my share in the common fund, your participation becomes something like 28 per cent, always provided that no change takes place in the position.

A change in the situation was now proposed, and, if it did take place, it would nullify the two men's 'friendly agreement'. Thus, for Gulbenkian to say that he was 'in no way committed to Shell' might be strictly accurate in a legal sense, but it was hardly an entirely frank explanation of the situation. Gulbenkian clearly – and understandably – was trying to make the very best of a very weak position.

Of more central importance to the Foreign Office than these internal Turkish Petroleum Company convolutions was the problem of getting all the parties to accept the main lines of the agreement. The Anglo-

1 William Knox D'Arcy, founder of the Anglo-Persian Oil Company

2 Charles Greenway (later Sir Charles and then Baron Greenway), managing director and later chairman of APOC

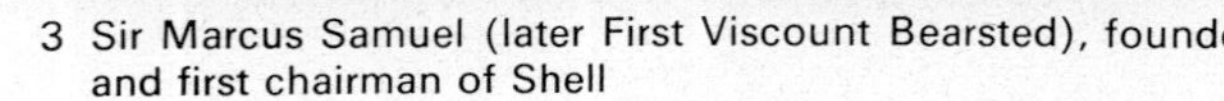

3 Sir Marcus Samuel (later First Viscount Bearsted), founder and first chairman of Shell

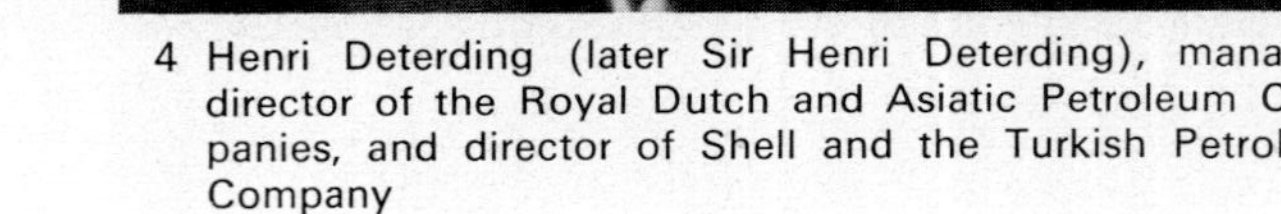

4 Henri Deterding (later Sir Henri Deterding), managing director of the Royal Dutch and Asiatic Petroleum Companies, and director of Shell and the Turkish Petroleum Company

5 Ibrahim Hakki Pasha, former Turkish Grand Vizir and diplomat

6 Calouste Sarkis Gulbenkian, financial adviser to the Porte and director of the Turkish Petroleum Company (a later photograph)

7 Sir Nicholas O'Conor, British Ambassador to Turkey, 1898-1908

8 Sir Gerard Lowther, British Ambassador to Turkey, 1908-13

9 Richard von Kühlmann, Counsellor at the German Embassy in London, 1908-14

10 Sir Henry Babington Smith, President of the National Bank of Turkey

11 Sir Edward Grey (later First Viscount Grey of Fallodon), British Foreign Secretary, 1905-16

12 Alwyn Parker, C.B., C.M.G., chief Foreign Office negotiator on the Anglo-Turkish negotiations

13 Sir Arthur Hirtzel, Secretary of the Political and Secret Department, India Office, 1909-17

14 Sir Mark Sykes, Arabist, Foreign Office adviser and joint-deviser of the Sykes-Picot Agreement

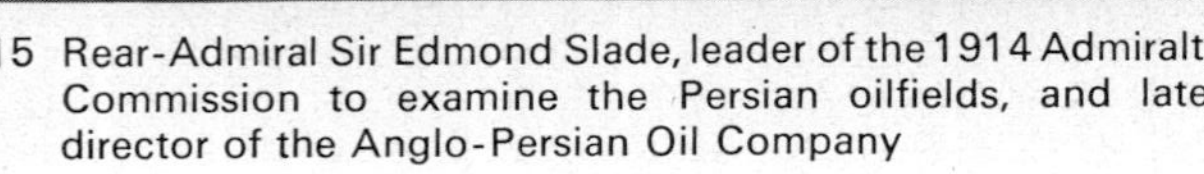

15 Rear-Admiral Sir Edmond Slade, leader of the 1914 Admiralty Commission to examine the Persian oilfields, and later director of the Anglo-Persian Oil Company

16 Sir John Cadman (later First Baron Cadman of Silverdale), director of the Petroleum Executive, and subsequently director and second chairman of APOC

Persian's efforts to obtain better terms for itself continued into mid-December, involving direct discussions with Stauss by Greenway and by the Board of Trade. These discussions were mainly concerned with certain conditions that the D'Arcy group, after hearing from the Deutsche Bank[97] that the latter group would not agree to the Anglo-Persian having more than a 50 per cent share in the new company, nor to its having a formal and permanent right to nominate the chairman of the company, had put forward as necessary to its acceptance of an agreement.[98] In order to maintain its own security, the Anglo-Persian required: first, that the members of the proposed new combine should form an independent exploration syndicate to test the Mesopotamian fields, and that their shares in the syndicate should be the same as they would be in the holding company; secondly, that should the syndicate's members be satisfied with the examination of the fields, they should undertake to form a working company having a capital of not less than £1 million, to be raised (if any member so desired) by a public issue of debentures and/or shares; thirdly, that the chairman of such syndicate and/or company should always be nominated by the D'Arcy group and have a casting vote, the other board members being nominated half by the D'Arcy group and half by the foreign group; and, fourthly, that the firm of Strick, Scott and Company Ltd of Baghdad (who were local agents for the Anglo-Persian Oil Company) should be appointed permanent managing agents of the new syndicate or company in Turkey.

Greenway's discussions with Stauss on these requirements were very amicable.[99] The Germans did not object to the first two conditions and had no strong objection to the fourth, although it seemed to them premature. The third condition, about the chairmanship, was the crux of the problem. The Germans, while being prepared to accept re-nomination of the Anglo-Persian's candidate should his performance be satisfactory and, particularly, should he be an eminent person, would not bind themselves formally to this. Indeed, in view of recent German parliamentary and press criticism of these negotiations, they did not dare to do so.[100] Stauss suggested also that the Anglo-Persian's second condition should not be pressed on Deterding, who might object, but he assured Greenway that, once the preliminary company had been formed and this point arose for discussion, the Deutsche Bank would support the Anglo-Persian on it. In addition, Stauss mentioned to the Board of Trade that his group would have no objection if the D'Arcy group simply replaced the National Bank in the Turkish Petroleum Company, thus dispensing with the formality of first offering the bank's shares to the two remaining partners; Gulbenkian's interest, he considered, was a purely internal matter for the National Bank to settle.

The net result of these discussions between the Anglo-Persian and Deutsche Bank interests was, despite their amicability and the fact that they served to clarify various points of detail, in fact nil.[101] The Board of Trade stated to the Foreign Office on 19 December[102] that it saw no reason to modify its opinion that, taking all the circumstances into account, the scheme outlined in the Board of Trade Memorandum of 14 November was the most satisfactory solution that could be found for a very difficult problem. Greenway should be told this, the Board insisted, and be asked to give a definite and early answer as to whether his group would participate in such an arrangement or stand out of the Mesopotamian concession altogether, as these were the only alternatives open to it. If the D'Arcy group did not wish to be included, the Board believed that the Deutsche Bank would not object to another British group participating. Finally, Sir Henry Babington Smith should be informed that, while HM Government could not object if his bank proceeded with the transfer of its shares to its two partners, it would be grateful if this action were deferred for another month. As for the matter of Gulbenkian's shares, this was purely a matter for him and the bank to arrange.

It took the Foreign Office a month to act on the Board of Trade's letter. This was surprising in view of its declared and demonstrated impatience to expedite the Turkish negotiations. It was even more surprising in view of the chauvinistic sentiments that had been voiced in the German parliament and press concerning the concession, and in view of the numerous reports of the renewed activities of the Standard Oil Company and of 'Baron' de Ward in Constantinople, the latter telling the Turks he had British Government support. The Foreign Office instructed its Ambassador to obstruct the efforts of both of these concession seekers.[103] On 14 January 1914 Sir Eyre Crowe wrote to Babington Smith as the Board of Trade had suggested. Babington Smith agreed that his bank should not transfer its shares for a month, but declared it would be impossible to delay matters longer than that.[104] On 16 January the Foreign Office sent off the proposed ultimatum to Greenway.[105] In addition to the points made by the Board of Trade, the letter included one most significant paragraph that showed up the somewhat cynical approach of the Foreign Office to the whole Mesopotamian oil affair. In this paragraph the Foreign Office contrasted the indisputable claims of the German interests, under the 1903 Baghdad Railway Convention, with these of Mr D'Arcy, which were based 'upon an oral assurance of later date, of which no record exists in the archives of the Ottoman Government'. The Foreign Office told Greenway that, while HM Government was anxious to secure the best possible terms for Mr D'Arcy, its representatives 'are of opinion that the provisions of the above convention do in fact debar him from any claim to a monopoly to the oil wells in the vilayets of Mosul and Baghdad, and that the only possible settlement of this question is by arrangement with the Germans.'

Despite Foreign Office pressure for a speedy settlement of the affair, the Anglo-Persian interests were reluctant to agree immediately.[106] This was partly because the company was nearing a more definite stage in its negotiations with the Admiralty for a contract, the conclusion of which would place it in a stronger financial position and thus make it better able to resist calculated financial demands by its prospective Turkish Petroleum Company partners. Another reason was that the Anglo-Persian was still unhappy about the question of the chairmanship of the proposed company – a point, incidentally, on which the Admiralty was in agreement with it[107] – although the Foreign Office advised Greenway not to put it forward as a *sine qua non* for a settlement.

The desire for haste was underlined both by the Constantinople Embassy and by Hakki Pasha.[108] The general negotiations with Turkey had made definite progress; the Ottoman Government was seriously embarrassed, financially and politically, by the delay in settling the Mesopotamian question, which it regarded as a domestic quarrel between British interests; and Hakki Pasha himself was in an unenviable situation: eight months previously he had advised his government to let the matter proceed at its own pace, and now he was being pressed for results. By the end of January, however, the Anglo-Persian Oil Company's negotiations with the Admiralty had progressed sufficiently to enable it, at long last, to reply formally to the Foreign Office's ultimatum.[109] The company was willing to accept the proposed arrangement whereby 50 per cent went to the D'Arcy group and 50 per cent to a Turkish Petroleum Company now consisting of Shell and the Deutsche Bank; the first chairman of the new company should be British. Since the Anglo-Persian Company's third and fourth conditions were unobtainable, the company assumed that its first two, which it regarded 'as of great importance if the continued participation in the concession of the British group is to be properly safeguarded'. were not unacceptable to the Foreign Office. Further, the company urged the Foreign Office to make every effort to ensure that the term of office of the first chairman should be not less than eight years.

Such progress seemed satisfactory enough to the Foreign Office,[110] but certain details still remained to be clarified. Although the National Bank of Turkey had now decided to remain in existence after all, this decision did not affect its resolve to withdraw from the Turkish Petroleum Company.[111] Thus, the future position of Gulbenkian in relation to the new company had yet to be arranged. At an interview at the Foreign Office on 27 January, Hakki Pasha told Parker[112] that he considered it very imprudent of the British Government not to enter into communication with Gulbenkian, who after all was a British subject, and reported that though Gulbenkian was prepared to cooperate with the Government about his share in the Turkish Petroleum Company he was not prepared to allow the National Bank to bargain away his rights, and if necessary would bring a lawsuit against it, which he was sure to win. The Foreign Office evidently decided at last that it should hear Gulbenkian's views, and, some weeks later, on 13 February, he was interviewed there by Alwyn Parker and a Board of Trade representative.[113] Gulbenkian confirmed the Government's supposition that he was the creator of the Turkish Petroleum Company, asserted that though he was in close touch with the heads of the Royal Dutch–Shell he was independent of them, and told the Government that its information concerning his 15 per cent share in the Turkish Petroleum Company was quite correct. As he was most unwilling to leave the Mesopotamian enterprise, he suggested that only the remaining 35 per cent of the National Bank's holding should be transferred to the D'Arcy group. In that event, he would be prepared to co-operate with the D'Arcy group if the latter were under the direction of the Government; if it were not, he would prefer to act with the other parties, since he knew them better and felt they had more experience in oil matters. He was eager for a round-table conference of himself, Deterding, Stauss and D'Arcy, and declared his readiness to meet any wishes of HM Government so far as he could; but, concluded the report of this meeting, 'he is evidently disposed to be very tenacious of what he regards as his rights'.

However much the British Government maintained to the members of the Turkish Petroleum Company that the question of Gulbenkian's rights was an internal matter for them alone to sort out, there was no denying that the question did present many difficulties. The Deutsche Bank told the British Government that it was most disturbed by the revelation of Gulbenkian's position, for it regarded his sub-participation as giving extra power to the Shell interests, something contrary to the spirit in which the Turkish Petroleum Company had been founded.[114] Stauss was in fact, sure, that, had the Deutsche Bank known about Gulbenkian's shareholding at the time when the Turkish Petroleum Company was formed, his group never would have joined the company. There were two alternative methods of arranging the combination of the Turkish Petroleum Company and the D'Arcy group: either the D'Arcy group should simply be substituted for the National Bank, or else the D'Arcy group and the Turkish Petroleum Company should form 50 per cent each of a new company, with the National Bank transferring its shareholding to the Deutsche Bank and the Anglo-Saxon. Because of Gulbenkian's position the first alternative now seemed clearly impossible. Stauss therefore declared, that either Gulbenkian's interest should be eliminated, or the Turkish Petroleum Company should be wound up completely. Personally he thought, that, if the National Bank could not come to a settlement with Gulbenkian, the Deutsche Bank would prefer a full liquidation of the Turkish Petroleum Company and a restoration of the *status quo*. Consequently Stauss announced his intention of suggesting to Berlin that Babington Smith be told of this. Such a course, Stauss thought, would bring a speedy settlement, though it would no doubt displease Deterding if he attached any importance to the maintenance of Gulbenkian's position. As regards other details of the proposed arrangement, Stauss declared that the Deutsche Bank was prepared to accept the Anglo-Persian Company's first two conditions, but that it could not change its attitude about the chairmanship.

Relations between the Foreign Office and the other members of the Turkish Petroleum Company, as represented by their spokesman, Babington Smith, now deteriorated markedly. Telephoning Parker early in March, the banker told him what he and Hakki Pasha had already reported three months before.[115] This was that Gulbenkian, 'after considerable pressure', was willing to agree that the voting rights of his 15 per cent should be held by the Anglo-Persian, provided that he retained the profits; in addition, he might possibly agree to a slight reduction of that percentage.[116] Parker, however, was not forthcoming, repeating that it was purely an internal matter for the Turkish Petroleum Company to arrange.[117] Babington Smith returned that it looked like a deadlock, for, despite what Gwinner appeared to think, legally the company could not be dissolved except by a three-quarters majority. Deterding was utterly against such a proceeding and the National Bank would not be willing to force it on him. Parker rejoined that the German and British Governments had it in their power to prevent the Ottoman Government from giving the concession to anyone of whom they did not approve, and 'neither the Anglo-Saxon nor Mr Gulbenkian could attach much importance to being shareholders in a paralytic company.' With this, Babington Smith could only agree, and, when Parker suggested that the best solution was for Gulbenkian and the Anglo-Saxon to share 25 per cent, he said he would pass this on. By this time Babington Smith had already written formally on behalf of the National Bank to both of the bank's partners in the Turkish Petroleum Company, offering them, on condition that satisfactory arrangements were made concerning Gulbenkian's interests, the shares belonging to the bank and to Cassel. On 2 March Deterding formally accepted this offer.[118]

The Foreign Office was even less forthcoming with Gulbenkian himself. The latter was, as has been seen, anxious to discuss the situation personally at a round-table conference, but he was consistently snubbed. When Babington Smith made the suggestion on his behalf it was refused; when Gulbenkian rang up Parker in person he was not granted an interview, and was told that a conference such as he and Deterding proposed was impossible, useless and undesirable, and if he had anything further to say he should put it in writing. When, accordingly, he wrote to the Foreign Office, he was again snubbed, and told that an official communication was being addressed to Babington Smith, as the official representative of the Turkish Petroleum Company.[119] This line of action by the Foreign Office was fully approved by the Board of Trade,[120] on whose suggestion the company was now told formally, on 6 March, that

> His Majesty's Government have reached a final decision that a 50 per cent interest as regards share capital, free of all encumbrance of any kind, must be obtained for the D'Arcy group in the Mesopotamian concession.
>
> The matter is one which cannot longer be delayed without grave inconvenience and consequently, if the Turkish Petroleum Company cannot see their way to participate in such an arrangement, His Majesty's Government will feel compelled to take such steps as they may think proper to secure the interests of the D'Arcy group.[121]

This was no idle threat. The British Government was already taking strong alternative action. The Constantinople Embassy and the Anglo-Persian Oil Company had informed the Foreign Office of the formation of a local Turkish group of wealthy and politically powerful oil concession seekers who were said to have significant connections in Germany.[122] Moreover, in early March the new Ambassador at Constantinople, Louis Mallet, reported the activities of a rival British group headed by the Central Mining and Investment Corporation, a London concern.[123] Both groups were pressing the Turkish Government to grant them an oil concession for the Mosul and Baghdad vilayets. Acceding to a suggestion made by Mallet, the Foreign Secretary gave the Ambassador permission to

> state categorically that if the concession for these fields is given to any company in which the D'Arcy company does not receive 50 per cent of the whole, I shall be compelled to break off all negotiations with Hakki Pasha and to reconsider the terms upon which His Majesty's Government could assent to the customs increase and the monopolies.[124]

Parker sent a similar note on 12 March to Hakki Pasha, spelling out in detail and even more strongly the British Government's requirements and the Ottoman Government's undertakings with regard to D'Arcy.[125] Mallet presented a formal note to the Grand Vizir, now Prince Saïd Halim Pasha, on 12 March. He also had an interview with Talaat Bey, Minister of the Interior, who rather dismissed the Ottoman company, and with the Grand Vizir, who did not, and who complained to him about the injustice to Turkey of the interminable delay in Britain's coming to terms with Germany.[126]

An attempt to speed up agreement with the German Government was the other, and major, part of the British Government's rearguard action. Whether it was a desperate bluff or a determined stand not to brook delay and distraction any longer, the two governments began negotiations aimed at forming a purely Anglo-German company for obtaining the Mesopotamian concession. On 11 March a preliminary discussion with Kühlmann took place at the Foreign Office.[127] Out of the discussion emerged the idea that the simplest course might be for the British and German Governments to inform the Ottoman Government that the Turkish Petroleum Company did not enjoy the support of either government and to urge that the concession be granted to a new company, in which the D'Arcy and German interests should have 50 per cent each. It was thought that the technical difficulty presented by the Deutsche Bank's undertaking of 1912, that it would not seek or exploit oil in Asiatic Turkey except through the Turkish Petroleum Company, might be overcome by the bank's putting forward a nominee to participate in the new company. The Turkish Petroleum Company, being deprived of a sphere of operations, would then presumably go into liquidation. The German Government was immediately informed, and on 13 March, after consulting the Deutsche Bank, the German Foreign Secretary, Herr von Jagow, told the British Ambassador, Sir William Goschen, that he agreed with the suggestion. He would immediately instruct the German Ambassador at Constantinople to confer with his British colleague, something that had in fact already occurred two days previously, on Mallet's initiative.[128] If the Deutsche Bank should make difficulties, the German Government was prepared to call in some other bank. Parker discussed the whole matter with the Board of Trade and Sir Frederick Black, the Director of Contracts at the Admiralty. With their assent the Foreign Office and the German Ministry of Foreign Affairs accordingly advised their ambassadors at Constantinople to tell the Ottoman Government that 'a definite scheme will be put before them by the British and German Governments on or before 23 March'.[129] It had only to be decided which scheme was preferable, 'support of the Turkish Petroleum Company or its supersession'. The careful wording of the message that the two ambassadors were to convey, plus the fact that the Foreign Office told the German Government that 'the attitude of the Anglo-Saxon group and Mr Gulbenkian now shows signs of becoming more reasonable' indicated that the question was still open. At any rate, the German Foreign Secretary told Goschen that Herr Bergmann, representative of the German oil interests, was shortly due to arrive in London to discuss the matter, news highly satisfactory to the Foreign Office.

IV THE LAST FEW DAYS: RESOLUTION AND AGREEMENT

Resolution of the negotiations was now imminent, assisted by two factors. In the first place Deterding was able to bring pressure to bear on the Foreign Office. He was still far from satisfied. On 13 March he had called on Churchill at the Admiralty and complained bitterly of the cavalier treatment he had been given by the Foreign Office.[130] As a result Churchill sent for Parker that evening to tell him that Deterding was extremely upset. He impressed upon the other that the Admiralty was under some obligation to Deterding, whom he considered a very distinguished man, and he wished Parker to 'smooth him over . . . as he might be of great service to the Government in the future'. Parker in turn explained that the Foreign Office had very good grounds to feel angry with Deterding, who had held back the information on Gulbenkian's interests in the Turkish Petroleum Company. He added that he thought Deterding was upset by the policy itself rather than, as he had insisted, the mode of pursuing it. Parker explained that in order to avoid endless complication the Foreign Office had to deal with principals – in this case the National Bank. This sounded very well, but Parker seemed to be forgetting the ambiguous position of the Deutsche Bank. If the bank was the protégé of the German Government, it was just as much a minor participant in the Turkish Petroleum Company as was Deterding's company.

The Foreign Office was now furious with the Admiralty.[131] Sir Eyre Crowe fumed that 'this is a complete "volte face" on the part of the Admiralty. It was owing to their direct request that we avoided entering into a discussion with the Shell Company.' Crowe's minute pointed out, moreover, that the delay in completing the current arrangements was entirely due to the contract that the Anglo-Persian was fixing up with the Admiralty, 'the whole idea being, as we were told, that so soon as the Admiralty had fixed up their agreement with D'Arcy, they could snap their fingers at the Shell'. This was indeed largely the case, although it is clear that the Foreign Office had always tended to take the Admiralty's private wish to be its manifest intention regarding its future relations with Shell.[132] Crowe was annoyed that the Foreign Office, which had, with the full concurrence of the Board of Trade and the Admiralty, put forward a new scheme for a purely Anglo-German company excluding both the National Bank and Shell because of 'their disingenuousness respecting the holding of Mr Gulbenkian and the latter's refusal to come to any acceptable arrangement', should now be asked by Churchill, under Deterding's influence, to go back on this. He asserted, with great feeling, 'I shall feel relieved when the Foreign Office ceases to be mixed up with these oil negotiations altogether.' The Foreign Secretary noted flatly, 'We cannot change about now. We can be as civil as possible in form, but it is too late for anything else.'

But it was not too late, for, despite its righteous indignation, the Foreign Office had never become firmly committed to the purely Anglo-German scheme. Indeed, an idea for a happier settlement had been mentioned when Babington Smith saw Crowe at the Foreign

Office on 12 March.[133] Two days later Crowe had sent him a telegram, asking him to set out his idea fully, in writing, and this he did on 16 March.[134] In this new scheme the Anglo-Saxon Company agreed to give Gulbenkian out of its holding in the new company a sub-participation of 2½ per cent without voting rights, provided the D'Arcy group would do the same. The latter 2½ per cent shareholding would stand in the name of the D'Arcy group, which would leave the corresponding voting right. On these conditions Gulbenkian agreed to take such a reduced participation, and, to remove any doubt on this point, was willing to sign any document deemed necessary. Further, he would bind himself not to transfer his holding to anyone without first offering it 'on definite terms' to the D'Arcy group.[135] As to the procedure by which the new company was to be formed, the National Bank did not mind which of the two methods was adopted. On the question of the exact territorial scope of the concession, Babington Smith thought that once the principle had been accepted the details could be settled without any difficulty by the parties involved.

It was as well for the Foreign Office that, on the Admiralty's and Babington Smith's persuasion, it had agreed to reconsider its plan for a purely Anglo-German deal concerning the proposed new oil company. Whereas Gulbenkian and the Anglo-Saxon, incredulous and dismayed at the willingness of the Foreign Office to abandon them, had quickly formulated the new conciliatory scheme that Babington Smith had proposed to the Foreign Office,[136] the Deutsche Bank had now retreated from the idea of a purely Anglo-German company. Though aware of its own insecure position *vis-à-vis* the German Government, the Deutsche Bank was even more aware of the need to retain at least some degree of amicability with the Anglo-Saxon. The two companies had business relations in other fields, and the bank faced the likelihood of litigation if it did not abide by its obligations to the Turkish Petroleum Company.[137] Thus, while it made clear to the Board of Trade that it would prefer to participate in a purely Anglo-German oil company, the Deutsche Bank now realised that it would not be possible to do so, and hastened to assure the Turkish Petroleum Company of its loyalty. Hence the Deutsche Bank decided that the new scheme provided an acceptable compromise. The Board of Trade thought so too, and advised the Foreign Office to try to bring about the Anglo-Persian's acceptance, for the scheme appeared to give the company as much as it could reasonably expect – 50 per cent of the control. In any event, the Board of Trade recommended a formal meeting of all the parties concerned, so that in the event of the Anglo-Persian's acceptance a record of the arrangement could be drawn up and signed.

This conference was what Deterding had been pressing for all along. Indeed, he had been so outraged by the Foreign Office's attitude that, imagining the negotiations about the proposed purely Anglo-German group to be almost complete, he had written to Churchill on 17 March threatening legal action against the Crown.[138] Further, as a result of intervention by his company's solicitor, two directors of Shell and the Anglo-Saxon, Robert Waley Cohen and Walter Samuel, had had a secret meeting with Parker at the Foreign Office on the afternoon of 18 March.[139] This meeting was not recorded at all for the Foreign Office, and only the Foreign Secretary and Deterding knew about it. Certainly none of the other government departments was to be told of it; nor were Babington Smith and Gulbenkian. At this meeting both sides explained their grievances, and in consequence understood each other far better.

Whether or not these last communications actually affected in any way the subsequent negotiations on the agreement is hard to say. The Shell/Anglo-Saxon interests obviously thought they did, since for the first time they were given the chance to view events directly through Foreign Office eyes. This was a rather sobering experience, but one that, as the company representatives pointed out, could well have been gained sooner. Much misunderstanding and ill feeling could have been avoided if the Foreign Office had previously not been so adamant in refusing Deterding's suggested round-table conference. Responsibility for this earlier attitude the Foreign Office laid squarely at the Admiralty's door. Thus Deterding's belief that Churchill's intervention was decisive in promoting and hastening a satisfactory settlement was correct only in a somewhat limited sense. Nevertheless, it brought Churchill Deterding's promise of unhesitating reciprocal service if ever it should be needed in the future.[140]

The conference for which Deterding – and now the Board of Trade – pressed was held the very next day. The participants were summoned by telegram on 19 March and met at the Foreign Office at four o'clock the same afternoon. Here they signed the so-called Foreign Office Agreement, more formally known as the 'Arrangements for Fusion of the Interests in the Turkish Petroleum Concession of the D'Arcy group and of the Turkish Petroleum Company.'[141] The signatories were R. von Kühlmann (for the Imperial German Government), Eyre A. Crowe (for His Britannic Majesty's Government), H. Babington Smith (for the National Bank of Turkey), [H.] W. Deterding and Walter H. Samuel (for the Anglo-Saxon Petroleum Company), C. Bergmann (for the Deutsche Bank), and C. Greenway and H. S. Barnes (for the D'Arcy group).

It is interesting to compare this agreement with the main points at issue during the negotiations of the previous ten months. The share percentages were indeed 50, 25 and 25 respectively (preamble), including the two $2\frac{1}{2}$ per cent holdings for Gulbenkian (Article 9).[142] The National Bank's shares were to be transferred equally to the Deutsche Bank and the Anglo-Saxon (Article 1), while the Turkish

Petroleum Company's capital was doubled by the creation of 80,000 new £1 shares (Article 2), which were to be allotted to the D'Arcy group (Article 3); the board of eight members would be divided in the proportions 4:2:2 (Article 4). Of the Anglo-Persian Oil Company's first two conditions about the exploration and working companies, the first was implicitly rejected and the second accepted only in principle and not in all details (Articles 5, 6 and 7). The self-denying clause in the 1912 Deutsche Bank–Turkish Petroleum Company agreement was retained in the new agreement, for all members of the reconstituted Turkish Petroleum Company undertook not to be interested, directly or indirectly, in oil production or manufacture in the Ottoman Empire (excepting Egypt, Koweit, or the 'transferred territories' of the Turco-Persian Frontier)[143] except through the new Turkish Petroleum Company (Article 10). It was agreed that, in order that these conditions might be carried out, the statutes of the old company would be altered as necessary forthwith (Article 8).

The Foreign Office Agreement was indeed an acceptance in principle of the absolute minimum. The most interesting omissions were those of any mention whatever of the chairmanship, the commercial control of the company, and the proportion and method of allocating its marketing. The agreement did not even mention the question of national allegiance in time of war, much less the two governments' options on the purchase of fuel oil. Nor did it make any provision for the protection of the Anglo-Persian Oil Company's local markets.

This was the agreement to which the negotiations of the previous ten months had been leading. Although it was thin and imperfect in content, it was an achievement, in view of the many delays and difficulties, that it had been produced at all. After each demanding a decisively controlling share in the proposed combine, the D'Arcy group and the Turkish Petroleum Company had eventually been brought to compromise and had decided to co-operate on equal terms. This decision was brought about by long months of hard negotiation, and had been encouraged by competition from outsiders in Constantinople, and by the fear that, if they did not sink their differences and co-operate, neither of the two governments' protégés would gain the concession. The agreement would never have been achieved but for the good offices of the British and German Governments, given because they were both concerned with their own imperial interests in the Ottoman Empire. Indeed, so determined were these two governments to secure their own interests, that at the last moment each was prepared to throw over its own protégé if it refused to reduce its demands and agree to compromises that, only months earlier, the governments would never have dreamed of demanding. Moreover, these protégés were the only competitors who had any sort of claim to the concession. Both governments, together with their protégés, disliked the Shell/Anglo-Saxon element in the Turkish Petroleum Company, and the British Government, especially, tried hard to exclude it from any settlement. One of the chief reasons for the success of these interests in resisting exclusion was the loyalty of the National Bank of Turkey in refusing to betray its associate – though Parker, Deterding, Waley Cohen and Gulbenkian did not seem to think so. Further important reasons were the tenacity of Deterding himself, the eventual if reluctant support of the Deutsche Bank, and the British Admiralty's unavoidable need of the group's fuel oil. Whatever reasons the British Government may have had for its hostility towards the Shell/Anglo-Saxon interests, they cannot be clearly deduced from the documentary record of these negotiations. What is clear is that all the 'blame' for the delays and difficulties encountered in these prolonged negotiations can not be placed on any one participant. Each of the parties involved – Government departments, banks, companies, and individuals – was responsible for some particular delay, misunderstanding or subterfuge. However, the relationship between the British Government and its protégé, the D'Arcy group – Anglo-Persian Oil Company is well documented, and has been described in this and the previous chapter. It can be seen that, while the relationship was, regarding Mesopotamia and Persia, mutually dependent, it was maintained only by pressure from one or the other side – and this, at times, almost amounted to blackmail. True, the British Government earnestly and even ruthlessly supported its protégé at Constantinople, but even the Foreign Office could not honestly admit to itself or to the company that the latter's claim to the Mesopotamian concession was worth as much as the Deutsche Bank's. By 19 March 1914 the situation appeared to be that a re-formed Turkish Petroleum Company, with the D'Arcy group replacing the National Bank, was going to attempt to gain the Mesopotamian concession once and for all. This undertaking did not turn out to be as simple and speedy as the new company expected.

6 The Concession Gained and Lost, 1914–15

Setting out the problems – Arranging details of the FO Agreement – Question of the chairman and vice-chairman – Principle of the degree to which the Government should be involved in the TPC – The question of its financial involvement in the company, and of indirect involvement through the APOC representatives on the board of the TPC – Statement to the press – Position of the National Bank of Turkey – Attitude of the APOC–D'Arcy group and of Government departments – Basic issue: the extent of the British Government's involvement in the TPC – Problem of the size of concession sought – Position of FO – TPC only to lease the concession – Turkish Government's difficulties – The case of R. H. Silley – His treatment by the FO – Baron de Ward's group and their treatment by the FO – British and Turkish Government deliberations – The leverage possessed by the British and German Governments with regard to Turkish monopolies – Ultimata to the Grand Vizir – The Grand Vizir formally promises the concession – The problem of the Turkish Government's participation in the concession and royalty negotiations – APOC – D'Aroy group claims regarding the concession as a result of Turkey's entering the war – Crystallisation of the FO, Admiralty, India Office and Board of Trade responses – Summary of chapter.

I ORGANISING THE NEW COMPANY AND DEFINING THE BRITISH GOVERNMENT'S ATTITUDE TOWARDS IT

Though the Foreign Office Agreement of 19 March 1914 had provided for amalgamation of the major competing interests seeking the Mesopotamian oil concession, the details of this merger had yet to be settled. Indeed, the grant of the concession, the *raison d'être* of the whole operation, had still to be secured. Bringing both matters to a successful conclusion continued to require the British Government's close attention, both in defining points of principle and in supervising their material outcome. Breaking in on these arrangements came war, first with Germany, and later also with Turkey. It disrupted negotiations but provided, in consequence, the germ of an alternative settlement.

There were a number of questions to be settled in reorganising the Turkish Petroleum Company according to the Foreign Office Agreement. Minor points on which an understanding had to be reached included the appointment of the company's representatives at Constantinople, and the nationality of the chairman and vice-chairman; in addition, it was considered desirable to reach agreement on the proportion of fuel oil produced that each government was to receive.

The matter of the company's representatives was settled the very day the Foreign Office Agreement was signed, with Stock, Whittall, and F. J. Günther appointed as joint representatives.[1] The somewhat premature question of allocating to the British and German Governments set proportions of fuel oil was also settled without difficulty. Each government was to take up to one-third of the total quantity produced for export.[2] Deterding did not believe that the Turkish authorities would allow such a large proportion of the fuel to be so allocated, and thought it even less likely that in the foreseeable future sufficient surplus oil would be produced for any significant amount to be exported.[3] This belief was, perhaps, simply a way of expressing a fear that the prices offered by the respective governments would not be on a par with current market prices otherwise obtainable by the Turkish Petroleum Company. If so, it was a more than understandable attitude for a large commercial company to hold, particularly in view of the current rumours that an agreement between the British Government and the Anglo-Persian Oil Company was imminent.

A point of rather more immediate concern in the amalgamation negotiations was that of the nationality of the chairman and vice-chairman of the new company. Indeed, this question had been an important subject of discussion among the two governments, the D'Arcy group and the Deutsche Bank before the Foreign Office Agreement.[4] As a result of further discussions between Greenway and Stauss, it was settled by 23 April that the D'Arcy group's representatives on the board of the re-formed Turkish Petroleum Company and any of its subsidiaries would, for a period of not less than ten years, vote annually for the appointment of a German subject, nominated by the Deutsche Bank and approved by the German Government, to the post of deputy chairman of such company or companies. Similarly, an Englishman, nominated by the D'Arcy group and approved by the British Government, would be elected chairman. The arrangement would be extended by five-year periods unless either of the parties refused.[5]

The importance of this arrangement, as indeed of the Foreign Office Agreement, to the German interests is shown in a letter of 20 May from the Deutsche Bank to the German Foreign Ministry.[6] The bank's directors stated plainly that German interests had 'full reason to be satisfied' with the outcome of the negotiations. The opening up of the Mesopotamian oilfields was secured for the Baghdad railway and was to be financed largely by British capital – German capital would have been far harder to secure, because of German stock-exchange conditions. The German Navy was now assured the same share of Mesopotamian oil as its British counterpart was, while, thanks to the company's deputy directorship being assigned to a German, German interests were assured of influence in the running of the new Mesopotamian company.

The agreement on the chairmanship formed an important codicil to the Foreign Office Agreement of 19 March, for it was to be ratified by an exchange of notes between the British and German Governments. The German note was sent almost immediately, on 25 April. The Foreign Office was anxious to do the same, and obtained the agreement of the D'Arcy Group and the Board of Trade. The Admiralty, however, despite its great interest in the whole matter, was, as often happened, almost pathologically unable to send an opinion reasonably quickly. There is in fact no documentary evidence that the Foreign Office was ever able to send a return note to the German Government, for on 20 July Alwyn Parker was still begging the Admiralty for a reply,[7] and on 4 August Britain declared war on Germany.

Such a delay in settling the principle of the nationality of the chairman and deputy chairman naturally affected the organisation of the details. From April to July the D'Arcy group and a number of British Government departments – the Foreign Office, the Board of Trade, the India Office and the Admiralty – discussed who was to be chairman of the new company.[8] Interdepartmental comments were frank, one otherwise acceptable candidate put forward by the Anglo-Persian Oil Company being described as 'remarkably dense', and its next candidate as too weak. The Admiralty's favourite candidate, on the other hand, declined, when approached, to take on yet another unpaid job for the Government.

The most important point of the whole arrangement, and the only one that the Government could insist that the D'Arcy group observe, was related to political objections raised by the Foreign Office. Since Parliamentary sanction was shortly to be sought for the buying of the British Government's majority shareholding in the Anglo-Persian Oil Company, and the matter would thus become public knowledge, the Government wished to avoid any accusation at home of using public money to invest indirectly in a company – the Turkish Petroleum Company – for which the money had not been sanctioned. Even more, the British Government needed to avoid both condemnation in Germany for trickery in its dealings over the amalgamation, and the danger of arousing a united opposition in Turkey to any grant of the concession to what appeared to be a British Government concern.

The seemingly straightforward matter of selecting a chairman for the proposed new Turkish Petroleum Company was thus shown to have a much deeper implication. It brought into question the extent to which the British Government should become involved in the new company. That the company and the concession it sought had become a significant factor in British foreign policy has already been shown; but was this political relationship to become also a financial connection, as with the Anglo-Persian Oil Company–British Government agreement? The Anglo-Persian Oil Company, the Admiralty and the Treasury certainly thought such a development would be highly advantageous.[9] The point at issue was the manner in which the D'Arcy group should make its financial contribution to the capital of the re-formed Turkish Petroleum Company. The D'Arcy group was, of course, virtually identical with the Anglo-Persian Oil Company, and the Anglo-Persian and the British Government were on the point of making public the Government's majority shareholding in that company. The Admiralty suggested that the Anglo-Persian Oil Company should directly provide the money for the D'Arcy group to invest in the Turkish Petroleum Company, on the grounds that this would not only be a profitable enterprise, but also secure for the Anglo-Persian Oil Company – and through it for the British Government – some knowledge and control of the Turkish Petroleum Company's proceedings. This control would obviously be increased and facilitated if the Anglo-Persian nominated one of its own directors – Sir Hugh Barnes – to be chairman of the new company a nomination, incidentally, of which the Deutsche Bank approved).

The Foreign Office could not agree with this line of argument. As that department was always more exposed to public criticism than was one dealing with the nation's defence, and as it was less directly concerned with the Anglo-Persian Oil Company and its products than was the Admiralty, it took strong exception to the Admiralty's arguments and proposals. Thcsc constituted, in the Foreign Office's opinion, the exact reasons why the Anglo-Persian should not be directly connected with the Turkish Petroleum Company.[10] The Foreign Office pointed out to the Admiralty that an essential condition of the Government's acquisition of control in the Anglo-Persian Oil Company, and one previously stressed by the Admiralty, was that, because of 'most formidable diplomatic difficulties . . . The D'Arcy group as distinct from the Anglo-Persian Oil Company should be the parties interested in the Mesopotamian concession'. Indeed, the British oil interests party to the Foreign Office Agreement had signed it 'on behalf of the D'Arcy group'. Further, Greenway had repeatedly and emphatically stated that the danger to his company, should the Mesopotamian oilfields fall into the wrong hands, was 'principally due to the relatively weak financial position of the Anglo-Persian Oil Company and its consequent inability to face competition'.[11] Now, having agreed to afford the Anglo-Persian financial support, the Admiralty was arguing that the British Government's financial and naval interests in Persian oil would be endangered if the Government did not participate in and control Mesopotamian oil. Even if this were so, wrote the Foreign Office, surely alternative means to those proposed by the Anglo-Persian Company and taken up by the Admiralty could be devised, to ensure 50 per cent British control of the Turkish Petroleum Company. The Anglo-Persian had suggested a device whereby the subsidiary company the D'Arcy group proposed to create to hold its Turkish Petroleum Company shares would be financed by making a loan of £100,000 (£80,000 direct capital, and £20,000 for the holding company's working expenses and to provide a reserve fund) to the Anglo-Persian's representatives in the holding company. In return for this loan the D'Arcy group's shares were to be lodged together with blank transfers for them, with the Anglo-Persian Oil Company. This device, the Foreign Office told the Admiralty, would not deceive any foreign government (notably France, Russia and Turkey) or any political opponent at home. It was for the same reason that the Foreign Office felt it undesirable for any director of the Anglo-Persian Oil Company to have a seat on the board of either the D'Arcy group's holding company or the Turkish Petroleum Company; thus, if Sir Hugh Barnes became chairman of the latter company, he should vacate his seat on the board of the Anglo-Persian.

The Board of Trade, which acted as mediator in these negotiations.[12] thought that the question of directors was of only subsidiary importance. In any case, it could not see why some, at least, of the British directors in the Turkish Petroleum Company should not also be directors of the Anglo-Persian Oil Company; a complete separation of the Anglo-Persian Oil Company from the Turkish Petroleum Company was not, it felt, advisable. On discussion with Greenway and Sir Hugh Barnes, however, agreement was reached that Barnes should not accept nomination as chairman of the Turkish Petroleum Company.

The main problem was undoubtedly the difficulty about the source of finance for the D'Arcy group's holding company. The Board of Trade's main objection to the scheme proposed by the Anglo-Persian and Admiralty was that, in exchange for the odium that would attach to it were it to become known as a shareholder in the Turkish Petroleum Company, the British Government would have only indirect and very limited control over that company. Yet to the Board of Trade some Government control or influence was desirable. As a result of discussions with the Anglo-Persian Company – D'Arcy group representatives, the Board of Trade proposed to the Foreign Office a compromise solution. This was that the holding company should be formed from a group having a permanent interest in the Anglo-Persian Oil Company – in other words, the Burmah Oil Company, the Anglo-Persian's largest single non-government shareholder. There was only one small difficulty.

The Burmah Oil Company would agree to put up the necessary £100,000 only if the Anglo-Persian would guarantee this sum against any loss arising from the operations of the Turkish Petroleum Company. This provision disturbed the Board of Trade on commercial grounds, for it meant that the Burmah Oil Company would have all the profit and the Anglo-Persian all the risk. But so long as neither the other government departments involved, nor the Anglo-Persian, objected to the scheme, the Board of Trade said it would not do so either. Indeed, both the Board of Trade and the Anglo-Persian advocated this proposal as the only practical solution that would meet the objections the Foreign Office had made to the previous scheme. The Foreign Office and, more doubtfully, the Treasury assented.[13]

A firm arrangement had yet to be made and many details settled. From June to November, the negotiations stretched on. The Foreign Office's concern to convince the other government departments and the Anglo-Persian Oil Company of the importance of His Majesty's Government having no financial stake, and as unobtrusive a control as possible, in the Turkish Petroleum Company was completely vindicated following the announcement of the British Government–Anglo-Persian Oil Company agreement.[14] Editorial comment in *The Times* on 24 June queried the connection between the British Government, the Anglo-Persian Oil Company and the Turkish Petroleum Company. In view of the arguments just examined, the Anglo-Persian Oil Company's 'correction', placed in the paper the next day, is worth quoting in detail:

> . . . *(2) No part of the funds of the Anglo-Persian Oil Company will be employed in developing any oil territory which may be acquired by the Turkish Petroleum Company. (3) The Anglo-Persian Oil Company has not acquired nor has it any intention of acquiring any share or control in the Turkish Petroleum Company, nor does it intend working in Mesopotamia in conjunction with the Shell Company.* (4) The British group interested in the Mesopotamian Oil Fields and which is acquiring a 50 per cent share in the Turkish Petroleum Company is one which was formed many years ago by Mr. W. K. D'Arcy, for the purpose of acquiring the Mesopotamian oil concession, and its interests are separate from those of the Anglo-Persian Oil Company.[15]

Not surprisingly, the Anglo-Persian Oil Company now accepted the Foreign Office's stipulation that only one of the company's directors should also join the board of the Turkish Petroleum Company; accordingly, D'Arcy himself was proposed.[16] On 22 July the Treasury wrote to the Anglo-Persian Oil Company, stating that, subject to the departments concerned approving the suggested scheme, 'generally speaking, it will not be the policy of His Majesty's Government to interfere in any purely business arrangement which the company may consider it desirable to make . . .'.[17]

This letter proved somewhat premature. The departments concerned had not yet all approved the revised scheme. Despite a conference at the Admiralty on 16 June to discuss details of the proposed holding company, the D'Arcy Exploration Company Ltd (it had been incorporated on 12 June as the Stanmore Investment Company Ltd),[18] the Admiralty more than a month later proposed a different arrangement altogether. The Treasury had always been unhappy about an arrangement whereby the Anglo-Persian Oil Company was to incur risk without profit, but had not been able to improve on the scheme. After discussing the matter with the Admiralty, however, the two departments decided that a far simpler arrangement would be for the Anglo-Persian Oil Company to make a loan, for general purposes, to D'Arcy.[19] They declared that the new plan was much better and less complicated than the Burmah Oil Company guarantee scheme, and it need not appear on any printed document. The Foreign Office decided it could not object to the new scheme, since any objection it might have was equally applicable to the scheme it had already approved.

The Foreign Office had a further aspect of the matter to consider. The National Bank of Turkey was pressing for the D'Arcy group to take over its shares in the Turkish Petroleum Company, for until this was completed both bank and company were in a most difficult position.[20] The bank had already been obliged to wait four months since the Foreign Office Agreement to release itself from participation in the Turkish Petroleum Company, and it was most anxious to be free of this burden. Indeed, unless the transfer of the shares could be effected quickly, the bank proposed to follow its old course of transferring the shares directly to the Deutsche Bank and the Anglo-Saxon Petroleum Company, leaving the D'Arcy group to obtain its holding from them. This would be unnecessary, replied the Foreign Office; Babington Smith would be hearing from the D'Arcy group, who expected to reach a settlement within a few days.[21]

On both counts the Foreign Office was mistaken. The settlement was never reached. Two months later, in September, Lord Inchcape, one of the Government's *ex-officio* directors on the Anglo-Persian's board, agreed with Sir John Bradbury, joint Permanent Secretary of the Treasury, that the best proposition was still the original one, by which the Anglo-Persian would take shares in the holding company 'and stand or fall with it'. He thought that in the present international situation, with Britain at war with Germany, previous Foreign Office objections to this course would surely not apply.[22] The Foreign Office could give no opinion at all while the Turkish situation was so confused.[23] Now that Turkey had gone ahead and announced an increase in its customs duties, together with various other measures, the whole affair of the

Mesopotamian oil concession might well have to be renegotiated after the war. Meanwhile the Foreign Office would, 'of course, refuse to allow the rights we have acquired to be impaired'. An India Office minute summed up the situation: 'War with Turkey will surely give the *coup de grâce* to this undertaking, which seems somehow to have survived war with Germany.'[24]

Another month passed and Babington Smith again complained to the Foreign Office that he had still not heard from the D'Arcy group.[25] The directors of his bank were placed in an invidious position: 'Legally as directors of the Company, they are responsible for whatever action is taken; but, practically, they have no further interest in the Company and are anxious to be relieved of their legal responsibility at the earliest possible moment.' Babington Smith realised that the interim arrangement he had suggested to the Foreign Office was now no longer possible, but he saw no reason why the National Bank directors should not resign and be replaced by British Government nominees.

Greenway strongly agreed with Babington Smith.[26] Carrying through the fusion arrangements without further delay would not only preserve the interests of the D'Arcy group, but also help avoid increasing the complications over financial liability for the expenses incurred by the Turkish Petroleum Company. The latest Treasury–Admiralty suggestion was accepted, but the Treasury's confirmation was required before the arrangements could be put into effect. Thus, the D'Arcy Exploration Company's shares had not yet been subscribed for, and consequently that company had neither applied for its shares in the new Turkish Petroleum Company nor nominated its directors.

The D'Arcy group saw its present position as dangerous. The only pre-war oil agreement that was unassailable was the Baghdad Railway Convention, ensuring to the railway company the best oil areas of Mosul and Baghdad, through which the railway would be carefully aligned. The insecurity of the D'Arcy group's Mesopotamian ambitions was underlined by the fact that before the war the group had been daily pressed, especially by the Shell interests, to conclude its arrangements with the Turkish Petroleum Company; since then, Shell had not once approached it. This Greenway interpreted as indicating that both Shell and the Deutsche Bank were well content with their current position, of owning 50 per cent, rather than merely 25 per cent, of the railway company's oil rights – and this under the aegis of a British company. After the war these rights would presumably be strengthened by the remainder of the oil concession being granted, as the Turkish Government had promised, to the Turkish Petroleum Company.[27] If the D'Arcy group carried out the 19 March agreement, it would ensure to itself the Baghdad railway's oil rights, and at the same time would not have prejudiced its own position regarding a post-war settlement of the remainder of the Mesopotamian oil concession, should it be decided to set up a purely British company. Its controlling share in the Turkish Petroleum Company would place the D'Arcy group

> . . . in a position to adopt whichever one of the following courses may later on prove to be the most expedient.
>
> (a) Wind up the company if it be found practicable to secure both the Baghdad Railway rights and the Mesopotamian concession for an all-British group, and work the rights and concessions under the aegis of the D'Arcy Exploration Company.
>
> (b) Carry it on for the purpose only of dealing with the Baghdad Railway rights, and let the D'Arcy Exploration Company deal with the Mesopotamian concession.
>
> (c) Carry on entirely in pursuance of the original arrangement.

By 5 November Britain was at war with Turkey. Two weeks later the Admiralty and Board of Trade sent their opinions on the situation to the Foreign Office.[28] The Admiralty had now decided that the Anglo-Persian Oil Company should not, after all, hold shares directly in the D'Arcy Exploration Company, but that the Burmah Oil Company plan should be proceeded with. It was clear that after the war a joint Mesopotamian company composed of its present members might not be possible, and, as Greenway had stressed, the best course at present was 'to maintain and in no way to prejudice the British interests and claims represented by the D'Arcy group.' The Board of Trade, on the other hand, felt that in view of the condition of international relations it was 'impractical for any further steps to be taken in this matter at present'. The Foreign Office's view was summed up in a monosyllabic minute: 'Wait'.

II OBTAINING THE CONCESSION

If organising the company by which the Mesopotamian concession was to be obtained was difficult to arrange, gaining the grant of the concession presented just as many problems. The basic issue in the one case was the extent of the British Government's involvement in the Turkish Petroleum Company; in the other, the British Government's main problem was the old question of the validity of the claims to the concession. This question took several forms. Was the concession to be a monopoly? Over what area was it to be sought? What was to be the Turkish Petroleum Company's – and therefore the British Government's – policy towards rival claimants, possibly with valid cases for compensation? These questions involved much difficult negotiation with the Turkish Government, and much legal opining over the interpretation of Ottoman law and practice.

Once the 19 March Foreign Office Agreement had been signed, the next step was to seek a concession for the new Turkish Petroleum Company, but over what area? The agreement specified which parts of the Ottoman Empire were excluded from the operations of the reorganised company; these were the areas administered by the Egyptian Government or the Sheikh of Koweit, and the 'transferred territories' on the Turco-Persian frontier. Yet the agreement had said nothing about the areas over which the Turkish Petroleum Company would seek its concession rights. The old 1904 German agreement had sought a concession over the whole of the Ottoman Empire; the D'Arcy group claimed rights over only the provinces of Mosul and Baghdad. By private agreement, however, the British and German Governments had decided that their ambassadors in Constantinople should first of all seek a concession for only Mosul and Baghdad, possibly seeking others later on. Accordingly, on 23 March, Mallet and the German Ambassador visited the Porte and asked the Grande Vizir to grant the Turkish Petroleum Company the concession.[29]

However, despite their previous understanding with the British Government, the Germans were still anxious to acquire the larger concession. This caused some difficulty, both between the two governments and with the Turkish Government. The German Ambassador attempted to make it plain to the Turkish Government that a much larger concession was envisaged; the D'Arcy group tried the same notion on the Foreign Office.[30] They were smartly rebuffed. Mallet was instructed to make the Foreign Office's views absolutely plain to his German colleagues and to Stock. Greenway was told that unless the offending clause were removed from the prepared draft contract, where it had been inserted 'in opposition to the clearly expressed wish of His Majesty's Government', the Government would have to withdraw its support. Greenway climbed down immediately,[31] but his protest that it was his Turkish Petroleum Company colleagues who had obliged him to include the clause was received with disbelief by the Foreign Office. Parker noted, 'this is a lie' – a view borne out by a letter Greenway had written Deterding on 26 March, pressing for the extended concession.[32]

The Foreign Office had several reasons for opposing a larger concession. The first reason was that, according to the draft contract, 'The concession will . . . be entirely based on German rights . . . [and accordingly] . . . there will perhaps be an implied admission that all D'Arcy's negotiations and our representations had no bases whatever and that D'Arcy has come into the company under the aegis of the Germans.'[33]

Further, both the Grand Vizir and the British Foreign Office held that the 1904 German contract had been annulled.[34] The German Ambassador, on the other hand, thought that basing the concession on the 1904 contract alone would obviate the most immediate complication holding up the grant of the concession.[35] That obstacle was the likelihood, if the new Turkish Petroleum Company were granted a monopoly concession for Baghdad and Mosul, of other countries making similar demands of Turkey – notably Russia for the eastern provinces, and France for Syria. In any case, granting a monopoly concession was against the Turkish mining law. The Turkish Government, however, saw this as a matter of lesser importance, and as early as 30 March the Grand Vizir told Mallet that his government would grant the Turkish Petroleum Company the concession, and that it had found a way of by-passing the legal difficulty.[36] In mid-April he outlined his plan.[37] The Turkish Government was ready to grant the Turkish Petroleum Company a practical, though not a formal monopoly, of oil in Mosul and Baghdad. The company would be granted all the wells already discovered that were in the possession of the Government and would be given *permis de recherche* for any other districts (in the same vilayets) where it thought oil was likely to be found. On Mallet's objection that such an arrangement would not exclude other companies, the Grand Vizir agreed, but said that by applying at once for *permis* the Turkish Petroleum Company would forestall anyone else. The Minister of the Interior went further and told Mallet that if other companies sought *permis*, they would be refused. Provided a secret, written undertaking were obtained from the Turks, this course did not seem impossible to Mallet and his German colleague.

The Foreign Office saw the force of the Turkish argument.[38] Although denying the analogy between the Russian and French claims and those of the new Turkish Petroleum Company, the department realised that in practice a French claim to a monopoly in Syria 'would be very inconvenient'. Rights in the area were held by a British subject, William Boxall, who, with Foreign Office support, was proposing to transfer them to the Turkish Petroleum Company. Grey thought, therefore, that 'there may be something to be said for agreeing to the Turkish suggestion'. Indeed, weakening under Deutsche Bank persuasion,[39] on 23 April the Foreign Secretary even telegraphed to Mallet, 'You know the formal objections felt here to basing application upon the 1904 Convention, which we have maintained had lapsed; but if there are great practical advantages in doing so, Your Excellency has full freedom of action in the matter. . . .'[40] Most surprisingly, this drew from a colleague the remark that, 'After all our opposition to the 1904 Convention, to support it now, when it suits our book, is rather cynical but it certainly does offer a solution of a tiresome point.'[41]

Mallet was completely opposed to the suggestion.[42] In his reply next day he pointed out to the Foreign Secretary that,

> As D'Arcy's application and our support were based on the argument that the German contract was annulled – a position which we and the

> Turkish Government have consistently upheld for years past – we should completely stultify ourselves by suggesting or recommending course favoured by Deutsche Bank, and it might even be dangerous to do so.

The Foreign Secretary's desire for haste was largely due to the need to settle with Turkey the questions of the customs increase and the monopolies grant, the operation of both agreements having been made contingent on the grant of the oil concession. Grey was anxious to be able to lay before Parliament, in good time before the summer recess, the whole series of Anglo-Turkish agreements.[43] But, while Mallet was waiting for a list of the Turkish Government's petroleum wells, the Foreign Secretary agreed to accept the enforced delay. The list arrived on 5 May, and, at a meeting at the German Embassy, Mallet, his German colleague, and the Turkish Petroleum Company's local representative developed what the Foreign Office described as a 'most satisfactory and ingenious' plan.[44] By this plan the concession was to remain in the Turkish Government's possession and the Turkish Petroleum Company would only lease it. Thus the company would evade the delicate question of whether to base the concession on the 1904 German contract or on the 1909 promise to D'Arcy. The plan would also remove the Porte's fears of French and Russian claims, and more important still, make it unnecessary for the Turkish Petroleum Company to obtain *permis de recherche*, while yet securing to the company the monopoly of all oilfields in Baghdad and Mosul. On May 18 the two ambassadors presented this plan to the Grand Vizir, who, Mallet reported, seemed to welcome the idea and promised a quick reply.[45] The British Ambassador reinforced this visit with one the same night to the Minister of the Interior.[46]

Mallet was too optimistic. He saw the Grand Vizir twice subsequently on the same matter. The Vizir now said he did not think the ambassadors' new proposal any help at all, for what was advocated still amounted to a monopoly.[47] Mallet agreed that it was indeed a monopoly on which the company was insisting, and reminded the Grand Vizir that he had promised the concession to the joint German–British company. The Ambassador's impression was that the Turkish Government was evidently unable to make up its mind how to proceed, but, in the long run, he thought, it would be compelled to accept the fact that the concession had been promised and must be granted to the new Turkish Petroleum Company.

The main reason for the Turkish Government's delay was apparent from its sudden preoccupation with the correct observance of the Turkish mining law. It was under the mining law that the *permis de recherche* system operated, and a number of oil *permis* relating to the Baghdad and Mosul vilayets had already been applied for by various individuals and, in some cases, granted. Yet, since the Imperial firmans of 1908–9 transferring ownership of oilfields in the Mosul and Baghdad vilayets from the Civil List to the Ministry of Finance, laws emanating from the Ministry of Mines could not affect territory under the control of the Ministry of Finance, and therefore *permis* granted under the mining law and relating to parts of Mosul and Baghdad should have no validity. This was the view maintained by the Foreign Office and the Turkish Petroleum Company; but, from the middle of April, the Grand Vizir became increasingly preoccupied with the problem.[48] This was apparent not only from his own statements, but also from a steadily expanding file of correspondence between the Foreign Office and a firm of solicitors, Treherne, Higgins and Company, representing one Roland H. Silley.

Silley was a young Englishman, formerly an employee of the Vacuum Oil Company and now an independent commission agent in Constantinople. Since 1910 he and his Turkish associates had applied to the Turkish Government for a number of *permis de recherche* for oil; these related to parts of the vilayets of Mosul, Baghdad, Basra and Nejd. In late August 1913 he first sought British diplomatic support of his applications for these concessions.[49] The Foreign Office made careful inquiries of the Constantinople Embassy and the local consulates at Basra and Suez about Silley and his applications, and after consulting the Board of Trade and the Admiralty, the Government's attitude was settled. Silley could not be supported regarding Mosul and Baghdad, because of D'Arcy and his prior claim to a monopoly, but Silley's interest in Basra and Nejd might be supported providing he were willing to give a written undertaking that his group was British-controlled and would not pass into non-British hands. In any case, Nejd and Basra were thought to be valueless for oil. Correspondence between the Foreign Office and Silley's solicitors continued till December. Silley disputed the Foreign Office's rejection of his request for diplomatic support regarding Mosul and Baghdad, and claimed that he had been granted *permis de recherche* by the Turkish Ministry of Mines in accordance with Turkish mining law. He maintained bitterly that the British Government's refusal to recognise the validity of these *permis* was entirely due to its partiality for D'Arcy and to its having been tricked into supporting the partly foreign Turkish Petroleum Company–D'Arcy combine.

There were aspects of the Foreign Office's behaviour towards Silley that could fairly be criticized. While waiting for the Grand Vizir finally to promise the concession to the new Turkish Petroleum Company, the department intentionally held back over important stages in its correspondence with Silley and thus delayed action by him.[50] Moreover once the Foreign Office had learnt that it was worthwhile for the Turkish Petroleum Company to become definitely interested in Basra, it grew less willing to support Silley's apparently valid applications for *permis* even there, and, together with the Constantinople Embassy, encouraged the Turkish Petroleum Company itself to file *permis* applications for the area.[51] (Under the mining law the granting of *permis* depended strictly on priority in applying for them, even if the licences were suspended.) The attitude of the Foreign Office was not without some justification, and derived partly from Silley's unwillingness, failing Foreign Office support for his claims in Mosul and Baghdad, to give the department the undertaking it required regarding Basra and Nejd. Also, despite what seemed to the Foreign Office and the Constantinople Embassy, Silley's questionable financial intentions,[52] they consistently encouraged him to come to an agreement with the Turkish Petroleum Company whereby he would sell it his Basra and Nejd rights; in return, they would guarantee him fair treatment from the company. On a more pragmatic level, this seemed the only way to ensure that the rights did not go to foreigners. When, eventually, Silley appeared willing to come to such an agreement, political events had made it impossible.

Even though Silley was unsuccessful in attempting to obtain British diplomatic support for his claims in Mosul and Baghdad, it is clear that he embarrassed the Turkish Government by his pressure. To add to the confusion Baron de Ward was again in evidence, seeking British diplomatic support in obtaining an oil concession for the whole of Mesopotamia.[53] He informed the Embassy that the previous year, when his negotiations with the Ministry of Mines had been suspended, he had been told that the concession could be granted only to an Anglo-German group. Consequently he had formed an Anglo-German group and he now requested the concession. His supporters undoubtedly included some prominent Englishmen. Two of these, Lord Cowdray and Lord Murray of Elibank, had personal interviews at the Foreign Office – but to no avail. De Ward's group received much the same answers as Silley had, but were unable even to expect support in Basra. In truth, de Ward was mistrusted by the Foreign Office (and even, to some extent, by some of his colleagues), and the Turkish Government obviously could not have granted him the concession he desired, even had it wished to do so, which is doubtful.

The two cases summarised above throw an interesting light on British diplomatic practice. 'First come, first served' appeared to have become Foreign Office policy for supporting its nationals abroad, at least with regard to oil in Mesopotamia. That one at least of the British Government's diplomatic staff saw the shortcomings of such an attitude is shown by a long minute contained in the Constantinople Embassy files; this observes that 'It seems to be a very dangerous position to take up, that only the first in the field are entitled to support to the exclusion of latecomers who may have made just as great financial sacrifices.'[54] This minute was not forwarded to London; nor would it have made any difference if it had been. The British Government was too deeply committed in its support of D'Arcy and the reorganised Turkish Petroleum Company to be able to support a British competitor, even had there been one with unquestionable rights.

The British Government's determination to secure for its protégé the Mesopotamian oil concession could, in one particular instance, be interpreted as interfering in the internal government of Turkey. Probably desiring on the one hand to gain time, and on the other to obtain from the state's chief advisory organ its backing for a controversial decision, early in May the Grand Vizir requested the Turkish Council of State to meet and consider the matter of the Mesopotamian oil concession.[55] On 4 June the Council gave its opinion. Despite advice to the contrary from the Ministry of Mines itself, the Council decided in favour of applying the mining law to oil in Mosul and Baghdad.[56] Silley's claims were thus encouraged; D'Arcy's disparaged. That this was not the answer expected by or from the Grand Vizir is evident from the resulting correspondence. The Foreign Office declared that, though the Council's decision was in itself unimportant – apart from muddling matters further – the Turkish Government was merely trifling with the matter. The British and German Foreign Offices accordingly instructed their Ambassadors that they should categorically inform Prince Saïd Halim Pasha that 'unless the question is satisfactorily settled at a very early date, the two Governments must withhold their consent to the monopolies.'[57]

The two ambassadors continued to press the Grand Vizir. Mallet was confident that the new Turkish Petroleum Company would eventually be granted the concession and he was anxious to delay as long as possible presenting an ultimatum to the Turkish Government.[58] On 16 and 18 June the Grand Vizir assured each ambassador separately that their demands would be conceded and that the only delay now would be for setting aside the Council of State's pronouncement.[59] This would require only a few days. When, by 18 June, the ambassadors had still received no definite answer, they sent their ultimata.[60] On 25 June the Grand Vizir finally gave the ambassadors a formal promise of the concession[61] and confirmed this in identic notes on 28 June.[62]

The Grand Vizir's note showed that the Turkish Government had accepted the ambassadors' 'ingenious plan'. It declared that 'the Ministry of Finance, being substituted for the Civil List concerning petroleum resources discovered and to be discovered in the vilayets of Mossoul and Baghdad, consented to lease these to the Turkish Petroleum Company'. The Turkish Government, however, reserved the right to determine thereafter its own participation in the project and in the general conditions of the contract. In addition, the note included the Turkish Government's own contribution to solving the difficulty about the *permis de recherche* that had already been issued for the area by the Ministry of Mines. 'The Company must undertake to indemnify, where necessary, any third parties who might be interested in the oilfields in those two vilayets.' The Grand Vizir's note was thus not entirely satisfactory, either to the Turkish Petroleum Company or to its British and German Government supporters, whose feelings were summed up in a minute written by Crowe: 'The Turkish Government are really hopeless, and are getting more and more muddled.'[63]

Although the Mesopotamian oil concession had now been formally promised to the Turkish Petroleum Company, the Turkish Government's additional stipulations needed to be dealt with. The question of compensating third parties was settled within a fortnight. The Council of State's decision of 4 June had, 'by the unfortunate indiscretion by which it has become generally known', immeasurably increased the risk of such claims; and, regarding Silley in particular, the Foreign Secretary 'anticipated much trouble'.[64] Silley and his lawyers maintained that the Council of State was not merely an advisory body to the Turkish Government, and declared that the Council's decision had been reversed 'in violation of justice and in consequence of diplomatic pressure'.[65]

The second of Silley's charges was accurate but was not considered worthy of notice by the Foreign Office. The first was the old question of the validity of the firmans granting the Mosul and Baghdad oil concession to the Turkish Ministry of Finance. If, as the Grand Vizir's note promising the concession to the Turkish Petroleum Company stated, the concession belonged to the Ministry of Finance (and was *ipso facto* outside the jurisdiction of the mining law), then it was logically and legally impossible that there could exist any valid claims to compensation for *permis* or concessions granted under the mining law. None the less, such *permis* had been granted, which was one reason why the Turkish Government had had such difficulty in making up its mind about the concession. Recognising this situation, the company was indeed prepared to make some small indemnification in some cases. What it objected to was an unlimited liability to do so, and that this should be a prior condition for the contract.[66] The Foreign Office felt that the Turkish Government, having got into this tangle, should sort it out. On 4 July Mallet and the German Ambassador wrote formally to the Grand Vizir pointing out the legal impossibility of the existence of third-party claims to the concession,[67] and on 9 July Hakki Pasha, in reply to similar representations in London,[68] replied from Claridges that the legality of the transfer was in no doubt whatever, and that any claims that did exist would be minimal.[69] Accordingly, this disputed second paragraph of the Grand Vizir's note might be set aside for discussion until after the Turkish Petroleum Company's contract had been signed. This satisfied the Foreign Office. Mallet was similarly satisfied and reported to the Foreign Office that at a meeting on 9 July with the Grand Vizir the latter had confirmed that the Council of State's function was merely advisory:[70]

> He ridiculed the idea that its decisions could impose any legal obligations on the Government. As the question is one of Turkish Constitutional Law, on which only the Turkish Government can express an authoritative opinion. I presume that this statement of the Grand Vizir may be taken as settling the matter for His Majesty's Government.

More difficult to settle, however, was the question of the Turkish Government's desired participation in the exploitation of the Mesopotamian concession. This question was basic to the whole arrangement, wrote Greenway to the Foreign Office, and it must be settled 'before the conclusion of the negotiations with Turkey, as otherwise quite impossible terms might at some later date be put forward by the Ottoman Government whereby the whole arrangement might be rendered nugatory'.[71] The Foreign Office continued to withhold its assent to the Turkish monopolies agreement until this matter was settled,[72] and to that end the Turkish Petroleum Company entered direct negotiations with the Turkish Government, keeping the Foreign Office acquainted with the progress made.[73] Essentially, what the Turkish Government wanted was both the royalty provided for it in the draft contract, and a share in the company's net profits. The company had already decided, in March, that the advance it would offer the Turkish Government in exchange for the concession would be £400,000 – £500,000.[74] It was now prepared to accede to the Turkish Government's further request, provided the royalty was decreased correspondingly.[75] The draft contract had provided for an 8 per cent royalty; the company was willing to allow the Government a 6–10 per cent share in its net profits provided that the royalty were reduced to 5 per cent.[76] An additional request made by the Turkish Government was for a Turkish director on the company's board. Although Mallet thought this a minor point, which he was willing to concede, the Foreign Secretary thought differently.[77]

These questions were not difficult in themselves but were never properly settled. In mid-July the Grand Vizir announced that his government would not be able to begin considering them until mid-August, after the Turkish Chamber had risen, and that an answer on them could not be expected before the end of October.[78] If this was the case, responded the Foreign Office, then the Embassy must inform the Turkish Government that neither the British nor the German Government would consent to the monopolies agreement or the customs increase. Further, it should be pointed out to the Turkish Government that the revenue it would thus lose would greatly exceed any possible

Turkish share in the oil concession.[79] The German and British Embassies both pressed the Turkish Government for a much quicker reply on its desired participation, but the reply when it came, on 31 July, was considered unsatisfactory by the company.[80] The Minister of Finance, Djavid Bey, asked for a 10 per cent participation in any exploitation company that was to be formed, but he was not yet ready to give a decision on the royalty.

III WAR AND THE CONCESSION

The grant of the Mesopotamian oil concession thus depended basically on the composition of the company that was to possess it. The coming of the war disturbed the negotiations concerning the Turkish Government's participation no less than it did the arrangements over the manner of the D'Arcy group's financial involvement in the Turkish Petroleum Company. War also drastically changed the attitude of the British Government towards the new Turkish Petroleum Company and the Mesopotamian concession. Previously the Foreign Office had been anxious to have all the negotiations completed. This was also the attitude of the D'Arcy group when Greenway wrote to the Foreign Office in November 1914 urging that his group should secure its rights by taking up immediately its shareholding in the Turkish Petroleum Company.[81] Although the Admiralty, predictably, and the India Office, hesitantly, supported the D'Arcy group in this course, the Foreign Office and the Board of Trade showed some caution.[82] Over the following months, lengthy consultations among these departments crystallised this caution into a definite policy.[83]

Greenway's letter of 3 November had been written on the assumption that the Foreign Office Agreement of 19 March was still in existence and would, at the very least, provide the basis for arranging the future of the Mesopotamian oilfields. On this assumption Greenway's proposal was quite justifiable, but the Foreign Office's Assistant Legal Adviser, H. W. Malkin,[84] questioned the assumption.[85] The effects of war on an agreement between British, German and Turkish interests must be either to dissolve it entirely or else to suspend its operation during the war. Had the agreement been entered into only by the various commercial parties, then it might only be suspended; but, since the three warring governments were parties to the agreement, since the territory it concerned belonged to the enemy, and since parts of that territory were in the actual occupation of British troops, so that it was doubtful whether the territory would remain Turkish after the war, the only possible conclusion seemed to Malkin to be 'that the agreement has completely come to an end and that the hands of the British parties to it are entirely free regarding the future'.

In addition, Malkin pointed out, that it was very much in Britain's interest to maintain this point of view. Whatever the future of the area in question, it seemed quite impossible that British and German interests should work together thereafter as previously intended. It was possible that considerable portions of the territories would pass under British rule after the war, and presumably Britain would be extremely careful to exclude German interests from them. Even if the territories did not become British, it would doubtless still be considered desirable to keep their development as far as possible in British hands: 'In either case, therefore, it seems to me necessary to get rid of any obligations which it might be contended compelled us to recognise any interests of the German parties to the agreement as still existing.'

Malkin's advice was therefore that the Foreign Office should announce at once that it regarded the Foreign Office Agreement as no longer having any validity whatsoever. The department must decline to take it into account at all when the time came to arrange the future of the Mesopotamian oil areas – a task simplified by the fact (hitherto regarded as unfortunate) that the Turkish Government had not actually granted the agreement's signatories any concession. It was particularly important that Greenway should be informed of the invalidity of the agreement. Otherwise he would continue to regard it as in force and hold the Foreign Office responsible for preventing him from securing his group's position. Malkin declared that the most satisfactory way of dealing with the matter thereafter would be to provide for it in the terms of peace.

The Foreign Office completely accepted the advice which supported and supplemented the department's own views. The other Government departments concerned were similarly convinced.[86] On 23 November 1915 the Anglo-Persian Oil Company was informed that HM Government regarded the Foreign Office Agreement as invalid and as inapplicable to future arrangements for the oil territories it concerned.[87] The company was advised to make no attempt to carry out the arrangements embodied in the agreement and was consoled with a promise that 'the necessity of safeguarding so far as possible the interests of the British parties to that agreement will not be lost sight of'.

By the end of 1915 the question of the Mesopotamian oil concession seemed to have completed a full, fruitless circle. The carefully wrought Anglo-German attempt at co-operation was upset by the outbreak of war, first between Britain and Germany, and then between Britain and Turkey. The British Government and its protégé, the D'Arcy group, would always have preferred a purely British concession, and the war – since it was not doubted that Britain would prove victorious – now provided the perfect chance of achieving this. But, before peace was restored and a settlement reached, much was to happen, both on the military and on the allied political front, and this would broaden beyond all recognition the scope of the problem.

Part III

Exigencies of War and Provision for Peace: Oil Policy and Territorial Desiderata

7 The War, 1914–18

Shell and the Government of India upset by the British Government's purchase of a majority shareholding in the APOC – APOC oil installations in Persia in relation to the landing of the Expeditionary Force at the head of the Persian Gulf – The Admiralty's reasons – Toluol – Oil and its role in the Mesopotamian campaign – Oil in relation to the British Government's political considerations – Alexandretta – Examination of British desiderata – Hirtzel's note – The Bunsen committee – The Sykes–Picot Agreement – Sykes's views on the importance of Mesopotomia – German interest in the region – Greenway's views – Admiral Slade's views and Sykes's and Hankey's reactions to them – Balfour and the dropping of Slade's proposals – The Imperial War Cabinet and War Aims – The French attitude to the Sykes–Picot Agreement – The Question of the British advance to Mosul – First amalgamation scheme, summer 1915 (Burmah–Shell) – Second amalgamation scheme (for an all-British oil company), January 1916 – The APOC's strategy in seeking a post-war oil monopoly in the Turkish Empire – FO, Board of Trade, India Office and Admiralty reactions – Third amalgamation scheme (Board of Trade's scheme for an Imperial Oil Company), August 1916 – Fourth amalgamation scheme (Admiralty's scheme for a National Oil Company), August 1916 – Cabinet decides in favour of the third scheme – Resulting negotiations – Press reports and denials – Formation of Petroleum Executive, December 1917 – Setting up of the Petroleum Imperial Policy Committee (PIPCo), May 1918 – Fifth (PIPCo) scheme – First phase of the negotiations, May–November 1918 – Summary of chapter.

I BRITISH WARTIME MILITARY AND POLITICAL ACTIVITIES IN THE MIDDLE EAST: THE BRITISH GOVERNMENT AND CONTROL OF SOURCES OF OIL SUPPLY

Though the outbreak of war meant that the quest for the Mesopotamian oil concession had temporarily to be abandoned, Middle East oil concessions still remained an important British Government preoccupation. War brought home forcibly to the Government its almost complete dependence on foreign oil supplies and obliged it to develop a policy and an organisation for ensuring that oil supplies were adequate, both for its wartime activities and for afterwards. Further, Middle East oil also became involved in questions of military strategy and post-war territorial ambitions. The wartime interdependence of strategy and supply thus meant that Middle East oil concessions played an important part in the evolution of British Government oil policy.

The basis of this policy had already been laid, through the Government's purchase of a majority shareholding in the Anglo-Persian Oil Company. This action, which was intended by the Admiralty to insure the Navy against oil shortages and high prices, did, however, greatly upset two parties with a particular interest in Government oil policy. One of these was, predictably, the Anglo-Persian Company's great rival, Shell, on behalf of which Sir Marcus Samuel protested bitterly, in private letters to the Admiralty and in a letter to the press.[1] He took the line that if a business was sound there was no difficulty in raising additional capital through public subscription, and that, by becoming financially involved in the Anglo-Persian, the Government was itself entering into competition with other commercial companies. Such competition was indeed very different from the free competition the Admiralty publicly declared it was assisting, because the company enjoying Government financial and diplomatic support would have an unfair advantage. Samuel's colleagues in the Royal Dutch–Shell Group ever continued to uphold this line.

The other party to which the Government's purchase caused particular upset was the Government of India. When it and the India Office heard of the action they were extremely perturbed, fearing additional military responsibilities in defending the Anglo-Persian Company's installations from attack.[2] With Turkey joining Germany in the war, on 5 November 1914, this likelihood became reality.[3] It should, however, be pointed out that protection of the oil installations was only one of a number of objectives behind the landing of the Expeditionary Force in the Persian Gulf port of Fao on 6 November. Although before the outbreak of war, Admiral Slade, a Government-appointed member of the company's board of directors, had strongly urged the defence of the Abadan refinery and the Anglo-Persian Company's pipelines, Churchill, First Lord of the Admiralty and progenitor of the company's agreement with the Government, did not appear to agree. He was content to note on a Naval Staff memorandum of 1 September that pressed such a move, that European and Egyptian defence had priority and that Britain could buy her oil from elsewhere – surely, a negation of his own arguments in favour of the agreement.[4] The Viceroy and Government of India agreed with him.[5] Only the fact that it was expected that Basra would be gained permanently for the empire finally persuaded India to support the maintaining of troops at Abadan.[6]

During the early part of the campaign, Mesopotamia was clearly not a major battleground, and oil, whether Persian or Mesopotamian, was not a major factor in planning military strategy. But, despite Churchill's attitude of September 1914, six months later the Admiralty began to increase its pressure on India to defend the Persian oil installations.

In addition to its need for marine fuel oil, there was another important reason why the Admiralty wished these installations to be working fully. Britain at this time had a shortage of explosives, and the Admiralty was supporting experiments aimed at distilling toluol, a basic ingredient of explosives, from Persian oil. As it was not until autumn 1915 that it was seen that the cost of extracting toluol from Persian oil was prohibitive and that Borneo oil was far more satisfactory, and as the Persian pipeline had already been damaged by Arab saboteurs, the Admiralty continued to impress on India[7] (and, indeed, did so right up to mid-1916)[8] the importance of deploying Indian troops to defend the pipeline. India had to comply, although the Viceroy's private correspondence shows clearly that he did not appreciate the Admiralty's arguments about toluol. In April 1915 he wrote,

> How I do hate that pipeline. I imagine that all they are thinking about are the dividends of the £2 millions that they have invested, for it is inconceivable that the Admiralty can be in any way dependent upon the supply of oil derived from Abadan. . . .[9]

It was the Admiralty, consequently, that in mid-1915 opposed further troop advances northwards, since this would imply the withdrawal of some troops from along the pipeline, at Ahwaz. The Viceroy, on the other hand, in writing to the King, made it quite clear that this was only an Admiralty fear, and in October 1915 he wrote jubilantly and, as it turned out, somewhat prematurely to the King's Private Secretary that 'My little show in Mesopotamia is still going strong and I hope that Baghdad will soon be comprised within the British Empire.'[10]

Such a triumph was, from some points of view, becoming a necessity, because of the unsatisfactory Dardanelles operations. In addition, there were signs that Russia too might be intending to advance to Baghdad – in her case, from the north. To forestall Russia and, among other reasons, to raise British prestige in the eyes of the Moslem world, it was eventually decided that the British force would advance towards Baghdad. From the arguments used in coming to this decision (these are dealt with at length in Moberly's official history of the campaign and in the official documents contained in the Asquith papers and the Cabinet records),[11] the conclusion must be drawn that oil, whether from Persia or from north of Baghdad, played very little part in the considerations. The story of the ensuing military movements is purely one of military campaign. (The very last phase of the Mesopotamian operations, the advance to Mosul after the armistice of Mudros on 30 October 1918, will, however, be considered in due course below, following an examination of various developments in intervening years.)

Seeing that the role of Middle East oil in the British Government's

Mesopotamian military strategy was clearly limited and only secondary, the question arises of whether it played any larger part in the Government's political considerations. These considerations concerned the future of the Ottoman Empire and were focused, in mid-1916, by the Sykes–Picot Agreement, which divided up the Ottoman Empire among Britain, France and Russia and which included Mosul in the French sphere of influence.

It may seem that after so many years of hard international struggle to support the claims of British nationals to oil rights in Mesopotamia the British Government had suddenly given up its resolve in the matter. This was hardly the case, for the future of Mesopotamia and the importance of British interests there and in Persia, the Persian Gulf and India were central considerations for Britain in her military involvement in the Middle East. When the question of occupying Alexandretta was being discussed, in the middle of March 1915, the future of Mesopotamia was the chief basis of discussion. Oil was one, though only one and rarely the chief, aspect of the question. Admiral Fisher certainly saw Alexandretta as having 'special importance as an outlet for the oil supplies of Mesopotamia and Persia,[12] a view strongly supported by an official Admiralty memorandum.[13] But Lord Kitchener (the Secretary of War) and Admiral Sir Henry Jackson (who succeeded Fisher in May as First Sea Lord), while feeling that British occupation of Alexandretta and its hinterland would indeed facilitate the working of minerals in Asia Minor and protect British interests in Persia, saw this as only one aspect among many.[14] In any event, the scheme met opposition from other members of the War Committee and was dropped, partly for military reasons and partly through fear of French hostility to it, a telling argument in time of war.[15]

If possession of Alexandretta was thought to require possession of its Mesopotamian hinterland, control over Mesopotamia, need not despite Kitchener's opinion to the contrary,[16] entail control over Alexandretta. In view of France's claims to extensive areas of the Ottoman Empire, following Russia's demand for Constantinople and the Straits, the British Government began serious investigations into which parts of the Ottoman Empire it, in its own interests, would desire to retain at the end of the war. Of central importance in the trail leading eventually to the Sykes–Picot Agreement was a long and detailed 'note' by Sir Arthur Hirtzel, Secretary of the Political and Secret Department, India Office.[17] It was on Hirtzel's note that the subsequent Bunsen report was largely based.[18] The most significant aspect of the note, from the point of view of oil considerations and the later Sykes–Picot Agreement, was the northern boundary Hirtzel suggested for British Mesopotamia. This was a line beginning at the Turco-Persian frontier, running up the Jabal Hamrin range to Fat-ha on the Tigris, and thence crossing either to Ana or to Hit on the Euphrates. In other words, it excluded almost the entire Mosul vilayet. Although he made a special point of including Hit in the British area, because of its bituminous deposits, Hirtzel was content to exclude– and, indeed, not mention at all – many well known oil seepage areas, such as Kirkuk and Tuz Khurmatli. He examined almost every aspect of Mesopotamia's economic potential except oil.

By the time of the Sykes–Picot Agreement the northern boundary proposed by Hirtzel had been amended so as to include in the British sphere of influence both the oil seepage areas mentioned above. In addition, Hirtzel's forthright opinion that the need for buffer regions between British and Russian spheres in Persia or Turkey was 'one of those superstitions which linger on in offices long after they have lost all reality in practice' made no impression on Kitchener and some of the makers of the Sykes–Picot agreement. It should also be noted that Hirtzel's opinions on the question of Mesopotamia's future were not those of all his colleagues, who were united only in the belief that Britain must retain, in some form, the vilayet of Basra. The Viceroy and the Military Department under General Sir Edmund Barrow preferred to strengthen rather than weaken Turkish rule over the rest of her Asiatic provinces, and to uphold the buffer state policy. The Viceroy, however, as has already been seen, was like Hirtzel in showing no interest in Mesopotamian oil.[19]

The Committee on Asiatic Turkey was set up by the Prime Minister, Asquith, on 8 April 1915, under the chairmanship of Sir Maurice de Bunsen, and it presented its report on 30 June.[20] It was empowered to consider 'the nature of British desiderata in Turkey in Asia in the event of a successful conclusion of the war with special reference to the [recent] memoranda on the subject . . .'. Nine British desiderata in the Persian Gulf and Asiatic Turkey were enumerated and of these only one, number four, mentioned oil, together with other economic interests. The committee declared that its aim was to achieve 'a final settlement, without the handicaps imposed upon us by the conditions under which Hakki Pasha was able to negotiate [before the war]'.

The committee examined four different kinds of territorial settlement. These were (1) direct annexation, (2) spheres of influence, (3) an independent but co-operative Turkish government organised as at present, though with some modifications, and (4) the most favoured course, an independent but decentralised Ottoman administration.[21] From the oil aspect the most interesting factor (common to all schemes except the third, least favoured, scheme, and also one of the annexation alternatives) was the northern boundary of the British area. The committee strongly approved Hirtzel's views but went further than he had done, proposing a boundary running at least as far north as from Acre in the west, to Zakho and Rowanduz in the north-east – thus including the Mosul vilayet in the British sphere. Among the very many reasons the committee put forward as justification for this was the consideration that 'oil again makes it commercially desirable for us to carry our control on to Mosul, in the vicinity of which place there are valuable wells, possession of which by another Power would be prejudicial to our interests'.

All the schemes assumed victory over Turkey and Germany. Nevertheless, the committee was careful to provide, at the end of its report, that, should peace be desirable before the war had reached the stage when German rights in Turkey could be entirely swept away, Britain's special present and future interests south of the Haifa–Rowanduz line 'should be formally recognised by the Treaty Powers' and Turkey.

The most that can be said of the Bunsen committee's attitude towards Mesopotamian oil is that oil, together with many other equally important factors, led the committee to define a British area of interest that included the Mosul province. As to the particular means by which Britain could best exercise influence over her area, other factors, broadly comprising Britain's commercial and political relations with her French and Russian allies, were what counted.

How was it, then, that the Sykes–Picot Agreement once again removed Mosul from the British sphere? The answer is simply that when the Anglo-French discussions finally got under way, towards the end of 1915, France claimed Mosul as part of her sphere. This, thought Lt-Col. Sir Mark Sykes MP, Arabist and War Office adviser on Arab matters, was the result of pressure from Franco-Levantine financiers, who wanted to link up France's Syrian railway concessions with the Trans-Persian railway.[22] In a memorandum of early January 1916 on the Arab question, Sykes set out clearly the claims of Britain, France and the Arabs: all three claimed Mosul.[23] By the end of the same month, however, Sykes and François Georges-Picot (former French Consul-general in Beirut and French government representative) had together worked out the division of Asiatic Turkey that provided the basis of the subsequent Sykes–Picot agreement. Northern Mesopotamia between Baghdad and Amadia–Zakho was to be divided between Britain and France in such a way that Britain received Kirkuk and France Mosul.[24]

In reaching this compromise the view of the War Office was decisive. The War Office held that, 'From a military point of view, the principle of inserting a wedge of French territory between any British zone and the Russian Caucasus would seem in every way desirable.'[25] The author of this remark, Brigadier-General G. M. W. Macdonogh, the Director of Military Intelligence, prefaced his comments by confessing that 'it seems to me that we are rather in the position of the hunters who divided up the skin of the bear before they had killed it'.

The Admiralty had to agree with the last statement, but all the same sharply criticised the proposed agreement. Its criticism had mainly to do with strategic considerations, but, in addition, the Admiralty pointed out that the economic benefit that Britain would derive from the agreement compared unfavourably with the benefit France would obtain.[26] Indeed, Admiral Fisher had written to the Prime Minister the previous November stating 'I hope you are not losing any time in annexing the Tigris and Euphrates!'[27]

Hirtzel, for the India Office, congratulated Sykes on securing 'a considerable abatement on M. Picot's original claim', but thought that 'the loss of the Mosul vilayet is a serious sacrifice for us'.[28] Hirtzel gave purely economic reasons for this opinion and recognised France's desire to work the oil deposits. If it were impossible for Britain to obtain Mosul, he said, then France should at least be 'very accommodating elsewhere' in return. The Permanent Under-Secretary, Sir Thomas Holderness, merely noted that 'it is clear that we shall have to make up our minds to the inclusion of Mosul in the French sphere'.

While Sykes was still pressing the Foreign Office for a final settlement of Britain's and France's partition plans, the Permanent Under-Secretary at the Foreign Office, Nicolson, was giving in his private correspondence his own opinion of the whole matter. He was not optimistic about the chances of any of these negotiations bearing fruit. The Anglo-French agreement was, of course, dependent on a pro-British Arab uprising and the eventual formation of an Arab state; and Nicolson, realising this, wrote, in a private letter to the Viceroy, that, although some progress was being made in the discussions with France over 'the question of the Northern limits of the future Arab state', that state was merely a 'shadow to which I doubt any real substance will be given'.[29]

The Foreign Office was surprised that France desired to extend her influence so far eastwards, and impressed on the French Government that this 'would entail the abdication of considerable British interests' – a point emphasised again in May, when the agreement was finally being settled.[30] Grey would not agree without Russia doing so also. While the British Ambassador, Sir George Buchanan, was to conduct the British side of these discussions, it was decided that Sykes should accompany Picot, France's chief negotiator, 'to keep an eye on the French discussion'.[31] This was just as well, for, in order to secure Russian agreement to France's eastwards expansion, Paléologue, the French Ambassador to Russia, continually impressed on Sazonov, the Russian Foreign Minister, that this extension was solely due to Britain's desire for a buffer region between her own and Russian territory.[32] Although this explanation correctly described the attitude of Kitchener and the War Office, it infuriated the Foreign Office, and official British denials were given verbally and by telegram to Sazonov. Privately, the Foreign Office's minutes declared Paléologue to be 'really incorrigible', and Sir Eyre Crowe raged that 'this is an intolerable impertinence. I consider the Russians to be preferable neighbours to the French anywhere in the East.'[33] Eventually, however, France and Russia adjusted their territorial difficulties to their general satisfaction, without affecting the proposed French and British spheres of influence south of the Zakho–Amadia line.[34]

Although, when first approached on the matter, Russia had not thought it necessary to examine and approve the Anglo-French negotiations, she was not, once the negotiations had indeed become three-cornered, as co-operative as either the French or British negotiators had hoped. Difficulties were smoothed out in time, however, and the Sykes–Picot Agreement, made official in the Grey–Cambon exchange of letters in May–August 1916, became a Franco-British-Russian agreement by a similar exchange of letters between governments in September–October 1916. The Grey–Cambon letters of 15 May[35] seemed to provide, in a general way at least, for the fears contained in the suggestion the India Office had made on 1 April that year. This suggestion was that, in regard to D'Arcy's claim to 'all oil deposits in the vilayets of Mosul and Baghdad . . . whether or not it may be possible to maintain this claim against the French in its entirety, it would seem advisable to keep in our hands, if possible, material for bargaining'.[36] In the letters of 15 May Britain and France gave reciprocal assurances to maintain, in their respective regions, each other's existing concessions, rights and privileges. The D'Arcy group's claims could hardly be described as an existing concession or, considering the group in isolation from the rest of the reorganised Turkish Petroleum Company, even a right. But the Mesopotamian oil concession it sought was indeed to become a most useful bargaining counter between the two governments in their immediate post-war territorial negotiations.

Even once the Sykes–Picot Agreement had been concluded, Mesopotamian oil continued to be an important background consideration for the British Government, and remained so for the rest of the war. Almost immediately after the agreement had been finalised the War Committee was again discussing Britain's interests in the Middle East. In an interview with the committee on 6 July 1916 Sir Mark Sykes stressed the great strategic importance of the Middle East for Britain.[37] He also mentioned the great value of the 'immense oil areas' to whoever should possess them. He believed that, even though the fields of Flanders might decide the battle, what Germany was fighting for was the Middle East. German writing that year gave point to his comment. Sir Arthur Hirtzel agreed with Sykes' opinion, in two memoranda on the subject,[38] dated 25 May and 31 October 1916. Greenway, similarly, pressed the Government to take note of the tenor of current German writing, and in April 1916 sent the Foreign Office translations of articles on the importance of Persian and Turkish oil.[39] These indicated the significance that Germany attached to securing possession of the

Mesopotamian and Persian oilfields, an important objective of Turco-German military operations in the Middle East.

Admiral Slade expressed such views even more strongly. In a Cabinet memorandum of 31 October 1916 he emphasised the importance of oil to the Admiralty and of securing control of all the oil rights in Mesopotamia, Koweit, Bahrein and Arabia.[40] Late in the war, when the question of defining War Aims was coming up for discussion, Slade brought all his ideas together in a long paper entitled 'The Petroleum Situation in the British Empire', which he wrote for the Admiralty on 29 July 1918.[41] In this paper he examined the problems and sources of British oil fuel supplies, and concluded that 'it is evident that the Power that controls the oil lands of Persia and Mesopotamia will control the source of supply of the majority of the liquid fuel of the future . . .'. Britain must therefore 'at all costs retain [her] hold on the Persian and Mesopotamian oilfields and any other fields which may exist in the British Empire and [she] must not allow the intrusion in any form of any foreign interests, however much disguised they may be'. He went on to declare that 'The interest that is most inimical to British control at the present time is the Royal Dutch Company', with its 'controlling interest in one of the most important so called British Companies'. 'This Company', he alleged, was 'in intimate relations with . . . Germany', and to allow it an interest in Persia and Mesopotamia would be synonymous with assisting Britain's enemies.

Slade's paper, which was endorsed strongly by the Admiralty as a useful contribution to both the general discussion of oil fuel sources, and the discussion on War Aims, was circulated by Sir Maurice Hankey, Secretary to the Imperial War Cabinet.[42] Hankey regarded 'the retention of the oil-bearing regions in Mesopotamia and Persia in British hands as well as a proper strategic boundary to cover them' as 'a first-class British War Aim'. He also recommended that before peace was discussed Britain should 'obtain possession of all the oil-bearing regions in Mesopotamia and Southern Persia, wherever they may be . . .'. The Chief of the Air Staff, Major-General F. H. Sykes endorsed Slade's views and recommendations 'with all possible emphasis'.[43] Sykes considered that 'the very existence of the Empire will depend in the first instance upon aerial supremacy'. Slade had shown that Persia and Mesopotamia held the world's largest oil reserves. Thus 'it is essential that steps shall be taken to monopolise all possible supplies. . . . Further, the area in which it is contained must be safeguarded by a very wide belt of territory between it and potential enemies'.

Balfour, however, now Foreign Secretary, was clearly not impressed. He saw Slade's recommendations as representing an entirely imperialistic War Aim. On 11 August 1918, the day before he was to make his statement on War Aims to the Imperial War Cabinet, he received a further letter from Hankey.[44] Hankey admitted that the Aim was imperialistic and would doubtless shock President Wilson and others of Britain's allies. He repeated his question, therefore, somewhat differently. Might not the British forces press forward in Mesopotamia in order to secure a proper water supply? This, incidentally, would also give Britain most of the oil-bearing regions.

Although it gave rise to such immediate interest, Slade's memorandum was shortly quietly dropped. On 17 September Balfour circulated his own memorandum to the War Cabinet.[45] The Foreign Secretary declared that there were passages in Slade's memorandum 'which deal with contentious questions of oil company politics', and thought that Slade's open hostility towards the Royal Dutch–Shell group led his memorandum to be 'read as an *ex parte* statement on behalf of the Anglo-Persian Company *vis-à-vis* its trade rivals, especially the Royal Dutch Company'. His own earlier endorsement of the memorandum, as also that of the First Sea Lord, referred only to the contention 'that the oil bearing districts of Mesopotamia and Persia are of very great national importance to us'.

The Imperial War Cabinet considered the question of War Aims at its meeting on 13 August 1918.[46] At this meeting the Foreign Secretary, Balfour, declared that Britain's 'chief diplomatic difficulties were created by the Sykes–Picot agreement, which, though still remaining as a diplomatic instrument, was historically out of date, and by the jealousy of France and Italy'. He pointed out also that there was a 'vital necessity for the British Empire to secure a [Mesopotamian] settlement which would not endanger our facilities for obtaining oil from this region'. The Eastern Committee of the War Cabinet had already carefully discussed the continued desirability and validity of the Sykes–Picot Agreement and had unanimously agreed that it was dead.[47]

If this was the British view, it was not that of France, which would not hear of cancelling an agreement that secured to her so many advantages. The British Government could not afford to estrange its ally, and thus had to secure a mutually acceptable revision of the agreement. But obviously it was desirable to do so from as strong a position as possible. In addition, the matter was urgent, for there now seemed to be a good chance of making peace with Turkey.

It is at this point that the question of the British advance to Mosul arises.[48] The advance, after the signing of the armistice of Mudros on 30 October, was indeed a deployment of the occupation garrisons as agreed in the armistice. But the minutes of the War Cabinet meetings of that month show clearly that it was undertaken also to put Britain in as strong a bargaining position as possible for negotiating peace with Turkey and a reorganisation of the Sykes–Picot Agreement with France. Oil was not specifically mentioned at these meetings, but the discussions that took place beforehand, and the succeeding negotiations with France, make it plain that it was an important factor in Britain's wish to regain influence over Mosul.

II BRITISH WARTIME OIL ADMINISTRATION PROBLEMS: THE GOVERNMENT'S ATTEMPTS TO GAIN CONTROL OF OIL SUPPLIERS

Despite the Government's pre-war attempt at ensuring national interests by 'taking-over' the more than willing Anglo-Persian Oil Company, British Government – oil company relations during the war were essentially a matter of British *versus* 'foreign' interests. War made the problem of finding a general British oil policy more acute, for the dependence of the British Empire on foreign, and particularly on American, oil became more marked and disquieting. It seemed therefore to the British Government that the most suitable way of solving the problem would be to attempt to bring important foreign oil interests under British control. Allied to this question, for it was an important basic factor in any British consideration of inter-company relations at this time, was the old matter of the Mesopotamian oil concession.

It was in the summer of 1915[49] that the question of amalgamating the companies supplying Britain's oil first arose. In July, or earlier, in conjunction with its plans for supplying to the Admiralty a large quantity of Borneo oil, valuable for toluol extraction, Shell had made an important proposal to the Admiralty. Extracting toluol from crude oil left a large residue (some 98·5 per cent) of by-products to be disposed of in the market, and tankers for transporting the oil to Britain for toluol extraction were acutely short, the Government using those belonging to Shell.[50] The company proposed, therefore, that an amalgamation be arranged with the Burmah Oil Company, the chief supplier of the Indian kerosene market, so as to provide the necessary tank storage and refining facilities and a market for the by-products.

The Admiralty, however, together with the Foreign Office and India, thought this proposal merely a pretext for a general extension of Shell's activities, in particular over the Persian and Baluchistan markets, and saw in it also a disguised threat to British interests in Mesopotamia.[51] Ever since Shell's first approaches to the Government, in 1902, the Admiralty had in fact consistently blocked its applications for oil concessions in Burma, on the grounds of the company's susceptibility to foreign influence,[52] and thus the rejection of its latest proposal was hardly a surprise. A compromise solution was reached by the end of the year, and, though not entirely satisfactory either to Shell or to the Admiralty, had at least the merit to the Admiralty of avoiding a Shell–Burmah Oil Company amalgamation.[53]

However, the question had not been settled, only introduced. The basic issue was that of ensuring the British character of the firms supplying Britain's oil. In meetings in January 1916 with the two main

British companies involved, the Government, as represented by the Foreign Office and the Admiralty, sought more detailed views on how an 'all-British oil company' might be set up.[54] Greenway, for the Anglo-Persian Oil Company, suggested a purely imperial company, with priority in Government contracts and in obtaining concessions in Britain and all her dependencies and spheres of influence, and receiving fiscal protection in return for price control.[55] The Shell representatives, Marcus Samuel and Robert Waley Cohen, however, clung to their scheme of an amalgamation with the Burmah Oil Company.[56] They had put this scheme forward again in December and in mid-January, 'in response to a strongly expressed desire of the British Government' that Shell's subsidiary, the Anglo-Saxon Petroleum Company, 'might be brought entirely under British control'. Waley Cohen was able to repeat his company's belief (frequently declared since the Government's purchase of a shareholding in the Anglo-Persian) that fiscal protection, through either a subsidy or a protective tariff, was 'inadvisable . . . and would lead to a conflict of interest with other Powers, which is not in the interests of the State'. He asserted that a purely British oil company could not provide the advantages, particularly that of security of supplies, that were proffered in his scheme. If the British Government would mellow its attitude towards his Dutch colleagues he was sure they would accept his scheme, which would go on to be a great success.

Later events were to show that this was rather too large a pill for the Government to swallow. The Government was still suspicious of and grudging in any praise it bestowed on the English side of the Royal Dutch–Shell Group, let alone the Dutch side; also, its guardianship of the Anglo-Persian Oil Company was too recent for it to be anything but protective of its new dependant which in February 1916, choosing its moment carefully, emitted a *cri de coeur*.[57] The company wrote to the Foreign Office that during the cold weather its geological staff in Mesopotamia had found favourable indications of oil in the Basra vilayet. The company was not, however, intending to file an application for the area, since in view of the Foreign Office's letter of 15 November last, the company understood that it would 'be given the complete oil rights over any portion of the Turkish Empire which may come under British influence'. But, as a guide to its present and future exploration work in Mesopotamia for the Admiralty, the company wished to be advised 'if the above understanding of the position is correct'.

However sympathetic the Foreign Office may have appeared to the Anglo-Persian interests, the latter could hardly have expected a simple, affirmative answer to their query. Their letter was clearly a less than subtle attempt to acquire, as an authority to which they could subsequently appeal, written Government sanction to larger claims than the company had ever been granted. This letter sparked off an inter-departmental correspondence that was to last for three months, and the issue of post-war foreign policy that it raised was to pervade all subsequent Government thinking on relations with the oil companies.

Greenway's letter was indeed instrumental in changing the Foreign Office's mind – though in the opposite direction to that he had intended. The Foreign Office felt that it was 'important that the [company's] assumption should at once be controverted',[58] and pointed out to the other departments that the D'Arcy group, interested in Mesopotamian oil through the Turkish Petroleum Company, was separate from the Anglo-Persian Oil Company, and that the D'Arcy group's claim to a monopoly was quite another question. In any case, neither the group nor the company had any claims recognised by the Foreign Office to other parts of the Turkish Empire, concerning which, the department considered, other British groups were entitled to 'careful and probably to preferential consideration'.

Sir Edward Grey felt strongly that it was 'essential that the whole attitude of His Majesty's Government towards the oil question should be reviewed at an early date'. There were two main reasons for this view. The first was that, apart from the American companies, Shell was Britain's main supplier. Shell also controlled the marketing of the oil produced by the Anglo-Persian and the Burmah companies – two British, but weak and local, companies.[59] Hence the Foreign Secretary felt that it was 'desirable to examine whether the Royal Dutch–Shell Group cannot be brought under British control, by an amalgamation with the Burmah and Anglo-Persian Companies, or otherwise'. The present moment, he felt, was extremely opportune for pursuing such a development; Shell favoured the idea and the Government should take advantage of the company's present patriotic and self-sacrificing frame of mind. Most important to the Foreign Office was the 'important bearing . . . [of] . . . the oil question . . . upon considerations of foreign policy'. The pre-war Mesopotamian negotiations 'afforded an example of the embarrassment which was caused to this department in dealing with a company like the Anglo-Saxon Petroleum Company Limited which, though British in domicile, is in fact controlled by the Royal Dutch Company'. Once the war was over, and in order to avoid German economic penetration of the Middle East, concessions should be handled by a British group. But, added Grey, 'Neither the Burmah Oil Company nor the Anglo-Persian Oil Company appear to dispose of the economic independence, the areas of supply, or the commercial ability to enable them to fulfil the necessary conditions.' Parker's private views on the matter are even more illuminating. As can be seen from a departmental minute he wrote,[60] he held strongly that the Foreign Office could not allow either the Anglo-Persian or the D'Arcy group an oil monopoly, even in Mosul and Baghdad. Although it had been decided that the 1914 Foreign Office Agreement, and consequently Shell's 25 per cent participation was no longer valid, he was firmly convinced, 'in case there is litigation hereafter as I am positive there will be if we admit Greenway's claim, that the Shell would be unfairly treated by His Majesty's Government if they are now jostled out of that 25 per cent'. He pointed out that 'Admiral Slade, who is a director of the Anglo-Persian Oil Company, is unable to see anything but perfection in that Company' and he contrasted this with the opinion of Lord Inchcape, Slade's fellow Government director on the company's board, who 'said that the best thing we could do would be to get the whole thing taken over, on terms, by the Shell and run on sound commercial lines'.

Parker echoed the Foreign Office's fears that 'a full and frank investigation by an independent committee under a strong chairman is being burked'. He was not entirely wrong, for at this time both the Board of Trade and the Admiralty saw no advantage for British interests in the only sort of amalgamation scheme that the Shell interests favoured.[61] Further, the Board of Trade together with the India Office,[62] felt that the Anglo-Persian Company had good grounds for claiming priority for oil rights in Mesopotamia, though not in other parts of the Ottoman Empire.

The Admiralty's views are worth quoting in some detail. Concerning Greenway's claims, the department declared that it appreciated the 'importance of giving provisional consideration' to the Mesopotamian oil question, and agreed that support of the D'Arcy group 'in the sphere to which the promised concessions relate should not extend to other territories . . . where other British interests have previously been supported'. It maintained, more strongly than ever, its 1914 attitude towards the rival companies and did not hesitate to point out the change that had taken place in Foreign Office thinking since the previous December.[63] The Admiralty stressed that 'oil fuel is of such vital importance to the British Navy that My Lords are not prepared to trust entirely to the goodwill and self-interest of commercial companies (whose interests are necessarily those of their shareholders) for the necessary exploitation on which supplies depend'. Further, the department thought that

> It does not seem possible that any concessions to H.M. Government which the shareholders' interests in their vast capital would permit the Dutch–Shell group to make would be in the slightest degree commensurate with the giving over to them of a privileged position and rights of immense commercial value in India, Persia and Mesopotamia. The maintenance of a strong independent group in these regions appears to be a cardinal act of policy.

The sort of company reorganisation that would best serve Britain's interests, suggested the Admiralty, would be that combining a closer union of British groups with strengthened Government influence – the acquisition of a controlling share in the Burmah Oil Company by the Indian Government.

Since all the other departments concerned seemed to be taking the opposite line to its own, the Foreign Office pressed for an interdepartmental conference where the whole matter could be 'thrashed out'.[64] But the Board of Trade, into whose area of activity the question of oil company reorganisation fell, preferred that the two main aspects of the matter, of Mesopotamian oil claims and Royal Dutch-Shell reorganisation should be dealt with separately.[65] The Foreign Office was obliged, therefore, to send an interim reply to the Anglo-Persian Oil Company. It informed the company that the Government was not 'prepared to express unqualified assent in the wide claims advanced' in the company's letter, but that the whole question would be 'considered at a later date when political conditions are altered and more settled'.[66] 'Political conditions' meant, of course, the arrangements included in the Sykes–Picot Agreement, settled the day before the Foreign Office replied to the company. On that ground alone, even had there been no other reasons, it was necessary that the Anglo-Persian Oil Company's broad claim be treated with great circumspection. The company, predictably, was not satisfied with the answer it was given but could obtain nothing firmer.[67] It was on this note that the interdepartmental correspondence on Mesopotamia ended for the time being. The Admiralty, writing to the Foreign Office on 20 June 1916, recognised 'that no settlement of this question, which [their Lordships] regard as of the very greatest importance, can be effected until the political situation in that region is more defined'.[68]

Although separate consideration of the claims of the D'Arcy group had thus temporarily to be set aside, the Government continued to examine the possibility of reorganising the oil companies. However, Mesopotamian oil claims could never be completely excluded from these discussions, since Mesopotamia and Persia were fundamental to the Admiralty's attitude towards the rival oil companies.

Two schemes put forward in August 1916 formed the basis of the discussions. The first was contained in a Board of Trade memorandum of 12 August.[69] The Board of Trade considered that a purely British company or combination could not provide sufficient supplies or facilities to meet the empire's needs. Any effective combination must include the Royal Dutch–Shell, although, clearly, British control in the capital and management of the new undertaking must be ensured. By this scheme the Anglo-Saxon Petroleum Company would amalgamate with the Burmah Oil Company to form a new concern, the 'Imperial Oil Company', which would be 51 per cent British (Burmah and Anglo-Saxon) and 49 per cent Royal Dutch. Dominance of the British membership would be ensured through the creation of British voting trusts. The memorandum detailed the organisation and operation of this scheme, and declared, in conclusion, that the scheme, having been 'provisionally obtained' 'by long and difficult negotiations with the representatives of the Shell Company', must serve to represent the maximum demands that could be made in obtaining Royal Dutch concurrence. The Government must decide, therefore, 'not whether something more advantageous could not be drafted, but whether on the whole the scheme . . . presents greater advantages than the alternative policy of declining to make any arrangement' at all, and risking the consequences.

The Admiralty did not immediately agree with this opinion. Twelve days later, on 24 August, it issued an alternative scheme, drawn up by Admiral Slade.[70] The Admiralty objected that the Board of Trade's scheme neither excluded foreign influence from the new company's policy and management, nor protected the consumer. A huge monopoly would be created that the Shell interests would dominate. The Admiralty suggested, therefore, the formation of a 'National Oil Company', through amalgamation of the Anglo-Persian and Burmah oil companies. Distributing facilities would be provided by reconstituting the British Petroleum Company (which until recently had been a German-dominated marketing organisation) so as to bring it under British Government control.[71] The Admiralty declared that as a result of such a reorganisation the British companies would absorb Shell, instead of Shell in effect absorbing the British companies. The Anglo-Persian Oil Company would then proceed to develop the Persian, Mesopotamian and other 'British' oilfields and generally make the British Empire and its dependencies self-supporting with regard to oil supplies and distribution. A further memorandum by Slade, 'Observations on the Board of Trade Memorandum on Oil', is notable chiefly for its constant attack on the Royal Dutch–Shell group. The Board of Trade's and the Admiralty's memoranda were considered by the Cabinet Oil Committee, together with a further Admiralty memorandum of 19 October. In this later memorandum the Admiralty declared its support of the principle of a Burmah–Shell amalgamation on the basis of the Board of Trade's scheme.[72] It warned, however, that 'any attempt to push the goods of any one company in preference to those of the Anglo-Persian Oil Company cannot, under any circumstances, be tolerated'. However, although, at its meeting on 1 November, the committee approved the Board of Trade's scheme and authorised that department to continue its negotiations, these broke down over the question of cancelling the marketing agreement between the Anglo-Persian Oil Company and the Asiatic Petroleum Company.[73]

There was one small flurry over the question of an 'all-British oil company' at the end of 1917. This was sparked off by Greenway's speech at the annual meeting of the Anglo-Persian Oil Company on 3 December 1917. His speech was widely reported in the press, particularly as regards his reference to the desirability of an 'all-British' oil company. This, he said, should be Government-controlled, like the Anglo-Persian, and 'free from foreign taint of any kind' to develop oilfields outside the British Isles and 'absorb all the existing British oil-producing companies . . .'.[74] On 6 December Sir Marcus Samuel wrote an extremely angry letter to Sir John Cadman at the Ministry of Munitions (Cadman was shortly to become director of the new Petroleum Executive), the matter was raised in the House of Commons on 10 December, and an official notice was issued to the press on 7 January 1918 denying that the formation of such a company was being considered.[75] What was particularly irritating to the Anglo-Persian's rival companies and to the Petroleum Executive was a revelation that arose in discussion of this incident and led to an official reprimand for Greenway. The revelation was 'that the Anglo-Persian Oil Company had been making use of the fact that the Government held a large financial interest in their company to unduly influence trade connections' and seek 'priority for [obtaining] materials'.[76]

Although, strictly speaking, the Government's denial to the press in January 1918 of its intention to form an all-British oil company was accurate, it was merely a verbal equivocation. Four months later, Government investigations into the question of oil company amalgamation were resumed, along the lines of the Board of Trade's 1916 recommendations. These investigations were part of a definite attempt by the British Government to evolve a general oil policy.

In 1917 a special organisation, the Petroleum Executive, had been formed, under the direction of Professor Sir John Cadman.[77] Until that time each Government department had run its own oil affairs; but the wartime pressure of competing claims on a constantly depleted tanker tonnage meant that co-ordination was becoming essential.[78] Throughout 1917 efforts were made to co-ordinate oil matters by reducing and recasting the various existing oil committees, and as a result the Petroleum Executive was brought into being in December and given advisory powers and powers of executive action. But it was found difficult to work satisfactorily without some sort of national policy guide. This was so particularly in relation to the Government's attitude to oil companies, British and foreign. For instance, Shell, in an effort to prove to the Government its patriotism, and feeling resentful of the special favour it (not inaccurately) felt was shown to the Anglo-Persian Oil Company, had asked for a Government director on its board.[79] It was decided, therefore, to set up a special committee to consider questions of national policy and reopen the oil company negotiations.

The investigations were undertaken by a committee set up in May 1918 by Walter Long, Colonial Secretary and Minister in Charge of Petroleum Affairs. Meeting under the chairmanship of Lord Harcourt, the Petroleum Imperial Policy Committee (or 'PIPCo') was instructed 'to enquire into and advise His Majesty's Government on the policy to be followed to ensure adequate supplies of oil for naval, military and industrial purposes'.[80] The lines the committee was to follow were indicated by Long. He pointed out Britain's present dependence on the USA for about 80 per cent of her oil supplies, and the consequent power America would have over Britain if she decided to be unfriendly.[81] The most immediate background factor was, none the less, Britain's 1917 oil shortage, resulting from enemy submarine action against tankers. Consequently, Long advised the Committee that

> the [oil] situation must be most carefully reviewed, and that ways and means must be devised by which we can attain a reasonably self-supporting position for the future. ... The Committee will, therefore, find it necessary to consider what steps should be taken to secure control of as much as possible of the world supply of natural petroleum ... [and in this connection] ... it will be important to examine the share which British capital is now taking in the exploitation of oilfields in His Majesty's dominions and in foreign countries, and to consider how far the operations and policy of the great oil groups are in accord with Imperial interests.

The three main cases for consideration were (1) whether or not the British Government should retain its financial interest in the Anglo-Persian Oil Company, (2) whether the Anglo-Mexican Oil Company should be allowed to come under the control of an American purchaser, and (3) whether and how the Royal Dutch–Shell group might be brought under British Government control. Generally, however, the committee, through its frequent meetings and its interviews with witnesses, examined closely all British oil holdings in the effort to evolve a broad British policy. Dominion and colonial oil affairs were discussed at the Imperial War Conference in July 1918, where the conference endorsed the urging of Lord Harcourt that 'it is absolutely vital to the British Empire to get a firm hold of all possible sources of petroleum supply, and the Government will welcome the introduction of any such measures [i.e. licences and strict leasing conditions] in the Dominions as may tend to this end ...'[82] Production in the empire was, however, small and unlikely ever to be able to meet the demands of Britain's expanding oil technology. Therefore, the greater part of the committee's time and activity was spent in the negotiations with the Royal Dutch–Shell Group, the only 'great oil group' that it might be possible to bring under British Government control. Already containing a large British element, it seemed that if acceptable terms could be arranged the group might be willing to come under British control. In time the negotiations brought about an agreement to transfer the group from Dutch to British control, and, its terms of reference then considered fulfilled, the committee subsequently disbanded.

The negotiations with the Royal Dutch–Shell fell into two phases, the first of which lasted from May to November 1918. There were two ways in which it seemed possible to achieve British control: either something could be added to the group – some or all of the Government holdings in the Anglo-Persian Oil Company – thus securing British predominance; or the present holdings could be rearranged in such a way as to change the Dutch majority in the group to a minority. Obviously, for the company to agree to the latter course, it would require something – say, new oil territories – in return. In either case, interference with the commercial side of the business was recognised throughout the negotiations as being neither possible nor desirable. During the first phase of the negotiations, the first of the two alternative methods of procedure was examined, with Sir Marcus Samuel and Sir Henri Deterding discussing with the committee an agreement along the lines of the Royal Dutch–Shell group acquiring some or all of the British Government holding in the Anglo-Persian Company, or of being given additional shares in the Anglo-Persian that could be created specially to enable Royal–Dutch Shell participation. The difficulty lay in the extent to which each side was prepared to make the sacrifices the other saw as necessary.

Shell offered to the British public a 51 per cent voting power in the British companies of the group, and to the British Government both a Government-appointed director with advisory powers, and some preference ('most favoured nation' status for the empire) in purchasing the British companies' oil. The Government negotiators recognised that such a voting power majority, residing in non-Government shareholders, represented no security at all for the British Government, which wanted control over the Shell companies' shares and directorates, together with a special oil price deal irrespective of current market prices. As for the 'bait' offered to the Royal Dutch–Shell, participation in the Anglo-Persian Oil Company, this was no attraction to the group so long as the British Government controlled that company or, as the Government alternatively suggested, the Burmah Oil Company, the largest minority shareholder in the Anglo-Persian. The British Government was as unwilling to give up its real control over the Anglo-Persian – which to it would make the whole exercise pointless – as was the Royal Dutch–Shell group to give the British Government real control over Shell affairs. The opinions of the Anglo-Persian representatives, Greenway and Slade, were coloured by their strongly antipathetic attitude towards the Royal Dutch–Shell directorate. These men they described as being 'out for large personal gains', unlike the Anglo-Persian's directorate, which they said was 'influenced solely by the desire to promote national interests.'[83] Both men declared that Government control of a company was a drawback, as their company had found out; but, if this control were to be retained and British companies reorganised, then they would prefer this to be achieved through a purely British 'National Oil Company', as the Admiralty had earlier suggested.[84] It is thus not surprising that these negotiations foundered. There could, perhaps, have been an accommodation if Deterding had not been the chief negotiator for the Royal Dutch interests; Samuel was rather more anxious to reach a settlement with the British Government, but he had little influence over his more powerful colleague, who had, for instance, blandly remarked to the committee, that Samuel had asked for a Government director simply out of vanity, because the Anglo-Persian had some. Further, despite the attitude of Greenway and Slade to the Royal Dutch–Shell Group, J. T. Cargill, a director of the Anglo-Persian and chairman of the Burmah Oil Company, was also anxious for a settlement, even on reduced terms.[85]

By the end of 1918, therefore, considerable progress had been made towards evolving an oil policy, and it was one in which Mesopotamia was to play a major part. The exigencies of war had brought Mesopotamia much more to the fore, in terms both of military and of political activity, than could have been predicted. After the British Government had realised the blunder it had made in 1916, by agreeing to partition the Ottoman Empire in a way that would allow France Mosul, efforts had to be directed towards rectifying the situation. At the same time a national oil policy began to be sought. Even in the early stages of working this out, it seemed undeniable that the twin objectives must be to obtain control over both supplies and suppliers of Britain's oil. The realisation that departmental oil policy committees needed to be streamlined and co-ordinated led to the setting up of the Petroleum Executive and the Petroleum Imperial Policy Committee (PIPCo). Oil policy-makers came up with the solution of trying to obtain British control over the Royal Dutch–Shell Group of companies. Initial efforts at securing this control were unsuccessful, but by October–November 1918, with peace imminent, conditions were favourable for a resumed effort.

8 Unmaking the Sykes–Picot Agreement: Oil Negotiations November 1918–April 1920

Setting out the problem – Resumption of negotiations between PIPCo and the Royal Dutch–Shell – The making of the Long–Bérenger Agreement: November–December 1918; differences in outlook between the FO and the British Peace Conference delegates; French claims and the FO's reaction; negotiations, January–February 1919; British Peace Conference delegates' views; FO pique at the method of proceeding; draft agreement, 13 March 1919; views of A. T. Wilson, Acting Civil Commissioner in Mesopotamia; revised draft agreement, 8 April; FO reaction; FO approval – The heads of agreement between the British Government and the Royal Dutch–Shell approved, 8 May – The Long–Bérenger Agreement confirmed officially by the FO on 16 May, but then cancelled (verbally on 21 May, officially on 22 July) – Canvassing continues throughout the summer and autumn – Anglo-French negotiations resumed in December 1920 – The Greenwood–Bérenger Agreement concluded on 21 December – Agreement jeopardised by ministerial conference, 23 January 1920 – The French retaliate – Pressure from the Admiralty, Board of Trade and Petroleum Department – Lloyd George–Millerand meeting of 18 April – Berthelot-Cadman (San Remo) Agreement initialled on 24 April, confirmed on 25 April – Provisions of agreement – Immediate aftermath – Final stages of the British Government–Royal Dutch–Shell agreement – General conclusion.

I NEGOTIATIONS TO AUGUST 1919: DRAFT 'MESOPOTAMIAN AGREEMENT' INITIALLED AND LONG–BÉRENGER AGREEMENT MADE AND CANCELLED

The last sixteen months in the twenty-year period covered by this study of the British Government's interest in the Mesopotamian oil concession demonstrate the way in which the threads of the preceding years had by now drawn together. The oil question was greatly affected by the conclusion of the armistice with Turkey on 30 October and with Germany on 11 November 1918. Not only was Britain a victorious power, whose friendship was therefore additionally valuable to an international oil combine, but in addition there were now material *quid pro quos*, such as Mesopotamian oil, to include in the bargaining.

Such bargaining occurred on two levels. On one level, the Government could pursue the policy it had evolved during the war. By this it sought to bring under British control other oil companies besides the Anglo-Persian, in an effort to achieve for the empire as secure a future position as possible. With British victory in the war the 'bait' was improved, and the Royal Dutch–Shell group was enticed by the prospect of a firm oil concession to be gained in a Mesopotamia that was now under complete British occupation. But did Britain actually *control* all of Mesopotamia? Under the Sykes–Picot Agreement much of Mosul was still allotted to France, which, despite Britain's strong position in Upper Mesopotamia by the end of the war, could be persuaded to give up Mosul only if Britain offered in exchange territories that France desired. Further, France was now acutely aware of her own lack of oil. If she gave up Mosul she wished to be assured of participation in its oil development, given which she would allow the developers to construct pipelines through her Syrian territories to the coast. The two levels of negotiation, British Government–Royal Dutch–Shell, and British Government–French Government, came together over the question of Mesopotamian oil. To some extent the course of the Anglo-French negotiations is already known, though a considerable amount of documentary evidence concerning them has now become available and will be analysed below; but little has been known, even in outline, about the negotiations between the British Government and the Royal Dutch–Shell group, or about the role that Mesopotamian oil assumed in them.

The post-war oil negotiations had two main aspects, of which the first was the territorial. The Foreign Office would have preferred that a decision on the question of a Mesopotamian oil concession be left until after the Peace Conference had delimited the boundaries of the various spheres of influence in the former Ottoman Empire; yet, before this happened, Britain needed France to concur in a modification of the Sykes–Picot Agreement. The Foreign Office fully intended that Mesopotamian oil should be exploited, once Britain received the mandate for Mesopotamia, and did not see why it should have to promise France what might turn out to be an unnecessary slice of the cake.

The second main aspect of the negotiations concerned the question of the *quid pro quo* to be given the Royal Dutch–Shell in exchange for coming under British control. The group, through its subsidiary the Anglo-Saxon Petroleum Company, had undoubtedly legally possessed a 25 per cent share in the Turkish Petroleum Company. Further, the group was certainly secretly encouraging the French Government to ask for the sequestrated German share in the Turkish Petroleum Company. If Britain granted France a share in the company, then the British Government would face litigation from the Royal Dutch–Shell if it denied the Anglo-Saxon its participation. Under the articles of association of the original Turkish Petroleum Company, the Anglo-Saxon, as a partner, was entitled to have equal first option with the other remaining partners on the shares of any of their number who left the company. But the Deutsche Bank's 25 per cent share had by now been sold by the Public Trustee to a 'British Government Nominee' (actually Lancelot H. Smith of the Board of Trade). Also, the remaining 50 per cent share, intended in 1914 for the Anglo-Persian Oil Company, had never been taken up by that company. The Anglo-Persian had, of course, been told by the Foreign Office in 1915 that the Turkish Petroleum Company and its promised concession were no longer valid, and in consequence it had assumed, as we have seen, that after the war it would hold the field alone.

The British Government was thus in an extremely tight corner. It seemed, therefore, that the only way out of it and the only way that would ensure the Anglo-Persian Company's participation at all in Mesopotamian oil exploitation was for the Government to regard the Turkish Petroleum Company and its promised concession once more as valid.

On the Royal Dutch–Shell front, negotiations between the group and PIPCo proceeded fairly satisfactorily. A provisional agreement was initialled by Lord Harcourt and Henri Deterding[1] on 31 January 1919, and, with a few amendments, was approved by the War Cabinet on 8 May 1919. This agreement provided that:

> His Majesty's Government will use their best endeavours to secure, either by re-arrangement of the capital in the Turkish Petroleum Company or otherwise that the Royal Dutch–Shell group . . . through . . . the Anglo-Saxon Petroleum Company . . . and the Anglo-Persian Oil Company shall be admitted to equal participation in the exploitation of all oilfields in Mesopotamia.[2]

In return for this assured participation it was agreed that 'The Shell Transport and Trading Company and its subsidiary companies' – in other words the British companies comprised in the Royal Dutch–Shell group – would be reconstituted in such a way as to secure British control, though without affecting their financial and commercial freedom.

The main outlines of the agreement were that Shell would become the chief company of the group, and that at least 75 per cent of the directors on its board would be British-born British subjects. The group's subsidiary companies were, so far as possible, to be registered in Britain and to be brought under 'Shell' control; their boards too (including those of the Anglo-Saxon and the Asiatic petroleum companies) were to contain a majority of British-born British subjects acceptable to the Government. For all these companies, a Government nominee was to have a right of veto over certain matters such as the sale of assets or any change in a company's articles of association without Government approval.

Despite the initialled draft and War Cabinet approval, negotiations between the Royal Dutch–Shell group and the Petroleum Executive continued throughout 1919 and 1920, giving substance to the agreement and settling, at tedious length, various points of detail. Cadman conducted the Government side of the negotiations, assisted by J. C. Clarke of the Petroleum Executive, with Harold Brown of Messrs. Linklater, Solicitors, dealing with the legal framing of detail. The Royal Dutch–Shell side was represented chiefly by directors H. Colijn (previously War Minister, and later to become Prime Minister, of Holland), Deterding and Walter Samuel, with G. F. Hotblack of Waltons as counterpart to Brown. The main points under discussion during these long months concerned such matters as indemnity from double taxation (British as well as Dutch) for the transferred companies and their shareholders – as it turned out an exceedingly difficult point to thrash out; the basic question of percentage allocations (especially after it became known that in the course of the Anglo-French negotiations it had been agreed that the native interests allocation be increased to 20 per cent); the extent of the area of Asia Minor over which the British Government would support the Turkish Petroleum Company's claim for concessions; and the unswervable determination of Deterding that Shell interests, and not the Anglo-Persian Oil Company should absolutely control management of the Turkish Petroleum Company. The Royal Dutch was indeed giving up a great deal in order to achieve essentially two things: first, and less specifically, an improvement in its relations with the British Government; and, secondly, recognition of its position in the Turkish Petroleum Company and of Shell's claim for managerial control of that company. In return, the Government could expect to ensure that Shell would permanently be British in law, nationality and sentiment, that Shell would control as many companies (especially producing companies) as possible in the Royal Dutch–Shell group, and that the British Government would be guaranteed precedence in supplies, all of which would substantially aid Britain's oil position in the world. The agreement, however, was dependent on a parallel Anglo-French agreement settling the question of Mosul, and it is these negotiations that must now be examined in some detail.

The story of the making of the Long–Bérenger Agreement and the succeeding Anglo-French oil agreements is something of a diplomatic saga, for it was typified by confusion and mishandling. However, most of the story can now be pieced together from the records of the Foreign Office, the Foreign Office Paris Peace Conference Delegation, and the private papers of the Prime Minister, David Lloyd George.

By the end of 1918 the French Commissioner-General for Fuel (*pétrole et combustibles*), Senator Henri Bérenger, and the French Prime Minister, Georges Clemenceau, had made known to their British counterparts their government's desires with regard to oil. As France had undergone an even worse oil shortage during the war than Britain had, it wanted to secure its future position through a continuation of the allied wartime co-operation and through a substantial participation in Mesopotamian and other oil.[3] Consequently, when he was in London between 16 and 23 November 1918, Bérenger made his views known to Walter Long.[4] On 1 December occurred the oft referred to, but never properly documented, meeting between Lloyd George and Clemenceau[5] at which Clemenceau agreed to give up Mosul in exchange for Syria and a share in Mosul's oil potential – a formal bargain that none the less appears to have remained unknown to the prime ministers' colleagues until months later. By 17 December, therefore, when British and French Government representatives met to discuss the French suggestions,[6] the negotiations that were to lead to the Long–Bérenger and subsequent Anglo-French oil agreements were effectively under way.

The negotiations were official at least from the point of view of the French side. But on the British side the crux of the problem surrounding the negotiations was their degree and method of authorisation. The chief British negotiator was Sir John Cadman, director of the Petroleum Executive and representative of the Petroleum Executive in the Economic Section of the British Peace Delegation, and he was backed up strongly in London by Walter Long. In Paris Cadman was instructed to liaise closely with members of the Foreign Office delegation to the Peace Conference: Balfour, Foreign Secretary until October 1919, and Mallet, assisted by Charles Tufton. The Foreign Office delegates were clearly strongly influenced by Cadman and Bérenger; the difficulty arose in communications with London. Back in the Foreign Office the acting Foreign Secretary, Curzon,[7] and his colleagues (chiefly, on this issue, Ernest Weakley, now Foreign Office Liaison Officer with the Petroleum Executive, and George Kidston) were consulted on the negotiations – when they heard of them – largely *post hoc*. Although their comment was usually adverse – Curzon protested strongly and repeatedly against French participation – it usually arrived too late to be able to have any effect. The Foreign Office's Peace Conference delegates would, by then, already have concurred in the proposals put forward at that particular stage of the negotiations, partly because they approved of the proposals and partly because they thought that their London colleagues had done so. Cadman, who conducted most of the negotiations, insisted that he was complying with the Foreign Office's directive that the negotiations with Bérenger remain only unofficial and tentative, and that the Foreign Office be kept informed of them. But when these had been nearly concluded and had been approved by the Foreign Office Peace Conference delegates, he brought them back to London for official War Cabinet approval.

The differences in opinion and action are explicable. While the Foreign Office Peace Conference delegates, who considered that they possessed fully delegated powers in the peace negotiations, thought that the Anglo-French oil problem should be ironed out before the Peace Conference arranged the terms and areas of the mandates, Curzon and his staff in London believed that the oil question should not be considered until after the Peace Conference had met and organised the mandates. Further, they believed that they should have been much more fully and officially informed of the content and progress of the oil negotiations that were taking place in Paris, and of which they heard only intermittently and then usually casually, through private conversation or correspondence. Cadman clearly considered the Peace Conference delegates as what they were – the executive extension of the Foreign Office for the peace arrangements – and since, both to himself and to them, the oil negotiations were a necessary preliminary to the peace negotiations, his liaison with them was accordingly close and, to his mind, exactly what was required of him; whenever he was back in London he paid the London-based members of the Foreign Office the courtesy of discussing the matter with them and answering their questions. Finally, matters were not helped by the time it took for correspondence to travel from Paris to London, and the even greater time-lag between its arrival at the Foreign Office and its reception by Curzon or his colleagues. As Curzon sourly commented, after documents that Cadman had handed to Weakley on 6 February, and that Weakley had immediately handed in for entering up, had returned to him only on 17 February, 'No policy can survive such a system.'[8]

What the French sought at the meeting of 17 December was a joint Anglo-French policy, and a general share in oilfield development – Roumania, the Caucasus, Mesopotamia and Persia being instanced. On Mesopotamia they suggested that the Deutsche Bank's share in the Turkish Petroleum Company be sold to the Anglo-Saxon Company, which would then hand it over to French interests. These views were formally written down in a letter of 6 January 1919 from the French Minister in London to the Foreign Secretary.[9] This letter, which was signed by the Chargé d'Affaires, M. de Fleuriau, confirmed that the French Government had already discussed the matter with the Royal Dutch company, and sought permission to discuss the matter officially with the British Peace Conference delegates.

The Foreign Office reaction was decidedly unfavourable to the French claims, even before the interdepartmental meeting held at the Admiralty on 15 January.[10] The Foreign Office representative at this meeting, Ernest Weakley, made clear Curzon's view that it would be wiser to refuse to discuss any of these matters with the French until the Peace Conference had decided the ultimate fate of the districts involved. But the Foreign Office was supported only in this by the Board of Trade and was overridden when the meeting concluded that the British Government should show itself willing to co-operate before the French (who were negotiating with the US Government and the Standard Oil Company) obtained American help, and at the Peace Conference forced on Britain the co-operation which they were at present seeking to obtain voluntarily. Further, as France, under the Sykes–Picot Agreement, already had rights in Mosul, and as it was at present impossible to know which was the best oil area in Mesopotamia, it seemed preferable to have a sharing agreement covering the whole territory and thus be sure of some oil rather than risk getting none at all. Persia, of course, could not be – and never was – discussed, except in relation to French proposals for a second pipeline from the Persian oilfields; this apart, the French must be assumed to have introduced Persia merely to help keep the British on their toes. However, as regards the proposed second pipeline – to run through 'French' territory to the Mediterranean coast – the Admiralty was particularly impressed by the French arguments for it, and remained so throughout the negotiations. Curzon, though, pooh-poohed the idea of 'two pipelines running for thousands of miles across the desert as a prey for the roving Bedouin'. More seriously he complained, 'while we are struggling hard to get rid of the iniquitous Sykes–Picot Agreement and refusing France permission to send relief missions or Consular Officers to Mosul we are once more to tie ourselves up with it'.

Clemenceau, however, stated that 'The petroleum question appears to be one of the most important economic questions at the Peace Conference. It affects crucially the future of France's national defence and her general prosperity.'[11] Thus, when the French Ambassador in London sent the Foreign Office a second note on the matter,[12] it was quite in keeping with this attitude. On reading the note, which was received on 1 February, Weakley was 'astounded and surprised', for it claimed that in a 'precise conversation' Bérenger and Cadman had agreed that the oil problems could be solved favourably. Accordingly the French Ambassador urged that the Public Trustee be authorised to sell the Deutsche Bank's former 25 per cent share in the Turkish Petroleum Company, and that the French Government be enabled to acquire all or most of the holding. Despite an urgent Foreign Office telegram to Balfour in Paris, asking him to ascertain personally how far Cadman had gone in his conversation with Bérenger, and repeating that for the time being the Foreign Office was unwilling to hold any such discussions with the French, it was not until nearly three weeks later that Weakley was able to ascertain the facts, which he learnt for himself directly from Cadman.[13] On 21 February, when he was back in London, Cadman assured Weakley that he had conversed with Bérenger only in generalities, carefully avoiding discussing any details. He quite appreciated that while the Foreign Office was in the throes of trying to get rid of the Sykes–Picot Agreement it wished to avoid discussions about oil, and he stated that nothing had been said to the French about pipeline wayleaves or anything else likely to compromise the present issue.

Meanwhile in Paris, on 1 February, members of the Foreign Office Peace Delegation had held their own interdepartmental conference with Board of Trade and India Office delegates, to discuss French participation in the Mesopotamian concession.[14] The conclusions reached were clearly important in moulding British views in Paris. It was decided, for instance, that whatever verdict the Attorney General reached concerning the legality of the Mesopotamian oil concession this could be 'righted' if necessary by a clause in the treaty or treaties with the Arab state. Further, however French participation came about, whether through territorial ownership or through a share in the company (the preferred method), Britain should take the line that if the terms of the Peace Treaty gave her an influential position in Mesopotamia she would then use her influence with the Arab state so as to support the oil concession holder. In addition, it was suggested, for the first time, that the Arab state should have a holding in the company of up to about 20 per cent; this would mean that the company would probably receive more favourable terms in its lease from the Arab state.

Following the discussions at this conference, Balfour and Mallet put to the Foreign Office a number of important reasons for acceding to the French Government's request for oil negotiations.[15] They wrote that it was extremely doubtful whether the pre-war promise of a concession could be regarded as having any substance, while the legality of the Turkish Petroleum Company was also in question. On the assumption, therefore, that both France and the Royal Dutch–Shell must be satisfied, making an agreement to admit the French would imply French recognition of both the 'concession' and the Turkish Petroleum Company. Leaving aside the difficulty of blankly refusing ex-enemy spoils – the Deutsche Bank's former share in the Turkish Petroleum Company – to Britain's ally (this was after all, a less important, sentimental consideration), concurrence in the French request would facilitate revision of the Sykes–Picot Agreement. By ensuring positive French support in upholding the concession, an Anglo-French oil agreement would also thereby avoid the threatened alternative: French opposition to the confirmation of the concession, and certain obstruction from the Americans when the question came to be submitted to the Peace Conference. Such an agreement would also encourage the French to be less unreasonable towards British participation in Algerian oil, and would ensure French co-operation in constructing a pipeline through the French sphere of influence, Syria, to the Mediterranean coast, to carry both Mesopotamian and Persian oil.

At this point the Foreign Office's confusion and pique at proceedings in Paris reached a new high, which was to last quite some time. On 20 and 22 February Curzon sent the Foreign Office delegates in Paris an unequivocal statement of the department's views.[16] He reiterated his conviction that it was inadvisable to try to settle the oil question before the fate of Mesopotamia and Syria had been finally decided at Paris, and pointed out the uncertainty over the route for a Mesopotamia–Mediterranean pipeline, let alone a Persia–Mediterranean one. He complained that

> while, on the one hand, we are resolutely declining to come to an interim agreement with the French Government regarding the revision of the Sykes–Picot agreement as a whole, Sir John Cadman appears to have been discussing details with M. Bérenger. His conversations will doubtless be taken as representing the views of His Majesty's Government and will be appealed to as undertakings on our part when the details referred to come up for discussion.

The despatch just quoted was sent on 22 February, the day after Weakley's interview with Cadman at which the latter had disclaimed having discussed any details with the French.[17] This may well have been so, but Cadman could now no longer claim ignorance of the Foreign Office's opposition to the negotiations over French participation in Mesopotamian oil. Yet he now returned to Paris and resumed discussions – in detail – with Bérenger, on 13 March sending a copy of the provisional Long–Bérenger Agreement both to the Foreign Office and to its Peace Conference delegates in Paris, informing Mallet that he had 'secured the best terms we could arrange from the British point of view' and Curzon that the question had been discussed in Paris with Foreign Office representatives and that the Petroleum Executive hoped he would 'concur in the action taken'.[18]

As the Peace Conference Delegation's minutes show, Mallet had not received this draft agreement by 17 March, when he replied on Balfour's behalf to Curzon's two despatches of 20 and 22 February.[19] Mallet concluded that 'on the whole' he agreed that, 'subject to Sir John Cadman being consulted, and so long as he made it clear to M. Bérenger that we were ready to admit French participation in the Turkish Petroleum Company, it would not appear profitable to pursue these negotiations in detail until the ultimate nature of the territorial settlement is more clearly indicated'. In addition he pointed out that the naval section of the British Peace Delegation favoured Haifa for the

Mediterranean terminal of the pipeline, since this port was almost certain to be in the British sphere of influence after the Peace Settlement.[20]

Nonetheless, Mallet's conclusions were flexible, as his reply to Cadman a fortnight later shows.[21] While pointing out areas for modification in the proposed agreement, he still gave Cadman the official go-ahead from the British delegation, commenting that he trusted that the arrangement, which seemed to be in accordance with the recommendations of the meeting of 1 February, would dispose of the French claims satisfactorily.

The Foreign Office, not surprisingly, was not so amenable to the arrangements. In a despatch of 2 April to Balfour, Curzon pointed out the obvious discrepancy between the date on the draft agreement (13 March) and that on the despatch Mallet had sent four days later (17 March) failing to mention it, and queried whether, in fact, the discussions resulting in the agreement had 'been conducted with your sanction and approval'.[22] He objected to a number of points in the draft agreement:

> The only . . . advantage [other than that of French interest in upholding the validity of the Turkish Petroleum Company's concession] which appears to have been secured is a promise of facilities for two pipelines which we may never be in a position to construct through a district in which the French may never be in a position to afford us the facilities promised.

In short, the agreement appeared to have gratuitously given up to the French oil privileges for which Britain would receive no *quid pro quo*. The Foreign Office's opposition to the agreement was strengthened on hearing from Lt-Col. A. T. Wilson, the Acting Civil Commissioner in Mesopotamia.[23] Wilson held strongly that oil was the only immediately available asset of the occupied Mesopotamian territories, and that therefore it represented the sole real security that the territory would be able to offer in return for any future loan. Indeed, Wilson felt, oil exploitation should remain the property of the Mesopotamian administration and not be placed in the hands of any existing commercial company. He saw the Turkish Petroleum Company's claim as no more than a doubtful paper one, and considered that, so far as he was the trustee of the interests of the future Iraqi state, he would not feel able to give the Turkish Petroleum Company the facilities that it desired and that the British Government had undertaken to use its influence to obtain for the company.

However righteous, and apparently right, the views of the Foreign Office and the Acting Civil Commissioner for Mesopotamia, their objections were soon to be overcome. The Foreign Office had, as the

Paris delegates pointed out, missed the whole crux of the Mesopotamian arrangements, which was to give the Royal Dutch–Shell group a share in the Turkish Petroleum Company in return for coming under British control.[24] On 8 April Tufton enclosed a revised draft agreement in a private letter to Sir George Clerk, Senior Clerk in the Foreign Office, and Curzon's private secretary; the Mesopotamian section had now, he mentioned, been concurred in by Edwin Montague, the Secretary of State for India, as also by Mallet.[25] The agreement was subject to confirmation by the British and French Governments, and the British delegates hoped that their government would give its confirmation as soon as possible, through the usual diplomatic channels. On 9 April Cadman left Paris for London to call on the Foreign Office and help explain the new draft agreement. He explained to Weakley that the revisions were designed to meet the Foreign Office's objections to the implied recognition, in the earlier draft of a French sphere of influence in the Mosul district. In addition, the new draft aimed to meet other objections: over the proposed Roumanian provisions, and over A. T. Wilson's claims for a much larger participation for the Iraqi state. The agreement had now been made conditional on Britain's receiving the mandate for Mesopotamia; native participation in the oil company would now be at the level of 10 per cent for the native government interest and of up to 10 per cent for local native interests; France was bound, if it received the mandate for the area through which the pipeline were to be laid, to use its good offices to secure all facilities for laying the pipelines; and, finally, French participation in the company would now be limited solely to the Mesopotamian oilfields, and could not be extended, as had hypothetically been possible under the earlier drafts, to other fields in which the company might be interested.

If the content of the draft agreement was now less unpalatable to the Foreign Office, it did not alter the fact that the department remained piqued over many aspects of the question.[26] Why should such important communications invariably be made by private letter? Why should such important matters, negotiated with official representatives of the French Government, not be negotiated through the proper British Government channel – the Foreign Office? Why, indeed, when such negotiations were conducted despite the express opposition of the Foreign Office, should the latter then be asked to ratify, and as soon as possible, a cut and dried agreement without even expressing an opinion on it?

It was thus not surprising that the interdepartmental conference of the Eastern Committee called by Curzon at the Foreign Office on 29 April started off in a somewhat prickly atmosphere.[27] However, it was explained that the Acting Civil Commissioner for Mesopotamia had now dropped his opposition to the agreement, having realised that the Mesopotamian administration was not being committed behind his back to any course of action, and that the whole 'object of the agreement was merely the formation of a company to take up any concession which the Mesopotamian Administration had at its disposal and nothing in it prevented their making any conditions they chose'. As the Treasury agreed, Wilson's arguments on financial grounds no longer applied, in view of the Mesopotamian administration's ability to levy royalties. And, since Wilson's attitude had been a major influence on the Foreign Office's views, Curzon now admitted that a good case had been made out for the agreement. As a result of this discussion, therefore, 'His Majesty's Government would concur in the proposed agreement with the French, subject to the final concurrence of the War Cabinet in the Shell agreement, and to Foreign Office concurrence in the French agreement.'

On 8 May the heads of the Royal Dutch–Shell agreement were approved by the War Cabinet, and on 16 May, in a letter from Curzon sent to the French Ambassador, Paul Cambon, the Foreign Office officially confirmed the Long–Bérenger Agreement and invited the French Government to do the same.[28] This the French never did. In the course of increasingly recriminatory relations between the French and British prime ministers in their discussions over Syria, Lloyd George, in an angry outburst on 21 May, cancelled the newly concluded oil agreement. It did not accord, he declared in his confirmatory letter,[29] with the agreement made between the two prime ministers the previous December.

For some time after this the situation was one of confusion. Apparently Lloyd George himself had only recently learnt of the Long–Bérenger Agreement, in casual conversation;[30] and it was not until Lord Eustace Percy, a member of the British Delegation in Paris, wrote privately on 5 June to Sir George Clerk in London, mentioning the differences between the two prime ministers and enclosing a copy of Lloyd George's private letter of 21 May to Clemenceau,[31] that the Foreign Office learnt that the agreement had been withdrawn. When Percy's letter and its enclosure were received at the Foreign Office on 11 June, they caused a paper uproar there, largely because an agreement discussed *ad nauseam* had now been arbitrarily withdrawn and the Foreign Office informed only in a private letter, but also because it was not clear from the wording of Lloyd George's short letter whether the withdrawal referred to the whole agreement or only to the pipeline clauses. In any case, the Foreign Office had not previously known of the secret agreement that Lloyd George now so casually mentioned had been made between himself and Clemenceau in December 1918. Only Kidston, who had been hostile to the agreement throughout (and abrasive all through the meeting of 29 April at which Curzon had finally come round), expressed pleasure at the news of its withdrawal, and this Lloyd George informed Curzon of only on 12 June in a telephone message.[32] Meeting the Prime Minister's request the Foreign

Office sent him a memorandum and copies of its correspondence on the negotiations.[33] In having this memorandum drawn up Curzon commented (and the comments reached the Prime Minister's files), 'I challenged the agreement at a meeting of the Eastern Committee, only to be confronted with a series of papers initialled by Sir Louis Mallet and Mr Balfour in Paris negotiating the agreement of which I had heard nothing here until it was concluded.'[34] The Prime Minister's own views on the oil negotiations in fact agreed with Curzon's. This is not really surprising, since the letter to Curzon in which they were expressed was drafted jointly by Lloyd George's secretary and confidant, Sir J. T. Davies, and by Curzon himself.[35] Lloyd George considered that no oil arrangement should be concluded with France until after the mandate boundaries had been determined; believed that the Long–Bérenger Agreement placed Britain's interests entirely in the hands of the French, and that this could be changed only if Britain achieved the aim of direct access to the Mediterranean; and, finally, felt that since the discussions were on important matters of policy they should not be mixed up with arrangements about oil in which private companies were involved.

This last point was given some substance by the growing pressure from American interests, which, aware at least since early May that Anglo-French oil negotiations were in progress, were seeking detailed information on them. Further in Britain rumours were rife about expected developments in the negotiations with Shell.[36] Curzon felt, therefore that the situation must at least be clarified; and, having first sought the Prime Minister's concurrence, he then wrote on 22 July to the French Ambassador, Cambon, officially annulling his note of 16 May.[37] His communication was acknowledged on 12 August in a note from the French Foreign Minister, Pichon, who wrote,

> So vanishes the last vestige of the conversations of the English and French Prime Ministers on the subject of the zones and interests of France and England in Syria and Mesopotamia such as had been laid down by the Anglo-French agreement of 1916, which stands as the only possible basis for all settlement between the two countries on the affairs of Asia Minor.[38]

Thus ended this stage of the Anglo-French oil negotiations over Mesopotamia, in frustration for those who had sought an agreement, success for those who had opposed it, and general ill feeling – represented at its highest level by the highly charged exchanges between the two prime ministers – between Britain and France.[39] The official cancellation of the Long–Bérenger agreement was reported to the War Cabinet at its meeting on 20 August, and the only significant point to come out in the discussion was the importance (described by Curzon as 'excessive') that the Prime Minister attached to having exclusively in British hands a railway and a pipeline from Mesopotamia to a Mediterranean port.[40] At the official level, matters were now to rest until early December.

II RESUMED NEGOTIATIONS, TO APRIL 1920: 'MESOPOTAMIAN AGREEMENT' DETAILED AND SAN REMO AGREEMENT SIGNED

If official negotiations for an Anglo-French oil agreement over Mesopotamia were halted, unofficially those who wished to see such an agreement continued throughout the summer and autumn to canvass support. The Admiralty and General Staff had the greatest interest in securing an unequivocal and favourable settlement of the matter, and they continued to exert pressure for the restoration of the Long–Bérenger Agreement. On 4 November Walter Long circulated to members of the Cabinet a memorandum[41] containing his own summary of the negotiations; he pointed out that he personally had been 'given an absolutely free hand by the Cabinet to act in all matters for the United Kingdom', and he urged the Cabinet to reconsider its decision: '. . . if we lose the opportunities which have grown out of the war, we shall probably never be able to regain our position, and shall undoubtedly suffer once again from a shortness of supplies which will gravely hamper our national action'.

The main point to emerge from this memorandum is that the differences between Long's and the Foreign Office's understanding of the situation were due to their basic disagreement over authority. To Long the 'Foreign Office' included its Peace Conference delegates; yet the Foreign Office itself, as can be seen both from the negotiations and from the annotations on the department's copy of the memorandum, differentiated between the Foreign Office in London and the delegates in Paris. In the light of Long's interpretation, therefore, his assertion that he had consulted the Foreign Office and kept it fully informed is perfectly understandable. The main complaint of the Foreign Office, however, in its minutes on Long's memorandum, was that, while it too had kept the Peace Delegation fully informed of its opinions, 'Neither the Petroleum Executive nor the Peace Delegation seems to have paid the slightest attention.'

Further pressure was exerted by the Secretary for War, Winston Churchill, who on 12 November circulated to the Cabinet a series of papers concerning the situation in Mesopotamia.[42] These included a memorandum by the General Staff stressing the vital strategic position of Mesopotamia as 'an important link in a chain of contiguous areas under British influence, extending from Egypt to India'. Especially important was its oil potential: 'With a railway and pipeline to the Mediterranean, which is forecasted within the next ten years, the position of England as a naval power in the Mediterranean could be doubly assured, and our dependence on the Suez Canal, which is a vulnerable point in our line of communications with the East would be considerably lessened'. Such considerations did not convince the Foreign Office, but its political objections to such a scheme were overruled on military grounds at the interdepartmental meeting held at the War Office on 29 October.[43]

Anglo-French conversations on oil were resumed early in December. On the eleventh of that month Clemenceau, with a supporting French staff, arrived on a three-day visit to London to discuss matters of common interest with members of the British Government.[44] On the first morning the two prime ministers had what Lloyd George described as an 'informal and friendly chat', with Clemenceau apparently very hopeful of a successful visit. Reporting afterwards to his colleagues on the conversation, Lloyd George indicated that Clemenceau was mainly interested in economic concessions in Asia Minor. At an official meeting held at 3 p.m. that day, Philippe Berthelot, director-general of foreign and commercial affairs in the French foreign ministry, gave Curzon a memorandum by Bérenger on the oil question and stressed the importance of co-operation between the two governments.

Bérenger's memorandum set out the reasons why France needed to come to an oil agreement with Britain, and sought an arrangement similar to the Long–Bérenger Agreement; Persia, however, was added to the list of French desiderata, and the memorandum was fairly heavily larded with nationalistic sentiments.[45] The new Minister in Charge of Petroleum Affairs, Sir Hamar Greenwood, had in a Cabinet meeting of 20 November already raised the question of reviving the Long–Bérenger Agreement, and Ernest Weakley, in reviewing Bérenger's new memorandum, likewise thought the agreement a good basis for joint co-operation, though rejecting the French claims regarding Persia.[46] A French note of 12 December similarly mentioned the need for Britain and France to co-operate over Mosul and oil.[47]

It was only a matter of time before the agreement was revived. On the same morning as Clemenceau and his entourage arrived in London and began their discussions at the Foreign Office, Greenwood had left for Paris to discuss the same matters.[48] By 21 December Greenwood and Bérenger were able to initial their agreement.[49] The main point on which it differed from the Long–Bérenger Agreement was in providing for two railways as well as the two pipelines. This concession by the French seemed to Cadman to be a triumph. Not only were no charges to be levied by the French for allowing oil out of, or materials in through, their sphere, but 'British oil interests now have the whole Eastern Mediterranean as an outlet for their oil.'[50] In addition, Cadman pointed out to Greenwood, the agreement restricted the French share in the Turkish Petroleum Company to a maximum of 25 per cent of the share capital and a minimum of 18 per cent (should the native interests take up their full 20 per cent share), and he believed that 18 per cent would be what the French would actually receive.

What does seem clear, both from Cadman's attitude (and it was he, after all, who personally negotiated all three oil agreements, irrespective of who signed them) and from the relevant documentation is that the French had climbed down considerably from their earlier position. Besides dropping their unrealistic claim to a 50 per cent participation in the Turkish Petroleum Company, and to participation in Persian oil, they had made important concessions with regard to the proposed piplines and railways – though in return the British had given up nothing. This assessment is clearly borne out by the way in which the agreement was discussed at the Anglo-French meeting held at the Foreign Office immediately after the agreement had been concluded.[51]

Nonetheless the agreement did not receive Cabinet ratification immediately. In fact, with sublime misunderstanding of the whole basis of the arrangement, a conference of ministers (in effect a Cabinet meeting) now proceeded to wreck the agreement. At its meeting at 10 Downing Street on 23 January 1920, the conference accepted French participation but resolved that 'as a matter of principle the profits arising from the exploitation of the oilfields of Mesopotamia should accrue for the benefit of the State rather than for the benefit of Joint Stock Companies'.[52] By this one decision the ministerial conference had, as Weakley later put it, 'practically cancelled the agreement of 8 May 1919 about the Shell agreement, an essential feature of which was the allocation to the Shell Company of a share in the Turkish Petroleum Company, and consequently also cancelled the agreement of 21 December 1919 made with the French'.[53]

It was, perhaps, fortunate that neither the French nor the Shell interests were yet familiar with the details of this confused situation, or their anger would undoubtedly have added to it. The Shell interests, in fact, did not hear until mid-February 1920 that the Greenwood–Bérenger Agreement had been signed, though this had happened on 21 December; and when they did get wind of the fact they thought the agreement had been signed only the previous week.[54] All this time the company had been pressing hard to get the agreement 'signed', and General Sir John Cowans (the former Quartermaster-General of the Army and now employed by the Anglo-Saxon Petroleum Company on behalf of the Turkish Petroleum Company) had impressed on Walter Long, as he had done the previous autumn,[55] the need for positive action.

By the time Shell had heard that the agreement had been signed the French had learnt of the British decision of 23 January to exclude private interests from participation in the Mesopotamian oilfields. Consequently they revived their claim to a 50 per cent share in the Turkish Petroleum Company, on the grounds that they had previously agreed to the quarter share only because of the commitment to the Shell interests. If these interests were to be abandoned then France required equal participation.[56] To back up French Government annoyance, a press campaign began, chiefly in *Le Temps*, that was so hostile to Britain in the Middle East, and particularly with regard to oil matters, that in its minutes the stunned Foreign Office registered only such remarks as 'outrageous' and 'disgustingly French'.[57] What is plain, however, particularly from the Shell correspondence, is that the French Government's virtual blackmail for a 50 per cent share was a necessary move resulting from the close relations between the French and the Shell interests over Mesopotamia; each depended on the other and the agreement depended on both.[58] The clear-sighted men who were absent from influencing British affairs in January 1920 knew this better than those dominating the ministerial conference of the twenty-third of that month.[59]

In response to all these pressures three strongly worded memoranda were circulated to the Cabinet by the First Lord of the Admiralty (Walter Long), the President of the Board of Trade (Sir Robert Horne), and the Minister in Charge of the Petroleum Department (Frederick Kellaway).[60] These three memoranda strongly argued that the express aim of the long months of intricate negotiation had been to secure British control of the Shell interests, something that had for some years been established as a 'leading principle' of Britain's petroleum policy but was now suddenly in jeopardy. If given up after so long, dire consequences were likely to follow. Shell would be antagonised, and might ally itself with either the Americans or the French, or even withdraw from its London headquarters altogether, thus leaving Britain more vulnerable than ever. More positively, it was insisted that, as Britain was so heavily dependent on Shell, the unique opportunity of bringing Shell under British control ought not to be missed. Retention of the Shell agreement also made it easier to reach a settlement with the French and avoid their claim for a 50 per cent participation. In any case, however attractive it might seem to some, the proposal to develop the oilfields as Government property was not realistic. The Government did not have the necessary organisation for the successful commercial exploitation of a large oilfield or for the marketing of its products, while the cost of creating one would be 'prohibitive', with no benefit to the country's revenues for some time to come. Moreover, the oil business was a particularly unsuitable one for governments to engage in, being speculative, very technical, and requiring 'exceptional audacity'; and private development would open up Mesopotamia far more rapidly than a Government concern could do. Once the concession had been granted the Mesopotamian administration could impose whatever royalties and duties it desired, and obtain a large revenue without any risk whatever. On grounds, therefore, both of policy and of practical expediency, the three memoranda strongly urged that both the Mesopotamian agreements (the Shell and the Anglo-French) should be adhered to and carried out without further delay.

Even before the third of these memoranda had been circulated, Lloyd George had become clearly persuaded of the need for the oil agreements. When he discussed this matter (among others) with the French Prime Minister, Millerand, on the morning of Sunday 18 April, he spoke very firmly.[61] Although, in an effort to calm troubled waters, he admitted that he 'had not really thoroughly mastered the previous proposals' and that his difficulties derived from the prevalent and growing distrust towards the large oil companies, making any Government involvement with them a Parliamentary risk, he riposted smartly to the other's response that in that case it would be best to do without the companies and simply give France a 50 per cent share. Lloyd George's answer was to ask Millerand whether France was then prepared to carry half the cost of the administration of Mosul. In any case, he pointed out, even the 25 per cent share that Britain was willing to concede France was arrived at only after deducting the very heavy administration costs. Lloyd George won the game of bluff and concluded the meeting by giving the Frenchman a face-saving way out, inviting him to put in writing France's precise proposals over oil. This was, of course, unnecessary, since Cadman and Berthelot were already hard at work in Paris drafting an agreement; and only six days later, on Saturday 24 April, the Berthelot–Cadman Agreement, better known as the San Remo Agreement, was initialled.[62] The next day (25 April) the two prime ministers gave it the required confirmation.[63]

Most of the Mesopotamian provisions of the San Remo Agreement were virtually identical to those of the previous, Greenwood–Bérenger Agreement. Native interests received up to a 20 per cent participation; pipeline facilities were granted free by the French; and Britain agreed to do the same should the oil need pipeline and railway facilities to the Persian Gulf. There were really only three changes from the previous agreement. The first was very slight: with regard to the French share of Mesopotamian oil, the French were now offered (Article 7) either 25 per cent of the net output of crude oil at current market rates (in the event of the oilfields being developed by Government action), or a 25 per cent shareholding in any private company that was used to develop the oilfields. In two new provisions the French and British sought to placate each other. By Article 9 the British Government agreed to support any arrangements by which the French Government might procure from the Anglo-Persian Oil Company, on terms to be agreed with it, a share (of up to 25 per cent) of the Persian oil piped through French-mandated territory. Included in Article 7 was an unequivocal statement that any private company used to develop the oilfields would be under permanent British control.

This, then, was the final agreement reached by the British and French in their long post-war negotiations over Mesopotamian oil. It had taken three attempts (four if one counts the first draft of the Long–Bérenger Agreement, or five if one includes the December 1918 Lloyd George–Clemenceau understanding) to reach it. Further, the saga was not over yet, for the agreement had to be submitted to the House of Commons (which it was on 23 July 1920, after weeks of awkward Parliamentary Questions) and to withstand the continual barrage of nationalistic criticism that, following 'leaks' immediately after the conclusion of the agreement, had begun to emanate from the press on both sides of the Channel. The agreement was eventually published on 24 July and was criticised strongly, in terms of the 'open door' doctrine, by the Americans, who showed an almost paranoiac sense of national injury at being left out.[64] Even so, however, the basic question of whether the concession was to be private or state-run remained in doubt throughout that year.[65]

Yet, though the question of an Anglo-French oil agreement had been settled, at least in the short term, the same was not true of the British Government's agreement with the Royal Dutch–Shell. Filling in the detail around the initialled heads of agreement was lengthy and tedious. In April 1920 the seventh draft of the so-called 'Mesopotamian agreement' was still being modified, and at the end of the year the resulting draft agreement was still awaiting Cabinet consideration. There is no evidence that it ever received it, for following the transformation of American protests against the Anglo-French agreement into demands for inclusion, and the beginning of lengthy negotiations towards that end, the mists of confusion were again descending. Meanwhile the participants in the two 1920 agreements had to look after their own interests as best they could. The Anglo-Persian Oil Company acquired the services of (among other individuals concerned with this affair) the former Acting Civil Commissioner of Mesopotamia, A. T. Wilson, and Sir John Cadman.[66] The French Government invited the Banque de l'Union Parisienne to set up a company to hold its interests in the Turkish Petroleum Company. This was done, and in the resulting Société pour l'Exploitation des Pétroles the Royal Dutch–Shell group quietly held a controlling interest.[67]

III CONCLUSION

By 1920 the two concerns of Mesopotamian oil and the evolving of a national oil policy had become closely associated. The outlines of national policy had become clear: that is, the British Government recognised the need to control as far as possible both the sources and the suppliers of Britain's oil. Control over sources was necessarily limited to the empire (which did not produce much and was not thought likely ever to do so), to areas of informal empire, such as Persia and

Mesopotamia, and to such foreign areas as might come indirectly under the influence of the British Government due to its possessing control over companies exploiting them. This last consideration did not mean nationalisation or control over the commercial running of a company, but, rather, control of voting and a power of veto, to be reserved for use if and when the considerations of British nationality and patriotism were not sufficient to induce the company to put the British national interest first. Into this category came the Government purchase in 1914 of 51 per cent of the shares in the Anglo-Persian Oil Company; the attempts during 1916 and 1917 to form a National Oil Company, by merging the Anglo-Persian Oil Company and the Royal Dutch–Shell group; and the negotiations from 1918 to 1920 to bring the Royal Dutch–Shell under British control. Although, in the event, this was not achieved, it was part of an evolving pattern, which was to continue during the 1920s.

Mesopotamia was throughout the twenty-year period covered by this study, a further important consideration in British Government thinking on oil. Mesopotamia had always appeared a rich potential source of oil, though one does well to remember that oil was not found there in commercial quantities until 1927 and was not brought into production until some time after that. For the first twelve years of this period the Government's involvement in Mesopotamian oil affairs was, in essence, undoubtedly only that of a government according to its nationals the diplomatic support they required in order to achieve thier aims. But one national, D'Arcy, became a virtual government protégé, a status he achieved through his usefulness as the monopoly concessionaire in Persia, the Government's main hope for fuel for the Navy. Consequently, when D'Arcy's claims in Mesopotamia seemed seriously threatened by competition from the Turkish Petroleum Company, the British Government was drawn into the struggle, eventually becoming a major participant in the arrangements for amalgamating D'Arcy's interests and those of the Turkish Petroleum Company. The amalgamation was, however, never completed, due to the outbreak of war.

The war brought to Mesopotamia an entirely new situation. The area, always of basic strategic interest to Great Britain, because of the Persian Gulf and India, now became a theatre of war. Britain became faced not only with military commitments (which at the end of the war led to her maintaining an occupied enemy-territory administration, followed later by a mandate administration), but also with claims from her allies for control over areas of the Ottoman Empire, obliging her to devote attention to defining her own territorial claims. Because, for the first half of the war at least, economic motives did not play a major part in her interest in the region, she allowed the potentially oil-rich area of Mosul to slip through her fingers to the French. Thereafter, her political preoccupations with regard to Mesopotamia were concerned with regaining Mosul for her own Mesopotamian sphere of influence. Her political relations with France were, accordingly, devoted to this end, and the immediate post-war years, 1918 to 1920, saw attempts to make an agreement that would regain Mosul for Britain and obtain for France a share in its oil. This was achieved in April 1920, in the San Remo Agreement, on which, in turn, the agreement between the British Government and the Royal Dutch–Shell group depended, due to the fact that the 'consideration' for which the group would come under British control was recognition of the legality of its title to Mesopotamian oil. Although this agreement too was ready in draft about April 1920, it never quite reached the Cabinet for ratification, and was overtaken by events requiring modification of the Anglo-French agreement. The main factors here were American opposition and demands for inclusion, which were eventually satisfied.

However, these later years of the period under discussion show the distance Britain had come in recognising the need to evolve a coherent oil policy and in attempting to operate one. The 1920 agreements show how closely the Mesopotamian question had become intertwined with this fundamental policy. By 1920 Mesopotamian oil, still commercially as hypothetical as ever, had come to occupy a major place in British diplomatic and military concerns in the Middle East. The First World War, with the drastic shortage of oil by 1917, gave added urgency to these concerns and to British concern with oil generally. After the war the change in the international scene – with the eclipse of Germany, the dismemberment of Turkey, and the attainment of a strong bargaining position by Britain's fellow victor, France – made the problem more complicated, and Mesopotamia and its oil potential became an important key to settling Anglo-French relations.

Britain's chief concern during the twenty-year period of this study was, essentially, the need to secure oil for her navy. During this time the lines of approach to the problem had been laid down and attempts were being made to follow them. Over the next twenty years some modifications in approach were necessary, but the quest for a successful oil policy continued, becoming crucial with the approach of the Second World War.

Appendixes

Appendices

Appendix I
The 1904 'Zander' Contract

CONTRAT

ENTRE LE MINISTÈRE IMPÉRIAL DE LA LISTE CIVILE ET LA SOCIÉTÉ DU CHEMIN DE FER OTTOMAN D'ANATOLIE CONCERNANT LES GISEMENTS PÉTROLIFÈRES EN MESOPOTAMIE.[1]

4/17 JUILLET 1904.

Entre

le Ministère de la Liste Civile, representé par Son Excellence *Ohannès Effendi Sakisian*,

d'une part,

et

la Société du Chemin de Fer Ottoman d'Anatolie, representée par Monsieur *K. Zander*,

d'autre part,

conformément à un Iradé Impérial de S.M.I. le Sultan, émané à cet effet en date du 3 Jumada al-Aula[2] 1322.

Il a été arrété et convenu ce qui suit:

Article 1

La Société du Chemin de Fer Ottoman d'Anatolie se charge d'éxécuter entièrement à ses frais, dans un délai d'un an, à partir de l'échange de la présente Convention, les études préliminaires (sondages et autres) concernant l'exploitation des gisements de pétrole dont la Liste Civile est concessionnaire en vertu des Firmans en date des 5 Chaban 1306, 5 Jumada al-Aula 1316 et 16 Ramadhan 1320, dans les Vilayets de Bagdad et Mossoul.

La Liste Civile s'engage à procurer aux spécialistes délégués par la Société du Chemin de Fer Ottoman d'Anatolie toutes les facilités désirables pour l'accomplissement de leur mission; elle leur remettra les cartes et croquis du terrain, les études existantes, les autorisations de circuler librement dans toute l'étendue des domaines dont il s'agit; elle leur procurera l'assistance absolue des autorités etc.

Les frais et les résultats de ces études seront communiqués intégralement et dans tous leurs détails à la Liste Civile.

Article 2

Si, à la suite de ces études, la Société demande à se charger de l'exploitation des dites mines, cette exploitation lui sera concédée pour une durée de quarante ans par une Convention spéciale sanctionnée par Iradé Impérial; elle aura lieu avec la coopération et sous le contrôle de la Liste Civile.

Article 3

Dans ce cas, la Société procurera par une émission spéciale d'Obligations, le capital nécéssaire pour les travaux d'installation (usines, puits, machines etc.) et pour les fonds de roulement, le tout à fixer d'un commun accord entre elle et la Liste Civile.

Article 4

Le service des intérêts et amortissement de ce capital, y compris les dépenses occasionnées par les études préliminaires, sera fait sur les recettes de l'exploitation.

Article 5

Les recettes nettes au delà des frais d'exploitation et du susdit capital, seront partagées entre la Liste Civile et la Société dans la proportion qui sera arrêtée entre elles.

Article 6

Si la Société, après achèvement des études, renonce à l'exploitation de ces mines, la Liste Civile pourra en disposer en faveur d'autrui, sans que la Société ait le droit de réclamer aucun frais ou indemnité, à quelque titre que ce soit.

Dans le cas où la Convention relative à la concession de l'exploitation à la Société ne pourra être conclue, pour tout autre motif, la Liste Civile sera tenue de lui rembourser, avec les intérêts calculés à 5% l'an, le montant constaté des dépenses effectuées pour les études préliminaires et la Société conservera un droit de préférence, à conditions égales, vis-à-vis de toute autre personne ou Société qui demanderait cette exploitation.

Fait en double à Constantinople, le 4/17 Juillet, 1904.

(s) Ohannès Sakisian,
Ministre de la Liste Civile.

(s) K. Zander,
Directeur Général de la Société du Chemin de Fer Ottoman d'Anatolie.

Appendix II
Correspondence between the Minister of the Civil List and the Anatolian Railway Company, August 1905–March 1907

Letter 1
Minister of the Civil List, Ohannès Effendi Sakisian, to the Ottoman Railway Company of Anatolia, 26 July/8 August 1905, no. 320.

Comme d'après les dispositions de la Convention conclue avec votre honorable Administration en date du 1/4 Juin 1904,[1] il y avait lieu d'effectuer, dans un délai d'une année, les études nécessaires concernant les gisements de pétrole situés dans les Vilayets de Bagdad et de Mossoul et concédée au Ministère de la Liste Civile, une Commission technique a été chargée de se rendre sur les lieux et de faire ces études.

Bien que les études nécessaires aient été faites et que le délai fixé à cet effet soit passé, le résultat obtenu n'ayant pas été communiqué à notre Département jusqu'aujourd'hui, nous vous prions de vous faire connaître les renseignements recueillis au sujet des gisements en question.

Letter 2
Huguenin, Ottoman Railway Company of Anatolia, to the Minister of the Civil List, 4 September 1905, no. 2114.

Nous avons l'honneur de porter à la connaissance de votre Excellence qu'il résulte d'une lettre que nous venons de recevoir de Monsieur le Professeur, Docteur Porro, Chef Spécialiste de la Mission que nous avons envoyée en Mésopotamie, pour y étudier la question des gisements de pétrole et leur exploitation éventuelle, que c'est seulement maintenant, après d'énormes difficultés et de longs retards, que les échantillons géologiques et autres, très nombreux et lourds, sont arrivés en Europe.

Or comme il est de la plus haute importance, dans l'intérêt du résultat cherché, que tous ces échantillons soient analysés en laboratoire avec un soin minutieux, et que les études complémentaires que ces analyses imposent, soient aussi l'objet de tous les soins des savants spécialistes qui en sont chargés, une prorogation suffisante, c'est à dire de dix à douze mois environ, du délai, d'ailleurs beaucoup trop court, fixé à l'origine, est devenue tout-à-fait indispensable.

Nous venons donc prier Votre Excellence de vouloir bien faire le nécessaire à cet effet.

Veuillez agréer, Monsieur le Ministre, les assurances réitérées de notre plus haute considération.

Letter 3

Minister of the Civil List to the Ottoman Railway Company of Anatolia, 9/22 October 1905, no. 442.

Répondant à votre honorée en date du 4 Septembre 1905 No. 2114, je vous prie de me faire parvenir les rapports concernant les gisements pétrolifères des Régions de Bagdad et de Mossoul, afin que mon Département puisse examiner les résultats des études et constatations effectuées par la Commission Technique, conformément aux dispositions de la Convention dressée et échangée au sujet de ces gisements, ainsi que les frais qui ont été effectués à cet effet.

Veuillez agréer, etc. etc.

Letter 4

Minister of the Civil List to the Board of the Ottoman Railway Company of Anatolia, 13/26 July 1906, no. 233.

En vertu d'un Iradé Impérial en date du 3/16 Jumada al-Aula 1322/ Juillet 1904, relatif aux mines de pétroles situées dans les parages de Mossoul et de Bagdad, une convention avait été conclue et échangée entre mon Ministère et votre Société.

Aux termes de l'article I de cette convention, votre Société s'était engagée à effectuer les recherches et études préliminaires et à adresser à mon Département les rapports y relatifs, dans le délai d'une année à partir de la date susmentionnée.

Votre Société nous ayant demandé, par la suite, de prolonger ce délai, de 12 mois, je vous ai répondu par ma lettre en date du 9/22 Octobre 1905, d'avoir à vous adresser tout d'abord le rapport relatif à vos recherches et études, ainsi que le relevé de vos dépenses.

Comme nous n'avons pas encore reçu une réponse à cette lettre, et comme le délai fixé pour les études dans la susdite convention est déjà expiré depuis longtemps, je vous prie de me faire parvenir d'urgence votre réponse catégorique, ainsi que les rapports voulus sur les résultats des recherches et études sur les mines de pétrol en question.

Letter 5
Minister of the Civil List to the Board of the Ottoman Railway Company of Anatolia, 27 July/9 August 1906, no. 355.

Ayant été stipulé dans l'Article I de la Convention préliminaire conclue et échangée avec votre Administration à la suite de l'Iradé Impérial en date du 3 Jumada al-Aula, concernant les gisements pétrolifères des régions de Mossoul et de Bagdad, que les études et constatations nécessaires seront effectuées dans le délai d'une année, comptée à partir de la susdite date, et que tous les résultats obtenus par ces études ainsi que les frais y relatifs seraient portés en détail à la connaissance de mon Département, je me suis basé sur cette disposition conventionnelle pour vous prier, par ma lettre en date du 13/26 Juin, de ma faire parvenir les rapports et documents y relatifs.

Or, cette lettre est restée jusqu'aujourd'hui sans réponse et le délai fixé pour les susdites études est également passé.

Il est vrai que votre Administration a demandé ultérieurement la prolongation de ce délai, mais comme une période de 13 mois s'est écoulée à partir de la date d'expiration de délai en question et comme les dispositions de l'Article VI de la Convention susmentionnée prescrivent que mon Département a la faculté de concéder à un autre l'exploitation des gisements en question si votre Société n'en veut pas, je vous prie de m'envoyer les documents ci-dessus mentionnés et de me faire connaître le plus tôt possible et d'une manière formelle si votre Administration entreprendra ou non l'exploitation des gisements en question afin d'agir conformément aux dispositions conventionnelles.

Veuillez agréer, etc. etc.

Letter 6
Huguenin, Ottoman Railway Company of Anatolia, to the Minister of the Civil List, 22 August 1906, no. 2162.

Nous avons l'honneur de porter à Votre Excellence que la Commission chargée des études préliminaires concernant l'exploitation des gisements de pétrole en Mésopotamie, vient de terminer ses travaux et de nous fournir son rapport definitif. Nous nous empressons de soumettre ce rapport à la bienveillante attention de Votre Excellence, suivant les ordres que Votre Excellence a bien voulu nous donner par les lettres en date du 13/26 Juin a.c. No. 233 et du 27/9 Août a.c. No. 355. L'œuvre approfondie des savants specialistes qui ont été chargés des études minutieuses et scientifiques, résumant les résultats de notre expédition, ne manquera pas d'expliquer et d'excuser auprès de Votre Excellence le retard qu s'est produit.

Les dépenses faites pour cette expédition se montent a 340,000 Frs.

Soucieux de servir, par tous les moyens en notre pouvoir, les intérêts de Sa Majesté Impériale le Sultan nous avons l'honneur de porter à la connaissance de Votre Excellence que notre Société, malgré les résultats malheureusement peu encourageants des recherches de la Commission d'Etudes, est prête à supporter les frais très considérables de sondages qui seuls peuvent démontrer s'il existe en Mésopotamie du pétrole en quantité suffisante pour une exploitation sur une grande échelle; mais il va de soi que notre Société ne pourrait se charger de cette lourde tâche qu'après établissement d'un accord équitable à intervenir entre la Liste Civile et notre Société.

Veuillez agréer, etc. etc.

Letter 7

Minister of the Civil List to the Ottoman Railway Company of Anatolia, 11/24 October 1906, no. 556.

Le rapport en allemand contenant les résultats de études faites au sujet des sources de pétrole situées dans les régions de Mossoul et de Bagdad, qui m'avait été soumis par votre honorée en date du 22 Août 1906, vous a été retourné alors de la main à la main, avec prière de le faire traduire en turc et en français.

Je vous avais prié, en même temps, d'envoyer a mon Département un projet de convention à ce sujet.

Malgré ce qui précède, aucun envoi ne m'ayant été effectué jusqu'aujourd'hui, veuillez me faire parvenir d'urgence les traductions du dit rapport ainsi que le projet de convention en question.

Veuillez agréer, etc. etc.

Letter 8

Minister of the Civil List to the Ottoman Railway Company of Anatolia, 13/26 November 1906, no. 586.

Je vous avais restitué jadis de la main à la main, pour être traduit en turc et en français, le rapport en allemand que vous m'aviez envoyé, rapport concernant les conclusions des études qui ont été faites au sujet des sources de pétrole des regions de Mossoul et de Bagdad, et je vous avais prié aussi d'élaborer un projet de convention et de ma l'envoyer. Malgré que je vous eusse réitéré la chose par une lettre en date du 11 Octobre 1322, vous n'y avez pas donné de suite jusqu'içi. Aussi, je vous prie de me faire parvenir, sans retard, les traductions dudit rapport et le projet en question.

Indépendamment de ce qui précède, je vous avais encore exposé dans mes deux lettres datées du 28 Juin et du 11 Octobre 1322 que comme le Ministère de la Liste Civile n'acceptait pas les dispositions de treize articles de projet de convention élaboré par votre Direction au sujet du mode et des conditions d'éxecution des fouilles, et des travaux nécessaires pour l'irrigation de la plaine de Konia, je vous avais restitué ledit projet et vous avais prié, en même temps, de me faire connaître votre manière de voir définitive à ce sujet. Malgré mes deux communications précitées, vous ne m'avez fait parvenir jusqu'ici aucun avis à cet égard.

Or, comme il est sérieux et urgent au plus haut point de donner le plus tôt possible, une solution à cette question aussi, je vous prie de m'en informer sans retard.

Veuillez agréer, etc. etc.

Letter 9

Ministry of the Civil List to the Board of the Ottoman Railway Company of Anatolia, 24/26 January 1907, no. 656.

Nous avons reçu votre lettre en date du 22 Août 1906, concernant l'exploitation des sources de pétrole situées dans les Vilayets de Bagdad et de Mossoul et dont le Ministère de la Liste Civile est concessionnaire, le rapport technique content les résultats obtenus à la suite des études préliminaires effectuées à cet effet, les documents accessoires y afférents ainsi que le projet définitif de Convention élaboré par votre Société.

En vertu des dispositions de l'Article I de la Convention conclue et échangée avec votre prédécesseur Monsieur Zander, votre Société avait entrepris d'éxécuter des travaux de sondage, comme étant le meilleur moyen pour établir la nature et le degré de richesse des gisements susmentionnés.

Ces travaux de sondage, qui auraient du être effectués dans le délai d'une année, fixé par la susdite convention, n'ayant pas été encore éxécutés, bien que ce délai ait été dépassé d'une année et demie encore, et le contexte du projet définitif de convention, expédié dernièrement, ne concordant nullement avec les dispositions de la Convention précédents, laquelle a été tenue par votre Société comme nulle et non avenue, nous vous informons qu'il n'y a plus lieu ni possibilité d'échanger des pourparlers entre notre Département et votre Société, et qu'il est naturel de considérer la première convention comme abrogée de fait.

Agréez, etc. etc.

Letter 10

Huguenin, Ottoman Railway Company of Anatolia, to the Minister of the Civil List, 9 February 1907, no. 354.

En réponse à la dépêche de Votre Excellence, No. 656 du 24/6 Janvier dernier, nous avons l'honneur de signaler à Votre bienveillante attention, Monsieur le Ministre, que l'Article 1 de notre convention du 4/17 Juillet 1904, auquel vous voulez bien vous référer, ne comportant aucunement, aussi bien l'interprétation que les conclusions qui nous sont communiquées par la dépêche en question. Nous ne pouvons que les repousser catégoriquement.

Nous sommes d'ailleurs persuadés qu'un nouvel examen impartial de cette affaire, vous convaincra, Monsieur le Ministre qu'en dehors de la grosse dépense de 340,000 Francs en résultant, nous avons encore fait et au-delà ce qui pouvait raisonnablement et scientifiquement être fait, et que nos droits acquis par la Convention précitée, restent intacts et exercent tous leurs effets.

Veuillez agréer, Monsieur le Ministre, les assurances de notre plus haute considération.

Letter 11

Minister of the Civil List to the Board of the Ottoman Railway Company of Anatolia, 19 February/4 March 1907, no. 753.

Vous ayant adressé une communication pour vous faire part que la Convention échangée précédemment au sujet des sources de pétrole, situées dans les Provinces de Bagdad et de Mossoul et concédée au Ministère de la Liste Civile, sera considérée comme abrogée, vous m'informez par votre honorée en date du 9 Février 1907, que ma communication susmentionnée est contraire aux dispositions de l'Article I de la Convention préliminaire, que les dispositions de cette convention restent en vigueur et que les droits y afférents sont maintenant [?maintenus] dans toute leur intégrité.

Ainsi qu'il est de votre connaissance, Monsieur le Directeur-Général, ma précédente communication repose, en principe, sur les deux points ci-dessous exposés.

(1). Bien que le délai fixé dans l'Article I de la Convention conclue avec votre Société, en date du 4 Juillet 1320, pour ce qui concerne les études préliminaires à effectuer par votre Société, soit dépassé une fois et $\frac{1}{2}$, et bien que votre Société se soit engagée, par le susdit Article I, a entreprendre des travaux de sondage, lesquels sont évidemment le moyen pouvant le plus contribuer à établir le degré de richesse des sources de pétrole en question, votre Société n'a pas fait effectuer ces travaux de sondage.

(2). D'après les dispositions de la Convention susindiquée, la Société jouit de la faculté de se charger ou non de l'exploitation des sources de pétrole. Toutefois, dans le cas où elle voulait se charger de cette exploitation, les principales conditions qui devaient servir de base à l'élaboration de la nouvelle Convention définitive étaient clairement énumérées et établies dans la Convention préliminaire.

Nonobstant ce qui précède, le projet de la Convention définitive, qui avait été communiqué par votre Société, ayant été d'une façon contraire et étrangère aux conditions susmentionnées et d'une manière annulant tous les droits et les avantages que la Liste Civile s'était assurés, nous avions constaté de ce qui précède, que votre Société avait mis a l'écart la convention préliminaire, en la considérant comme nulle et non avenue.

Quoique les susdits deux points eussent été invoqués dans ma communication antérieure, votre Société ne donne aucun éclaircissement et explication touchant ces deux importants points, dans sa lettre responsive du 9 Février 1907, et se contente de confirmer, simplement sa prétention, d'une façon absolue et dans le but de sauvegarder ses droits.

Je m'empresse, par conséquent, de vous informer que mon Département ne peut que réitérer et confirmer le sens et la teneur de ma précédente communication et qu'il ne lui est point possible d'ajouter autre chose à ce sujet.

Agréez, etc. etc.

Appendix III
Arrangements for Fusion of the Interests in Turkish Petroleum Concessions of the D'Arcy Group and of the Turkish Petroleum Company,[1] 19 March 1914

It is agreed that the interests shall be divided as follows:

Fifty per cent to the D'Arcy group, Twenty-five per cent to the Deutsche Bank, Twenty-five per cent to the Anglo-Saxon Petroleum Company, and that, in order to carry out this division,

1. The shares in the Turkish Petroleum Company now held by the National Bank of Turkey shall be transferred in equal moieties to the Deutsche Bank and the Anglo-Saxon Petroleum Company.

2. The capital of the Turkish Petroleum Company shall be increased to 160,000 by the creation of 80,000 new £1 shares each of the same class as those now existing.

3. These 80,000 new shares shall be allotted to the D'Arcy group on terms to be agreed upon between the parties.

4. The Board of the Company shall consist of eight members, of whom four will be nominated by the D'Arcy group, two by the Deutsche Bank, and two by the Anglo-Saxon Company.

5. The capital of the Turkish Petroleum Company shall be employed only in exploring, testing, and proving oilfields, a separate public company or companies being formed to work any field or fields the examination of which has proved satisfactory.

6. Such working company or companies shall issue to the Turkish Petroleum Company fully paid ordinary shares as consideration for the acquisition of the rights of the company to the properties to be acquired; such ordinary shares shall carry full control of the working company or companies, which control shall in no circumstances be parted with by the Turkish Petroleum Company.

7. The working capital required by such working company or companies shall be raised by means of preference shares and (or) debentures which shall be offered to the public to such extent as the members of the Turkish Petroleum Company or any one of them shall elect not to subscribe for themselves.

8. The alterations in the memorandum and (or) articles of association of the Turkish Petroleum Company necessary to carry out the above conditions shall be made forthwith.

9. Mr. C. S. Gulbenkian shall be entitled to a beneficiary five per cent interest without voting rights in the Turkish Petroleum Company, this five per cent being contributed equally by the D'Arcy group and the Anglo-Saxon Company out of their respective holdings. The shares representing Mr. Gulbenkian's interest shall be registered in the names of the nominees of the D'Arcy group and of the Anglo-Saxon Company, and shall be held by them but undertakings shall be exchanged between these parties whereby

(1) Mr. Gulbenkian undertakes to pay the calls on the shares, and
(2) The D'Arcy group and the Anglo-Saxon Company undertake that Mr. Gulbenkian shall be entitled to all financial benefits of the shares.

If Mr. Gulbenkian shall desire to dispose of this interest, and also in the event of his death, the D'Arcy group and the Anglo-Saxon Company shall have the option of purchasing the interests standing in their names on the terms defined in Article 36 (b) of the articles of association of the Turkish Petroleum Company.

10. The three groups participating in the Turkish Petroleum Company shall give undertakings on their own behalf and on behalf of the companies associated with them not to be interested directly or indirectly in the production or manufacture of crude oil in the Ottoman Empire in Europe and Asia, except in that part which is under the administration of the Egyptian Government or of the Sheikh of Koweit, or in the 'transferred territories' on the Turco-Persian frontier, otherwise than through the Turkish Petroleum Company.

[signed]	(For the Imperial German Govt.)	R. von Kühlmann
	(For His Britannic Majesty's Govt.)	Eyre A. Crowe
	(For the National Bank of Turkey)	H. Babington Smith
	(For the Anglo-Saxon Petroleum Co. Ltd.)	W. Deterding, Walter H. Samuel
	(For the Deutsche Bank)	C. Bergmann
	(For the D'Arcy Group)	C. Greenway, H. S. Barnes

Appendix IV
Oil Agreements, 1919–20

I THE LONG–BÉRENGER AGREEMENT[1]

Text of original agreement	*Text of final agreement*
MESOPOTAMIA	MESOPOTAMIA
The British Government places at the disposal of the French Government a share capital of 25 per cent in the Turkish Petroleum Company, or such company as may be formed for the exploitation of the Mesopotamian oilfields, with all the rights of representation and other rights which may be attached to the said shares. The company shall be under permanent British control. If it is decided to apply the terms of the agreement to the Turkish Petroleum Company as already constituted, the price to be paid by the French Government shall be that paid by the British Government to the Public Trustee for the shares belonging to the Deutsche Bank plus 5 per cent interest on said price since the date of payment. The capital of the Company shall then be divided as follows: British interest 75% French interest 25% If it is necessary to give participation to any native	*In the event of His Majesty's Government receiving the mandate in Mesopotamia they undertake to make it their duty to secure from the Mesopotamian Government for the Turkish Petroleum Company or the Company to be formed to acquire the interests of that Company, the rights acquired by the Turkish Petroleum Company in Mesopotamia under arrangements made with the Turkish Government.* *The French Government to have a share in the capital in the Company as herein indicated,* with all rights of representation and other rights which may be attached to the said shares. The Company shall be under permanent British control. If it is decided to apply the terms of the agreement to the Turkish Petroleum Company as already constituted, the price to be paid by the French Government shall be that paid by the British Government to the Public Trustee for the shares belonging to the Deutsche Bank, plus 5 per cent interest on said

Text of original agreement

interest it is agreed that this may be provided up to a maximum of 10 per cent of the original share capital in equal parts from the British and French holdings.

In consideration for said participation the French Government shall agree to facilitate by every means in its power as soon as application is made, the construction of two separate pipe-lines for the transport of oil from Mesopotamia and Persia to a port or ports on the Eastern Mediterranean. The port or ports shall be chosen in agreement between the two Governments.

Should the pipe-line cross territory within the French sphere of influence France undertakes to give every facility for the rights of crossing without asking for any royalty or wayleaves on the oil transported. Nevertheless compensation shall be payable to the landowners for the surface occupied.

In the same way France will give facilities at the terminal port or ports for the acquisition by the Mesopotamian Company and the Anglo-Persian Oil Company of the land necessary for the erection of depots, refineries, loading wharves, etc. Oil thus exported shall be exempt from export and transit dues. The materials necessary for the construction of the pipe-lines, refineries and other equipment shall also be free from import duties.

This agreement in so far as it

Text of final agreement

price since the date of payment.

The capital of the Company shall be divided as follows:

British interest 70%
French interest 20%
Native Government interest 10%

If the Native Government do not desire to participate to the extent of 10% the balance shall be divided equally between the British and French holdings.

It is understood that one of the terms to be embodied in the lease to be granted to the Company to work the oilfields will provide that local native interests may participate, if they so desire, up to 10% in the share capital of any subsidiary company which may be formed to work any of the oilfields or in the event of subsidiary companies not being formed, up to 10% of the share capital of the original company will be specially provided for this purpose in addition to the amount allocated to native government interests. This additional participation shall be provided by each group in proportion to their holding.

In consideration for said participation the French Government shall agree to facilitate by every means in its power as soon as application is made, the construction of two separate pipe-lines for the transport of oil from Mesopotamia and Persia to a port or ports on the Eastern Mediterranean. The port or ports shall be chosen in agreement between the two Governments.

Text of original agreement

refers to pipe-lines is subject to the French Government possessing territorial rights in the country which it is desired to traverse and this part of the agreement is entered into solely to facilitate the supply of petroleum and is in no way to be taken as implying that any such territorial rights are in existence.

Should the Mesopotamian Company desire to lay a pipe-line to the Persian Gulf the British Government will agree to the laying of such pipe-line on similar terms to those agreed by the French Government in regard to the pipe-line to the Mediterranean.

Text of final agreement

Should the pipe-lines cross territory in which France has received a mandate, France undertakes to use her good offices to secure every facility for the rights of crossing without any royalty or wayleaves on the oil transported. Nevertheless, compensation shall be payable to the land-owners for the surface occupied.

In the same way France will give facilities at the terminal port or ports for the acquisition by the Mesopotamian Company and the Anglo-Persian Company of the land necessary for the erection of depots, refineries, loading wharves, etc. Oil thus exported shall be exempt from export and transit dues. The materials necessary for the construction of the pipe-lines, refineries, and other equipment shall also be free from import duties.

This agreement in so far as it relates to pipe-lines, *storage, refineries, depots, loading wharves, etc. is entered solely to facilitate the supply of petroleum and is in no way to be taken as implying that any territorial rights are in existence.*

Should the Mesopotamian Company desire to lay a pipe-line to the Persian Gulf the British Government will use its good offices to secure similar facilities for that purpose.

II THE GREENWOOD–BÉRENGER AGREEMENT[2] AND THE BERTHELOT–CADMAN (SAN REMO) AGREEMENT[3]

Greenwood–Bérenger Agreement

MESOPOTAMIA

9. As regards Mesopotamia participation has been guided by the fact that the Turkish Petroleum Company had secured before the war from the Turkish Government the petroleum rights in the vilayets of Mosul and Baghdad, and its shares are now all in British hands.

10. The British Government places at the disposal of the French Government a share of twenty-five per cent in the Turkish Petroleum Company with all the rights of representation and other rights which may be attached to the said shares. The price to be paid by the French Government shall be that paid by the British Government to the Public Trustee for the shares belonging to the Deutsche Bank, plus five per cent interest on said price since the date of payment.

Berthelot–Cadman (San Remo) Agreement

MESOPOTAMIA

7. The British Government undertake to grant to the French Government or its nominee 25 per cent of the net output of crude oil at current market rates which His Majesty's Government may secure from the Mesopotamian oilfields, in the event of their being developed by Government action; or in the event of a private petroleum company being used to develop the Mesopotamian oilfields, the British Government will place at the disposal of the French Government a share of 25 per cent in such company. The price to be paid for such participation to be no more than that paid by any of the other participants to the said petroleum company. It is also understood that the said petroleum company shall be under permanent British control.

Greenwood–Bérenger Agreement	*Berthelot–Cadman (San Remo) Agreement*
POSTSCRIPT	
1. In connection with the agreement entered into on the twenty-first day of December, 1919, between the undersigned on behalf of the British and French Governments, it is clearly understood that native government or other native interests shall be allowed if they so desire to participate in the Turkish Petroleum Company up to a maximum of twenty per cent of the share capital. The French shall contribute one-half of the first ten per cent of such native participation and the additional participation shall be provided by each group in proportion to their holdings.	8. It is agreed that, should the private petroleum company be constituted as aforesaid, the native Government or other native interests shall be allowed, if they so desire, to participate up to a maximum of 20 per cent of the share capital of the said company. The French shall contribute one-half of the first 10 per cent of such native participation and the additional participation shall be provided by each participant in proportion to his holdings.
	9. The British Government agree to support arrangements by which the French Government may procure from the Anglo-Persian Company supplies of oil, which may be piped from Persia to the Mediterranean through any pipe-line which may have been constructed within the French mandated territory and in regard to which France has given special facilities, up to the extent of 25 per cent. of the oil so piped, on such terms and conditions as may be mutually agreed between the French Government and the Anglo-Persian Company.
11. In consideration of said participation the French	10. In consideration of the above-mentioned arrangements,

Greenwood–Bérenger Agreement	*Berthelot–Cadman (San Remo) Agreement*
Government shall agree, if it is desired and as soon as application is made, to the construction of two separate pipe-lines and railways necessary for their construction and maintenance and for the transport of oil from Mesopotamia and Persia through French spheres of influence to a port or ports on the Eastern Mediterranean. The port or ports shall be chosen in agreement between the two Governments.	the French Government shall agree, if it is desired and as soon as application is made, to the construction of two separate pipe-lines and railways necessary for their construction and maintenance and for the transport of oil from Mesopotamia and Persia through French spheres of influence to a port or ports on the Eastern Mediterranean. The port or ports shall be chosen in agreement between the two Governments.
12. Should such pipe-lines and railways cross territory within a French sphere of influence France undertakes to give every facility for the rights of crossing without any royalty or wayleaves on the oil transported. Nevertheless, compensation shall be payable to the landowners for the surface occupied.	11. Should such pipe-line and railways cross territory within a French sphere of influence, France undertakes to give every facility for the rights of crossing without any royalty or wayleaves on the oil transported. Nevertheless, compensation shall be payable to the landowners for the surface occupied.
13. In the same way France will give facilities at the terminal port or ports for the acquisition by the Turkish Petroleum Company and the Anglo-Persian Oil Company of the land necessary for the erection of depots, railways, refineries, loading wharves, etc. Oil thus exported shall be exempt from export and transit dues. The material necessary for the construction of the pipe-lines, railways, refineries, and other equipment shall also be free from import duties and wayleaves.	12. In the same way France will give facilities at the terminal port for the acquisition of the land necessary for the erection of depots, railways, refineries, loading wharfs, etc. Oil thus exported shall be exempt from export and transit dues. The material necessary for the construction of the pipe-lines, railways, refineries and other equipment shall also be free from import duties and wayleaves.

Greenwood–Bérenger Agreement	*Berthelot–Cadman (San Remo) Agreement*
14. Should the Turkish Petroleum Company desire to lay a pipe-line and a railway to the Persian Gulf the British Government will use its good offices to secure similar facilities for that purpose.	13. Should the said petroleum company desire to lay a pipe-line and a railway to the Persian Gulf, the British Government will use its good offices to secure similar facilities for that purpose.

III HEADS OF AGREEMENT OF THE ROYAL DUTCH–SHELL/BRITISH GOVERNMENT AGREEMENT AS INITIALLED BY DETERDING AND HARCOURT, 6–7 MARCH 1919[4]

It is desired to secure that the Shell Transport and Trading Company, Ltd., and certain other companies included in the Royal Dutch–Shell Group shall be brought permanently under British control. It is not, however, desired to interfere with the commercial policy or financial or business management of the companies concerned.

It is agreed that these objects can be secured as follows:

(a) 1. His Majesty's Government will be advised to use their best endeavours to secure, either by rearrangement of the capital in the Turkish Petroleum Company or otherwise, that the Royal Dutch–Shell Group by the medium of the Anglo-Saxon Petroleum Company (or such other British Company owned by the Shell Group as may be deemed preferable by His Majesty's Government) and the Anglo-Persian Oil Company shall be admitted to equal participation in the exploitation of all oilfields in Asia Minor, including what is usually called Mesopotamia. The interest of any other participant shall be held as may be arranged hereafter. Certain shares with a special majority voting power in the company operating in Mesopotamia shall be controlled by His Majesty's Government and the management shall be permanently British.

2. Percentage of holdings by His Majesty's Government, the Anglo-Persian, and the Anglo-Saxon Petroleum Company.

   The combined votes of these three parties shall be put into a Voting Trust and the majority of the votes in this Voting Trust shall instruct how the 70 per cent. block shall vote.

3. The shareholdings of the Anglo-Persian and the Anglo-Saxon shall be 34 per cent. each, and His Majesty's Government 2 per cent., which would leave 30 per cent. for other interests, which interests if of less amount the balance would be divided equally between the Anglo-Persian and the Anglo-Saxon

Companies. The partners in the company so formed shall be simultaneously informed as to all arrangements. The Articles of Association shall provide that the directorate will be appointed by the interests concerned in proportion to their shareholdings.

4. Notwithstanding the necessity for the company so formed to lay a pipe-line from its fields to the Mediterranean, it will not oppose or obstruct directly or indirectly the laying at any date of a similar line connecting the Anglo-Persian fields with that shore on the understanding that the above is a Trans-Continental line to convey oil to the Mediterranean and not to be used directly or indirectly for distributing oil in Asia Minor.
5. The management of the company shall be entrusted by contract to the Shell Company Group for a period of seven years from the date of the Company's formation, and thereafter for such term as the Board may decide.
6. The Shell Group management of the company so formed shall be under the orders of the Board and therefore under the control of the Voting Trust. The Board shall not permit the Managers to conclude any marketing arrangements with the Anglo-Persian Company or its subsidiaries or its associations without the Shell Company's consent, nor shall the Board permit the Managers to conclude any marketing arrangements with the Shell Company or its subsidiaries or its associations without the consent of the Anglo-Persian Company. In any dispute under this clause the only interest which shall be considered shall be that of the company so formed. The company so formed shall construct and control its own pipelines, shall erect and run its own refineries, and shall arrange its own marketing. The Board of the company so formed, in deciding through which channel surplus oil for export whether crude or refined shall be dealt with, shall take as their only guidance the financial interests of the company so formed.

(b) The said Shell Transport and Trading Company, Ltd., shall make arrangements with His Majesty's Government that no change in its directorate as at present constituted shall take place without the consent and approval of the Governor of the Bank of England, and/or some person of similar standing nominated by His Majesty's Government.

Further, the said Shell Transport and Trading Company and certain other companies in the group shall remain or become registered in Great Britain and shall be so constituted that 75 per cent. of the directors of the said company, and a majority of the directors in the other companies shall be British born British subjects, and be precluded from selling or disposing of their capital assets so as to place the same outside British control.

(c) The Anglo-Saxon Petroleum Company, Ltd., which company, by virtue of various contracts controls and manages the companies detailed in the schedule hereto annexed, shall be reconstituted so that the control of all these companies shall be permanently vested in the Shell Transport and Trading Company.

(d) As arranged, any of the companies specified in the schedule hereto annexed, which are not now registered in the United Kingdom, shall be brought under British control as soon as practicable, with the exception of the company specified in paragraph 4 of the said schedule.

(e) None of the properties, leases, concessions, or ships of the companies and none of the other capital assets of the companies of a value exceeding £ shall be sold, leased, mortgaged or otherwise dealt with in any way which shall have the effect of vesting the control thereof in anyone other than the Board of Directors of the companies or other companies similarly constituted without the approval of an extraordinary resolution of the companies in general meeting, and any contract or arrangement in contravention of this provision shall, notwithstanding any other provision of the Articles of Association of the companies and any powers conferred upon the directors of the companies, be absolutely void and of no effect.

(f) Fresh interests in production, transport and marketing other than interests which have holdings under French control, and interests in territories under Dutch rule, shall always be entered into or acquired by the Royal Dutch–Shell Group through the medium of the Anglo-Saxon Petroleum Company unless the British nominee as hereinafter defined consents that such interests shall be otherwise controlled.

(g) The Articles of Association of the companies concerned shall provide or be altered by special resolution to provide for the following points:

1. If possible there shall be a special class of shares to be called British Control Shares of small nominal amount, say £ in each case. If this is impossible some other method shall be adopted giving to the British nominee mentioned below special powers as detailed in the following section.
2. The Governor of the Bank of England or some such nominee as may be agreed between the parties to be called the "British nominee" shall be entitled to one vote only on all questions at general meetings, other than the following, viz:

(a) Any resolution for the alteration or cancellation of any of the special provisions herein referred to;
(b) Any resolution for the approval of any arrangement for sale, lease, mortgage or other disposition of the capital assets of the companies as above mentioned;
(c) Any resolution for liquidation, except where the company is actually shown to be trading at a loss;
(d) Any resolution for alteration of the Articles of Association on which questions the British nominee shall exercise a number of votes exceeding by one vote the total number of votes which can be cast by the other parties entitled to attend and vote at such meetings.

The British nominee will also be entitled at all times to veto the election of any new British Director.

3. For any General Meeting convened for any of the purposes (a), (b), (c) and (d), referred to in paragraph g2 above, there shall not be a quorum present at any such meeting unless the British nominee is present or represented by proxy.
4. Any person whether a shareholder or not may be appointed to act as proxy for the British nominee.
5. At least three-fourths of the Directors of the Shell Transport and Trading Company and the majority of the directors in the companies specified in the schedule hereto annexed shall always be British-born British subjects.
6. The consumers of the British Empire and of France and its Colonies shall receive as regards prices, quantities and deliveries the advantages of the most favoured nation.
7. Taxation clause protecting Dutch shareholders to be provided.
8. This agreement is initialled by Lord Harcourt and Mr. Deterding as a recommendation by the former to His Majesty's Government and by the latter to his Dutch colleagues, but is not binding on either until confirmed by each.

Int'd. H.
Int'd. H.D.

SCHEDULE

1.	The Ural Caspian Petroleum Company	Russia
	The New Schibaieff Petroleum Company	Russia
	The North Caucasian Oilfields, Ltd.	Russia
	The Grosny Sundja Oilfields, Ltd.	Russia
	The Anglo-Egyptian Oilfields, Ltd.	(Egypt)

The Caribbean Petroleum Company	Venezuela
Venezuela Oil Concessions	Venezuela
The Colon Development Company	Venezuela
United British Oilfields of Trinidad and subsidiaries	(Sales only)

2. The Asiatic Petroleum Company, Ltd., for itself and affiliated Companies, viz:
   - The Asiatic Petroleum Company (Egypt), Ltd.
   - The Asiatic Petroleum Company (Ceylon), Ltd.
   - The Asiatic Petroleum Company (India), Ltd.
   - The Asiatic Petroleum Company (Straits Settlements), Ltd.
   - The Asiatic Petroleum Company (Federated Malay States), Ltd.
   - The Asiatic Petroleum Company (Siam), Ltd.
   - The Asiatic Petroleum Company (Philippine Islands), Ltd.
   - The Asiatic Petroleum Company (North China), Ltd.
   - The Asiatic Petroleum Company (South China), Ltd.
   - The British Imperial Oil Company, Ltd., Australia.
   - The British Imperial Oil Company South Africa, Ltd.
   - The British Imperial Oil Company New Zealand, Ltd.
   - The Lisbon Coal and Oil Company, Ltd., Portugal.
   - Compagnie Franco-Asiatique des Pétroles, Saigon.
   - The Rising Sun Petroleum Company, Ltd., Japan.
3. The Royal Dutch–Shell Mexican interests.
4. The Astra Romana Company of Roumania.

Note.—subject to negotiations with the French and Roumanian Governments the directorate to be Dutch, English, French and Roumanian, while the Executive Board of the Company shall be transferred to London and be controlled by the Shell Company.

Appendix V
The 'Transferred Territories'

The 'transferred territories'[1] were two areas lying between Khaniqin and Mandali.[2] They had been considered Persian, but, under the rectification of the Turco-Persian frontier in 1913–14, were declared by the internationally constituted Frontier Commission to be Turkish territory. They were accordingly, as part of the mutual exchange of territory between the two countries, awarded to Turkey.

The main point of concern regarding these transferred territories was the way the transfer would affect the Anglo-Persian Oil Company's concession in central and southern Persia. If the territories in question were definitely to be awarded to Turkey, the company faced losing an important part of its concession.

The problem was solved through the use of the words 'cession' and 'transferred territories'. Not only was this a tactful way of avoiding giving offence either to Persia or Turkey, but in addition, and more importantly these words implied that Turkey was taking over Persia's rights and obligations in the area. These rights and obligations included, of course, the Anglo-Persian Oil Company's concession in the area and any royalties accruing from it. This was indeed the arrangement eventually reached, through negotiations between the British and Russian Governments on the one side, and the Turkish Government on the other.

The Anglo-Persian Oil Company was thus secured against any claim from rival companies to an oil concession in the transferred territories. The chief threat came from the Turkish Petroleum Company, whose claim for a concession over the area could be argued to date from the Zander contract of 1904.[3] At the time of the negotiations over the Anglo-Persian Oil Company's rights in the transferred territories (August to November 1913) negotiations were also in progress over the fusion of Anglo-Persian and Turkish Petroleum Company interests relative to the Turkish oil concession.[4] The Anglo-Persian Oil Company, however, did not feel confident enough of the outcome of these negotiations to be able to rely on the proposed fusion to secure its interests in the transferred territories. Indeed, the company tried to persuade the Foreign Office to secure it even larger rights in the area than it held there while the area was still under Persian jurisdiction. The Foreign Office refused to support these larger claims, pointing out that not only were they unlikely to be granted, but also that they would greatly complicate and delay the negotiations with the Turkish Government.[5]

Appendix VI
Note on Government Mincral Oil Organisation during the First World War[1]

At the beginning of 1917 there existed a number of departmental committees dealing with various aspects of petroleum supply, organisation, and distribution. These committees were:

(1) *The Petrol Control Committee*, set up in April 1916 to control the supply and distribution of petrol in relation to war needs and the civilian population. It reported to the Board of Trade.
(2) *The Committee for the Regulation of Petroleum Supplies*, set up in August 1916 and dealing with the maintenance and distribution of general petroleum supplies, particularly in view of tanker shortages. It included representatives of the Admiralty, War Office, Board of Trade and Ministry of Munitions, to which it reported.
(3) *The Colonial Office Inter-Departmental Committee on Oil Leases in Crown Colonies.*
(4) The *Standing Admiralty Committee*, which dealt exclusively with Admiralty requirements.

To co-ordinate all these committees, in February 1917 the *Inter-Departmental Committee on Petroleum Products* was set up, including representatives of the Admiralty, Board of Trade, War Office, Ministry of Munitions, Colonial Office, and Controller of Shipping, with Foreign and India Office occasional representatives. The committee was chaired by E. G. Pretyman, MP, Civil Lord of the Admiralty.[2] Subsequently, on a War Cabinet decision, the question of safeguarding supplies of essential petroleum products was handed over to a further committee, the *Inter-Departmental Petroleum Committee*, headed by the Colonial Secretary, Walter Long. Long had recommended that in order to reduce the confusion and overlapping of the existing committees a controlling authority be set up as a final decision-making body, with executive action to be taken by the Government departments concerned and arrangements made for co-operation. The

Colonial Secretary was accordingly appointed as the controlling authority, to act as arbiter in any dispute. The terms of reference of the Petrol Control Committee and the Inter-Departmental Committee on Petroleum Products were cancelled and the Board of Trade took over their function, with authority over both the allocation of supplies of petroleum products for industrial and civil needs and the distribution of such products. The new committee was to include representatives of all the departments that had participated in the old Interdepartmental Committee and of the Board of Agriculture as well; it was to advise all Government departments concerned with petroleum and to co-ordinate their work and arrange co-operation, but it would have no executive function.

The Colonial Secretary, as controlling authority, presided over meetings of a new *Petroleum Committee* made up of the chairman of the Inter-Departmental Petroleum Committee, the Pool Board (see below), Professor Cadman (Long's technical adviser and liaison officer, co-ordinating the departments and committees involved), and Admiralty, Colonial Office and other departmental representatives. First meeting in July 1917, the committee aimed to deal with questions of general policy and departmental co-ordination. In December the *Petroleum Executive*[3] was formed, with Cadman as director, to formulate policy and co-ordinate departmental programming and executive action. At its suggestion the *Inter-Allied Petroleum Conference* was founded, with Cadman as chairman, to exchange information with Britain's allies and examine and deal with the petroleum problems of the allies in general. In May 1918, Long, as Minister in Charge of Petroleum Affairs and head of the Petroleum Executive, set up the *Petroleum Imperial Policy Committee*[4] under the chairmanship of Viscount Harcourt. It included four unofficial members, plus representatives of the Foreign Office, Admiralty, Board of Trade, Ministry of Shipping, and Petroleum Executive.

Apart from these committees there were also the *Munitions Petroleum Supplies Department*, which was concerned with importation, home production and distribution of petroleum products, chiefly in order to secure uninterrupted essential services, and the *Petroleum Research Department*. This was a sub-department of the Munitions Petroleum Supplies Department (though for a time under the Admiralty), was directed by Sir Boverton Redwood and was concerned with undeveloped sources of mineral oil within Great Britain. In April 1917 the *Pool Board* was formed to regulate the supply, importation and disbution of petroleum products. It remained in existence until December 1918 and consisted of six importing and distributing companies: the Anglo-American Oil Company (controlled by Standard Oil), the Shell Marketing Company, the Anglo-Mexican Petroleum Company (including the Bowring Petroleum Company), the British Petroleum Company (including the Homelight Oil Company), the Union

Petroleum Products Company, and Messrs H. P. Wheatley and Co. The Board of Trade supervised the policy and conduct of the Pool Board, though leaving its organisation and management alone, and the Government purchased its immediate requirements of petroleum products through it. In July 1917 the *Munitions Mineral Oil Production Division* was formed from the Committee for the Regulation of Petroleum Supplies (see above), to deal with the home production and distribution of petroleum and other mineral oils. It was attached to the Director-General of Munitions Supply and directed by Cadman, as Controller of Mineral Oil Production. An advisory board, of which Sir Frederick Black was a member, worked with the division and aimed to facilitate contact with and technical assistance from those departments directly interested in production; its recommendations were submitted to the Inter-Departmental Committee. Also in mid–1917, the Petroleum Research Department was transferred from the Ministry of Munitions to work under the Chairman of the Inter-Departmental Committee. Sir Boverton Redwood left it, becoming Director of Technical Investigation in the Petroleum Executive. In September 1917 the Munitions Mineral Oil Production Division was integrated into the Department of Explosives Supply. Colonel Sir Arthur Churchman became director and Cadman his chief technical adviser.

The post-war history of the Petroleum Executive is worth noting. Its functions ended with the cessation of control in December 1918, but part of its staff were retained and transferred to the Board of Trade, and special advisers such as Sir John Cadman continued to conduct important oil negotiations (for instance, those with the French between 1919 and 1920).[5] During 1919 Long, now First Lord of the Admiralty, pressed the Cabinet to reconstitute the Petroleum Executive into a permanent ministerial department. He stressed the growing importance of petroleum as one of the new 'key' industries, underlined Britain's great need of petroleum (particularly if she were to retain her naval and mercantile supremacy), and pointed out the great benefit that would be derived if the Petroleum Executive were able to operate as an independent organisation. The remaining staff of the Executive were resigning, in quick succession, owing to uncertainty about their future, and Sir John Cadman's was among the resignations. Long had himself been asked to control petroleum matters, but he found this increasingly difficult to cope with on top of his work at the Admiralty.

In 1920 Long achieved his aim. The Petroleum Executive was reconstituted and renamed the Petroleum Department. It was directed by Sir John Cadman, was placed under the auspices of Secretary for Overseas Trade, and had its own minister, Sir Hamar Greenwood. But once its chief concerns – the negotiations with the French Government and with the Royal Dutch–Shell group – had been taken as far as they could be (and by 1922 the negotiations had been suspended), the department lost its independent status and was once again absorbed into the Board of Trade, where it thereafter acted solely as adviser to other Government departments. In 1923 Sir John Cadman joined the board of the Anglo-Persian Oil Company.

Appendix VII
Directors of the Anglo-Persian Oil Company and the Shell Transport and Trading Company, 1911–28, and of the Turkish Petroleum Company, 1912–28

TABLE 1

Directors of the Anglo-Persian Oil Company and the Shell Transport and Trading Company 1911–28[1]

Year	*APOC*		*Shell*
1911	Donald Alexander Smith, Lord Strathcona, PC, GCMG, GCVO:[2] chairman Charles William Wallace[3] Charles Greenway (in 1919 First Bart. and in 1927 First Baron Greenway of Stanbridge Earls):[4] managing director Sir Hugh Shakespear Barnes, KCSI, KCVO[5] John Traill Cargill[6] William Knox D'Arcy William Garson James Hamilton[7]		Sir Marcus Samuel (in 1921 Baron Bearsted of Maidstone, and in 1925 Viscount):[29] chairman and managing director Samuel Samuel:[30] managing director Walter Horace Samuel:[31] managing director William Foot Mitchell:[32] managing director Sir Reginald MacLeod KCB[33] Robert Waley Cohen (later Sir Robert Waley Cohen)[34] Robert James Black (later Sir R. J. Black, Bart.) Henry Neville Benjamin[35] Henri Wilhelm August Deterding (later Sir Henri Deterding KBE)[36] Andrew Vans Dunlop Best Dr Arnold Jacob Cohen Stuart[37]
1912	Sir Campbell Kirkman Finlay[8]	joined	no change
1913	no change		no change
1914	Strathcona Garson Duncan Garrow[9] James Lyle MacKay, Lord Inchcape of Strathnaver, GCSI, GCMG, KCSI, KCIE[10] Vice-Admiral Sir Edmond John Warre Slade, KCIE, KCVO[11] Greenway became chairman and managing director	deceased resigned joined joined (*ex officio*) joined (*ex officio*)	no change

Year	APOC		Shell	
1915	Wallace	resigned	no change	
	Herbert Edward Nichols[12]	joined		
	Col. Sir Trevredyn Rashleigh Wynne, KCSI, KCIE[13]	joined		
1916	no change		Best	deceased
1917	D'Arcy	deceased	no change	
	Frederick William Lund[14]	joined		
	Frank Cyril Tiarks	joined		
1918	Finlay	resigned	no change	
	Robert Irving Watson[15]	joined		
	Francis John Stephen Hopwood, Lord Southborough, PC, GCB, GCMG, GCVO, KCSI[16]	joined		
1919	John Buck Lloyd[17]	joined	no change	
	Sir Frederick William Black, KCB[18]	joined		
1920	Hamilton	resigned	Brig.-Gen. Hugh Henry John Williams Drummond, CMG[38]	joined
	John Douglas Stewart[19]	joined		
	Sir Edward Hussey Packe (to replace Slade, now a director in his own right and soon to be vice-chairman[20]	joined (*ex-officio*)		
1921	no change		Marcus Samuel	resigned
			Stuart	deceased
			Hendrikus Colijn[39]	joined
			Archibald Scott Debenham[40]	joined
			Lt-Col. Bertram Abel Smith, DSO, MC[41]	joined

Year	*APOC*		*Shell*	
1922	no change		Colijn	resigned
			Dr August Philips[42]	joined
			Walter Samuel appointed Chairman	
			Waley Cohen appointed Managing Director	
1923	William Fraser, CBE[21]	joined	Andrew Agnew, CBE	joined
	Sir John Cadman, KCMG (in 1929 GCMG, First Baron Cadman of Silverdale).[22]	joined		
1924	Garrow	resigned	Sir George Ambrose Lloyd, PC, GCSI, GCIE, DSO, (1925, Baron Lloyd of Dolobran)[43]	joined
	Hubert Bryan Heath Eves[23]	joined		
1925	Stewart	resigned	Dr Joseph Theodore Erb	joined
	Inchcape	resigned		
	Southborough	resigned		
	John Swanwick Bradbury, Lord Bradbury of Winsford, GCB[24]	joined (*ex-officio*)		
	Gilbert Campbell Whigham[25]	joined		
	Thomas Lavington Jacks[26]	joined		
1926	no change		Lord Lloyd	resigned
			Black	deceased
			Col. Sir (Arthur) Henry McMahon, GCMG, GCVO, KCIE, CSI, CIE[44]	joined
			Sir Thomas Royden, Bart., CH (in 1944 Baron Royden)[45]	joined

Year	*APOC*		*Shell*
1927	Bradbury	resigned	no change
	Sir George Lewis Barstow, KCB[27]	joined (*ex-officio*)	
	Cadman became chairman		
	Greenway became president		
1928	Slade	resigned	no change
	Nichols	resigned	
	Arthur Charles Hearn (in 1945 Sir A. C. Hearn)[28]	joined	

NOTES ON TABLE 1

1 Compiled from the annual Registers of Shareholders, Companies Register Office, London. Additional information given below is from *Who was Who*, *The Dictionary of National Biography*, Walter R. Skinner's *Oil and Petroleum Year Book* (London, annual) and *The Times*.

2 *Lord Strathcona and Mount Royal*: in 1911 aged 93 (6 Aug. 1818–21 Jan 1914). Various positions and directorships in Canada, including governorship of the Hudson's Bay Co., director of the Canadian Pacific Railway, and honorary president of the Bank of Montreal.

3 *C. W. Wallace*: director of the Burmah Oil Co.

4 *C. Greenway*: originally agent in India of the Burmah Oil Co. Senior partner in the firms of Shaw, Wallace and Co., India and Ceylon, and R. G. Shaw and Co., London; prominent in banking and commerce in Britain; managing director and (from 1914) chairman of the APOC; also director of its subsidiary companies and the Turkish Petroleum Company; Grand Officier of the Lion and Sun, Persia. Additional detail in text, *passim*.

5 *H. S. Barnes*: entered the Indian Civil Service in 1874; Foreign Secretary to the Government of India 1900–3; Lt-Governor of Burma 1903–5; member of the Government of India Council 1905–13. Director of various companies, including the Imperial Bank of Persia (chairman 1916–37), the APOC and its subsidiary companies (the Bakhtiari Oil Co., the British Tanker Co., the First Exploitation Co. the D'Arcy Exploration Co.), the Burmah Oil Co., the Burmah Corporation, Burmah Ruby Mines, United British Refineries and the Anglo-Malay Rubber Co.

6 *J. T. Cargill*: chairman, Burmah Oil Co., and director of concessions Syndicate Ltd.

7 *J. Hamilton*: director of the Burmah Oil Co. and a number of APOC companies.

8 *C. K. Finlay*: member of the Legislative Council, Burma. Director of the Burmah Oil Co.

9 *D. Garrow*: director of the First Exploitation Co., D'Arcy Exploration Co., and other companies.

10 *Lord Inchcape*: member of the Indian Legislative Council 1891–3; member of the Government of India Council 1897–1911 (participated in various Government committees and prominent in matters concerning Indian Railways); also on many wartime committees, including the Imperial Defence Committee 1917, and the Commercial Intelligence Committee 1919. Member of the council of the Corporation of Foreign Bondholders; senior partner in many companies based in India, Australia, London, etc.; director of a great many companies, including – besides APOC subsidiaries – banking, insurance, telegraph, trading and shipping companies

(chairman and managing director of several major shipping companies, notably the P & O Steam Navigation Co.); vice-president of the Suez Canal Co.; and Government director of the APOC, the First Exploitation Co., and other companies.

11 *Admiral Slade*: Commander-in-Chief, East Indies, 1909–12; headed Admiralty Oil Commission to Persia 1913–14; Rear-Admiral 1908, Vice-Admiral April 1914, retired from Navy 1917. Director of First Exploitation Co. and vice-chairman of the APOC.

12 *H. E. Nichols*: director of a great many companies, including all APOC subsidiaries – the British Tanker Co., Broxburn Oil Co., Homelight Oil Co., National Oil Refineries, Oakbank Oil Co., Pumpherson Oil Co., Scottish Oil Agency, Scottish Oils, and Tanker Insurance Co.; became Managing director of the Turkish Petroleum Company.

13 *Sir T. R. Wynne*: member of the Railway Board of India 1905–14, and president 1908–14; member of the Indian Legislative Council 1908–14; Government director of Indian railway companies, 1914–15; director of the Burmah Corporation, and director (managing director from 1915, and chairman from 1930) of the Bengal Nagpur Railway Co.

14 *F. W. Lund*: shipowner; director of the Petroleum Steamship Co. British Tanker Co., Société Générale des Huiles du Pétrole.

15 *R. I. Watson*: director of the D'Arcy Exploration Co., First Exploitation Co., and other companies.

16 *Hopwood, Lord Southborough*: Permanent Secretary to the Board of Trade 1901–7; Permanent Under-Secretary for the Colonies 1907–11; Additional Civil Lord of the Admiralty, 1912–17; member of various Government committees and royal commissions, including, during the war, chairman of the Grand Committee on War Trade. Created First Baron Southborough in 1917. Director of several companies, including Armstrong, Whitworth and Co., and the National Provincial and Union Bank of England.

17 *J. B. Lloyd*: director of a vast number of oil companies within and outside the APOC orbit.

18 *Sir F. W. Black*: Director of Naval Stores 1903–6; Director of Naval Contracts 1906–19; Director-General of Munitions Supply from August 1915, and sent to India to assist Indian Government on Munitions Service, March 1917; acting chairman of the British War Mission, USA, November 1917–February 1918; resigned from Admiralty 1919. President of the Institute of Petroleum Technologists and managing director of the APOC from 1919; director of the First Exploitation Co. and other companies, including the Steaua Romana oil companies (British and Roumanian).

19 *J. D. Stewart*: shipbroker; director of many companies, including the British Oil Bunkering Co., British Tanker Co., National Oil

Refineries, Broxburn Oil Co., Oakbank Oil Co., Pumpherson Oil Co., Scottish Oil Agency, Scottish Oils, Tanker Insurance Co., and D'Arcy Exploration Co.

20 *Sir E. H. Packe*: Assistant Private Secretary to the Marquis of Lansdowne at the War Office, 1900; to the Earl of Selborne at the Admiralty, 1901–5; to Lord Cawdor, 1915; to Balfour, 1916; to Sir Eric Carson, 1916–17. Private Secretary to Sir Eric Geddes, 1917–19, and to Walter Long, 1919. Attached to the Admiralty Staff 1914–19. Government director of the APOC and the First Exploitation Co.

21 *William Fraser* (1888–1970), Baron Strathalmond (1955): managing director of Pumpherson Oil Co., and founder and director of Scottish Oils, as a subsidiary of the APOC; managing director and director of many oil companies associated with the APOC; chairman of the Inter-Allied Petroleum Conference Specifications Commission in World War I, and from 1935 honorary petroleum adviser to the War Office; a member of the Petroleum Board in World War II.

22 *Sir J. Cadman*: Professor of Mining and Petroleum Technology at Birmingham University 1908–20; consulting petroleum adviser to the Colonial Office and the Government of Trinidad; adviser to the Coal Mines Department, Board of Trade; member of Admiralty Oil Commission to Persia 1913–14; consulting petroleum adviser to the British Government, and from 1917 Controller of Mineral Oil Production and director of the Petroleum Executive; chairman of the Inter-Allied Petroleum Conference, 1918. Director, and later chairman of the APOC and the Iraq Petroleum Company; director of the D'Arcy Exploration Co., of the Suez Canal Co., and of the Great Western Railway. President of the Institution of Petroleum Technologists; of the Institute of Fuel; of the Society of British Gas Industries; and of the Institution of Mining Engineers.

23 *H. B. H. Eves*: director of the Homelight Oil Co.

24 *Lord Bradbury*: Joint Permanent Secretary to the Treasury, 1913–19; principal British delegate to the Reparation Commission, Paris, 1919–25; various positions in banking.

25 *G. C. Whigham*: director of the Hungarian Oil Syndicate and in 1920 of the Burmah Oil Corporation.

26 *T. L. Jacks*: joint general manager of APOC 1921–4; resident director of the APOC at Tehran 1924–36; director of the Khanaqin Oil Co.

27 *G. L. Barstow*: Government representative on the APOC and associated companies.

28 *A. C. Hearn*: Admiralty, 1899–1919, chairman of the Anglo-French Mission to Roumania, 1919–20; oil adviser to the Admiralty and the Petroleum Division of the Ministry of Fuel and Power; member

of the Executive Committee of the Oil Control Board; knighted 1945; retired 1946. Director of the APOC 1920–38, and of the D'Arcy Exploration Co.

29 *Marcus Samuel*: founder and chairman of Shell Transport and Trading Co.; director of the Royal Dutch–Shell group and its major subsidiaries, such as the Anglo-Saxon Petroleum Co., the Asiatic Petroleum Co., and Anglo-Egyptian Oilfields. In 1902 Lord Mayor of London; in 1921 created Baron Bearsted of Maidstone; and in 1925 created Viscount.

30 *S. Samuel*: Conservative MP for Wandsworth, 1913–19, and Putney from 1919; Director of various companies, including the Anglo-Saxon Petroleum Co., Shell Marketing Co., Shell Mex, and the Capital and Counties Bank.

31 *W. Samuel*: director of many companies, including major Royal Dutch–Shell group subsidiaries – Anglo-Mexican Petroleum Co. N. Caucasian Oilfields, Societate Anonima Astra Romana, Société Maritime des Pétroles, Egyptian Engineering Co.

32 *W. F. Mitchell*: director of various companies, including De Bataafsche Petroleum Maatschappij; Shell Marketing Co.; N. Caucasian Oilfields; Chartered Bank of India, Australia and China; and the Tampico-Panuco Valley Railway Co.

33 *Sir R. MacLeod*: director of a number of companies, including the Shell Marketing Co., Shell Mex, De Bataafsche Petroleum Maatschappij, N. Caucasian Oilfields, and the Anglo-Egyptian Oilfields. A former Under-Secretary of State for Scotland.

34 *R. Waley Cohen*: director of a great many companies, including numerous Royal Dutch–Shell group subsidiaries – British Imperial Oil Co. (Britain, South Africa, and New Zealand), Anglo-Egyptian Oilfields, Eagle Oil Transport Co., Shell Mex, New Schibaieff Petroleum Co., Grozny-Sundja Oilfields, N. Caucasian Oilfields, Société Commerciale et Industrielle de Naphte Mazout, Yugo Slav Petroleum Co., Compagnie Franco-Asiatique des Pétroles, 'United British' interests, Lisbon Coal and Oil Fuel Co., Tank Storage Co. (India), and Tampico-Panuco Valley Railway Co.

35 *H. N. Benjamin*: director of many companies, including numerous Royal Dutch–Shell group subsidiaries – British Imperial Oil Co. (Britain, South Africa, and New Zealand), 'United British' interests, New Schibaieff Petroleum Co., Grozny-Sundja Oilfields, Colon Development Co., Burlington Investment Co., James Bartle and Co., and the Tampico-Panuco Valley Railway Co.

36 *H. W. A. Deterding*: director of a great many companies, including numerous Royal Dutch–Shell group subsidiaries – the British Imperial Oil Co. (Britain, South Africa and New Zealand), Anglo-Egyptian Oilfields, New Schibaieff Petroleum Co., Grozny-Sundja Oilfields, N. Caucasian Oilfields, Ural-Caspian Oil Corporation,

Société Standard Russe de Grozny, société Anonyme pour l'Industrie de Naphte, Société Maritime des Pétroles, Société pour l'Exploitation des Pétroles, Societate Anonima Italiana Importazione Olii, Societate Anonima 'Astra Romana', Compania Mexicana de Petroleo 'El Aguila', Petroleum Maatschappij 'La Corona', Geconsolideerde Hollandsche Petroleum Compagnie, and the Turkish Petroleum Company.

37 *A. J. C. Stuart*: director of many companies, including many Royal Dutch–Shell subsidiaries – British Imperial Oil Co. (Britain, South Africa, and New Zealand), Compagnie Franco-Asiatique des Pétroles, Geconsolideerde Hollandsche Petroleum Compagnie, Petroleum Maatschappij 'La Corona'.

38 *H. H. J. W. Drummond*: director of companies including De Bataafsche Petroleum Maatschappij, National Provincial and Union Bank of England, Alliance Assurance Co., British Italian Corporation.

39. *H. Colijn*: director of many companies, including many Royal Dutch–Shell subsidiaries – Geconsolideerde Hollandsche Petroleum Compagnie, Petroleum Maatschappij 'La Corona', Nederlandsche-Indische Industrie en Handel Maatschappij, Nederlandsche Indische Tankstoomboot Maatschappij, Société Maritime des Pétroles, Société Commerciale et Industrielle de Naphthe Caspienne et de la Mer Noire, Societate Anonima 'Astra Romana', Compania Mexicana de Petroleo 'El Aguila', Yugo Slav Petroleum Co.

40 *A. S. Debenham:* director of many companies, including Royal Dutch–Shell subsidiaries – British Imperial Oil Co. (Britain, South Africa, and New Zealand), Mexican Eagle Oil Co., Eagle Oil Transport Co., Shell Mex, Anglo-Mexican Petroleum Co., Tank Storage Co. (India) Ltd., Lisbon Coal and Oil Fuel Co. Ltd., Yugo Slav Petroleum Company, and the Ceram Oil Syndicate.

41 *B. A. Smith*: extraordinary director of Shell Transport and Trading Co., and of the National Provincial and Union Bank of England.

42 *Dr. A. Philips*: director of a number of companies in the Royal Dutch orbit, including Royal Dutch subsidiaries, and also the Société pour l'Exploitation des Pétroles and the Nationale Revensverzekerung Bank.

43 *Lord Lloyd*: from 1905 attaché at Constantinople Embassy; in 1907 special commissioner to inquire into the future of British trade in Turkey, Mesopotamia and the Persian Gulf; in 1910 became Conservative MP for West Staffs; during the war mainly in staff posts and on special missions in the Near East (in 1916 was sent to Basra to help Sir Percy Cox and later to the Hejaz; subsequently was attached to the Arab Bureau for special duties concerning the Arab Revolt and T. E. Lawrence's activities); Governor of the Bombay presidency 1918–24; in 1924 elected MP for Eastbourne,

but in 1925 succeeded Allenby as High Commissioner in Egypt, becoming Baron Lloyd of Dolobran; resigned in 1929; in 1940 became Secretary of State for the Colonies and in 1941 leader of the House of Lords. Director of many companies, including the British South Africa Co.

44 *Sir Henry McMahon*: Foreign Secretary to the Government of India 1911–14; First High Commissioner for Egypt, 1914–16 (conducted the 'Hussein–McMahon correspondence'); British Commissioner on the Middle East International Commission to the Peace Conference in 1919.

45 *Sir T. Royden*: on various Government advisory committees during the war (including shipping control) and at the Paris Peace Conference represented the Shipping Controller; Conservative MP for Bootle 1918–22. Director of many companies including the Anchor Line, the Midland Bank, the Suez Canal Co., the Phoenix Assurance Co., the Union Marine and General Insurance Co.; from 1905 director of Cunard and Cunard White Star Ltd (1909–22 deputy chairman, and 1922–30 chairman).

Table 2

Directors of the Turkish Petroleum Company, 1912–28[1]

1912	Sir Henry Babington Smith, Calouste Sarkis Gulbenkian, the Hon. Hugo Baring, Frederick Edwin Whittall, H. W. A. Deterding, Frederick Lane, E. G. Stauss, F. J. Günther
1913	No change
1914	Deterding not listed
1915	Harry Pugh Kingham joined in place of Lane; Stauss and Günther lost positions, as 'aliens'
1916–17	No change
1918	Edward Nathan Meyer joined in place of Babington Smith
1919	Lancelot Hugh Grey Smith, and Sir Charles Eric Hambro joined as 'additional appointments'
1920	Meyer, Baring, Whittall and Kingham not listed
1921	Sir Charles Greenway, Herbert Edward Nichols, John Buck Lloyd. and John Douglas Stewart joined
1922–3	No change – i.e. Greenway, Gulbenkian, Nichols, Lloyd, Deterding, Stewart, Smith, Hambro
1924	Ernest Mercier and Léon Martin replaced L. H. Smith and Hambro
1925	Sir John Cadman replaced Stewart, Nichols listed as managing director, Sir George Mark Watson Macdonogh listed as 'alternate to Deterding', Nubar Gulbenkian as 'alternate to C. S. Gulbenkian', and Louis Tronchère as alternate to Martin and Mercier
1926	Robert Cayrol replaced Martin; Macdonogh, Nubar Gulbenkian and Tronchère unlisted
1927	Arthur Charles Hearn replaced Nichols (deceased), Andrew Agnew replaced C. S. Gulbenkian
1928	Hearn unlisted; Harry George Seidel, William Fraser, Montagu Piesse, and Ja'far Pasha al-Askari joined

NOTES ON PEOPLE MENTIONED IN TABLE 2

Babington Smith: chairman of Mortgagee Co. of Egypt; Oriental Telephone and Electric Co.; Telephone Co. of Egypt; China and Japan Telephone and Electric Co.; Société des Baux du Liban; and the Pacific Cable Board. Director of the British-Italian Corporation, Compagnie Italo Britannica, Central London Railway Co., Agricultural Bank of Egypt, Bank of England; president of the National Bank of Turkey. Additional details in text, *passim*.

Gulbenkian: director of various companies, including the Ural-Caspian Oil Corporation, North British Diesel Engine Works, Societate Anonima, 'Astra Romana', Société pour l'Exploitation des Pétroles, Participations and Investments, Mexican Eagle Oil Co, and the National Bank of Turkey. Additional details in text.

Baring: directorships included London County Westminster and Paris Bank, Anglo-Egyptian Oilfields, and the National Bank of Turkey.

Meyer: director of the National Bank of Turkey.

Hambro: director of the Great Eastern Railway, Royal Exchange Assurance Co., Hambro's Bank of Northern Commerce.

Mercier: president of the Compagnie Français de Pétroles.

Cayrol: director of the Compagnie Français des Pétroles.

Agnew: director of the Asiatic Petroleum Co.

Seidel: director of the Compagnie Standard–Franco–Americaine (US national).

Ja 'far Pasha al-Askari: 'Iraq Diplomatic Agent' (Iraqi citizen).

Appendix VIII

TABLE 3

World Production of Petroleum, 1913–20[a] (long or English tons)[b]

	1913	1914	1915	1916	1917	1918	1919	1920
United Kingdom	289,684	285,464	263,083	247,472	249,598	242,501	213,886	234,000
Egypt	12,618	103,605	34,961	54,800	134,700	272,494	232,148	155,578
Canada	32,583	30,686	30,781	28,303	30,547	43,534	34,352	28,134
Trinidad	70,506	90,092	147,015	129,903	224,324	291,489	257,746	297,588
India	1,110,211	1,037,371	1,148,374	1,188,759	1,131,038	1,146,340	1,222,607	1,000,000
Australia	5,435	16,016	4,952	5,576	10,121	10,366	10,000	8,000
New Zealand	444	412	556	560	600	600	500	400
Sarawak	19,953	45,039	55,460	90,570	76,738	71,366	85,143	148,633
France							47,225[d]	55,000[e]
Galicia	1,095,506	645,077	666,063	912,535	887,415	667,733	818,333	752,528
Germany	142,252	142,252	142,252	142,252	142,252	186,000	32,775	30,000
Italy	6,466	5,453	6,007	6,922	5,577	4,828	4,773	5,400
Roumania	1,854,927	1,755,276	1,646,255	1,224,099	56,567	1,194,705	905,064	1,017,382
Russia	8,976,337	9,574,360	9,792,580	10,400,159	8,362,903	3,143,960	3,642,571	3,483,143
Mexico	3,670,899	3,747,915	4,701,501	5,792,245	7,898,967	9,118,332	12,439,000	22,800,000
United States	35,492,319	37,966,076	40,157,729	42,966,737	47,902,229	50,846,817	53,959,857	63,343,143

	1913	1914	1915	1916	1917	1918	1919	1920
Argentina	18,970	40,073	74,650	118,755	166,193	180,790	172,169	207,301
Peru	271,709	248,605	357,325	357,670	341,514	329,618	343,000	360,000
Venezuela					17,962	49,895	63,589	67,429
Japan and Formosa	273,522	371,628	412,808	417,645	403,371	342,814[f]	285,000	280,000
Dutch East Indies	1,509,566	1,543,998	1,617,032	1,702,374	1,660,272	1,679,246	2,125,017	2,250,000
Persia[c]	243,621	381,890	474,553	587,502	937,902	1,131,489	1,194,000	1,712,267

a Imperial Mineral Resources Bureau, *The Mineral Industry of the British Empire and Foreign Countries*, Statistical Summaries 1913–20 (HMSO, 1921), p. 66.

b 1 long or English ton equals 1·01605 metric tons, 1·12 short tons or 2240 lb.
1 short ton equals 0·892857 long tons, 0·907185 metric tons, or 2000 lb.
1 metric ton equals 0·98421 long tons, 1·10131 short tons, or 2204·6 lb.

c In Henry Longhurst (*Adventure in Oil. The Story of British Petroleum* p. 56) the Persian production increase is given as being from 2–4,000 tons in 1914 to 1,385,000 in 1920.

d Alsace-Lorraine only.

e Including Alsace-Lorraine.

f Japan only.

FIGURE 1

OFFICIAL LONDON FUEL OIL PRICES 1911–1924

POUNDS STERLING (CONTEMPORARY VALUES)

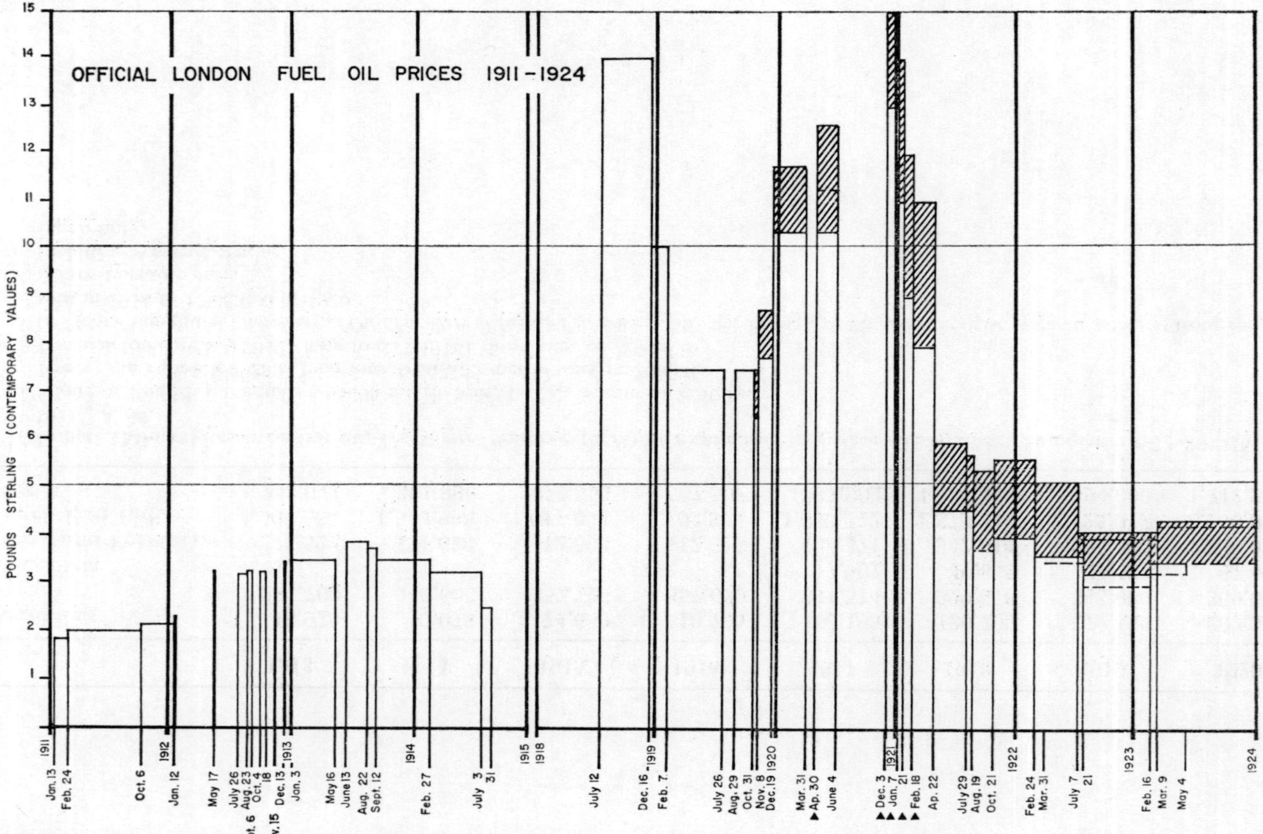

Source: BENJAMIN and COMPANY'S (formerly Benjamin and Gee's) reports published in the 'PETROLEUM REVIEW' called after 1919

NOTES ON FIGURE 1

All prices quoted are per ton, to be purchased in bulk ex-wharf, except for those marked ▲, which are quoted ex-pipeline, and therefore represent a much higher real price than that quoted. Further, prices were frequently arranged by private negotiation.

From 31 October 1919 onwards price was differentiated into two. The cheaper price was called 'bunker fuel oil' until 8 November and thereafter 'furnace fuel oil'. From 30 April to 4 June 1920 and from 31 March 1922 onwards prices for furnace and diesel oil included also, where specifically indicated, (marked – – –), a lower price for bunker oil.

Blank periods when no official listing given, are:

1912:	8 Mar–3 May	No stocks available
	31 May–12 July	Only small quantities available; freight prices 'higher than old selling price of oil', no dealings
	20 Sept, 1 Nov, and 27 Dec	Small quantities, high prices, no official quotation
1913:	23 May–6 June	Same
1915–18:	Aug–July	Wartime. Stocks taken over by Government, no official quotation
1920:	9 April, and 11 June –26 Dec	Small quantities, high prices, no official quotation.

All prices from August 1921 onwards were to include an additional 10s. per ton delivery charge.

Price reductions of 16 December 1918, 7 February 1919, 7 January, 18 February, 22 April, and 19 August 1921 were 'controlled' price reductions, made by announcement.

Prices from 17 to 31 December 1920 are described as 'approximate', although still being officially listed.

50s. price for 3 July, 1914 was for 'ordinary' fuel oil. Fuel oil to Admiralty specification cost 55s. (from 17 July 60s.), while Mexican fuel oil was 40s. per ton.

FIGURE 2

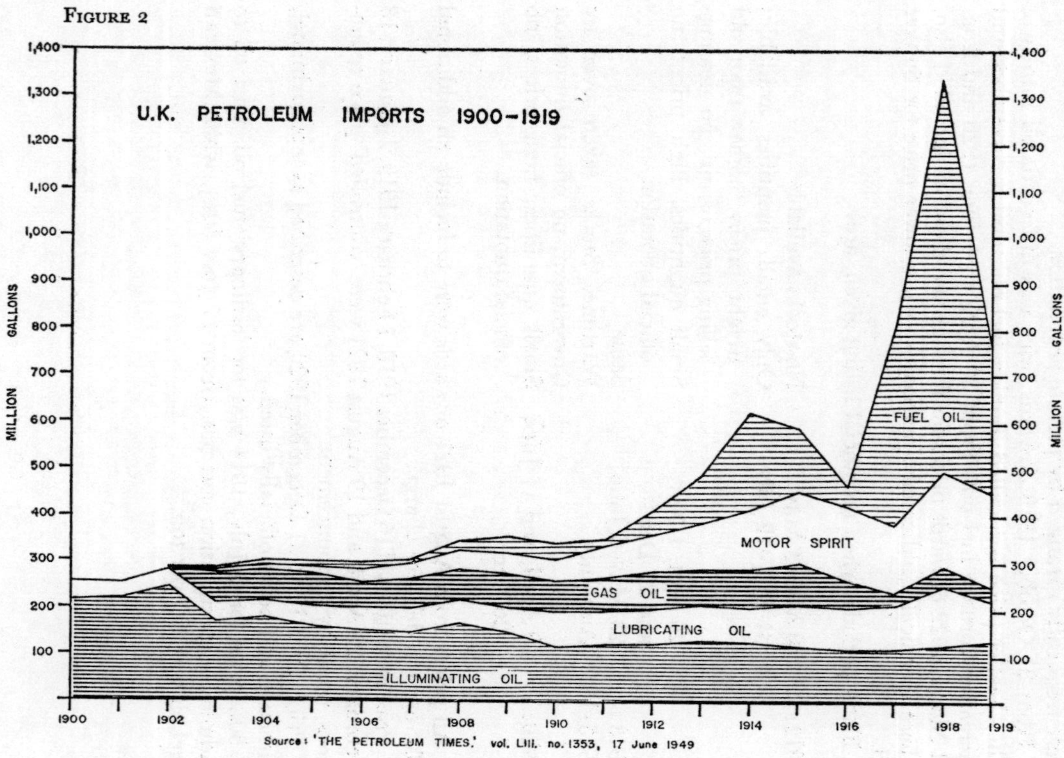

Source: 'THE PETROLEUM TIMES,' vol. LIII. no. 1353, 17 June 1949

FIGURE 3

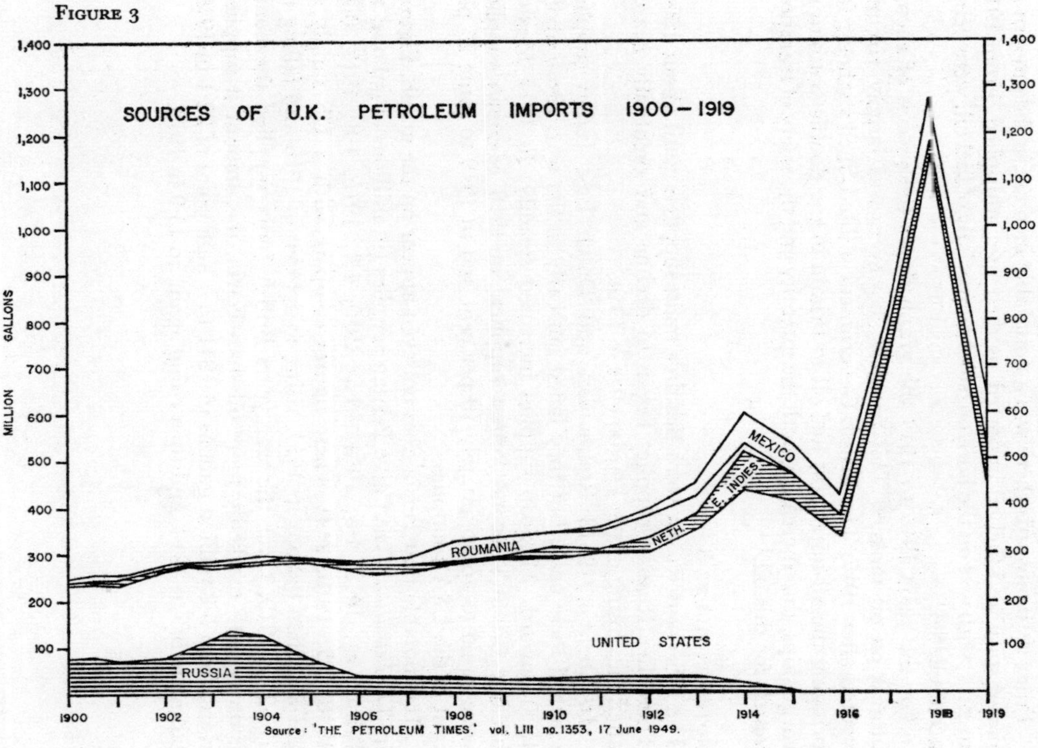

Source: 'THE PETROLEUM TIMES.' vol. LIII no. 1353, 17 June 1949.

NOTES ON FIGURE 2

This graph shows that in the years after 1902 fuel oil was only gradually becoming important to Britain. Until about the turn of the century the term 'petroleum' had tended to refer simply to illuminating oil, but after that it came to signify lubricating oil as well.

From 1910 onwards there was a noticeable increase in the amount of motor spirit and fuel oil imported, as their uses multiplied. From 1912 to 1914, with war on the horizon, stocks, especially of fuel oil, were being accumulated.

For the years 1915 to 1917 the graph shows the success of enemy attacks on oil tankers. This problem, however, was largely circumvented after 1917. The British Government utilised Shell's scheme for bringing the all-important fuel oil to Britain in the double bottoms of cargo ships, thus increasing both the quantity and the safety of transport vessels for this oil.[1]

NOTES ON FIGURE 3

The USA and Russia were Britain's main suppliers until about 1904. Thereafter Russian supplies began to decline and eventually ceased after the closing of the Dardanelles in 1914.

In about 1910–13 Roumanian and Dutch East Indies supplies reached their peak, but they faded out early in the war. From about 1910 onwards Mexican supplies increased steadily: in 1917 Mexico became Britain's second largest supplier; in 1918 Mexican supplies were equal to approximately 10 per cent and in 1919 to some 25 per cent of the USA's supplies.

It is notable that Persia does not even appear on the graph. Figures in *The Petroleum Times*[2] give Persian supplies (in millions of gallons) to Britain as: 1913, 1·5; 1914, 13·5; 1915, 4·8; 1916, 1·8; 1917, 0·7; 1918, 0·5; 1919, 24·0. These figures compare with a US supply of 251·8 million gallons in 1911, rising to 1,145·6 in 1918 and falling to 476·2 in 1919. Over the war years British India supplied the home country with markedly more oil than Persia, the amount it supplied rising from 5·8 million gallons in 1911 to a high point of 22·1 in 1915, falling to 5·5 in 1918, and then rising again, to 15·9 in 1919.

TABLE 4

ESTIMATE OF RETURN OBTAINED BY H.M. GOVERNMENT ON THEIR ORIGINAL INVESTMENT OF £2,200,000 IN THE ANGLO-PERSIAN OIL COMPANY LTD[3] (APOC, 25 January 1922)

		£
(1)	In dividends, interest, income tax, E.P.D., and corporation tax, from 31.3.17 to 31.3.21.	5,360,000
	(If the government had not supplied the above capital to the Company, thereby enabling it to (a) preserve its independence, (b) largely increase its output, (c) to contract with the Admiralty for large supplies of oil on very favourable terms, it is more than doubtful whether the Company would have been able to make profits on so large a scale or have been in a position to pay income tax, E.P.D., etc.)	
(2)	Gain on Admiralty and War Office Contracts as compared with what they would have had to pay had they been dependent on other supplies:	
	Fuel oil delivered from July 1914–June 1922:	5,400,000[4]
	Petrol and kerosene from July 1914–June 1922:	1,650,000[5]
		12,410,000
(3)	Gain on purchases of oil from other suppliers due to Anglo-Persian competition, say:	5,000,000
	(This is a purely hypothetical figure but it is unquestionable that the Admiralty contract with the Anglo-Person enabled them to contract with other suppliers on much more favourable terms than would otherwise have been the case. Probably £5,000,000 is a very considerable underestimate of the actual advantage obtained)	
	Total	17,410,000
	Apart from the above, the 2 million Ordinary shares originally acquired by the Government have appreciated in value to the extent of, say:	4,500,000
	Total gain up to date on Government's original investment of £2,200,000	
		£21,910,000

N.B. The above calculation takes no account of the Government's later investments in the Company because these had not begun to fructify during the period for which these figures stand. These later investments will in due course give large additional gains, apart from the following which are already in sight:

(1) Appreciation in value of the £3,000,000 Ordinary shares subsequently acquired:	6,750,000
(2) 13 years delivery of Admiralty fuel oil contract still to run = 5,200,000 tons at say £2 per ton:	10,400,000
	£17,150,000

Appendix IX
Maps

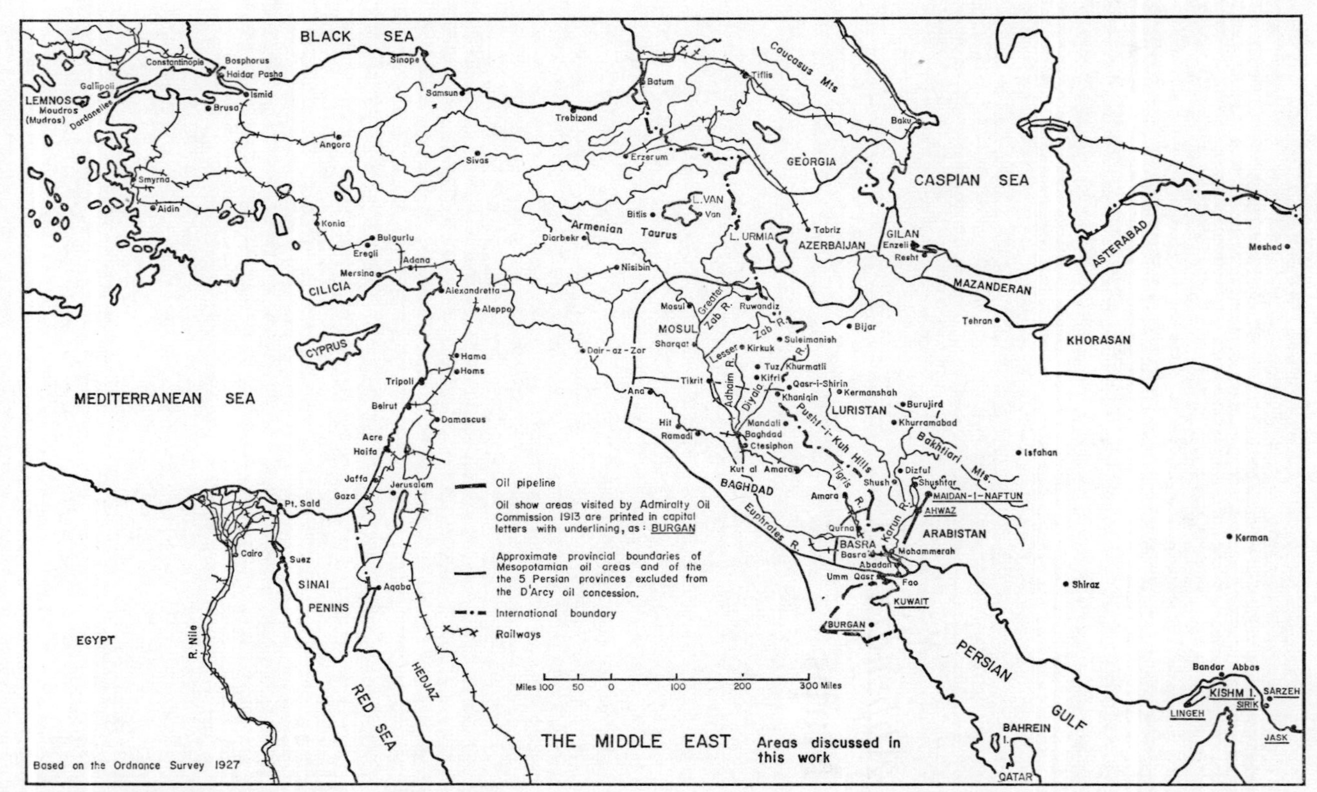

THE MIDDLE EAST Areas discussed in this work

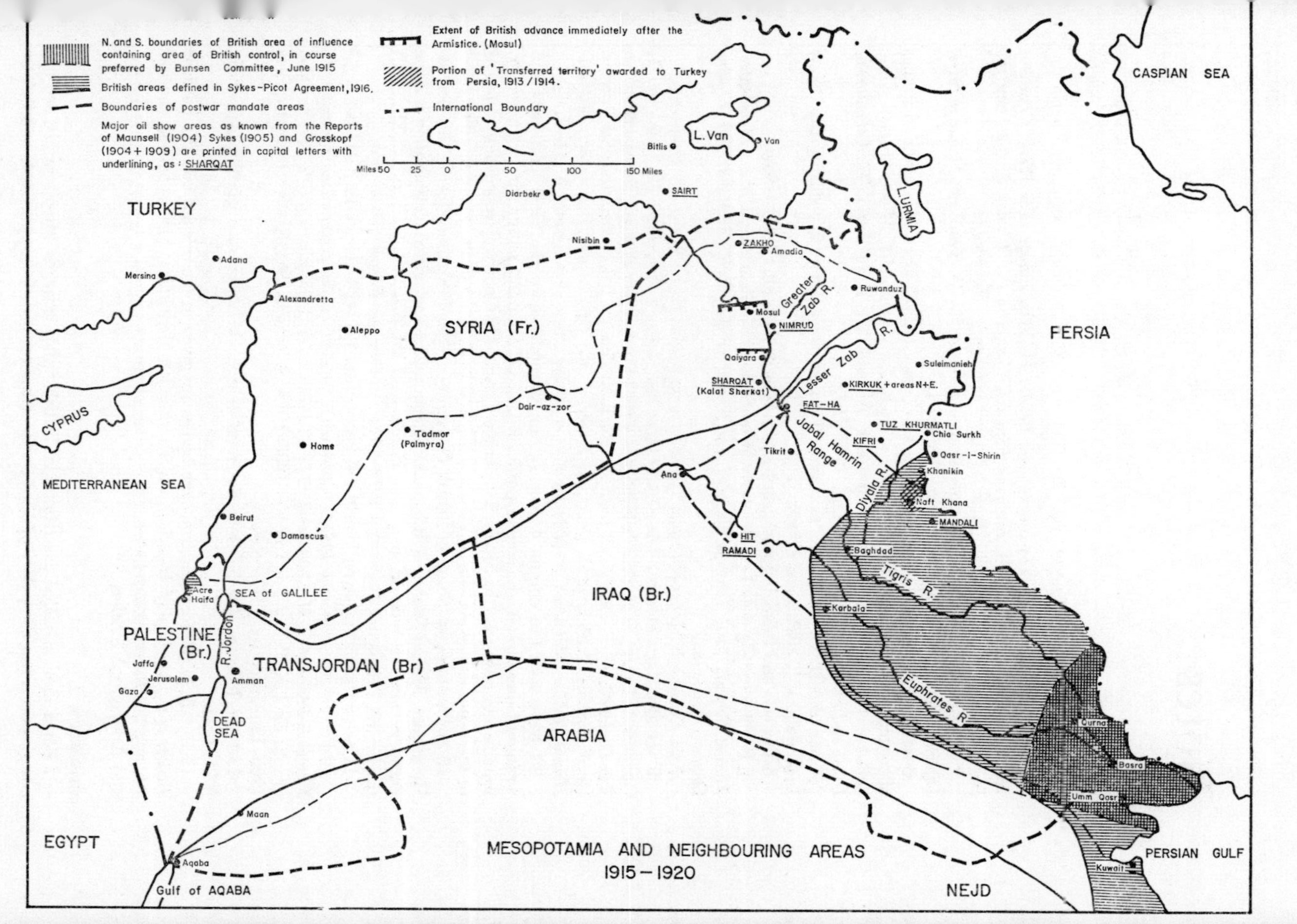

N. and S. boundaries of British area of influence containing area of British control, in course preferred by Bunsen Committee, June 1915
British areas defined in Sykes-Picot Agreement, 1916.
Boundaries of postwar mandate areas
Major oil show areas as known from the Reports of Maunsell (1904) Sykes (1905) and Grosskopf (1904 + 1909) are printed in capital letters with underlining, as: SHARQAT
Extent of British advance immediately after the Armistice. (Mosul)
Portion of 'Transferred territory' awarded to Turkey from Persia, 1913 / 1914.
International Boundary
Miles 50 25 0 50 100 150 Miles
CASPIAN SEA
TURKEY
L. Van
Van
Bitlis
Diarbekr
SAIRT
L. URMIA
Nisibin
ZAKHO
Amadia
Adana
Mersina
Alexandretta
Aleppo
SYRIA (Fr.)
Greater Zab R.
Ruwanduz
Mosul
NIMRUD
FERSIA
Qaiyara
Suleimanieh
SHARQAT
(Kalat Sherkat)
Lesser Zab R.
KIRKUK + areas N+E.
FAT-HA
CYPRUS
Dair-az-zor
Tadmor
(Palmyra)
Homs
Jabal Hamrin Range
TUZ KHURMATLI
Chia Surkh
KIFRI
Qasr-i-Shirin
Tikrit
Khanikin
MEDITERRANEAN SEA
Ana
Diyala R.
Naft Khana
MANDALI
Beirut
Damascus
HIT
RAMADI
Baghdad
Tigris R.
Acre
Haifa
SEA of GALILEE
IRAQ (Br.)
Karbala
PALESTINE
(Br.)
R. Jordan
Jaffa
Jerusalem
Gaza
Amman
TRANSJORDAN (Br)
Euphrates R.
DEAD SEA
ARABIA
Qurna
Basra
Umm Qasr
Maan
EGYPT
MESOPOTAMIA AND NEIGHBOURING AREAS
1915 – 1920
PERSIAN GULF
Kuwait
Aqaba
Gulf of AQABA
NEJD

Notes

INTRODUCTORY

1 See A. S. J. Baster, *The International Banks;* H. Feis, *Europe, The World's Banker: 1870–1914;* D. C. Blaisdell, *European Financial Control in the Ottoman Empire;* and E. Borchard and W. H. Wynne, *State Insolvency and Foreign Bondholders.*

2 A list of such interests and concessions is given in W. W. Gottlieb, *Studies in Secret Diplomacy during the First World War*, chapter 1.

3 Bernard Lewis, *The Emergence of Modern Turkey*, p. 207. Useful background studies of contemporary Turkey are to be found in E. G. Mears (ed.), *Modern Turkey*, while detail on the revolution may be found in F. Ahmad, *The Young Turks. The Committee of Union and Progress in Turkish Politics, 1908–1914.*

4 See also D. C. M. Platt, 'Economic Factors in British Policy during the "New Imperialism"', in *Past and Present*, 39.

5 For this and following paragraph see graphs in Appendix VIII below.

6 For interesting detail on the early years of the oil industry see Robert Henriques, *Marcus Samuel, First Viscount Bearsted and founder of the 'Shell' Transport and Trading Company 1853–1927.*

7 Cf. Elizabeth Monroe, *Britain's Moment in the Middle East, 1914–1956*, chapter 4.

8 See also Zara Steiner, *The Foreign Office and Foreign Policy, 1898–1914*, chapter 3; Gordon A. Craig, 'The British Foreign Office from Grey to Austen Chamberlain', in *The Diplomats 1919–1939*; and John A. Murray, 'Foreign Policy Debated: Sir Edward Grey and his Critics, 1911–1912', in *Power, Public Opinion and Diplomacy: Essays in Honour of Eber Malcolm Carroll by his Former Students.* See also chapter 8 below.

9 I have used this common abbreviation throughout for the Shell Transport and Trading Company; in the contemporary British Government minutes it was, however, usually referred to as 'the Shell'. The Anglo-Persian Oil Company was usually referred to by its full title or as 'the Anglo-Persian', and both forms of usage are retained here.

10 For an understanding of British Government–Shell relations during this period, Henriques, *Marcus Samuel*, is indispensable reading. A specialised examination is to be found in Marian Jack (Kent), 'The Purchase of the British Government's Shares in the British Petroleum Company 1912–1914', in *Past and Present*, 39.

11 See statistical table on World Oil Production 1913–20, Appendix VIII below.

12 Petroleum Imperial Policy Committee, *Report of the Negotiations regarding the Petroleum Policy of H.M. Government 1918–1919*, FO 371/2255, file 87900, S 347. See also graphs on UK Petroleum Imports 1900–19, and Sources of UK Petroleum Imports 1900–19, Appendix VIII below.

13 Lord Jellicoe, *The Crisis of the Naval War*, p. 147. See also graphs, Appendix VIII below.

14 Details of the formation of these bodies are given in the printed but unpublished *History of the Ministry of Munitions*, vii, chapter 10; Henriques, *Marcus Samuel*, chapter 10, and *Sir Robert Waley Cohen, 1877–1952*, chapters 11 and 12. See also chapter 7 and Appendix VI below.

CHAPTER 2

1 For a more detailed description of British policy towards Mesopotamia, see my contributions (on the policy of Sir Edward Grey towards Constantinople and Asiatic

Turkey) to a symposium on British Foreign Policy under Sir Edward Grey. This will appear shortly with C.U.P., edited by Professor F. H. Hinsley. On the British Government's attitude towards financiers and banking opportunities see my article 'Agent of Empire? The National Bank of Turkey and British Foreign Policy', in *The Historical Journal*, XVIII, 2, 1975.

2 See, for example, *British Documents on the Origins of the War, 1898–1914*, v, pp. 43–4; Annual Report for Turkey for 1907, and private letter from S. H. Fitzmaurice (then Chief Dragoman at the Constantinople Embassy) to W. G. Tyrrell (then Senior Clerk, FO, and Private Secretary to Sir Edward Grey), 12 Apr 1908, ibid., v, no. 196, p. 247; also Sir Edward Grey's memoirs, *Twenty-Five Years*, I, pp. 172–3 and 258–60.

3 For detailed information see J. B. Kelly's 'The Legal and Historical Basis of the British Position in the Persian Gulf, in *St Antony's Papers*, no. 4, and the same author's *Britain and the Persian Gulf 1785–1880*.

4 The best detailed published account of the Baghdad railway negotiations is in M. K. Chapman, 'Great Britain and the Baghdad Railway 1888–1914' (*Smith College Studies in History*, XXXI), although the author relies heavily on the published German documentation in *Die grosse Politik der europaischen Kabinette, 1871–1914*. For a short account of the British negotiations and their implications see my study of the policy of Sir Edward Grey (further details in note 1 above). Particularly useful is the long draft despatch by Alwyn Parker to Sir Louis Mallet, drafted 24 July 1914 and printed some years later as a draft despatch, although it was included in the contemporary FO file (FO 371/2125, no. 33655). Parker was at this time Assistant Clerk at the FO and became the chief FO negotiator during the later stages of the Baghdad railway and general Anglo–Turkish negotiations. From 1914–1917 he headed the FO Contraband Department and in 1918 became FO Librarian. He was Private Secretary to Lord Hardinge of Penshurst and attended the Paris Peace Conference in 1919 as an Embassy Counsellor. In 1919 he resigned from the FO. He died in 1951, at the age of 74. Sir Louis Mallet was Assistant Under-Secretary of State, FO, until 1913, and again from 1918 to 1920. During 1913–14 he was HM Ambassador at Constantinople.

5 The Shatt el Arab convention is in *British Documents*, x, part 2, enclosure I to no. 124, pp. 183–7. For detail on the waterway and the convention, see Parker's draft despatch, FO 371/2125, no. 33655.

6 The river navigation concession as finally signed on 12 Dec 1913 is in *British Documents*, x, part 2, no. 188, pp. 283–8.

7 For details on this aspect of the frontier delimitation, see below, Appendix V. For details on the commission's work in general, see A. T. Wilson, *South West Persia. A Political Officer's Diary, 1907–1914*.

8 See *British Documents*, x. part 2; report, 3 May 1913, in editor's note, p. 114; declaration of 29 July 1913, pp. 188–9; and correspondence in nos 141 and 142, pp. 216–17.

9 For the text of the 1899 agreement see *British Documents*, x, part 2, p. 107; also despatch from Marling to Grey, no. 14 (secret), 4 Jan 1911, in ibid., no. 6, p. 12. On the 1907 agreement see FO 371/532 and 371/351 (1908); FO memo. of 12 Feb 1908 (confidential print), FO 881/9161; and CID sub-committee report, 26 Jan 1909, Cab. 16/10. Mr (after 1916, Sir) Charles M. Marling was Counsellor at the British Embassy at Tehran in 1906–9, and at Constantinople in 1908–10, Chargé d'Affaires at Tehran in 1910, Counsellor and sometimes Chargé d'Affaires at Constantinople in 1910–5; and Minister at Tehran in 1915–19, at Copenhagen in 1919–21, and at the Hague in 1921–6.

10 Despatch from Grey to Lowther (to be read to and given to the Turkish Government), no. 107 (secret), 20 Apr 1910, *British Documents*, VI, no. 352, p. 470. The whole despatch is a most illuminating statement of Britain's aims and history of involvement in Mesopotamia and the Persian Gulf. Sir Gerard Lowther was brother of the Speaker of the House of Commons; on 1 July 1908, after the death of Sir Nicholas O'Conor, he

was appointed HM Ambassador at Constantinople, where he stayed till his recall in October 1913 and replacement by Sir Louis Mallet.

11 See my study of the policy of Sir Edward Grey (further details in note 1 above); Grey, *Twenty-Five Years*, II, pp. 164–6, 167 and 174–7; Churchill MSS., document nos 21/36 and 13/45, cited in Martin Gilbert, *Winston S. Churchill*, III, pp. 194–5, 198 and 828–9; and ibid., pp. 207–10 and 216.

CHAPTER 3

1 For details of the situation in 1900 see S. H. Longrigg, *Iraq, 1900–1950*, p. 27.

2 Ibid., p. 27.

3 S. H. Longrigg, *Oil in the Middle East: its Discovery and Development*, 3rd ed. p. 14, mentions those by A. F. Stahl in 1893, Lt-Col. T. R. Maunsell in 1897 (see Maunsell's article 'The Mesopotamian Petroleum Field', in the *Geographical Journal*, IX, pp. 523–32), and Baron von Oppenheim in 1899.

4 Calouste Sarkis Gulbenkian, an Armenian educated in the West, later became financial adviser to the Turkish Government, director of various oil companies and of the National Bank of Turkey, and a millionaire. For a brief biographical summary see R. Hewins, *Mr Five per cent*, p. xvi.

5 In addition, the administration's attention was drawn to the oil areas by the interest of Ottoman nationals, most notably Tahsin Pasha, who in about 1883 obtained a *permis de recherche* for petroleum in the Mosul vilayet and, in 1902, after this was declared lapsed, sued the Sultan – unsuccessfully. For details and texts of firmans, see 'The Mesopotamian Oilfields', in *Oil Engineering and Finance*, III, 17 Feb 1923. Late in 1911 Tahsin Pasha was still claiming to possess preferential rights in the Baghdad and Basra vilayets and attempting to sell them to the D'Arcy syndicate; see FO 371/1263 (1911), file 48964, and FO 371/1487 (1912), file 911. Longrigg (*Oil in the Middle East*, p. 25) mentions that the revised mining code of 1906 enabled Ottoman subjects to obtain licences, which they then proceeded to resell to credulous foreigners.

6 'Mesopotamian Oilfields', p. 197.

7 For details of the company and concession, see: J. B. Wolf, 'The Diplomatic History of the Baghdad Railway' *University of Missouri Studies*, chapter 2; H. Feis, *Europe the World's Banker*, chapter 15, pp. 343–6; and H. S. W. Corrigan, *British, French and German Interests in Asiatic Turkey 1881–1914*, Ph.D. thesis, chapter 2. The company was registered under Turkish law on 4 October 1888 as the société du Chemin de Fer d'Anatolie. The line, started in 1889, reached Angora in 1893 and, at the Sultan's wish, was extended to Konia by 1896, thus becoming the main line of the future Berlin–Baghdad railway. This concession marked the beginning of German financial interest and economic influence in Turkey.

8 For details see Wolf, 'Diplomatic History of the Baghdad Railway' chapters 3 and 4, Corrigan, 'British, French and German Interests', chapters 5 and 6, and M. K. Chapman, 'Great Britain and the Baghdad Railway' *passim*. In November 1899 the German interests, combined with Anglo–French interests, were awarded the concession for continuing the line to the Persian Gulf. The award was made definitive in January 1902, and on 5 March 1903 the Baghdad Railway Company was organised under a convention and registered under Turkish law by the Deutsche Bank, British and French interests having both by then withdrawn.

9 The Rt. Hon. Sir N. R. O'Conor was appointed HM Ambassador to Turkey on 1 July 1898 and died in office on 19 Mar 1908.

10 O'Conor to the Marquis of Salisbury (Foreign Secretary, until November), despatch 231 (confidential), 3 July 1900, FO 78/5102.

11 *Die Bagdadbahn* (18 Jan 1902), pp. 43–4, summarised and translated in FO 424/206, enclosure to print 66.

12 The convention is to be found in British Parliamentary Papers, *Baghdad Railway no. 1*, Cd 5635 (1911), pp. 37–48. Also reproduced in J. C. Hurewitz, *Diplomacy in the*

Near and Middle East. A Documentary Record, I, *1535–1914* (Van Nostrand: Princeton, 1956), document 103.

13 The complete contract is given in the original French as Appendix I below; taken from FO 371/344 (1907), no. 36290.

14 For instance, the German concession to excavate for antiquities at Kelat Sherkat, situated in the centre of the petroleum districts and at a junction of trade routes; see O'Conor to Lansdowne, despatch 794, 10 Nov 1905, FO 78/5399. But a Russian request to send to the Baghdad and Mosul vilayets in 1903 a 'scientific' expedition for archaeological and geographical surveys was not favourably received by the Turkish Minister of Foreign Affairs; see O'Conor to Lansdowne, despatch 291 (confidential), 20 May 1903, FO 424/206.

15 A British-born mining millionaire whose early Persian exploration syndicate became finally, in 1909, the Anglo-Persian Oil Company (APOC), of which he was a director. He died in 1917.

16 Longrigg, *Oil in the Middle East*, p. 28. For a fully documented account of the support the Government gave D'Arcy with regard to his Persian concession between 1901 and 1910, see a confidential FO memorandum 'Mr. W. K. D'Arcy's Oil Concession in Persia', FO 371/2075, no. 10146. An interesting and novel interpretation is given in a letter from Sir Guy Fleetwood Wilson (member of the Viceroy's Council, India) to Lord Hardinge, 27 Apr 1913; see Hardinge MSS., vol. 85, part I, no. 221. Lord Hardinge of Penshurst was from 1910 to 1916 Viceroy of India. Previously, as Sir Charles Hardinge, he had been Permanent Under-Secretary of State, FO, a post he resumed in 1916.

17 He, in turn, was later supplemented – with the Government's help – by a 'more energetic' agent (see p. 44 below). Later still, however, he was to become a director of the Anglo-Persian Oil Company and managing director of the Turkish Petroleum Company. For further detail on Nichols, see Appendix VII below.

18 Referred to in O'Conor to Lansdowne, despatch 178, 16 Mar 1904, FO 78/5330. The original document is not in the file and cannot be found elsewhere.

19 O'Conor to Lansdowne, despatch 732 (secret), 20 Sep 1904, FO 78/5336.

20 In November 1904 Walter Townley (in 1904 Embassy Secretary, Constantinople, in 1905 also Embassy Counsellor) sent to the Foreign Secretary a copy secretly obtained by the Embassy's Military Attaché, Lt-Col. T. R. Maunsell, of a map, prepared by Herr Grosskopf for the Anatolian Railway Company, of the Mesopotamian petroleum districts, with a corresponding tract of the main line of the Baghdad railway; see Townley to Lansdowne, despatch 871 (secret), 15 Nov 1904, FO 78/5337. In October 1905 Capt. Mark Sykes (Honorary Attaché at the Constantinople Embassy 1905–8) drew up a report 'based on a private report to the Civil List by a German engineer'. As Syke's description of the Mesopotamian oil areas, together with the names mentioned, accorded almost exact with the markings on Grosskopf's map, he had very likely seen an early draft of Grosskopf's report. Grosskopf pointed out, significantly, that many of the springs named could be profitably worked via pipeline to the sea, before the completion of the Baghdad railway. See enclosure in O'Conor to Lansdowne, despatch 716 (secret), 15 Oct 1905, FO 78/5398. A pretentious twenty-two page report by Grosskopf (dated May 1909) is to be found in the Shell files, MEP 20. See also map 2 in Appendix IX below, indicating major oil areas discussed in these three reports. On Sykes's later activities, see pp. 122–4.

21 O'Conor to Lansdowne, despatch 563, 16 Aug 1905, FO 78/5396.

22 Townley to Lansdowne, despatch 45, 17 Jan 1905, and O'Conor to Lansdowne, despatch 563, 16 Aug 1905, FO 78/5392. The expedition, which set off from Constantinople on 16 January 1905, was led by an Italian and included a Swiss and two Germans. Its expenses were to be borne entirely by the Deutsche Bank and it was given every facility by the Sultan (who was to share in any eventual profit). Townley further reported that in the event of a successful report a trust was to be formed to work the deposits.

23 O'Conor to Lansdowne, despatch 794, 10 Nov 1905, FO 78/5399.

24 Cf. Longrigg, *Oil in the Middle East*, p. 28. His account has provided the basis for all subsequent writing on the subject.

25 This correspondence is given below as Appendix II.

26 O'Conor to Grey, despatch 184 (secret and confidential), 20 Mar 1906, FO 371/148, no. 10397. Sir Edward Grey was Foreign Secretary from December 1905 to December 1916. He became Viscount Grey of Fallodon in July 1916.

27 In 1905 this company was persuaded by the Admiralty to help D'Arcy's first Persian syndicate – the First Exploitation Company – out of its financial difficulties, and together they formed the Concessions Syndicate Ltd for the purpose of continuing the Persian oil search.

28 O'Conor to Grey, despatch 81 (confidential), 6 Feb 1907, FO 371/345.

29 The inclusion of Whittalls would seem to be doubtful, as one of the brothers was son-in-law to, and a member of the firm of, Gilchrist, guardian of the D'Arcy interests. This 'group' probably represented the early stages of the Lynch–Lt.-Col. Henry Picot association, incorporated in November 1908 into the Eastern Petroleum Syndicate Ltd; see below, p. 25.

30 Correspondence between Grey, Hardinge, O'Conor and D'Arcy during February 1907, FO 371/345, nos. 4700, 5749, 6080, 6287.

31 They formed two new companies, the Bataafsche Petroleum Maatschappij in The Hague (for production), and the Anglo-Saxon Petroleum Company in London (for distribution, transport, storage and subsidiary businesses), on a basis of 60 per cent Royal Dutch and 40 per cent Shell shares. The Royal Dutch and Shell became merely holding companies.

32 Longrigg, *Oil in the Middle East*, p. 29. According to Hewins, (*Mr Five per cent*, p. 71), it was Gulbenkian who persuaded the Shell interests to open this office, ostensibly to deal with oil shipments from Russia, but in reality so that Gulbenkian could use it as a cover for his own intrigues with the officials of the Civil List and the Turkish Government.

33 Block to Hardinge, May–Nov 1907, FO 371/344, nos 23141, 25693, and 36290. In addition Block thought that German obstruction was partly due to Britain's attitude towards the Baghdad railway. Sir Henry Drummond Wolf, former British Ambassador to Persia, was also of opinion that D'Arcy and the Germans should combine; see Wolf–Mallet correspondence, 31 May–12 June, FO 371/345, nos 17864 and 18784.

34 O'Conor to Hardinge (private), 2 Apr 1907, FO 371/343, no. 12713.

35 O'Conor to Hardinge (private), 16 Oct 1907, FO 371/344, no. 35694.

36 For details of the Revolution see Bernard Lewis, *The Emergence of Modern Turkey* chapter 5, and F. Ahmad, *The Young Turks*.

37 See Longrigg, *Oil in the Middle East*, pp. 28–9; also *Oil Engineering and Finance*, pp. 200–2.

38 D'Arcy to Hardinge, 1 Nov 1908, FO 371/560, no. 31179. He also assured the FO that his group intended itself to work the concession, and not to use it for speculative purposes.

39 Although the FO records do not contain this piece of detail, nor suggest quite this timing,the Grand Vizir and the Minister for the Civil List had, according to Dr Lawrence Lockhart, who knew Nichols personally, approved Nichols's contract at the beginning of April 1909, and on 13 April had formally applied for the Sultan to issue the necessary irade. On the next day Nichols and Lowther were to go to the Palace to receive this irade, but were prevented by the disturbances then breaking out. See also Bernard Lewis, *The Emergence of Modern Turkey*, pp. 211–13.

40 Lowther to FO, telegram 212, 21 June, and letter from Mallet to D'Arcy, 28 June 1909, FO 371/777, no. 23256. Longrigg (*Oil in the Middle East*, p. 28) notes Nichols's claim that he had been given a written promise of the concession in 1903.

41 Lowther to Grey, despatch 674, 17 Aug 1909, FO 371/777, no. 31632.

42 Presumably he meant the Steaua Romana, controlled by the Deutsche Bank.

43 Lowther to Grey, despatch 707, 31 Aug 1909, FO 371/767, no. 33347.

44 Grey to Lowther, despatch 633, 30 Aug 1909, FO 371/759, no. 32962.

45 This letter, dated 27 June 1910, is no. 54 in the large file of 'Cospoli' correspondence examined in Constantinople in 1920 by Sir William Mitchell Ramsay, the noted scholar and archaeologist of Asia Minor antiquities. He described the file as the 'confidential correspondence found at the German Railway offices, relative to the Baghdad Railway and the connection of that Railway with the Deutsche Bank and with the Imperial German Government' (letter to the British Ambassador at Washington, 11 Nov 1920). Other particularly relevant letters in the file are nos. 2 and 5. After unsuccessfully searching for this correspondence in the contemporary Government records and, with the assistance of Miss Elizabeth Monroe, through surviving members of Ramsay's family, I found it in the then newly opened 1921 FO records, FO 371/5638. The correspondence is indeed invaluable for a proper understanding of the thought and actions of the German interests. J. A. De Novo (*American Interests and Policies in the Middle East, 1900–1939*, p. 212, n. 6) appears to know of the correspondence but not to have used it. It was, however, read and reported on briefly by John Carter in his article 'The Bitter Conflict over Turkish Oilfields', in *Current History*, XXIII, p. 495. This correspondence supplements that in the Shell files.

46 See p. 22 above. Hewins (*Mr Five per cent*, p. 71) and Longrigg (*Oil in the Middle East*, p. 29) say it was not until 1910 that the D'Arcy group became aware of Gulbenkian/Shell competition; but the correspondence cited in notes 47 and 48 below shows it was a year earlier.

47 FO correspondence with Sir Marcus Samuel and Mr (later Sir) Robert Waley-Cohen, FO 371/777, nos 28640, 28858, 31930 and 32301.

48 Letters between Mallet and D'Arcy, 30 Aug and 8 Sep 1909, FO 371/777, no. 32838.

49 A substantial businessman, partner in the firm of Lane and MacAndrew, oil merchants, and director of various oil companies in the Royal Dutch–Shell orbit. See his evidence to the Royal Commission on Fuel and Engines in a letter of 4 Dec 1912 to Capt. Philip Dumas RN, a secretary to the Commission, Adm. 116/1208, p. 457.

50 Minutes by Mallet, 8 Sep, and Hardinge, 25 Sep, and a letter from Lane to Hardinge, 14 Oct 1909, FO 371/777, nos 34707, 35669 and 38169; letter from Lane to Hardinge, 6 Nov 1909, FO, 371/467, no. 41111. Lane said that if his group did not acquire the monopoly of importation and distribution then the Standard Oil Company would. An Embassy report informed the Foreign Office otherwise, stating that the Standard was seeking only tank installations. See Marling to Grey, despatch 976, 17 Dec 1909, FO 371/777, no. 46724; also letter from Gulbenkian to Alwyn Parker (confidential), 13 Feb 1914, FO 371/2131, no. 6788.

51 In his letter of 1 Nov 1908 to Hardinge (see note 38 above), D'Arcy denies such a charge (see also note 56 below). In succeeding years the various rivals were continually making this accusation about each other.

52 Minute by Hardinge, 25 Sep, and letter from FO to Lane, 27 Sep 1909, FO 371/777, no. 35669. The question of an oil marketing monopoly in Turkey was one of the issues included in the general Anglo-Turkish-German negotiations of 1913–14, and the Turks' own desire to possess this monopoly provided a useful lever for the European powers in their later oil concession negotiations with Turkey (for instance, see p. 109 below).

53 'Cospoli' correspondence, no. 42, 15 Mar 1910.

54 Ibid., no. 43.

55 See note 29 above. A very brief, rather general mention is given in Dr F. C. Gerretson's official *History of the Royal Dutch* (III, p. 244). More precise documentation is contained in the Shell files (MEP 72).

56 FO correspondence with D'Arcy and Harmsworth, Aug–Dec 1909, FO 371/777, nos. 32316, 35669, 40277, 42198 and 44808. Harmsworth had been engaged in oil

enterprises in New South Wales since 1906, and Egypt since 1908, and was stated to have financed the Egyptian Oil Trust almost entirely by himself.

57 For details of the schemes and negotiations, see De Novo, *American Interests*, chapter 3 ('Dollar Diplomacy in Turkey: the Chester Project, 1908–13'), and Leyland James Gordon, *American Relations with Turkey*, chapter 14. The German Foreign Office records (on microfilm, GFM 10/417/ 51 and 52, and GFM 10/418/55) contain some material for 1910–11 on the Chester project but little that is not contained in FO 371, vols 777, file 23256 (1909); 995, file 184 (1910); 1004, file 5693 (1910); 1002, file 27482 (1910); 1240, file 330 (1911); and 1242, file 1074 (1911). A little material is also included in *Die grosse Politik der europäischen Kabinette*, XXVII, XXVIII, XXXI and XXXIII. Further details on the Glasgow and Chester schemes are contained in the 'Cospoli' correspondence, which gives Huguenin's comments (Ramsay thought his private source of information very bad). Helfferich was clearly worried by the Glasgow scheme's chances, although he was very rude about it. The chief German method of opposition was to play off rival contenders (for instance, E. Whittall and Nichols) against each other.

58 The application also included the Constantinople telephone concession. Ever since his visit to the country in 1900, Admiral Chester had been interested in the commercial possibilities and great need for Turkey's economic development.

59 Moore represented his father, Charles Arthur Moore, president of Manning, Maxwell and Moore, a railway supply company, whose treasurer was Colby M. Chester Jr. Other principal investors in the syndicate were E. G. Converse, a director of US Steel; MacArthur Bros, prominent railway builders; the Foundation Company, general contractors; and the banking firm of Laidlaw and Co. (see Gordon, *American Relations with Turkey*, p. 259, and De Novo, *American Interests*, p. 60). In November, 1909 the Ottoman–American Development Corporation was formed, with Colby M. Chester Jr as its secretary. In 1912–13 it was re-constituted as the Ottoman–American Exploration Company, and in 1922 it became the Ottoman American Development Corporation. See De Novo, *American Interests*, chapter 7, pp. 218ff.

60 A further scheme, by a Belgian group headed by Colonel Schaeffer, asked for a concession for a very similar route, but, though it was more favourably received in the Turkish press, did not meet with much consideration from the Turkish parliament. See FO 371/767, no. 43491; FO 371/995, file 184, no. 19854; and FO 371/1004, no. 13057.

61 Lowther to Grey, despatch 815, 15 Oct 1909, FO 371/767, no. 39223. Lowther also threw doubt on the financial ability of both Chester's and Glasgow's supporters to muster sufficient capital to build the proposed railways.

62 Enclosure in Marling to Grey, despatch 929, 22 Nov 1909, FO 371/767, no. 43491, and 'Memorandum as to Mineral and Railway Concessions in Asia Minor', May 1911, FO 371/1248, no. 18688. The death knell of the Glasgow scheme was sounded by an official notice from the Ottoman Public Works Department; this was published in the local press on 16 November 1909 and stated that all applicants at present seeking concessions must give the Department proof of their financial capacity, by 1/14 December 1909 at the latest, or their applications would not be considered. Glasgow's preliminary deposit was £T5,000, to be increased to £T30,000 should his group, after preliminary exploration, decide to take up the option. His group held that proof of financial capacity should be consequent on obtaining the option, and not a prerequisite; in fact, it seemed as if outside rumour that the group lacked sufficients financial backing were only too true.

63 FO 371/1248, file 18688, and FO 371/1242, file 1074; private letter from Lowther to Sir Arthur Nicolson (Permanent Under-Secretary of State, FO, 1910–16), 24 May 1911, Nicolson MSS., 1911, II, FO 800/348. Both Glasgow and the Denbigh schemes were supported by Dr Pasdermadjian, member for Erzeroum in the Turkish Chamber of Deputies, who was anxious for his own area of Turkey to be opened up to commercial and mineral development. See also 'Cospoli' correspondence, no. 62.

64 De Novo, *American Interests*, p. 63.

65 In addition to those interests mentioned in note 59 above, the group was supported by the New York Chamber of Commerce and the New York Board of Trade.

66 By the new Concessions Law published on 10/23 June 1910 all concession schemes had to come before parliament. A copy of the law is in FO 371/1011, no. 34731.

67 De Novo, *American Interests*, p. 75.

68 Lowther thought, apparently rightly, that it was the hope of the Grand Vizir (who was strongly pro-German) and opponents of the scheme generally that continued postponement and delay would disgust Chester and his group and thus cause the plan to suffer a lingering though natural death; see Lowther to Grey, despatch 316, 10 May 1911, FO 371/1242, no. 18257.

69 The granting to the Baghdad Railway Company of the concession for the branch line to Alexandretta was a death blow to the Chester project. As the FO noted in March 1911, 'The whole story is eloquent testimony to the strength of German influence at Constantinople' (FO 371/1242, no. 1003). An even more potent blow came from the fact that by September 1911 the Anatolian Railway Company was negotiating with the Ottoman Government for the construction of lines to link the Angora branch line with the Samsoun–Sivas line, and to extend it to Diarbekir and Harput (see FO 371/1240, no. 37334, which encloses and comments on an article from the *Gazette Financière* of 5 Sep 1911). After the 1912–14 effort the Chester concession claim was not revived until 1920–2.

70 Correspondence between the FO and the syndicate during September–October 1909, FO 371/767, nos 35504, 36195, 37249, 38134, 38359 and 39519.

71 From Sinope or Samsoun to Sivas, via Ammassia; from Ammassia to Angora; from Sivas to Diarbekir via Eghin; from Eghin to Erzeroum; any necessary branches or prolongations.

72 See De Novo, *American Interests*, pp. 68–72 and 77; Gordon, *American Relations with Turkey*, p. 261; and Carter, in *Current History*, XXIII. German opposition is detailed in the 'Cospoli' correspondence.

73 FO 371/1004, nos 12165 and 26770 (Apr–July 1910), and FO 371/1240, no. 48326 (Nov–Dec 1911). The attitude of the French Embassy at Constantinople, expressed through M de la Jonquière, was that the project was 'a bluff and doomed to failure' because of its impracticality, while that of the Russian Ambassador, Tcharykov, was favourable, for Russia was anxious for German influence in northern Asia Minor to be diluted. See Miguel, German Embassy, to German Government, July 1910, GFM 10/417/51, no. 12773; also note 69 above.

74 Telegrams between Grey, Bryce (HM Ambassador, Washington) and Lowther, June 1910, FO 371/1004, nos 21729 and 21874. See also Gordon, *American Relations with Turkey*, p. 261. Grey speculated to Bryce that if the mining rights did turn out to cover the districts for which D'Arcy was applying, it might be arranged that the American concession should not apply to oil in that district – a somewhat naïve supposition, since Arghana copper and Mosul oil were the two most important minerals along the route.

75 Correspondence between Lowther and Grey, Mar–May 1910, FO 371/1004, nos 10510, 9639 and 17340. See also 'Cospoli' correspondence, no 7.

76 FO minute, FO 371/1004, no. 21874. Lowther had also pointed out that the entire route had to be laid down and approved before the commencement of mining operations (Article 21), and, though mining could be begun as soon as the route was approved, the minerals extracted could bot be removed until the railway was working in the section where the mine was situated. Ibid., no. 10510.

77 FO correspondence with D'Arcy and Lowther, Apr–Nov 1910, FO 371/1004, nos 12060, 17340 and 41228.

78 This was amply demonstrated by the APOC's frustration of American interest in the five northern Persian provinces during the 1920s.

79 FO to Lowther, despatch 313, 5 Oct 1909, FO 371/777, no. 35669.

80 Lowther to Grey, despatch 548, 2 Aug 1911, FO 371/1240, no. 30989. On 29 July a convention was signed between the Régie Générale des Chemins de Fer and the Turkish Minister of Public Works, concerning railway construction in Rumelia and Anatolia; the Germans asked for compensation for this extension of French interests (see note 69 above). The FO noted that the French and Germans were acquiring all the railways in European and Asiatic Turkey, and that Britain would be left out in the cold; Britain must therefore insist on the Mesopotamian irrigation and the D'Arcy oil concessions.

81 Greenway (managing director of the Anglo-Persian Oil Company) to Mallet, 3 Jan, and minute by Alwyn Parker, 4 Jan 1912, FO 371/1486, no. 472.

82 Lowther to Grey, despatch 101, 2 Feb, and Grey to Lowther, despatch 65, 20 Feb 1912, ibid., no. 5242.

83 Lowther to Grey, despatch 308, 14 Apr 1912, ibid., no. 16795.

84 See chapters 4 and 5 below.

85 Marling to Grey, despatch 944, 30 Dec 1910, FO 371/1240, no. 330.

86 FO to Lowther, 8 Sep 1909, FO 371/777, no. 34128.

CHAPTER 4

1 Marling to Grey, despatch 637, 27 July 1912, FO 371/1486, no. 32932. The (Anglo-Turkish) National Bank of Turkey was founded in 1909 on Turkish initiative and with strong FO encouragement. Its other British directors were Lord Revelstoke, Sir Ernest Cassel (president) and C. S. Gulbenkian. Regarding the National Bank of Turkey, see M. Kent, 'Agent of Empire'. The National Bank of Turkey and British Foreign Policy', in *Historical Journal*, XVIII, 2, 1975.

2 See pp. 36–7 and note 15 below.

3 Letter from Babington Smith to FO (confidential), 29 Aug 1912, FO 371/1486, no. 36674.

4 In other words, the Royal Dutch–Shell group of companies and associated interests.

5 This was promised formally on 23 October 1912. Already, by a letter to the TPC on 12 October, the Deutsche Bank had formally given up all direct or indirect interest in producing or manufacturing oil in the Ottoman Empire, other than through the TPC. These two documents, together with the TPC's memorandum and extracts from its articles of association, are in FO 371/1761, no. 38738. See also below, pp. 46, 49–50, and Longrigg, *Oil in the Middle East*, pp. 29–30.

6 Letter from Mallet to Greenway, 23 Aug 1912, FO 371/1486, no. 35252.

7 Greenway to the FO, 2 Sep 1912, ibid., no. 37181 (letter following an interview); and minute by Mallet, ibid., no. 36674. These arguments were repeated continuously throughout the resulting negotiations, but especially clear statements of them may also be found in letters from Greenway to the FO, Oct–Dec 1912, ibid., nos. 44428 and 53280.

8 In 1905 Lord Selbourne, First Lord of the Admiralty, persuaded the Burmah Oil Company to buy shares in the Persian oil syndicate, the First Exploitation Company, then on the point of selling out its concession to foreigners because of a paucity of positive results and a lack of further finance. According to information given me by Dr Lawrence Lockhart, the Burmah Oil Company was, through the Concessions Syndicate (which it had specially formed), to repay D'Arcy a large proportion of the amount he had spent in endeavouring to find oil.

9 The fallacy of this argument was shown up in less than two years, when the British Government began passing its wartime security legislation. Between 1914 and 1918 there were no fewer than seven 'Trading with the Enemy' Acts to deal with this same problem.

10 The company's strong belief in the sanctity of the British Empire was constantly stressed in Greenway's arguments, especially with regard to Lord Strathcona, Sir Hugh

Barnes and D'Arcy. See memorandum by Mallet, 15 Nov 1912, FO 371/1486, no. 48688.

11 Grey to Marling, telegram 608, 12 Sep 1912, and letter from Marling to R. P. Maxwell (Senior Clerk, FO, 1902–13), 18 Sep, ibid., no. 36674; Marling to Grey, 17 Sep, telegram 378, ibid., no. 39178.

12 Note from Mallet to Grey, 10 Sep 1912, Grey MSS. FO 800/93; letters from the FO to the Admiralty, (immediate and very confidential) 13 Sep, Admiralty to the FO (confidential) 26 Sep, FO 371/1486, nos 36674 and 40516.

13 See pp. 40 and 44 below.

14 Letter from Nicolson to Babington Smith (confidential), 28 Sep, and Grey to Marling, telegram 672, 28 Sep 1912, FO 371/1486, no. 40516; letter from Nicolson to Marling, 30 Sep Nicolson MSS., 1912, VI, FO 800/358, and letter from Babington Smith to the FO, 9 Oct and accompanying Minute by Lancelot Oliphant (Acting Third Secretary, Diplomatic Service, 1905–16; Assistant Clerk, FO 1916–20), 11 Oct, FO 371/1486, no. 42490.

15 On the other hand, in private correspondence among the TPC's members, it is clear that they all thought that the British Government had indeed been informed, through Lowther, while Babington Smith and F. E. Whittall were quite definite that they had, from time to time, personally discussed the matter with the Ambassador. The most likely inference is thus, that Lowther did not at the time grasp the significance of what was being discussed, omitted to make any official report, and then forgot all about it. Whittall's views on the founding of the TPC, and his own role in it, are detailed in a private memorandum entitled 'The Story of the Birth of the Present Iraq Petroleum Company', signed and dated Istanbul, 16 July 1945.

16 Note from Maxwell to Nicolson, 10 Oct 1912, FO 371/1486, no. 42763.

17 Letter from Greenway to Maxwell, 30 Oct 1912, with enclosed Asiatic Petroleum Company correspondence, ibid., no. 47482.

18 Memorandum by Mallet, 6 Nov 1912, ibid., no. 47486.

19 Minutes by Grey, Nicolson and Mallet, 6–11 Nov, 1912, ibid., no. 46486.

20 Letter from the Admiralty to the FO (confidential) 26 Sep, 1912, ibid., no. 40516.

21 This is stated particularly clearly in a memorandum by Parker, 19 Nov 1912, on Greenway's report of his meeting with the Admiralty, ibid., no. 49500. See also memorandum by Mallet, 15 Nov, ibid., no. 48688.

22 Admiralty memorandum, Appendix II to Churchill's Cabinet memorandum (secret), 16 June 1913, Cab 37/115.

23 Correspondence between the APOC and the Admiralty, Mar–Oct 1912, FO 371/1486, nos. 51935 and 17709; India Office, Public Works Department (PW) file 929/13, vol. 858. The Indian Government Railways Board had indeed long been considering the question seriously; since 1902–3 it had made periodic though inconclusive trials of oil fuel. 'see A. J. Chase *et al.*, 'Oil Fuel Trials on the North-Western Railway of India, 1913–1916,' *Railways Department Technical Paper* no. 193.

24 In his memorandum of 19 November Parker continued 'I read this record of the conversation over to Greenway, who said it fairly represented in summary what he had said. . . .' (FO 371/1486, no. 49500). Detail on Parker is in chapter 2, note 4 above.

25 Letter from the FO to the Admiralty, 15 Nov 1912, ibid., no. 40516.

26 The conference proceedings are described in a minute by Nicolson, 20 Nov 1912, no. 50815.

27 Letter from Mallet to the Admiralty (immediate and confidential), 28 Nov 1912, ibid., no. 49186. For more details on Sir Frederick Black, see below, Appendix VII.

28 Semi-official letter from Sir Thomas Holderness (Permanent Under-Secretary of State, IO) to Mallet, 3 Dec 1912, ibid., no. 51935. IO views on the APOC were recorded by Drake and Hirtzel; see IO, Political and Secret Subject Files (P & S), v. 104, 1912, nos P 3877 and P 4743. Francis C. Drake was Secretary of the Revenue and Statistics Department, IO, until 1915; Sir Arthur Hirtzel was Secretary of the Political

and Secret Department, IO, until 1917, when he became Under-Secretary of State, IO.

29 Letter from Mallet to the IO (immediate and confidential), 9 Dec 1912 FO 371/1486, no. 51935.

30 Letter from Holderness to the FO, 13 Dec 1912, ibid. no. 53280. See also minute by Hirtzel, 30 Dec, IO, P & S, vol. 104, 1912, no. P 4969.

31 The private correspondence between the Secretary of State and the Viceroy shows very plainly their own, strongly negative attitude on the question. See Hardinge MSS., vols. 97, 118–120 (1912–14).

32 Minute by Parker, 16 Dec 1912, FO 371/1486, no. 53280.

33 Letter from Holderness to FO (immediate), 4 Jan 1913, FO 371/1760, no. 722.

34 Letter from the Admiralty to the FO (immediate and confidential), 28 Dec 1912, FO 371/1486, no. 55654.

35 It took only until May 1914 for the Government, on behalf of Admiralty interests, to buy a 51 per cent share in the APOC. This arrangement provided for two British Government representatives to sit on the board, and, until November 1914, for British troops to land in Persia, at least partly to defend the pipelines and tank installations of the APOC. In any case, since 1908 Indian troops had been defending the company's personnel. See A. T. Wilson, *South-West Persia, A Political Officer's Diary, 1907–1914* pp. 18, 24.

36 Letter from the Admiralty to the IO, 26 Mar 1912, FO 371/1486, no. 51935.

37 See, for example, letter from Greenway to the FO, 12 Feb 1913, FO 371/1760, no. 7026.

38 See p. 47 below.

39 See p. 48 below.

40 Minutes by Parker and Mallet on Admiralty letter, FO 371/1486, no. 55654.

41 Minute by Mallet for Grey, 9 Jan 1913, FO 371/1760, no. 2463.

42 Greenway to the Admiralty and to the FO, 29 Jan, and minute by Parker, 31 Jan 1913, ibid. no. 4559. An unsigned article in *Financial News*, 14 Nov 1912, entitled 'Will Germany Control the Oil Supply for our Navy?', gave point to this matter by contrasting the strong German state control over its oil interests with the opposite situation in Britain, which, the author thought, should follow Germany's example. The article caused some excitement in the Royal Commission on Fuel and Engines, then in session. On the other hand, Dr Lawrence Lockhart tells me that the official Admiralty opinion (which I did not locate in the Admiralty records) was that it had no objection to the APOC supplying the German Navy providing that the British Navy's demands were satisfied. See also p. 96 below.

43 Mallet to Greenway (confidential and immediate), 5 Feb 1913, FO 371/1760 no. 2463 (my italics).

44 See letter from Nicolson to Lowther, 14 Oct 1912, Nicolson MSS., 1912, VII, FO 800/859.

45 Letter from Greenway to the FO, 4 Dec 1912, FO 371/1486, no. 51845. See also note from Parker to Mallet (immediate and confidential), 15 Nov. Parker thought that there were ways by which the British Government need not actually figure in the matter, and the importance of the question certainly made it necessary to consider every expedient.

46 Mallet to the Admiralty (immediate and confidential), 28 Nov, and Grey to Lowther, telegram 1092R, 6 Dec 1912, FO 371/1486, nos. 49186 and 51845.

47 Private letter from Lowther to Maxwell, 11 Dec 1912, ibid., no. 53729. On Nichols's later positions see Chapter 3, note 17. Lowther was himself recalled from Constantinople in October 1913 and replaced by Mallet, his ambassadorship in Turkey having generally been regarded in FO circles as a failure. See Hardinge MSS., vol. 93, part I, nos 35, 65, and 168, and part II, nos 25, 26 and 42. See also Steiner, *The Foreign Office*, pp. 102, 106, 176–7.

48 Lowther to Grey, despatch 1097, 22 Dec 1912, and letter from Mallet to Greenway, 31 Dec 1912, FO 371/1486, nos 55372 and 55479.

49 Lowther to Grey, telegram 63, 1 Feb 1913, FO 371/1760, no. 4989; Grey to Lowther, telegram 71, 31 Jan, and minute by Parker, 31 Jan, ibid., no. 4977, and FO 195/2449, file 18. Correspondence on the subject continued till June, for the appointment had led to some difficulty for the FO due to Edwin Whittall's mistaken belief that the FO was discriminating against him personally.

50 Grey to Lowther, telegram 1115 (confidential), 23 Dec 1912, FO 371/1486, no. 53729. This advice was based on a memorandum dated 20 Dec 1912, drawn up by the FO's Assistant Legal Adviser, C. J. B. Hurst (who later, as Sir Cecil Hurst, became the FO's Legal Adviser).

51 These claims were set out by Greenway, on the FO's request, in a letter to Parker, 23 Jan 1913, FO 371/1760, no. 3606.

52 Minute (no date) by Mallet on Hurst's memorandum.

53 Memorandum by Weakley, 27 Dec, in Lowther to Grey, despatch 1125, 28 Dec 1912, FO 371/1760, no. 16 (1913). Lowther elaborated his views, on request, in a further despatch to Grey: despatch 1132, 31 Dec 1912, ibid., no. 573 (1913), and in telegram 8R, 6 Jan 1913, ibid., no. 810. See also minutes by Parker and Mallet on this telegram.

54 Already, between December 1911 and February 1912, an Admiralty committee under Capt. Pakenham had considered some of the problems of oil fuel; some of its proceedings are described in Henriques, *Marcus Samuel*, pp. 531–9. Further useful background for this period is contained in an article written, from printed sources, by Joseph E. King: 'The New Broad Arrow: Origins of British Oil Policy', in *Mariner's Mirror*, XXXIX, pp. 187–200. Arthur J. Marder's *From the Dreadnought to Scapa Flow*, I, and his *Fear God and Dread Nought*, II, are indispensable background reading for general naval policy in this period. The brief account of this matter given by Randolph Churchill in his *Winston S. Churchill*, II, is highly inaccurate. For the only full discussion of the subject, see Jack (Kent), in *Past and Present*, 39.

55 The commission, generally known as the Royal Commission on Fuel and Engines, commenced proceedings on 24 Sep 1912, submitted its first report to the King on 27 Nov and its second exactly three months later. By then most of the important evidence had been collected, and the chairman, Admiral Fisher, had long been bombarding Churchill with his findings. The commission's full proceedings are in Adm. 116/1208–9. These were kept strictly confidential at the time (save for a brief, general report in 1914), to encourage witnesses to speak freely – which they did.

56 Samuel spoke on 19 Nov 1912 and Deterding on 26 Feb 1913. They had also protested against this Admiralty prejudice in Dec 1911 before Pakenham's committee; see note 54 above, and, for further biographical detail, Appendix VII below.

57 These arguments were repeated in a letter from Sir Reginald MacLeod, a director of Shell, to Mallet, 28 July 1913, FO 371/1761, no. 34933.

58 Samuel stated that he himself held a majority of his company's shares, while Deterding said that in the Royal Dutch this contingency had been guarded against by the creation of special preference shares.

59 For the membership of the board, see comparative table of directors of the Anglo-Persian Oil Company and the Shell Transport and Trading Company, 1911–28, Appendix VII below.

60 See p. 24 above. It is clear from Samuel's evidence to the commission (see Adm. 116/1208, pp. 362, 368), and from the following chapter, that the Shell–Deutsche Bank alliance was a most uneasy one. The contrast between Samuel's and the Germans' account of the formation of the TPC is striking. According to the German Chargé d'Affaires in London, Richard von Kühlmann, the German Government approached Gwinner of the Deutsche Bank to come to terms with the British; Gwinner thereupon approached Cassel, since the latter's bank was regarded as being in close touch with the

British Government and it was Cassel who had entered into negotiations with the Anglo-Saxon Petroleum Company. See Memorandum by Parker (secret), 16 July 1913, FO 371/1761, no. 32788; and *British Documents*, x, part 2, no. 117.

61 'Memorandum in regard to Outline Scheme for Supply of Oil Fuel' (secret), 7 Mar 1913, Adm. 116/1219. This along with other more technical aspects of the question, is treated in more detail, by Jack (Kent), in *Past and Present*, 39.

62 Recommended in the second report, of 26 Feb 1913.

63 Adm. 116/1209, pp. 47, 80–4. The reason why Persia and Mexico could offer large forward contracts was stated to be that both lacked a developed local market and both refined their own crude oil, thus making possible a more accurate assessment of their own manufacturing costs.

64 Fuel oil prices were listed regularly by Benjamin and Company (formerly Benjamin and Gee) and printed in *The Petroleum Review* (from 1919, *The Petroleum Times*). All prices mentioned here are, unless otherwise stated, taken from the company's London listing. See graph on price movements between 1911 and 1924, Appendix VIII below. For the system of oil pricing, see C. Issawi and M. Yeganeh, *The Economics of Middle East Oil* pp. 64–5;) Edith T. Penrose, *The Large International Firm in Developing Countries. The International Petroleum Industry*, pp. 180 ff.; and Helmut J. Frank, *Crude Oil Prices in the Middle East. A Study in Oligopolistic Price Behaviour.*

65 If in some areas (especially in the USA) relations between oil companies certainly helped to raise petrol prices, these relations were not co-operative but bitterly hostile. See Henriques, *Marcus Samuel*, pp. 517–64.

66 See notes 80 and 85 below.

67 Letters from Greenway to the FO, 12 Feb, and to the Admiralty, (confidential), 6 Mar 1913, FO 371/1760, nos. 7026 and 11238. Also detailed in Churchill's memorandum to the Cabinet, 'Oil Fuel Supply for His Majesty's Navy', 16 June 1913, Cab. 37/115. Minutes of 1913 Admiralty Board meetings are in Adm. 167/47.

68 See above, pp. 38–9 and 41–2.

69 Greenway's letter of 12 Feb, referred to in note 67 above; Report by Railways Board, Simla, to Government of India, 29 Jan 1913, FO 371/1760, no. 17709, and Adm. 116/1208, p. 344.

70 Letter from the Admiralty to the FO, 26 Feb 1913, FO 371/1760, no. 9375.

71 Admiralty to the IO, no date, enclosed in Admiralty to the FO, 13 May 1913, ibid., no. 22113.

72 Admiralty to the IO, 18 June 1913, FO 371/1761, no. 28100; reported to the Cabinet in Churchill's 'Supplementary Note' on the 'Proposed Arrangement with the Anglo-Persian Oil Company for a Supply of Oil Fuel', 4 July 1913, Cab. 37/116.

73 Telegram from the Viceroy to the Secretary of State, IO, 22 May (forwarded to the Admiralty, 24 May), IO, PW file 929/13, vol. 858; Hardinge MSS., vol. 97, part II, no. 312. India's views were repeated to the Admiralty in subsequent letters; see, for example, IO to the Admiralty, 2 Apr 1914, FO 371/2131, no. 14940.

74 Letter from the APOC to the FO, 23 June 1913, FO 371/1761, no. 28805; Churchill's Cabinet note of 4 July (see note 72 above); minute by Holderness to Crewe, 25 June, IO, P & S, vol. 105; private letter from Crewe to Hardinge, 27 June, Hardinge MSS., vol. 119, part I, no. 30; and private telegram, 28 June, ibid., vol. 97, part I, no. 355.

75 Asquith MSS., vol. 7 (or Cab.41/34). Meetings on 9 and 11 July 1913.

76 Cab. 37/115.

77 This was in his speech in the debate on the estimates for 1913–14. The wording for the speech was discussed in the Cabinet meeting of the previous day (see Asquith MSS., vol. 7).

78 The commission's members were Professor John Cadman, Professor of Mining at Birmingham University and petroleum adviser to the Colonial Office; E. R. Blundstone, a geologist; E. H. Pascoe, of the Geological Survey of India; and J. C. Clarke of

the Admiralty (secretary). During this time Rear-Admiral Slade also took part in an oil conference at Delhi and investigated possible oilfields at Bahrein and Koweit, recommending that steps should be taken to ensure that any development at these two places should be British – which was achieved. See papers sent by the IO to the Admiralty, 6 Mar 1914, FO 371/2131, no. 10237; also IO, P & S, vol. 186, 1913, nos. P 4159 and P 771. Slade became Vice-Admiral in April 1914.

79 Final Report of the Commission, 6 Apr 1914, attached to Cd 7419 (1914), *Navy (Oil Fuel) Agreement with the Anglo-Persian Oil Company (Ltd): Anglo-Persian Oil Company (Acquisition of Capital) Act, 1914.*

80 For a detailed account of these later negotiations see Jack (Kent), in *Past and Present*, 39, pp. 158–62. The final agreement is in Cd 7419 (1914). This agreement is, incidentally, incorrectly named, dated and described by Randolph Churchill in *Winston S. Churchill*, II, p. 611.

81 This price was first revealed by Jack (Kent), in *Past and Present*, 39, pp. 162, 165–6. On the APOC's estimate of the benefit from this arrangement see Appendix VIII.

82 This function of the Government directors was explained in a letter from the Treasury sent to the APOC on 20 May 1914. It is to be found in Adm. 116/1687D and was summarised as para. 4 in the Explanatory Memorandum to the APOC Agreement, Cd 7419 (1914), but was not published in full in the press until 1929 (see Elizabeth Monroe, *Britain's Moment*, p. 99. Details on the settling of all these matters are in Adm. 116/1687B–E.

83 *Parliamentary Debates*, series 5, 1914, LIX, cols 1907–9, and LXIII, cols 1131–53.

84 This attack was widely regarded as gratuitous, provocative and particularly unfair, as Shell was not able to defend itself by revealing either the prices the Government had paid for its oil or the price it had offered for a future forward contract. Both of these were actually regarded within the Admiralty as being very fair. See Adm. 116/1667C, CP 14171, also R. Henriques, *Waley Cohen*, pp. 189 and 194, and *Marcus Samuel*, pp. 576–90. The irony of Churchill's dislike of Samuel is that Samuel was British, strongly patriotic and prepared for reasonable compromise, while Deterding, whom Churchill admired, was a foreigner and, if anything, the uncompromising businessman.

85 On reactions to the passing of the bill, see Jack (Kent), in *Past and Present*, 39, pp. 163–4.

86 Letter from Greenway to the FO, 17 Feb 1913, enclosing letter to Nichols, FO 371/1760, no. 7820; Lowther to Grey, despatch 192 (confidential), 10 Mar, ibid., no. 11986; FO minute, and Grey to Lowther, telegram 151, 24 Mar, ibid., no. 13851.

87 See note 5 above. The TPC had in fact made several other applications in the period covered by this chapter – some to the Ministry of Commerce and Agriculture and some to the Ministry of Mines. All were for *permis de recherche* for particular areas, and especially (partly as a technical move to protect the company's legal position) for one over the whole of the Baghdad railway zone from Mosul to Takrit. It also protested against *permis* being granted to others, while continuing to defend the validity of its actions under Article 1 of the 1904 convention, or, conversely, under Article 6, demanding repayments of its expenses. For correspondence and (especially memoranda) see 'History of the Turkish Petroleum Co.: Summary of Board and General meetings' and 'Extracts from Documents bearing on Claims by, and Position of, the Turkish Petroleum Company,' in Shell files, MEP 20. See also below, p. 51.

88 Minute by Parker, 18 Feb 1913, FO 371/1760, no. 7820. The FO was very interested to learn for certain of the promise of 23 Oct 1912 to transfer the Deutsche Bank's rights to the TPC (see note 5 above). But it should be noted that this was only a written *promise* to transfer these rights, at some future convenient date, although the TPC's subsequent demands for the concession were based on it. (The transfer was in fact never carried out, and litigation in the 1920s could not enforce it.)

89 Grey to Lowther, telegrams 105 and 116, 20 and 28 Feb (confidential), FO

memorandum to Tewfik Pasha, 24 Feb, and note from Parker to Mallet, 28 Feb 1913, all in ibid., no. 7820. Ibrahim Hakki Pasha (1863–1918) was formerly Professor of International Law, adviser to the Porte, 1906, Minister of the Interior and of Public Instruction, 1908–9, Ambassador at Rome, 1909–10, and Grand Vizir, 1910–11.

90 Lowther to Grey, telegram 115R (confidential), 1 Mar 1913, ibid., no. 9772.

91 Lowther to Grey, telegram 117R (confidential), 1 Mar 1913, no. 9776, missing from FO files but located in IO, P & S, vol. 104. If genuine, the loan was probably offered by Baron Thomas de Ward, concerning whom see p. 63 below. The FO kept the APOC informed of progress made (see letter of 3 Mar, FO 371/1760, no. 9772).

92 Letters from Greenway to the FO, 10 Mar 1913, enclosing Stock to the APOC; APOC to the FO, 4 Mar, and reply, 10 Mar; ibid., nos 11393 and 10327. The FO had already decided to warn Greenway against payments to the Turks before peace was made, for Britain had urged Germany not to make any advance meanwhile and might be accused of double-dealing; minute by Parker, 3 Feb 1913, ibid., no. 4989.

93 Lowther to Grey, telegram 121R, 3 Mar; despatch 180, 4 Mar; telegram 139R, 11 Mar; despatch 192, 10 Mar 1913: ibid., nos. 10067, 10821, 11475 and 11986.

94 See letter from the APOC to the FO, 4 Mar 1913, ibid., no. 10317; Grey to Lowther, telegram 125R, 4 Mar, ibid., no. 10067; also letter from Greenway to Parker, 23 Jan 1913, ibid., no. 3606.

95 Lowther to Grey, despatch 197, 13 Mar 1913. ibid., no. 12194.

96 See p. 22 above.

97 See p. 23 above.

98 FO minutes on FO 371/1760, no. 12194.

99 Lowther to Grey, telegram no. 117R, 1 Mar 1913, IO, P & S, vol. 104, 1912, no. 9776; and despatch no. 192 (confidential), 10 Mar, FO 371/1760, no. 11986.

100 FO memorandum to Hakki Pasha, 18 Mar, and minute by Mallet, 25 Mar 1913, ibid., nos 11393 and 13851.

101 Lowther to Grey, telegram 147R (confidential), 15 Mar 1913, ibid., no. 12157. This possibility had also been raised in 1909 (see p. 23 above).

102 Grey to Lowther, telegram 149R, 19 Mar, FO 371/1760, no. 12608. See also note by Mallet, ibid., no. 15561.

103 Report, 29 Mar 1913, sent by Stock to Lowther, enclosed in Lowther to Grey, despatch 257, ibid., no. 15561.

104 FO minute, 25 Mar, and Grey to Lowther, telegram 151, 25 Mar 1913, ibid., no. 13851.

105 The interviews were on 24 and 30 Mar. See Lowther to Grey, telegram 165R, 26 Mar; despatch 239, 24 Mar; despatch 257, 31 Mar enclosed in letter from Stock to Lowther, 31 Mar 1913; ibid., nos. 13902, 14250 and 15561.

106 Minute by Maxwell, ibid., no. 14250.

107 Grey to Lowther, telegram 157, 28 Mar 1913, and minute by Mallet, ibid., no. 13902.

108 FO minute, ibid., no. 15561.

109 Lowther to Grey, despatch 227 (confidential), 20 Mar 1913, ibid., no. 13760. Sir Henry Babington Smith sent the FO a confidential 'Memorandum concerning the Petroleum Rights in Turkey acquired by the TPC', 23 Apr, enclosed in a letter to Maxwell, FO 371/1814, no. 19018.

110 Shell files, MEP 102; see also the arguments presented in chapter 3 above.

111 Shell files, MEP 102. This article corresponded to Article 22 of the Baghdad Railway Convention.

112 Polish orientalist and legal expert; appointed head of the Legal Department of the Ottoman Public Debt in 1893, legal adviser to the Ottoman Ministry of Mines and Forests in 1898, judical adviser to the Ottoman Government in 1909, and adviser to the Sublime Porte, ranking as Minister Plenipotentiary, in 1913. He was a member of the Polish delegation to the Paris Peace Conference in 1919. See also Sir Telford Waugh's *Turkey Yesterday, Today and Tomorrow*.

113 This letter is quoted in a memorandum, 'Extracts from Documents bearing on Claims by, and the Position of, the Turkish Petroleum Company' (no date, but later than Oct 1916), Shell files, MEP 20. It was clearly as a result of this opinion that the German Embassy in Constantinople wrote to the Porte on 21 Mar 1913 demanding either its rights under Article 1 of the 1904 contract or repayment of expenses as under Article 6 (see ibid.).

114 See p. 24 and note 15 above.

115 When, in September 1913, the TPC learnt of this infringement (which dated from 1910) by the Turkish Government's granting of three *permis* over the Kirkuk area to two Turkish subjects, Raghib Bey and Nazim Bey, it protested strongly to the Government. See Shell files, MEP 20 and 21.

116 Minutes on FO 371/1814, no. 19018, and FO 371/1760, no. 13760.

117 Letter from the APOC to the FO, 2 Apr, with FO minutes, and Grey to Lowther, telegram 113, 21 Apr 1913, ibid., no. 15220.

118 See p. 53 above.

119 FO 195/2449, file 18; also minutes on FO 371/1760, no. 15220.

120 Lowther to Grey, despatch 316, 17 Apr, 1913, ibid., no. 18135.

121 Lowther to Grey, despatch 336, 21 Apr 1913, ibid., no. 19321. Confirmed by Stock next day. See Lowther to Grey, despatch 348, 24 Apr, ibid., no. 19791; and Stock to Lowther, 22 Apr, FO 195/2449, file 18.

122 The basis for the Grand Vizir's hypothetical contract could well have been the *application* that the TPC made for a *permis de recherche* covering the Mosul–Takrit area. See p. 53 above.

123 The committee members included Shevket Bey, Director of the Mining Department, and Kennan Bey, its Chief Engineer. Stock's 'contact' was the Chief Clerk, Muslim Effendi, who was well rewarded for his constant and invaluable services to the D'Arcy interests.

124 Lowther to Grey, despatch 349, 25 Apr 1913, FO 371/1760, no. 19792.

125 A further scheme for economic partition of Mesopotamia was being put forward at the same time, as a solution to Turkey's desperate financial position. A despatch from Lorimer, Consul at Baghdad, to Lowther discussed the parts Britain ought to claim. Lorimer placed Baghdad and Basra first, with the possibility also of including Mosul, because of its oil potential. Enclosed in Lowther to Grey, despatch 354, 26 Apr 1913, FO 371/1816, no. 19797.

126 FO minutes on FO 371/1760, nos. 19792 and 20063, and FO 371/1816, no. 19797. At the time there was no minute by Alwyn Parker on this question. Later, however, he was to wonder whether the problem might not best be settled by allotting Mosul to Greenway and Baghdad to Babington Smith. See note by Parker, 10 June 1913, FO 371/1761, no. 27463.

127 Letter from Mallet to Greenway, 28 Apr 1913, FO 371/1760, no. 18135. Greenway was also sent copies of Lowther's recent despatches, with a letter from Mallet, 30 Apr, ibid., no. 19321.

128 Letter from the APOC to the FO, 29 Apr 1913, ibid., no. 20063.

129 See p. 37 above.

130 Letter from Sir Hubert Llewellyn Smith (since 1907 Permanent Secretary to the Board of Trade) to the FO, 16 May 1913, FO 371/1760, no. 22678.

131 Lowther to Grey, despatch 407, 13 May 1913, ibid., no. 22579.

132 FO note to Hakki Pasha, 23 May 1913, ibid., no. 23945.

133 Details of the conference, which was advocated first by Parker and was to include representatives of the FO, IO, Board of Trade and Admiralty, together with Greenway and Babington Smith, are given in the following chapter. See minutes on FO 371/1760, no. 20063; and Mallet to the various departments, 22 May 1913, ibid., no. 22579.

134 It should be added that the APOC's association with the Burmah Oil Company was also, of course, a source of strength.

CHAPTER 5

1 Report by Llewellyn Smith to the FO (secret), 20 June 1913, FO 371/1761, no. 28398.

2 Letters from Babington Smith to Llewellyn Smith, 10 June, and from Greenway to Llewellyn Smith, 11 June 1913, ibid., no. 28398. Note by Alwyn Parker, FO, 10 June, ibid., no. 27463.

3 FO minute, ibid., no. 26929.

4 Letters from Greenway to G. J. Stanley (Board of Trade), (confidential), 12 and 13 June, and from Stanley to Greenway (confidential), 13 June 1913, ibid., nos 26986, 27134, and 28398.

5 Letter from Llewellyn Smith to Babington Smith, 18 June, and reply, 19 June 1913, ibid., no. 28398.

6 Letters from the Board of Trade to the APOC (confidential), 20 June and to the FO (secret), 20 June 1913, ibid., no. 28398.

7 Letter from Mallet to Board of Trade, 21 June 1913, ibid., no. 28398. My italics.

8 Letter from Mallet to Babington Smith, 30 June 1913, ibid., no. 29070.

9 Minute by Parker, 24 June 1913, ibid., no. 28805.

10 Lowther to Grey, telegram 255, 3 June 1913, FO 371/1760, no. 25396.

11 Letter from Greenway to Mallet, 3 June 1913, enclosing Stock's 'Memorandum of Interview with Minister of Mines', ibid., no. 25622.

12 Ibid., no. 23945. See also p. 57 above.

13 Grey to Lowther, telegram 239R (urgent), 5 June 1913, FO 371/1760, no. 25396.

14 Letter from E. Narracott, for Admiral Fisher, to Sir W. G. Tyrrell, (Senior Clerk, FO, 1907–18; Private Secretary to Sir Edward Grey, 1907–15; Assistant Under-Secretary of State, FO, 1918–25), 5 June 1913, FO 371/1761, no. 26038. This was not, however, a TPC move. On 9 June, in a private letter to Mallet, Hakki Pasha was complaining of the National Bank's refusal to join the French and Germans in making a loan available to Turkey, and he begged Mallet for 'a word of encouragement and sympathy from the Foreign Office' (ibid., no. 27463). Indeed, by 20 June the TPC was discussing the question of an advance to the Turks but still would not make a firm offer until it had received an equally firm offer of the concession. See letter from Babington Smith to Deterding, 20 June 1913, Shell files MEP 20.

15 Minutes by Parker on interviews with Hakki Pasha, 11 and 14 June 1913, FO 371/1817, nos 26908 and 27464, and *British Documents*, x, part 2, nos. 95 and 97.

16 Lowther to Grey, despatch 521, 12 June 1913, no. 27372. This document was missing from the FO files (FO 371/1761), but was located in IO, P & S, vol. 104, no. P 2617.

17 Stock's memorandum, FO 371/1760, no. 25622; Grey to Lowther, telegram 237, 4 June 1913, ibid., no. 25608; Lowther to Grey, telegram 260, 4 June, ibid., no. 25644; Embassy minute for Lowther, 5 June, FO 195/2449, file 18. In October 1912, and again in April 1913, de Ward had unsuccessfully approached the British Embassy in Constantinople for official government support in obtaining the Mesopotamian concession; see FO 371/1487, no. 44663, and FO 371/1760, no. 17970. His activities were reported to the German Government by the German Embassy in Constantinople on 3 May 1913; see GFM 10/418/61, no. A 9370. For further details see above, chapter 4, note 91, and below, chapter 6, p. 108 and note 53.

18 Letter from Mallet to Hakki Pasha (immediate), 5 June 1913, FO 371/1760, no. 25644; Lowther to Grey, telegram 266R, 6 June, ibid., no. 25928.

19 Marling to Grey, telegram 313 (confidential), 4 July, and 315, 5 July 1913, FO 371/1761, nos. 30716 and 30909.

20 Grey to Marling, 7 July 1913, telegrams 306 and 310R, ibid., nos. 30716 and 30909.

21 Letter from Babington Smith to Grey (confidential), 11 June 1913, FO 371/1826, no. 26928.

22 Letter from Mallet to Babington Smith, 13 June 1913, ibid., no. 26928.

23 Minutes by Parker, 14 June 1913, on Babington Smith's letter, ibid., nos. 26928 and 27272; memorandum by Edward Parkes (Librarian's Department, FO 1905–14; Assistant, 1914–18; Acting Librarian and Keeper of the Records, 1918–19) on history of the National Bank, 26 June, ibid., no. 29346. The FO and the Embassy also considered at length, and even started, some preliminary negotiations concerning a possible successor to the bank.

24 Grey to Lowther, telegram 274R, 24 June 1913, FO 371/1761, no. 28729; Lowther to Grey, telegram 294, 24 June, ibid., no. 28828; note by Mallet, 30 June, ibid., no. 30628. See also the discussion of this question, pp. 34, 36–7 above.

25 Minute by Parker, 14 June 1913, FO 371/1826, no. 27272.

26 Babington Smith to the FO, 27 June 1913, ibid., no. 30276, in reply to Mallet's private letter of 25 June, ibid., no. 29250.

27 Minutes by Mallet, 7 July, and by Parker, 10 July 1913, FO 371/1761, no. 31596.

28 Departmental minutes on ibid., no. 32788.

29 Minute by Parker, 2 July 1913, FO 371/1791, no. 30443, and *British Documents*, x, part 2, no. 107; German Ambassador, London, to the German Government, 4 July, GFM 10/418/63, no. A 13368, and *Die grosse Politik*, XXXVII, no. 14762.

30 Günther to the Deutsche Bank, Constantinople, 2 July 1913, GFM 10/418/63 no. 13667.

31 Letter from the FO to the German Ambassador in London, 12 July 1913, FO 371/1761, no. 31596.

32 Letter from Parker to the Board of Trade (urgent and confidential), 14 July 1913, ibid., no. 32340; and Board of Trade to the FO, 17 July, ibid., no. 33052 (missing from file but described in index volume, Ind. 27985).

33 Memorandum by Parker (secret), 16 July 1913, FO 371/1761, no. 32788, and *British Documents*, x, part 2, no. 117.

34 Minute by Parker, 10 July 1913, FO 371/1761, no. 31596.

35 German Ambassador, London, to the German Government, 16 July 1913, GFM 10/418/63, no. A 14482.

36 Minute by Parker, 17 July 1913, FO 371/1791, no. 32991, and *British Documents*, x, part 2, no. 119. Parker wondered whether the APOC should not also make an advance, or at least get some firm assurance on its position. It is interesting to compare Hakki Pasha's attitude at this time with that of a few weeks before; see p. 62 above.

37 Note from Mallet to Parker, 24 July 1913, FO 371/1761, no. 34408.

38 Letters from MacLeod to Mallet, 28 and 30 July 1913, ibid., nos. 34933 and 35263. See also chapter 4, note 57 above. Further details are in Appendix VII.

39 For full argument see p. 46 above.

40 Llewellyn Smith to Mallet, 30 July 1913, FO 371/1761, no. 36361. My italics.

41 Letters from Hopwood to Mallet, 29 July and 1 Aug 1913, ibid., nos. 35070 and 35778. For biographical detail on Hopwood, see Appendix VII.

42 Letter from Mallet to Hopwood, 29 July 1913, ibid., no. 35070.

43 FO to the Board of Trade and to the Admiralty, and Mallet to Hopwood, 1 Aug 1913, ibid., nos. 35263 and 35778.

44 FO to the Board of Trade, 12 July 1913, ibid., no. 31596. This was indeed the case, and became a material point in the later negotiations; see p. 91 below.

45 Llewellyn Smith to Mallet, 30 July 1913, FO 371/1761, no. 36361. Concerning these projects, see chapter 4, II above.

46 Correspondence between Mallet and MacLeod, 10 July–16 Aug 1913, FO 371/1761, nos 35263 and 37961. A further approach, in early October, was also rebuffed. See letters from Sir Eyre Crowe (Assistant Under-Secretary of State, FO, 1912–20) to Board of Trade, 13 Oct; Board of Trade to the FO, 16 Oct; and Parker to MacLeod, 17 Oct: ibid., nos. 45716 and 47108.

47 Letter from Llewellyn Smith to FO (secret) 8 Aug 1913, ibid., no. 36771.

48 Here were listed a number of reasons, similar to those given on p. 35 above.

49 Letter from the Admiralty to the FO (secret), 14 Aug 1913, FO 371/1761, no. 37623.

50 Letter from Greenway to Parker, 16 Aug, 1913, ibid., no. 38082.

51 Minute by Parker, 19 Aug 1913, ibid., no. 38541, and *British Documents*, x, part 2, no. 139.

52 Minutes by Parker, 15 and 19 Aug 1913, FO 371/1761, nos. 37623 and 38541.

53 Minute by Parker, 20 Aug 1913, ibid., no. 38738, and *British Documents*, x, part 2, no. 140; letter from Kühlmann to Parker (private), 20 Aug no. 38574 (missing from FO file 371/1761 but located in IO, P & S, 1912, vol. 104).

54 Kühlmann to the German Chancellor, Bethmann-Hollweg, 21 Aug 1913, no. 481, *Die grosse Politik*, XXXVII, no. 14772, and GFM 10/418/63, no. 17168.

55 Letter from Llewellyn Smith to the FO (confidential), 28 Aug 1913, FO 371/1761, no. 39788.

56 Letter from Parker to Babington Smith (private and confidential), 5 Sep 1913, ibid., no. 39788. The fact that in their correspondence the two men addressed each each other by their Christian names indicates a degree of friendship between them not otherwise demonstrated in these difficult negotiations.

57 Minute by Parker, 10 Sep 1913, ibid., no. 41919.

58 Letter from Babington Smith to Parker, 12 Sep 1913, ibid., no. 42363.

59 Correspondence between Babington Smith and Parker, 12 Sep 1913 ibid., nos. 41919 and 41956. Details of the conference are in a memorandum from the Board of Trade to the FO, 23 Oct, ibid., no. 48236. Babington Smith repeated his views to Crowe on 7 Nov (ibid., no. 50638).

60 He did so almost immediately; see letter from Babington Smith to Gwinner, 17 Sep, and reply, 1 Oct 1913, Shell files, MEP 102.

61 *British Documents*, x, part 2, no. 124 (7).

62 Minute by Parker, 10 Sep 1913, and FO's 'Memorandum communicated to Hakki Pasha, September 10, 1913', FO 371/1817, nos. 42886 and 40854.

63 Letter from Greenway to the FO, 2 Sep 1913, no. 40669 (missing from FO file 371/1761), but described in index volume, Ind. 27986).

64 Letter from the FO to Kühlmann (immediate and confidential), 4 Sep 1913, FO 371/1792, no. 40843.

65 IO memorandum by Mr Monteath on 'Mesopotamian Oil Concessions', 19 Sep 1913, IO, P & S, 1912, vol. 105, no. P 3888.

66 Marling to Grey, telegrams 478R, 22 Sep, 485, 26 Sep, and 488R, 29 Sep 1913, FO 371/1761, nos 43612, 43981 and 44152.

67 FO correspondence with the Constantinople Embassy, Board of Trade, and Babington Smith, 10–17 Oct 1913, ibid., nos. 46362, 46363, and 47459.

68 Board of Trade memorandum, 23 Oct 1913, ibid., no. 48236. Babington Smith's suggestion of bringing Deterding to this conference was turned down by the Government.

69 Ibid. There is also considerable correspondence on the subject in FO 371/1826.

70 Minute by Parker, 24 Oct 1913, FO 371/1761, no. 48596.

71 Letter from Kühlmann to Bethman-Hollweg, 24 Oct 1913 no. 589, *Die grosse Politik*, XXXVII, no. 14785.

72 Letter from Gwinner to the German Government, 26 Oct 1913, GFM 10/419/65, no. 21604.

73 Letters from Babington Smith to Crowe, 29 Oct, and to the FO (confidential), 7 Nov 1913, FO 371/1761, nos. 49309 and 50638.

74 Letter from Crowe, FO, to the Board of Trade, 10 Nov 1913, no. 50638 (missing from FO file but located in IO, P & S, 1912, vol. 105, no. P 4714).

75 Ibid., and subsequent correspondence between Llewellyn Smith and Crowe, 11–13 Nov 1913, FO 371/1761, no. 51389.

76 Reported by Crowe to Llewellyn Smith, 13 Nov 1913, ibid., no. 51680.

77 Letter from Crowe to Llewellyn Smith, 13 Nov 1913, ibid., no. 51680, and minute

by Llewellyn Smith, 14 Nov, enclosed in letter from Percy Ashley, Board of Trade, to Parker, 17 Nov, ibid., no. 52280, and confirmed in letter from Stauss to Ashley, Berlin, 20 Nov, ibid., no. 54729.

78 Minute by Ashley, 28 Nov 1913, ibid., no. 54729. The APOC – D'Arcy group representatives were Messrs D'Arcy, Greenway and Wallace, and Sir Hugh Barnes.

79 Minute by Ashley, 1 Dec 1913, ibid., no. 54729.

80 FO minute, 4 Dec 1913, ibid., no. 54909.

81 Minute by G. S. Barnes, Board of Trade, 1 Dec 1913, ibid., no. 54909.

82 Deterding's correspondence with Stauss, Sir Frederick Black, and Llewellyn Smith, 17–18 Nov 1913, Shell files, MEP 20 and 120.

83 Minute by Ashley, 18 Nov 1913, FO 371/1761, no. 54729; letters from Ashley to Parker (very confidential), 18 Nov, and Parker to Ashley (very pressing), 18 Nov, ibid., no. 52517.

84 Letter from Llewellyn Smith to Deterding, 1 Dec 1913, ibid. no. 54729.

85 Letter from Llewellyn Smith to Deterding, 22 Nov 1913, ibid., no. 54729.

86 Letters from Deterding to Llewellyn Smith, 24 Nov and 2 Dec 1913 (confidential), ibid., no. 54729.

87 Letter from Deterding to Llewellyn Smith, 24 Nov 1913, ibid., no. 54729.

88 Minute by Ashley, 28 Nov 1913, ibid., no. 54729.

89 Letter from Llewellyn Smith to Deterding, 1 Dec 1913, ibid., no. 54729.

90 Memorandum by Parker, 28 Nov, 1913 and accompanying minutes, ibid., no. 53892. This opinion of Gulbenkian's role was confirmed by Babington Smith (in his letter to Crowe, 9 Dec, ibid., no. 55551), by Deterding (as reported in minute by Ashley, 12 Dec, ibid., no 57611), and by Gulbenkian (in an interview at the FO on 13 Feb 1914, FO 371/2120, no. 7067).

91 Letter from Crowe to Babington Smith (confidential), 4 Dec 1913, FO 371/1761, no. 53892.

92 Minute by Parker, 1 Dec 1913, ibid., no. 54440.

93 Minute by Parker, on Babington Smith's two letters to Crowe, 9 Dec 1913, ibid., no. 55551.

94 See p. 34 above.

95 Minute by Parker, 10 Dec 1913, FO 371/1761, no. 55859.

96 Private letter from Gulbenkian to Deterding, 24 Oct 1913, Shell files, MEP 120.

97 Letter from Stauss to Greenway, 5 Dec 1913, ibid., no. 57611.

98 Letter from Greenway to Barnes, Board of Trade, 9 Dec 1913 (confidential), FO 371/1761, no. 57611. Greenway also suggested to the Board of Trade that perhaps the British Government itself might take half of the 50 per cent share to be allocated to his group, since the German Government seemed to be taking all or part of the Deutsche Bank's share, but this suggestion received no further consideration.

99 Minute by Ashley, 12 Dec 1913, ibid., no. 57611.

100 Details in despatch from Sir William Goschen, HM Ambassador, Berlin, to the FO, despatch 453, ibid., no. 56358; and letter from Lord Cowdray to Grey, 10 Dec 1913, ibid., no. 55846. Llewellyn Smith's tentative proposal for solving the problem of the chairmanship – the formation of a small, extra, neutral group, to hold the balance of shares and guarantee to support the commercial development of the oilfields – was considered by Stauss to be interesting but unnecessary. See letters from Llewellyn Smith to Stauss, 5 Dec, and Stauss to Llewellyn Smith, 6 Dec, ibid., no. 57611.

101 According to Dr Lawrence Lockhart, Deterding and Greenway met on 13 December and Greenway recorded that 'Deterding seemed to appreciate the strength of the D'Arcy Group's position'. There is, however, no record of this meeting in the FO or Shell archives.

102 Letter from the Board of Trade to the FO (confidential), FO 371/1761, no. 57611.

103 Correspondence between Mallet and Grey, 8–17 Jan 1914, 19 Dec 1913, FO

371/2120, nos 1067, 1870, 2096 and 5513, letter from Greenway to Grey, 13 Jan ibid., no. 1870; telegram from the German Ambassador, Constantinople, to the German Government, 30 Jan, GFM 10/419/70, no. 1878.

104 Letter from Crowe to Babington Smith (confidential), 14 Jan, and reply, 27 Jan 1914, 371/2120, nos. 2221 and 4004.

105 Letter from W. Langley, (Assistant Under-Secretary of State, FO, 1907–18) to Greenway (confidential), 16 Jan 1914, ibid., no. 2221.

106 Minute by Nicolson (confidential), 23 Jan, and letter from Greenway to the FO, 23 Jan 1914, ibid., nos. 3468 and 3288.

107 Letter from the Admiralty to the FO (confidential and immediate), 16 Jan 1914, ibid., no. 2362.

108 Mallet to Grey, telegram 61R, 26 Jan, and minute by Parker, 27 Jan 1914, ibid., nos. 3778 and 3952. Deterding, also, was worried at the delay; see letter from Deterding to Babington Smith, 3 Feb, Shell files, MEP 20.

109 Letter from Greenway, APOC, to the FO (private and confidential), 30 Jan 1914, FO 371/2120, no. 4452.

110 Minute by Parker, 2 Feb, on Greenway's letter to the FO, 30 Jan 1914, ibid., no. 4452.

111 Mallet to Grey, despatch 34 (confidential), 21 Jan 1914, FO 371/2127, no. 3544.

112 Minute by Parker, 27 Jan 1914, FO 371/2120, no. 3952.

113 'Mesopotamian Oil', Board of Trade minute by Ashley, 13 Feb 1914, ibid., no. 7067.

114 Board of Trade minute, recording conversation between Stauss and Ashley, 14 Feb 1914, ibid., no. 7068.

115 See pp. 81–2 above.

116 Letters from Parker to Ashley: 2 Mar 1914, FO 371/2120, no. 9311; and 5 Mar, (urgent and confidential), enclosing note from Gulbenkian to Parker, 5 Mar, ibid., no. 9869.

117 Crowe, however, was tempted by the suggestion, as a way of saving the APOC some capital, but it was quashed by the Board of Trade.

118 Letter from the National Bank of Turkey to the Anglo-Saxon Petroleum Company, 18 Feb and reply, 2 Mar, 1914, Shell files, MEP 120.

119 Note from Gulbenkian to Parker, 5 Mar 1914, FO 371/2120, no. 9869.

120 Letter from Ashley to Parker, 6 Mar 1915, ibid., no. 10010.

121 Letter from Langley, FO, to Babington Smith, 6 Mar 1914, ibid., no. 10010.

122 Letters from the APOC to the FO, 10 and 11 Mar, 1914, ibid., nos. 10880 and 10920; Mallet to Grey, telegram 157, 11 Mar, ibid., no. 10926, and FO 195/2456, file 64. The *Frankfurter Zeitung* of 5 Mar reported that Ghazi Mukhtar Pasha (father of the Turkish Ambassador at Berlin, and formerly Turkish Grand Vizir) headed the company. The APOC quoted Stock's opinion that the group wished to obtain the concession merely to resell it either to the Deutsche Bank or to the proposed re-formed TPC. Stock also reported that Huguenin and Whittall were said to be interested in the group and that the Young Turks, particularly Halil Bey and Djemal Pasha, strongly supported it.

123 It also included two other London companies – A. Hirsch and Co., and S. Pearson and Son Ltd. See Mallet to Grey, telegram 155R and despatch 156, 10 Mar 1914, FO 371/2120, nos. 10784 and 11485; and L. Reyersbach (director, Central Mining and Investment Corporation) to Crowe, 4 May, ibid., no. 19856. Hirsch had long maintained an interest in the Mesopotamian oil and railway competition: as early as Aug 1909 the firm was keeping the German group informed about Glasgow's group (see 'Cospoli' correspondence, nos 3 and 4).

124 Grey to Mallet, telegram 133R, 11 Mar 1914, FO 371/2120, no. 10926.

125 Note from Parker to Hakki Pasha, 12 Mar 1914, ibid., no. 10926.

126 Mallet to Grey, telegrams 159R, 11 Mar, and 165, 12 Mar 1914, ibid., nos. 10928 and 11107 and FO 195/2546. file 64.

127 Grey to Goschen, telegram 69R, 11 Mar 1914, FO 371/2120, no. 11062; note from Goschen to the German Government, 12 Mar, GFM 10/419/71, no. A 50178.

128 Goschen to Grey, telegrams 33R (confidential), 12 Mar, and 34R, 13 Mar 1914, FO 371/2120, nos. 11112 and 11267; and telegram from the German Ambassador, Constantinople, to the German Government, 11 Mar, GFM 10/419/71, no. 4964.

129 Minute by Parker, 14 Mar 1914, FO 371/2120, no. 11267; Grey to Goschen, telegram 75R, 14 Mar, and reply, telegram 35R, 15 Mar, ibid., nos. 11267 and 11459; German Ambassador, London, to the German Government, 14 March, GFM 10/419/71, no. 5109.

130 Minute by Parker (secret), 13 Mar 1914, FO 371/2120, no. 11273.

131 FO minutes, ibid., no. 11273.

132 See pp. 68 and 78 above.

133 Letter from Babington Smith to Gulbenkian, 12 Mar 1914, Shell files, MEP 20 and 120.

134 Telegram from Crowe to Babington Smith, 14 Mar, and letters from Babington Smith to the FO, 16 Mar, and the FO to Babington Smith, 18 Mar 1914, FO 371/2120, nos 11675 and 11676. See also GFM 10/420/72, no. 5502.

135 Gulbenkian's claim, in his memoirs (see Hewins, *Mr Five per cent*, pp. 80–2, and C. W. Hamilton, *Americans and Oil in the Middle East* p. 88), that he daily urged Deterding to settle with the APOC on an equitable basis, generously offering to sacrifice two-thirds of his holding, appears to apply only to the end of the negotiations. Although he was probably (and indeed generously) ready to make the sacrifice if eventually absolutely necessary (as shown by Hakki Pasha's and Babington Smith's confidential comments: see p. 81 above), he did hold out against the Government as long as possible, and agreed only when it seemed that he and his colleagues might be completely excluded from the concession.

136 Letters from Gulbenkian to Deterding (strictly private), 2 Mar, Deterding to S. Samuel, 10 Mar (not sent), Gulbenkian to Deterding, 14 Mar, and to Babington Smith, 15 Mar, and Babington Smith to Deterding, 17 Mar 1914, Shell files, MEP 20 and 120.

137 Memorandum by Ashley, 17 Mar 1914, FO 371/2124, no. 11963; telegram from Gwinner to Babington Smith, 14 Mar, Shell files MEP 20 and 120.

138 Two letters from Deterding to Churchill, 17 Mar 1914, ibid.

139 Letter from Waley Cohen to Deterding (strictly private), 18 Mar 1914, ibid.

140 Letter from Deterding to Churchill, 20 Mar 1914, ibid. Britain received this service during the war (see below, chapter 7), and Deterding subsequently received a knighthood for it; see FO 372/1509, no. T5765, May 1920, for correspondence on this point).

141 FO 371/2120, no. 12324. Although the agreement has been printed many times, for ease of reference it has been included below as Appendix III.

142 To say, as Gulbenkian did in his memoirs (see Hewins, *Mr Five per cent.*, p. 84), that he was 'stupefied' at discovering the role to which the FO Agreement limited him shows a faulty memory on this point. He may well have been upset, earlier, on realising he must reduce his participation, but he did in fact offer to do this, and his shares did not carry any voting rights anyway. See pp. 82 and 91 above.

143 Dr F. C. Gerretson's statement, in his official *History of the Royal Dutch*, 2nd ed., IV, p. 287, that the FO Agreement was a 'painful surprise' to the Royal Dutch Petroleum Company and that the British claimed (only) 25 per cent in the TPC – 'on the ground of the Turco-Persian Frontier Treaty' – is incorrect in every respect

CHAPTER 6

1 Correspondence of Babington Smith and Greenway with the FO, and between the FO with Constantinople of 20–27 Mar 1914, FO 371/2120, nos 12617, 12973 13538 and 13733. Günther was joint director-general of the Anatolian Railway Company.

2 Admiralty – Board of Trade correspondence, 20 May–8 June 1914, FO 371/2121, nos 22640 and 25842. Letter from the Deutsche Bank to the German Government, 20 May, GFM 10/420/75, no. 10051.

3 Reported in FO minute on Admiralty letter to the FO, 6 May 1914, FO 371/2121, no. 20259.

4 See above pp. 82, 83, 85, 87 and 93 above. Documentary material on the subject from 20 Mar to late June may be found in FO 371/2120, nos 12324, 15496 and 16749.

5 Letters from Greenway to the FO, 23 Apr 1914, ibid., no. 17856; Lichnowsky to Grey, 25 Apr, and Crowe, to the Board of Trade and to Greenway, 30 Apr, ibid., no. 18659; Greenway to the FO, 1 May, ibid., no. 19492; and Board of Trade to the FO, 6 May, FO 371/2121, no. 20355. See also correspondence between the Deutsche Bank, German Government and the German Embassy, London, 20–27 Apr, GFM 10/420/74, nos. 7729, 8061 and 8188, and *Die grosse Politik*, XXXVII, no. 14878.

6 Letter from the Deutsche Bank to the German Foreign Ministry, Berlin, 20 May 1914, *Die grosse Politik*, XXXVII, no. 14888.

7 Letter from Parker to Black, Admiralty, 20 July 1914, FO 371/2121, no. 20355.

8 The relevant correspondence is in FO 371/2120, nos 17742, 18773, 18950, 19492 and 20175, and FO 371/2121, nos 26445, 31791 and 20259 (minute by Parker, 8 May). See also letter from Hopwood to Grey, 19 May 1914, Grey MSS., FO 800/87, 'Admiralty, 1910–1914'.

9 Letter from the Admiralty to the FO, 6 May 1914, FO 371/2121, no. 20259.

10 FO minutes on Admiralty's letter of 6 May, and letters from Parker to Black (urgent and confidential), 8 May, and from Crowe to the Admiralty, 13 May 1914, ibid., no. 20259. It appears from the IO's minutes that that department had no objection to the Admiralty's proposals; see IO, P & S, 1912, vol. 106, no. P 1771.

11 See pp. 35, 38–9 above.

12 Letters from G. S. Barnes, Board of Trade, to Crowe, 14 May, and Parker to Ashley (Board of Trade), 15 May 1914, FO 371/2121, no. 21617; memorandum by Ashley, 14 May (sent privately to the FO, 20 May), ibid., no. 22742; letter from the Board of Trade to the FO (secret), 20 May, ibid., no. 22639.

13 Letters from the FO to the Board of Trade, 23 May, from the Treasury to the Admiralty, 10 June, and from the Admiralty to the FO, 11 June 1914, ibid., nos 22639, 26226 and 26365.

14 Letter from the Board of Trade to the FO, 25 June, and from the FO to the Admiralty, 26 June 1914, ibid., no. 28711.

15 My italics.

16 Letters from Greenway to the Admiralty, 10 July, and from the Admiralty to the FO, 15 July 1914, FO 371/2121, no. 32209.

17 Sir John Bradbury, Treasury, to the *ex-officio* directors of the APOC, and to the Admiralty, 22 July 1914, ibid., no. 33561. This was, in fact, a second 'Treasury letter', the first having been sent on 20 May, the day the British Government–Anglo-Persian Oil Company agreement was signed; it defined the interests of the Government's two *ex-officio* directors on the company's Board in similar terms. See Adm. 116/1687D; also, p. 49 above.

18 Letter from the APOC to the Admiralty and FO, 16 June 1914, enclosing memorandum of the conference, and memorandum and articles of association of the Stanmore Investment Company Ltd, FO 371/2121, no. 27229.

19 Letter from the FO to the Board of Trade, 23 July 1914, describing discussion with Vice-Admiral Sir Edmond Slade, 22 July, ibid., no. 33485. It was Slade who, in Oct 1913–Jan 1914, had led the Admiralty commission to examine the Persian oilfields.

20 Letter from Babington Smith to the FO, 18 July 1914, ibid., no. 32914.

21 Letters from the FO to Greenway and to the Treasury (pressing), 21 July, Nichols for Greenway to the FO (pressing), 24 July, and Crowe to Babington Smith (urgent), 27 July 1914, ibid., nos 32914 and 33641.

22 Letter from Lord Inchcape to Crowe, 8 Sep 1914, ibid., no. 47848.

23 Letter from Crowe to Inchcape, 22 Sep 1914, ibid., no. 47848.

24 Minute by Hirtzel on FO documents, no. 62196, IO, P & S, 1912, vol. 106, no. P 4245.

25 Letter from Babington Smith to the FO, 21 Oct 1914, and FO to Greenway, FO 371/2121, no. 62196.

26 Letters from Greenway to the FO, 2 and 11 Nov 1914, ibid., nos 66612 and 70310.

27 See p. 109 below.

28 Letters from the Admiralty to the FO, 19 Nov, Board of Trade to the FO, 20 Nov, and FO minute, 23 Nov 1914, FO 371/2121, nos 73320 and 74291.

29 Telegrams between Grey and Mallet, 19–25 Mar 1914, FO 371/2120, nos 12324, 12926 and 13294; telegram from the German Ambassador (Baron von Wangenheim), Constantinople, to the German Government, 27 Mar, GFM 10/420/72, no. 5846.

30 Letter from Greenway to Parker, 30 Mar 1914, enclosing draft contract; Grey to Mallet, telegram 173, 30 Mar, FO 371/2120, no. 14157.

31 Telegram from Greenway to Parker, 31 Mar, ibid., no. 14157, and letter to the FO, enclosing revised draft contract, 7 Apr 1914, ibid., no. 15558. Later, however, the advantages that would result if such a joint venture were prohibited became apparent to the D'Arcy group: Stock wrote to Mallet on 1 July pressing that applications for *permis de recherche* in the Basra area should be only in the D'Arcy group's name, so as to avoid Shell and German participation (FO 195/2456, file 64).

32 Letter from Greenway to Deterding, 26 Mar 1914, Shell files, MEP 120.

33 Minute by Weakley, Constantinople, on the draft contract, FO 195/2456, file 64.

34 This view was repeated by the Grand Vizir to Mallet and by Mallet to Wagenheim, 31 Mar 1914. Reported in Mallet to Grey, telegram 203, 31 Mar, FO 371/2120, no. 14293.

35 Letter from the Deutsche Bank to the German Government, 20 Apr 1914, GFM 10/420/74, no. 7793.

36 Mallet to Grey, telegram 203, 31 Mar 1914, FO 371/2120, no. 14293.

37 Telegrams between Mallet and Grey, 17–24 Apr 1914: ibid., nos 16914, 17090, 17675 and 18024; telegram from the German Ambassador to the German Government, 20 Apr, GFM 10/420/74, no. 7680.

38 Minute by Parker on Mallet's telegram, 31 Mar 1914, FO 371/2120, no. 14293; Grey to Mallet, telegram 202R, 20 Apr, ibid., no. 16914.

39 Letter from Greenway to the FO, 23 Apr 1914, reporting interview (22 Apr) with Stauss, ibid., no. 17857.

40 Grey to Mallet, telegram 209R, 23 Apr 1914, ibid., no. 17857.

41 Minute by George (later Sir George) Clerk (then Senior Clerk, FO), 23 Apr 1914, ibid., no. 17857.

42 Mallet to Grey, telegram 257, 24 Apr, ibid., no. 18024.

43 Grey to Mallet, telegram 212, 25 Apr, ibid., no. 18024, and telegram 258R, 10 June 1914, FO 371/2121, no. 25738.

44 Mallet to Grey, telegram 277, 5 May 1914, ibid., no. 20048. This plan also had the advantage of avoiding the land tax payable under the mining law, which was assessed on the area of the concession.

45 Mallet to Grey, telegram 290R, 18 May 1914, ibid., no. 22310; letter from Stock to Mallet, 13 May, FO 195/2456, file 64.

46 Mallet to Grey, telegram 328R, 9 June 1914, FO 371/2121, no. 25924.

47 Mallet to Grey, despatch 379, 27 May 1914, ibid., no. 24363.

48 Mallet to Grey, telegrams 255 and 257, 22 and 24 Apr 1914, FO 371/2120, nos 17675 and 18024; Mallet to Grey, despatch 379, 27 May, FO 371/2121, no. 24363.

49 Correspondence between the FO and Silley and his solicitors, 28 Aug–9 Sep 1913,

FO 371/1844, nos 40363 and 40830. All subsequent correspondence is in FO 371/2115, file 188.

50 This is evident from the correspondence as a whole, and is explicitly stated in a minute by Parker, 2 July 1914, FO 371/2115, no. 29859.

51 Mallet to Grey, telegrams 395R, 401 and 430, 30 June, 2 and 14 July 1914, FO 371/2121, nos 29575, 29930 and 31998.

52 Mallet to Grey, despatch 354, 20 May 1914, FO 371/2115, no. 23204.

53 On de Ward's antecedents, see FO 371/1487, no. 44663, and FO 371/1760, no. 17970. For subsequent correspondence, see FO 371/2120, nos 16102, 16139, 19856, 21386, 22542, 23386, 25938 and 29575 and FO 195/2456, file 64.

54 Minute by H. H. D. Beaumont (Counsellor to the Constantinople Embassy), 1 June 1914, on letter from the Central Mining and Investment Corporation to the FO, 19 May (FO 371/2121, no. 22542), FO 195/2456, file 64.

55 On the advisory status and non-binding character of the Council's pronouncement, the FO was guided by the legal opinions of its Assistant Legal Advisers, Ryan in Constantinople and Hurst in London, 11 and 16 July 1914, FO 371/2115, nos 29859 and 32183.

56 Memorandum by Weakley, no date, enclosed in Mallet to Grey, despatch 379, FO 371/2121, no. 24363; Mallet to Grey, telegram 323R, 8 June 1914, ibid., no. 25738.

57 Grey to Mallet, telegram 258R, 10 June 1914, ibid., no. 25738; German Ambassador, London, to the German Government, GFM 10/420/76, no. 11687.

58 Mallet to Grey, telegram 334, 11 June, and Grey to Mallet, telegram 262R, 12 June 1914, FO 371/2121, no. 26369.

59 Mallet to Grey, telegrams 347R and 352, 16 and 18 June, and Grey to Mallet, telegram 269R, 18 June 1914, ibid., nos 27143 and 27628.

60 Hurewitz, *Diplomacy in the Near and Middle East*, I, document 114 gives an English translation of the Grand Vizir's subsequent note of 28 June, in which he referred to the date of the ambassadors' ultimata as 19 June. According to the French original in the FO files, however, the ultimata were dated 18 June. Mallet's telegram of 18 June is not explicit about which day the ultimata were sent, but 18 June seems probable.

61 Mallet to Grey, telegrams 380 and 382, 24 and 25 June 1914, FO 371/2126, nos 28703 and 28705; *British Documents*, x, part 2, nos 253 and 255; German Ambassador, Constantinople, to the German Government, 25 June, GFM 10/420/77, no. 12577; Mallet to Grey, telegram 393R 30 June, FO 371/2121, no. 29578.

62 Mallet to Grey, despatch 472, 1 July 1914, enclosing note from Grand Vizir, 28 June, ibid., no. 30306; Hurewitz, *Diplomacy in the Near and Middle East*, I, document 114 (English translation).

63 Minute by Crowe, 1 July 1914, on Mallet to Grey, telegram 393R, FO 371/2121, no. 29578.

64 Grey to Mallet, telegram 292R, 2 July 1914, ibid., no. 29578; Mallet to Grey, telegram 412, 6 July, ibid., no. 30629.

65 Treherne, Higgins and Co. to the FO, 28 July 1914, FO 371/2115, no. 34530.

66 Mallet to Grey, telegram 405R, 3 July 1914, FO 371/2121, no. 30089.

67 Letter from Mallet to the Grand Vizir, 4 July 1914, ibid., no. 30615.

68 Grey to Mallet, telegram 298, 7 July 1914, ibid., no. 30629.

69 Letter from Hakki Pasha to Parker, 9 July, and Crowe to Greenway (pressing), 10 July 1914, ibid., no. 31135.

70 Mallet to Grey, telegrams 424 and 427R, 10 July 1914, ibid., nos 31307 and 31322.

71 Letter from Greenway to the FO 10 July 1914, ibid., no. 31453.

72 Grey to Mallet, telegrams 292R, 297R and 307R, 2, 7 and 13 July 1914, ibid., nos 29578, 30089 and 31307.

73 Details of these negotiations are to be found in the Shell files, MEP 120. In particular, see Nichols's notes of a meeting with Parker and Hakki Pasha at the FO on 1 July.

74 Letter from Greenway to Parker, 27 Mar 1914, FO 371/2120, no. 13736.

75 Letter from Greenway to the FO, 10 July 1914, ibid., no. 31453.

76 Shell files, MEP 120.

77 Mallet to Grey, telegram 405R, 3 July and Grey to Mallet, telegram 297R, 7 July 1914, FO 371/2121, no. 30089.

78 Beaumont to Grey, telegrams 437R and 444R, 16 and 21 July 1914, ibid., nos 32277 and 33150.

79 Grey to Beaumont, telegram 319R, 22 July 1914, ibid., no. 33150.

80 Beaumont to Grey, telegrams 451R and 462, 24 and 31 July 1914, ibid., nos 33511 and 35007.

81 See pp. 102–3 above.

82 See p. 103 above, and letter from the IO to the FO, 19 Jan 1915, FO 371/2475, no. 7504. IO departmental minutes are in IO P & S, 1912, vol. 106, nos P 186/15, P 3552/15, and P 3980/15.

83 Correspondence between Greenway, the FO, the Board of Trade, the Admiralty and the Treasury, 9–25 Jan 1915, FO 371/2475, nos 3884, 6532 and 9762.

84 Herbert W. Malkin (later Sir Herbert Malkin, KC) was the FO's Assistant Legal Adviser from 1914 to 1929. In 1929 he became Legal Adviser.

85 Minute by Malkin, 14 Sept 1915, FO 371/2475, no. 123844.

86 Interdepartmental correspondence, 27 Sep–16 Nov 1915, ibid., nos 123844, 145709, 147676, 154618, 155286 and 172576.

87 De Bunsen, FO, to the chairman of the APOC, 23 Nov 1915, acknowledged 'with satisfaction' by Greenway, 1 Dec, ibid., no. 172576.

CHAPTER 7

1 Two letters from Samuel to Hopwood, 29 May, Cab. 37/120, and one to the *Daily Telegraph*, 9 June 1914.

2 See Jack (Kent), in *Past and Present*, 39, pp. 162–4 and note 79; also, private letter from Hardinge to Holderness, 20 July, 1914, Hardinge MSS. vol 120, part II, no. 360.

3 Cd 7628 (Misc. no. 13, 1914), *Events leading to the Rupture of Relations with Turkey*.

4 Asquith MSS., 124/117–20, and 128/50–60. See also Brig.-Gen. F. J. Moberly's official history of *The Campaign in Mesopotamia 1914–1918*, I, pp. 78–133. The excellence and accuracy of this history can be verified and additional information obtained by referring to the original documents included in the Asquith MSS. See especially the 'Précis of Correspondence regarding the Mesopotamian Expedition – Its Genesis and Development', I, prepared in the Military Department of the IO (no date), and 'Brief for the defence of the Mesopotamian Campaign', amended copy (July 1916). See also Cd. 8074, *Despatches regarding Operations in the Persian Gulf and Mesopotamia*; A. T. Wilson, *Loyalties: Mesopotamia 1914–1917*, *passim;* and Philip Graves, *The Life of Sir Percy Cox*, pp. 175ff.

5 Private letter from Hardinge to Nicolson, Simla, 8 Oct 1914, Nicolson MSS., 1914, IV, FO 800/375.

6 Private letters from Hardinge to Sir Valentine Chirol, 2 and 10 Dec 1914, and to Nicolson, 6 Jan and 4 Feb 1915, Hardinge MSS., vol. 93, part II, nos 263, 266 and 290, and Nicolson MSS., 1915, I, FO 800/377.

7 See for example, Secretary of State for India to Viceroy, telegram 1728, 20 Mar 1915, and letter from the Admiralty to the IO, 20 Apr 1915, 'Precis of Correspondence regarding the Mesopotamian Expedition' III, Asquith MSS. 120/8 and 125/30; Moberly, *The Campaign in Mesopotamia*, I, p. 222, and II, p. 153; and *The History of the Ministry of Munitions*, VII, chapter 10, p. 136.

8 Moberly, *The Campaign in Mesopotamia*, III, p. 23.

9 Private letter from Hardinge to Chirol, 21 Apr 1915, Hardinge MSS. vol. 93, part II, no. 325. Repeated in more formal phraseology in a private letter to Nicolson, 26 Apr, ibid., vol. 93, part II, no. 327.

10 Moberly, *The Campaign in Mesopotamia*, I, p. 303; letters from Hardinge to HM the King-Emperor, 14 Aug and 8 Oct 1915, and to Lord Stamfordham, Hardinge MSS, vol 105, part II, nos 111, 114, 115.

11 See, for example, with regard to the meetings of the Dardanelles Committee, 14 and 21 Oct 1915, Cab. 42/4/9 and 15, and Moberly, *The Campaign in Mesopotamia*, II pp. 18–19, 22–4, 28–9.

12 Minutes of War Council meeting, 10 Mar 1915, Cab. 42/2/5.

13 'The War. Alexandretta and Mesopotamia' (secret), 17 Mar 1915, Committee of Imperial Defence (CID) paper no. G13, Cab. 24/1.

14 'Remarks on the Importance of Alexandretta as a Future Base' (secret), 15 Mar 1915, by Jackson, CID paper no. G15, Cab. 24/1; 'The War: Alexandretta and Mesopotamia' (secret), 16 Mar 1915, by Kitchener, CID paper no. G12, Cab. 24/1. An article by Yukka Nevakivi ('Lord Kitchener and the Partition of the Ottoman Empire 1915–1916', in *Studies in International History*) examines some aspects of the question, as does the same author's *Britain, France, and the Arab Middle East*.

15 Meetings of the War Committee, 15 and 19 Nov 1915, Cab. 42/5/12 and 16.

16 Minutes of the War Council, 19 Mar 1915, Cab. 42/2/14.

17 'Note', 14 Mar 1915, included in 'Notes and Private Telegram from the Viceroy concerning the Future Settlement of Eastern Turkey in Asia and Arabia' (secret), CID paper no. G16, Cab. 24/1, and Nicolson MSS., 1915, I, FO 800/377. See also map no. 2, Appendix IX below.

18. See pp. 121–2 below.

19 War Council meeting, 19 Mar, 'Note by General Sir Edmund Barrow on the Defence of Mesopotamia', and private (most secret) telegram from the Viceroy to the Secretary of State for India, 15 Mar 1915, included in CID paper no. G16, Cab. 24/1; private letter from Hardinge to Nicolson, 26 Apr, Nicolson MSS., 1915, I, FO 800/377.

20 CID paper no. 220–B, Cab. 4/6/1 (or Cab. 42/3/12). See also Nevakivi, *Britain, France and the Arab Middle East*, pp. 18–24, and my 1914–16 chapter in Hinsley, *British Foreign Policy under Sir Edward Grey*. De Bunsen was formerly HM Ambassador at Madrid, from 1906–13, and at Vienna, from 1913–14.

21 See map no. 2, Appendix IX below.

22 'Evidence of Lt.-Col. Sir Mark Sykes, Bart, MP, on the Arab Question,' CID paper no. G46, Cab. 42/6/10. Sykes was attached to the Directorate of Military Operations, advising on Arab matters, and was in the British delegation to the Peace Conference. Detail on the Sykes–Picot Agreement is in my 1914–16 chapter in Hinsley, *British Foreign Policy under Sir Edward Grey*. See also above, chapter 3, note 20.

23 Secret memorandum for the War Department, received at the FO on 5 Jan 1916, FO 371/2767, no. 2522.

24 The original version of the 'Arab proposals' is in FO 371/2767, no. 14106, together with minutes of a meeting of the War Council; the (slightly) amended version is in ibid., no. 25379, attached to an explanatory note by Nicolson, 2 Feb 1916. See also letter from Sykes to the FO, 16 Jan, ibid., no. 11844. A useful article on this subject is Elie Kedourie's 'Cairo and Khartoum on the Arab Question, 1915–18', in *The Historical Journal*, VII, 2, pp. 280–97. See also map no. 2, Appendix IX below.

25 Macdonogh to Nicolson, 6 Jan 1916, FO 371/2767, no. 3851. See also Elie Kedourie, *England and the Middle East*, p. 34, quoting Balfour's memorandum of 9 Sep 1919 (included in *Documents on British Foreign Policy*, series 1, IV, p. 374).

26 Memorandum by Capt W. R. Hall, 12 Jan 1916, FO 371/2767, no. 8116. Director of the Intelligence Division at the Admiralty from 1914–18, he became by 1919 Rear-Admiral Sir William Reginald Hall MP.

27 Letter from Fisher to Asquith, 5 Nov 1915, Asquith MSS. 15/124.

28 Note by Hirtzel to the FO, 10 Jan, enclosing letter from Sir Thomas Holderness to Nicolson, 13 Jan 1916, FO 371/2767, no. 8117.

29 Private letter from Nicolson to Hardinge, 26 Jan 1916, Nicolson MSS., 1916. I, FO 800/381. See also his letter of 16 Feb 1916, FO 371/2767, no. 8117.

30 Letter from Grey to Cambon, French Ambassador in London (secret), 15 May 1916, *Documents on British Foreign Policy*, series 1, IV, p. 245.

31 Note from Nicolson to Grey, 16 Feb 1916, and FO to Sir George Buchanan (HM Ambassador to Russia), 23 Feb 1916, FO 371/2767, no. 35529.

32 Note on the Arab question (secret), by Sir Maurice Hankey, Secretary to the CID and to the Cabinet, 20 Mar 1916, Cab. 42/11, and telegrams between Buchanan and the FO, 11–13 Mar 1916, FO 371/2767, nos 47088, 47950 and 48551.

33 FO minutes, ibid., no. 47088.

34 Buchanan to the FO, telegram 370, 15 Mar 1916, ibid., no. 50225; minutes of War Committee meeting, 23 Mar, Cab. 42/11/9.

35 *Documents on British Foreign Policy*, series 1, IV, pp. 244–5.

36 Letter from Hirtzel to the FO (immediate), 1 Apr, and notes to Oliphant, 20 Apr, and to Clerk, 14 May 1916, FO 371/2768, no. 62655.

37 Cab. 42/16.

38 'The War with Turkey', IO Political Department memorandum, 25 May 1916, Cab. 42/16; and 'Germany, Turkey, England and Arabia', 31 Oct 1916, Asquith MSS., 130/223–8. The works Hirtzel discussed were Dr Rohrbach's article in *Deutsche Politik*, 11 Feb 1916; Professor H. Delbrück's article in *Preussische Jahrbücher*, May 1916; an article by Professor Gerhard Schott of Hamburg, 'The Persian Gulf and the Commercial Policy of the Central Powers'; and Dr Franz Stuhlmann's recently published work, *The Fight for Arabia between Turkey and England*. Holderness did not however, agree with all Hirtzel's conclusions; see 'The War with Turkey. Note by the Under-Secretary of State, India Office', 13 June 1916, Cab. 42/16.

39 Letter from Greenway to the FO, 3 Apr 1916, FO 371/2721, no. 63619. He cited an article on 'The Presence of Petroleum on the Turkish–Persian Border' (which had appeared in Germany's main petroleum journal, *Petroleum*), and one by Otto Debtin on 'Germany and the Oil Deposits of Mesopotamia' (which had appeared in the *Frankfurter Zeitung*). See also 'Economic and Political Review of Turkey', memorandum by the General Staff, War Office 24 Oct 1917, Milner MSS., 108/132–7. For a useful account of the German Government's economic interest in the Ottoman Empire during the First World War, see U. Trumpener, *Germany and the Ottoman Empire 1914–1918*, chapters 10 and 12.

40 'The Political Position in the Persian Gulf at the End of the War', memorandum by Vice-Admiral Sir Edmond Slade, 31 Oct 1916, Cabinet paper G 118, Cab. 24/3.

41 Admiralty memorandum no. GT 5267, Cab. 21/119. There is a file of Government correspondence attached, and it is from this that the present discussion is drawn.

42 Note to the Imperial War Cabinet by Admiral R. E. Wemyss, 30 July 1918; letters from Hankey to Sir Eric Geddes (then First Lord of the Admiralty), 30 July, to Lloyd George (very secret, important), 1 Aug, to Balfour (secret), 1 Aug, and additional correspondence, Cab. 21/119.

43 'Notes by Chief of the Air Staff on Admiralty Memorandum GT 5267', GT 5376 (secret), 9 Oct 1918, Cab. 21/119.

44 Letter from Hankey to Balfour (personal and secret), 12 Aug 1918, Cab. 21/119.

45 'A Note in Reference to Admiralty Memorandum GT 5267', memorandum to the War Cabinet by the First Lord of the Admiralty, (secret), GT 5710, 17 Sep 1918, Cab. 21/119.

46 Cab. 23/7.

47 Minutes of the Eastern Committee of the War Cabinet, Milner MSS., vol. 119. See especially minutes of the meetings of 11 and 18 July, and 27 Nov 1918.

48 See map no. 2, Appendix IX below.

49 Not the Autumn, as is stated in the *History of the Ministry of Munitions*, VII, p. 136.

50 The Admiralty's alternative suggestion, that the company should erect additional tank storage in Borneo, was unrealistic in view of the great quantity of oil involved and the great loss in sales from an accumulation of oil products that could not be transported to their markets. Understandably, the proposal was turned down.

For details of Shell's general (difficult) relations with the Admiralty at this time, see Henriques, *Waley Cohen*, chapter 11, especially pp. 207–13.

51 Letter from the Admiralty to the IO, FO, Board of Trade, and Treasury, 28 July 1915, FO 371/2426, no. 103311; letters from the FO to the Admiralty, 6 Aug, from the IO to the FO, 18 Aug and 23 Sept, from the IO to the Admiralty (confidential), 18 Sep, and from the FO to the Admiralty, 14 Dec, ibid., nos 103311, 115230, 137673 and 185185.

52 Henriques, *Marcus Samuel*, pp. 390–1, 483–6 and 533–4. Until 1907 Shell was still an independent, purely British company.

53 Borneo crude oil was to be refined at the Shell group's Egyptian refinery. See letter from the Admiralty to the FO (confidential), 4 Dec 1915, enclosing letter from the Admiralty to the Ministry of Munitions (confidential and urgent), 1 Dec, FO 371/2426, no. 185185.

54 Conferences: 4 Jan 1916 at the Board of Trade, the FO, Admiralty and Greenway participating; 20 Jan 1916 at the FO, Parker, Marcus Samuel and Waley Cohen participating. See FO 382/1096, nos 4767 and 13409.

55 'Proposed All-British Oil Company. Memorandum Communicated by Mr. Greenway, 6 Jan 1916. "Nature of Suggested Support"' ibid., no. 4046. See also 'Memorandum on Course of Prices of Motor Spirit on the United Kingdom during the Last Seven Years', sent by Greenway to Parker, 7 Jan, and minute by Barnes, Board of Trade, 7 Feb 1916, ibid., nos 4767 and 26185.

56 Letter from Waley Cohen to Parker (private), and reply, 21 Jan 1916, ibid., no. 13409.

57 Letter from Greenway to the FO (confidential), 24 Feb 1916, FO 371/2721, no. 36846.

58 Letters from the FO to the IO, Admiralty., Board of Trade, and Treasury, 2 Mar 1916, ibid., no. 36846.

59 He was referring here to the Asiatic Petroleum Company's marketing agreements with the two companies. The agreement with the Burmah Oil Company chiefly concerned the quantity and price of kerosene for the Indian market. The ten-year agreement with the Anglo-Persian was made in 1912 and concerned crude oil. See also Gerretson, *History of the Royal Dutch*, III, pp. 211–16, and IV, p. 185.

60 Minute from Parker for O'Beirne, War Department, 17 Mar 1916, FO 371/2721, no. 53167.

61 Letter from Llewellyn Smith, Board of Trade, to the FO, 5 Apr 1916, enclosing confidential memorandum of a conference held with Admiralty (including Slade) and IO representatives, ibid., no. 49379; and letter from the Admiralty to the FO, 15 Apr, ibid., no. 72085. See also departmental minutes on these letters, and private letter from Crowe to Barnes, 9 Mar, ibid., no. 36846.

62 Letter from Hirtzel, IO, to the FO (immediate), 11 Mar 1916, ibid., no. 47758.

63 See pp. 125–6 above.

64 De Bunsen, FO, to the Board of Trade, 14 Apr, and to the Admiralty, Treasury and IO, 17 May 1916, FO 371/2721, nos 65047 and 86698.

65 H. Fountain, Board of Trade, to the FO, 6 May 1916, ibid., no. 86698.

66 Letter from the FO to the APOC, 17 May 1916, ibid., no. 86698.

67 Letters from Greenway to the FO, 22 May, and from de Bunsen, FO, to Greenway, 6 June 1916, ibid., no. 100625.

68 Letter from the Admiralty to the FO, 20 June 1916, ibid., no. 119250.

69 Included as appendix A to 'Report of the Negotiations regarding the Petroleum Policy of H.M. Government, 1918–1919', Petroleum Imperial Policy Committee, FO 368/2255, file 87990, S 347.

70 'Petroleum Supplies and Distribution. Memorandum by Vice-Admiral Sir Edmond Slade' (secret). This was one of three memoranda circulated to the Cabinet by Balfour, then First Lord of the Admiralty (afterwards Foreign Secretary, 1916–19, and then Lord President of the Council 1919–22 and 1925–29). The two supporting

confidential memoranda were entitled 'Observations on the Board of Trade Memorandum on Oil' and 'Strategic Importance of the Control of Petroleum' (Cab. 37/154). See also confidential Cabinet paper by Balfour, 18 Aug 1916 Cab. 37/154.

71 The German majority shareholding in this company had been sequestrated by the British Government a few months previously and vested in the Public Trustee. See *History of the Ministry of Munitions*, VII, p. 136; and Board of Trade memorandum, 'The British Petroleum Company', 7 Feb 1916, FO 382/1096, no. 26185. The British Petroleum Company's associated companies, the Homelight Oil Company and the Petroleum Steamship Company had also been German-controlled. They had all been sequestrated and their shares vested in the Public Trustee. The BP Company was acquired by the APOC in June 1917, and it acquired the other two companies shortly after. See Robert Henriques, *Marcus Samuel*, pp. 518 and 594, note.

72 Memorandum prepared by the Admiralty for the Cabinet, 'Progress of the Negotiations with regard to the Burmah–Shell Amalgamation', circulated by Balfour, 19 Oct 1916, Cab. 37/158.

73 Letters from Llewellyn Smith to the FO, 12 Feb 1917, and from Lancelot Hugh Smith, Board of Trade, to Lord Robert Cecil, KC, (Under-Secretary, FO, 1915–16), 22 Feb 1917, FO 371/2979, nos 34164 and 43051. For Cecil's opinion of Waley Cohen, see his confidential letter to Balfour, 21 Oct 1916, Balfour MSS., vol. 49738.

74 See, for example, *The Financial Times*, 4 and 8 Dec, *The Times*, 5 Dec, and *The Saturday Review*, 15 Dec 1917.

75 'Proposals to form an all-British Oil Company' Petroleum Executive (P.Ex.) file S 60. The file contains a considerable amount of correspondence on this matter.

76 Report of a meeting held at the Petroleum Executive, 21 Dec 1917, ibid.

77 'The Need for a Permanent Petroleum Department. Petroleum Executive Memorandum for the Cabinet', by Walter Long, 27 Feb 1919, FO 368/2255, file 87990, S 347, Appendix H, or Cab. 24/76, GT 6930. Accompanying letter to the Prime Minister, 5 June 1919, Lloyd George MSS., F/33/2/50. See also the *History of the Ministry of Munitions*, VII, p. 147; Cab. 24/6, GT 51; FO 368/1864, nos. 43920 48439 and 244699; FO 370/287, no. L 7970; and FO 370/301, no. L 395. Long's memorandum incorrectly dates the existence of the Petroleum Executive from April; the *History of the Ministry of Munitions* and the PIPCo report (see note 80 below) date it from December 1917. The only other account of it is a brief one in the official civil history of World War II: D. J. Payton-Smith, *Oil. A Study of War-time Policy and Administration*, p. 40.

78 See 'Note on Government Mineral Oil Organisation during the First World War', Appendix VI below. Also, War Cabinet minute no. 5, 24 May 1917, Cab. 23/2; letter and note from the Shipping Controller to the Secretary of the War Cabinet and to the First Lord of the Admiralty, Cab. 24/23, GT 1704; Cabinet memorandum by Long, 'The 'Petroleum Position', 16 Aug, ibid., GT 1756; and Cabinet memorandum from Fourth Sea Lord Tothill, 7 Aug, ibid., GT 1640.

79 'Report of the Negotiations regarding the Petroleum Policy of H.M. Government, 1918–1919', FO 371/2255, file 87900, S 347. See also confidential FO memorandum, 'Oil Interests in which the Anglo-Persian Oil Company are concerned outside the Area Covered by their Persian Concession', 12 Mar 1918, and FO–Petroleum Executive correspondence, FO 368/2041, file 65418.

80 All references to the work of the committee come from its report and proceedings, FO 371/2255, file 87990, S 347 (cited hereafter as the 'PIPCo report'). The committee consisted of four unofficial members, together with representatives of the FO, Admiralty, Board of Trade, Treasury, Ministry of Shipping and Petroleum Executive. Among these were Alwyn Parker (FO), Sir Frederick Black (Admiralty), Lancelot Smith (Board of Trade), B. A. Kemball Cook (Ministry of Shipping), Sir John Cadman (Petroleum Executive), Viscount Inchcape (Treasury), E. G. Pretyman (Admiralty), Sir Harry MacGowan, Sir John Ferguson, Sir Robert Horne and Col. R. S. Williamson. Harcourt had himself been Colonial Secretary from 1910–15.

81 Memorandum by Long, read to the committee at its inaugural meeting, 29 May 1918, PIPCo report, pp. 7–8. See also Table of World Oil Production, 1913–20, and graphs (UK Petroleum Imports, 1900–19, and Sources of UK Petroleum Imports, 1900–19), Appendix VIII below.

82 'Memorandum by the Right Hon. Viscount Harcourt. Presented to the Imperial War Conference, 22nd July, 1918. "Petroleum Position of the British Empire. Measures Suggested to Improve the Position"', FO 368/2255, Appendix C. In October 1918 British policy was defined thus: 'The Policy of the Colonial Office is not to deny to foreigners the owning or developing of property in the Colonies. Our policy is to restrict the exploitation of Crown lands for certain materials which are essential to our national safety to British Corporations. . . .' (War Cabinet memorandum by Long, 'Investment of Foreign Capital in the British Empire', 28 Oct 1918, Cab. 24/68, GT 6141.

83 'Memorandum by Mr C. Greenway on the National Oil Policy', 19 Sep 1918, PIPCo report, appendix G, p. 144.

84 See, especially, details of the meetings of 19 Sep and 4 Oct 1918, PIPCo report.

85 Memorandum by John T. Cargill, 8 Oct 1918, read to the committee the same day (PIPCo report, pp. 136–8). Further detail on Cargill is in Appendix VII below.

CHAPTER 8

1 Brief and somewhat inaccurate discussions occur in Glyn Roberts, *The Most Powerful Man in the World. The Life of Sir Henri Deterding*, pp. 200–1, and E. H. Davenport and S. R. Cooke, *The Oil Trusts and Anglo-American Relations*, pp. 40–3. Henriques includes a handful of documents in *Marcus Samuel* (pp. 625–30), admitting, however, that he does not really understand very much about them. In order to follow these negotiations between the Royal Dutch–Shell and the British Government, the PIPCo minutes and report are essential. Some material is to be found in FO 368/2237, file 3919; FO 368/2255; FO 371/4209; FO 608/227 and 231; Cab. 21/119; and Cab. 24/76, CP 6961.

2 PIPCo report, pp. 17–19.

3 André Tardieu, 'Mossoul et ses Pétroles', in *L'Illustration*, 19 June 1920; Henri Bérenger, *Le Pétrole et la France*; and Pierre L'Espagnol de la Tramerye, *La Lutte Mondiale pour le Pétrole*. See also Nevakivi, *Britain, France, and the Arab Middle East*, p. 90.

4 Stated by Bérenger at the meeting in Paris on 17 Dec 1918 between British and French Government oil representatives on the question of a common oil policy, FO 368/2095, no. 3593, PEx. file S 275, and Lloyd George MSS., F/92/14/3.

5 Described in a private letter from Lord Eustace Percy (member of the British Peace Conference Delegation) to Sir George Clerk, 5 June 1919, FO 368/2095, no. 85781; printed, minus this description, in *Documents on British Foreign Policy*, series 1, IV, no. 686, note 2, and referred to in letter from Lloyd George to Clemenceau, 21 May 1919, FO 368/2095, no. 85781, and Lloyd George MSS., F/33/2/66 (printed in *Documents on British Foreign Policy*, series 1, IV, no. 684 note 2), note by Clemenceau, 10 Oct 1919, enclosed in despatch no. 1931 from Crowe (Paris) to Curzon, 10 Oct 1919, ibid., series 1, IV, no. 314. For the Prime Ministers' personal descriptions of this meeting see D. Lloyd George, *The Truth about the Peace Treaties*, II, p. 1038; and Jean Martet, *Clemenceau*, pp. 189–90. See also Nevakivi, *Britain, France, and the Arab Middle East*, pp. 90–3, and B. C. Busch, *Britain, India, and the Arabs, 1914–1921*, pp. 303–16.

6 Present at the meeting were Sir John Cadman, assisted by Mr Ashdown and Mr J. C. Clarke (Petroleum Executive), and Senator Bérenger, supported by the Marquis de Chasseloup-Laubart and Lt Bénard.

7 Balfour resigned in October 1919, and Curzon thereafter held the post officially until January 1924.

8 See minutes by Curzon and Weakley, 19 and 17 Feb 1919, FO 608/231, no. 2642.

9 FO 368/2095, no. 3251, and Lloyd George MSS., F/92/14/3.

10 See minutes by George Kidston and others, 8 Jan 1919, FO 368/2095, no. 3593.

These views were adopted strongly by Curzon. Record of and minutes on the meeting are in ibid., no. 12790; Lloyd George MSS., F/92/14/3; and summarised in *Documents on British Foreign Policy,* series 1, IV, enclosure to no. 684. The meeting was held the very day after Walter Long became First Lord of the Admiralty.

11 My translation. Letter from Clemenceau to Bérenger, 30 Jan 1919, forwarded to the FO in February by the Petroleum Executive, no date, FO 368/2242, no. 21777, and P. Ex. S 275.

12 Note from the French Ambassador, London, to the FO, 29 Jan 1919, and accompanying FO minutes, FO 368/2095, no. 18150. Also in FO 608/231, no. 2633; Lloyd George MSS., F/92/14/3; and briefly summarised in *Documents on British Foreign Policy,* series 1, IV, enclosure to no. 684.

13 Telegram 115 (urgent) from the FO to Balfour, 4 Feb 1919, FO 368/2095, no. 18150; and note by Weakley of interview with Cadman, 21 Feb, FO 371/4209, no. 29705 (also in Lloyd George MSS., F/92/14/3, and described in *Documents on British Foreign Policy,* series 1, IV, enclosure to no. 684).

14 Details to be found only in Lloyd George MSS., F/92/14/3; mentioned in *Documents on British Foreign Policy,* series 1, IV, enclosure to no. 684.

15 Memorandum initialled by Balfour and Mallet, Paris, 3 Feb 1919, FO 608/231, no. 2642; Lloyd George MSS., F/92/14/3.

16 FO memorandum, 19 Feb 1919 (drafted 12 Feb), enclosed in Tilley to Balfour despatch 754, 20 Feb, FO 368/2095, no. 27792; unminuted versions in FO 608/231, no. 2633, and Lloyd George MSS., F/92/14/3. See also Tilley (for Curzon) to Balfour, despatch 822, 22 Feb, FO 608/231, nos 2896 and 2642, and Lloyd George MSS., F/92/14/3. J. A. C. (later Sir John) Tilley was Chief Clerk, FO, 1913–19, Acting Assistant Under-Secretary, 1919, and Assistant Secretary, 1919–21.

17 See pp. 143–4 above.

18 Letters from Cadman to Mallet (Paris) and to the Under-Secretary, FO, 13 Mar 1919, enclosed in private letter from C. Tufton (FO representative in the Economic Section of the Paris Peace Conference Delegation) to Sir George Clerk, 31 Mar, FO 608/231, nos. 2642 and 6336; see also FO 368/2095, no. 50701, and Lloyd George MSS., F/92/14/3.

19 Mallet (for Balfour) to Curzon, despatch 265, 17 Mar 1919, with minutes, FO 608/231, no. 2896; see also FO 371/4209, no. 42678, and Lloyd George MSS., F/92/14/3; mentioned in *Documents on British Foreign Policy,* series 1, IV, enclosure to no. 684.

20 This view repeated the conclusions of the interdepartmental meeting of 15 Feb 1919 on the future of the Baghdad railway; at this the Admiralty stressed that its main interest was the pipeline and the need for its terminal port or ports to be under British control in time of war, with Haifa being strategically preferable. See memorandum by Hardinge, 26 Feb 1919, 'The Future of the Baghdad Railway', FO 608/231, no. 2633.

21 Letter from Mallet to Cadman, 31 Mar 1919, enclosed in Tufton to Clerk, 31 Mar 1919.

22 Curzon to Balfour, despatch 1837, 2 Apr 1919, FO 608/231, no. 2642. The reply was based on Kidston's minutes of 18 Mar, FO 368/2095, no. 41123.

23 Wilson's views, known since the latter part of 1918, were given publicity at a conference at the India Office on 8 April 1919; FO 368/2095, nos 56571 and 27792. In addition, he wrote India Office paper no. 1518 – 'Mesopotamia. Future of Oil Concession', 13 Mar 1919 – which was circulated by the Admiralty with its own comments; Adm. 116/3248, Peace Conference Naval Section, no. 4385.

24 Minute by Tufton, 9 Apr 1919, on FO 608/231, no. 6336.

25 Private letter from Tufton to Clerk, enclosing revised draft agreement in parallel text, 8 Apr, and accompanying FO minute by Weakley, 12 Apr 1919, FO 368/2095 no. 56571, and Lloyd George MSS., F/92/14/1 and 3. See also Appendix IV below.

26 See, for example, minute by Kidston on draft agreement, 13 Apr 1919, FO 368/2095, no. 56571.

27 FO print (secret), 17th minutes of the Interdepartmental Committee on Eastern Affairs, (IDCE), missing from file, but located in Lloyd George MSS., F/92/14/3; also discussed in *Documents on British Foreign Policy*, series 1, IV, enclosure to no. 684. Present at the conference were Curzon (chairman) and representatives of the FO, Petroleum Executive, IO, War Office, Admiralty and Treasury.

28 Originally initialled on 31 Jan 1919, the final draft of the heads of agreement was initialled by Sir Henri Deterding on 6 Mar and by Lord Harcourt on 7 Mar 1919; it is included in file S 315. Copies are in FO 368/2255 and FO 371/4209, nos. 62702 and 66675. See also letter from Victor Wellesley (for Curzon) to Cambon, 16 May 1919, and Lloyd George MSS., F/92/14/3.

29 Private letter from Lloyd George to Clemenceau, 21 May 1919, FO 368/2095, no. 85781, and Lloyd George MSS., F/33/2/66 and F/51/1/26; also *Documents on British Foreign Policy*, series 1, IV, no. 684, note 2. Descriptions of the quarrel are in Nevakivi, *Britain, France, and the Arab Middle East*, pp. 153–5, and C. E. Callwell, *Field Marshal Sir Henry Wilson. His Life and Diaries*, II, p. 194.

30 Mentioned in private letter from Sir George Clerk to Philip Kerr (Private Secretary to Lloyd George), Paris, 17 June 1919, recording telephone message of 13 June (for Curzon from Lloyd George) to that effect, FO 368/2095, no. 91135, Lloyd George MSS., F/92/14/3, and *Documents on British Foreign Policy*, series 1, IV, no. 684.

31 FO 368/2095, no. 85781; extract printed in *Documents on British Foreign Policy*, series 1, IV, no. 686, note 2.

32 See note 30 above.

33 This memorandum is the enclosure to *Documents on British Foreign Policy*, series 1, IV, no. 684, cited frequently above. Original in FO 368/2095, no. 91135, and Lloyd George MSS., F/92/14/3 and 4.

34 Lloyd George MSS., F/92/14/3.

35 Reported in letter from Davies (10 Downing St) to Curzon, 11/14 July 1919, FO 368/2095, no. 102249; Lloyd George MSS., F/12/1/25; and *Documents on British Foreign Policy*, series 1, IV, no. 689. Davies was also a treasurer of the Lloyd George Fund and a director of the Suez Canal Company.

36 See documents printed in *Documents on British Foreign Policy*, series 1, IV, nos. 685, 687, 688, 692, 693, 695 and 696. The correspondence was with one of the American Peace Conference delegates in Paris, Leyland W. Summers, but Standard Oil interest and activity in Paris and Mesopotamia was (intentionally) making things awkward for the FO and anti-British statements were being made in the US Senate.

37 Letter from Clerk to Kerr (Paris), 4 July, and note from Curzon (signed Wellesley) to the French Ambassador in London, 22 July 1919, FO 368/2095, nos. 94556 and 102249, and *Documents on British Foreign Policy*, series 1, IV, nos 686 and 691.

38 My translation. Pichon's note was enclosed in a note from the French Chargé d'Affaires, London, to Curzon, 12/13 July 1919, FO 368/2095, no. 115404, and *Documents on British Foreign Policy*, series 1, IV, no. 702. Cf. Nevakivi's version of these negotiations: *Britain, France, and the Arab Middle East*, pp. 154–5, 173–4.

39 For a good general account of Anglo-French relations at this time, see ibid., chapters 5–11.

40 FO 371/4233, no. 10930; letter from Curzon to Balfour, 20 Aug 1919, Balfour MSS., LII, no. 49734.

41 'Oil Supplies. Memorandum for the Cabinet by the First Lord of the Admiralty', 4 Nov 1919, with covering letters to Curzon and to Lloyd George, FO 368/2095, no. 149381, and Lloyd George MSS., F/33/2/82.

42 Cab. 24/93, CP 120 (secret). The question of a Baghdad–Haifa railway/pipeline had been under consideration since mid-1918 (FO 371/3409, file 112342).

43 'Proceedings of Meeting held at the War Office on 29 October, 1919, to Discuss Preliminary Arrangements for a Reconnaissance for an Oil Pipeline Across the Arabian Desert', FO 371/4231, no. 148291.

44 *Documents on British Foreign Policy*, series 1, II, no. 55, minute 6 and note p. 727,

and IV p. 111, note 1. A very full account is in the 'Secretary's [Sir Maurice Hankey's] notes of a Conference held at no. 10, Downing St., Thursday Dec. 11, 1919, at 1 p.m.', Cab. 21/203.

45 The memorandum is discussed at length in a memorandum by Weakley, 13 Dec 1919, FO 368/2095, no. 166303, and *Documents on British Foreign Policy*, series 1, IV, no. 703. On Berthelot see Nevakivi, *Britain, France, and the Arab Middle East*, p. 229.

46 See minute by Curzon, 21 Nov 1919, FO 371/4209, no. 153393, and Weakley's memorandum cited in note 45 above.

47 Cab. 24/95; relevant sections of the French note and the British Peace Delegation's comments on it are contained in *Documents on British Foreign Policy*, series 1, IV, nos 398 and 404.

48 Shell files, MEP 102A.

49 The agreement is reprinted in Appendix IV below. Sources are FO 368/2095, no. 166303; FO 371/4241, no. 164667; *Documents on British Foreign Policy*, series 1, IV, no. 1705; and Lloyd George MSS., F/19/2/2 (with a covering letter from Greenwood to the Prime Minister, 23 Dec 1919). See also FO 368/2095, no. 166395.

50 Letter from Cadman to Greenwood, 23 Dec 1919, Lloyd George MSS., F/19/2/2.

51 Cab. 24/95, and *Documents on British Foreign Policy*, series 1, IV, no. 404. The meeting was the third meeting of the Anglo-French conference, and included Berthelot, Fleuriau, Curzon (chairman), and representatives of the FO, War Office, and Treasury.

52 Cab 23/20.

53 Minute by Weakley, 27 Dec 1920, FO 371/5213, no. 15201. Nevakivi is unaware of this Cabinet decision and the ripples emanating from it; see *Britain, France, and the Arab Middle East*, p. 235.

54 Correspondence in Shell files, MEP 22 and MEP 102A.

55 Notes by Cowans, 13 Oct 1919, Shell files, MEP 21.

56 See note 59 below.

57 See correspondence and reports in FO 371/5181, file 443.

58 See especially correspondence in Shell files, MEP 22 and MEP 102A.

59 Present at the ministerial conference (which was in effect a Cabinet meeting) were Lloyd George, A. Bonar-Law (Lord Privy Seal), Churchill (Secretary for War and Air), Montagu, Hardinge, Barstow (Treasury), and Sir S. J. Chapman and H. F. Carlill (both from the Board of Trade). Cowans had blamed Churchill and Lloyd George for the difficulty, and from the details of the conference's conclusions this would appear to be correct: the conclusions represented a victory for the War Office in its long-running quarrel with the FO over military (and quasi-military) exploration for and exploitation of oil, and over similarly organised pipeline surveys, in Mesopotamia. At the same time the FO was having to refuse permission to individuals, companies and, especially, foreign governments who desired facilities for the same things. See, for example, correspondence in FO 371/4209, file 19165, and FO 371/4231, file 102161; also *Documents on British Foreign Policy*, series 1, IV, nos 370 and 693.

60 'Oil Supplies. Memorandum to the Cabinet' by the First Lord of the Admiralty, 18 Mar 1920, CP 903; 'Mesopotamian Oilfields. Memorandum by the President of the Board of Trade', 16 Apr 1920, CP 1085; 'Mesopotamian Oilfields. Memorandum by the Minister in Charge of the Petroleum Department', 22 Apr 1920, CP 1118: Cab. 24/103, pp. 306–7, Cab. 24/104, pp. 71–4, and FO 371/5086, no. 14471.

61 'Notes of a Conversation between the Prime Minister and M. Millerand on Sunday, April 18, 1920, at 9.30 a.m.', *Documents on British Foreign Policy*, series 1, VIII, no. 2.

62 *Memorandum of Agreement between M. Philippe Berthelot, Directeur des Affaires Politiques et Commerciales au Ministère des Affaires Etrangères, and Professor Sir John Cadman,* KCMG, *Director in Charge of His Majesty's Petroleum Department*, 24 Apr 1920, Cmd. 675, Misc. no. 11 (1920); also in FO 371/5085, no. E8622. The text of the Mesopotamian section of this agreement is reproduced below in Appendix IV, parallel to the text of the

Greenwood–Bérenger Agreement, for ease of comparison. It can thus easily be seen that, despite statements in some books to the contrary, the 25 per cent share allocated to France remained unchanged in the later agreement.

63 25 April is the date printed on the original command paper, and, since the notes of the conversation between Lloyd George and Millerand on 24 April show only a desultory discussion of what was still an unseen agreement, and since Curzon telegraphed Sir Auckland Geddes (British Ambassador in Washington) on 30 July that the confirmation had been given on 25 April, it appears clear that the confirmation date of 24 April given in *Documents on British Foreign Policy*, series 1, VIII, p. 145, note 1, is incorrect. For notes of conversation see ibid., series 1, VIII, no. 14. For Curzon's telegram to Geddes (no. 645, 30 July 1920), see FO 371/5085, no. 9124.

64 On these matters see, for example, FO 371/5084–6; FO 371/5181, file 443; FO 371/5212–3; and Cmd 1226, Misc. no. 10 (1921).

65 See documentation in FO 371/5086.

66 See Appendix VII below.

67 On the history of this French oil company the reader should treat with great caution the early chapters of Jean Rondot, *La Compagnie Français des Pétroles*.

APPENDIX I

1 FO 371/344, no. 36290.

2 The spelling of this month has been standardised in both Appendixes I and II.

APPENDIX II

1 This date appears to be a mistake. From the copies of the convention preserved in the FO files (see Appendix I above) and from letters 4 and 10 of this correspondence, the date of the convention seems to have been quite clearly 4/17 July. But this and the later correspondence from this file (discussed on p. 23 above) would not have reached their present company location before 1911 or 1912 at the earliest, and it is not really surprising that when they did so it was in the form of a faulty French translation.

APPENDIX III

1 FO 371/2120, no. 12324.

APPENDIX IV

1 'Memorandum of Agreement between Senator Henry Bérenger, Commissioner-General of Petroleum Products in France, representing the Government of the French Republic, and the Right Honourable Walter H. Long MP, His Majesty's Minister in Charge of Petroleum Affairs', 8 Apr 1919 FO 371/4241, no. 164667, and *Documents on British Foreign Policy*, series 1, IV, pp. 1089–92. Parallel text in FO 368/2095, no. 56511.

2 Memorandum of Agreement between Lt.-Col. Sir Hamar Greenwood, Bart., MP, His Majesty's Minister in Charge of Petroleum Affairs, and Senator Henry Bérenger, Commissioner-General of Petroleum Products in France, representing the Government of the French Republic', 21 Dec 1919, FO 368/2098, no. 166303; and *Documents on British Foreign Policy*, series 1, IV, no. 705.

3 *Memorandum of Agreement between M. Philippe Berthelot, Directeur des Affaires Politiques et Commerciales au Ministère des Affaires Etrangères, and Professor Sir John Cadman* KCMG, *Director in Charge of His Majesty's Petroleum Department*, 24 Apr 1920, Cmd 675, Misc. no. 11 (1920).

4 This amended version is based on the February 1919 draft contained in FO 371/4209, nos. 62702 and 66675, and FO 368/2255, file 87990, and on Petroleum Department file S 315. The subsequent draft agreements, of which the seventh draft was completed in about April 1920, are, of course, much larger.

APPENDIX V

1 FO correspondence on the Turco-Persian frontier rectification of 1913–14 is

contained in FO 331/1431–2, file 52; FO 371/1713–5, file 261 (Persia 1913); and FO 371/2062–3, file 601 (Persia 1914).

2 See map no. 2, Appendix IX.

3 See Chapter 3 and Appendix I.

4 See Chapter 5 above.

5 This effort by the company has not hitherto been known. See minute by Malkin, 16 May, enclosed in Grey to Lowther, despatch, 6 June 1913, FO 371/1713, no. 20331; Lowther to Grey, despatch 546, 19 June, and Grey to Marling, telegram 300R, 4 July, FO 371/1714, nos 28576 and 30556; letter from Greenway, APOC, to the FO, 3 Sep, and accompanying FO minutes, FO 371/1432, no. 37308; letters from Crowe, FO, to Greenway (confidential), 15 Oct, and from Greenway to the FO (confidential), 12 Nov, FO 371/1715, nos. 44672 and 51583.

APPENDIX VI

1 Except where otherwise stated, this account is based on *The History of the Ministry of Munitions*, VII, chapter 10.

2 For detail see correspondence and memoranda in Cab. 24/6, GT 51 (also in Cab. 23/1, no. 80, appendix III, and CP 73605), and FO 368/1864, no. 48439, which also lists membership of the committee.

3 See p. 133 above.

4 See pp. 133–6 above.

5 See Chapter 8 above.

APPENDIX VII

1 Compiled from the annual Registers of Shareholders, Companies Register Office, London, and Walter R. Skinner's *Oil and Petroleum Year Book* (London, annual).

APPENDIX VIII

1 See Henriques, *Marcus Samuel*, pp. 605–10, and *Waley Cohen*, pp. 214–20.

2 *The Petroleum Times*, LIII, 1353 (17 June 1949), p. 435.

3 Cab. paper O.S.C. 4 (secret), 25 Jan 1922, Cab. 27/180. This estimate, drawn up by the APOC, aroused some scepticism in both the Petroleum Dept and the Admiralty as to the accuracy of the figures under headings (2) and (3), Adm. 116/3452. For further detail on this see p. 47 above, and Jack (Kent) in *Past and Present*, 39, *passim* but esp. pp. 165–6.

4 Admiralty annotation: 'tons at £1 per ton'.

5 Admiralty annotation: 'at £3·5'.

Bibliography

I PRIMARY SOURCES

(a) Manuscripts

Public Record Office

Foreign Office records
- Confidential print: FO 424
- Turkey, diplomatic, 1900–20: FO 78 and 371
- Embassy and consular, 1900–14: FO 195
- Persia, diplomatic, 1900–20: FO 60 and 371
- Turkey and general, commercial, 1914–20: FO 368 and 382
- Peace Conference files: FO 608
- Treaty series: FO 372
- Miscellaneous: FO 370

Cabinet records
- Committee of Imperial Defence, 1900–14: Cab. 1, 6, 16, 17, 18, 41
- Cabinet registered files, 1917–20: Cab. 21
- War Cabinet minutes, 1916–19: Cab. 23
- War Cabinet memoranda, 1915–20: Cab. 24
- Cabinet papers, 1912–16: Cab. 37
- War Council etc. papers, 1914–16: Cab. 42

Admiralty records
- Secretary's Department, 1912–14: Adm. 116
- Correspondence, 1912–14; Adm. 1
- Admiralty Board minutes and memoranda, 1912–14: Adm. 167

German Foreign Ministry

Microfilms of material from the German Foreign Ministry: GFM 10, reels 417, 418, 419, 420

India Office

Political and Secret Department memoranda
Political and Secret Department external files
Railways Department correspondence, 1912–14

Ministry of Power

Petroleum Executive and Petroleum Department papers, series S, 1917–20

Oil companies

Shell International Petroleum Company Ltd files (designated 'MEP') and Bataafse Internationale Petroleum Maatschappij NV files, 1900–20

Individual MSS. collections

Asquith, H. H., Earl of Oxford and Asquith	Bodleian Library, Oxford
Balfour, A. J., Earl of Balfour	British Museum
Bertie, Sir F., Vt Bertie of Thame	Public Record Office
Chamberlain, Sir Austen	Birmingham University Library
Graham Green, Sir W.	National Maritime Museum, Greenwich
Grey, Sir E., Vt Grey of Fallodon	Public Record Office
Hardinge, Sir C., Baron Hardinge of Penshurst	Cambridge University Library
Lansdowne, 5th Marquess	Public Record Office
Lloyd George, D., Earl of Dwyfor	Beaverbrook Library, London
Lowther, Sir G.	Public Record Office
Milner, A., Vt Milner	Bodleian Library, Oxford
Nicolson, Sir A., Baron Carnock	Public Record Office
Samuel, Sir, M., Vt Bearsted	The late Robert Henriques
Sykes., Sir M. (microfilm)	St Antony's College, Oxford
Wilson, Sir A. T.	The London Library
Yale, Capt. W. (microfilm)	St Antony's College, Oxford

(b) Printed primary sources

Collected documents

British Documents on the Origins of the War: 1898–1914, ed. G. P. Gooch and H. W. V. Temperley (HMSO, 1926–38), v, vi, x, parts 1 and 2.

Documents on British Foreign Policy, 1919–1939 (HMSO) series 1: ii (1948) and iv (1952), ed. E. L. Woodward and R. Butler; viii (1958) and xiii (1963), ed. R. Butler and J. P. T. Bury.

Die grosse Politik der europäischen Kabinette, 1871–1914, ed. J. Lepsius, *et al.* (Berlin, 1922–7), xxvii, xxviii, xxxi, xxxiii and xxxvii.

Diplomacy in the Near and Middle East. A Documentary Record, Hurewitz, J. C., 2 vols, *1535–1914*, *1914–1956* (Princeton, N. J., 1956).

Papers relating to the Foreign Relations of the United States (U.S. Government Printing Office, Washington, 1936): 1920, ii; 1921, ii.

British Parliamentary Papers

Cd 5635 (1911): *Baghdad Railway no. 1.*

Cd 7419 (1914): *Navy, (Oil Fuel) Agreement with the Anglo-Persian Oil Company (Ltd): Anglo-Persian Oil Company (Acquisition of Capital) Act, 1914.*

Cd 7628 (Misc. no. 13, 1914): *Events leading to the Rupture of Relations with Turkey.*

Cd 8074: *Despatches regarding Operations in the Persian Gulf and Mesopotamia.*

Cmd 53 (1919): *Armistice of Mudros.*

Cmd 675 (Misc. no. 11, 1920): *Memorandum of Agreement between M. Philippe Berthelot, Directeur des Affaires Politiques et Commerciales au Ministère des*

Affaires Étrangères, and Professor Sir John Cadman, KCMG, *Director in charge of his Majesty's Petroleum Department* ('San Remo Oil Agreement').

Cmd 1226 (Misc. no. 10, 1921): *Correspondence between H.M. Government and the U.S. Ambassador regarding Economic Rights in Mandated Territories.*

Cmd 5957 (Misc. no. 3, 1939): *Correspondence between Sir Henry McMahon and the Sharif of Mecca.*

Cmd 5964 (Misc. no. 4, 1939): *Statements made on behalf of His Majesty's Government during the year 1918 in regard to the Future Status of Certain Parts of the Ottoman Empire.*

Cmd 5974 (16 March 1939): *Report of a Committee set up to Consider Certain Correspondence between Sir Henry McMahon and the Sharif of Mecca in 1915 and 1916.*

Other official publications

Great Britain:

Admiralty, *A Handbook of Mesopotamia* (London, 1920).

Foreign Office Historical Section, Handbooks nos. 63 (*Mesopotamia*) and 76 (*The Persian Gulf*).

Imperial Institute and Petroleum Department, *Petroleum* (monographs on mineral resources with special reference to the British Empire) (London, 1921).

Imperial Mineral Resources Bureau, *The Mineral Industry of the British Empire and Foreign Countries*, Statistical Summaries 1913–20, 1920–2, 1921–3, 1922–4, 1923–5 (HMSO, 1921, 1924, 1925, 1926).

Moberly, Brig.-Gen. F. H., *Official History of the Great War. The Campaign in Mesopotamia 1914–1918*, 4 vols (HMSO, 1923–7).

Newbolt, Sir H., and Corbett, Sir J., *Official History of the Great War. Naval Operations* (London, 1920–31), IV and V.

Petroleum Department, *The History of the Ministry of Munitions* (not published, but printed in 1922) VII.

Further material has been obtained from the *Parliamentary Debates*, House of Commons and House of Lords, and biographical material from the Foreign Office, India Office and Navy Lists, and *The Dictionary of National Biography* and *Who Was Who*.

Government of India:

Pascoe, Dr. E. H., 'Geological Notes on Mesopotamia with Special Reference to the Occurrence of Petroleum', *Memoirs of the Geological Survey of India* (Calcutta, 1922), XLVIII.

United States Government:

The International Petroleum Cartel, Report to the US Senate Select Committee on Small Business (Government Printing Office: Washington, 1952).

II SECONDARY SOURCES

(a) Books

Addison, C., *Four and a Half Years. A Personal Diary from June 1914 to January 1919* (London, 1934), I.

Addison, C., *Politics from Within, 1911–1918*, 2 vols (London, 1924).
Ahmad, F., *The Young Turks: the Committee of Union and Progress in Turkish Politics, 1908–1914* (Oxford, 1969).
Amery, L. S., *My Political Life* (London 1953), II.
Anderson, M. S., *The Eastern Question* (London, 1966).
Antonius, G., *The Arab Awakening* (London, 1938).
Arthur, Sir G., *Life of Lord Kitchener* (London, 1920), III.
Ash, B., *The Lost Dictator: Field Marshal Sir Henry Wilson* (London, 1968).
Asquith, H., *Memoirs and Reflections* (London, 1928).
Azami, Z., *Le Pétrole en Perse* (Paris, 1933).
Bacon, Sir R., *Life of Lord Fisher of Kilverstone* (London, 1929).
Baster, A. S. J., *The International Banks* (London, 1935).
Beaverbrook, Lord, *Decline and Fall of Lloyd George* (London, 1963).
Beaverbrook, Lord, *Politicians and the War, 1914–1916*, 2 vols (London, 1928–32).
Beaverbrook, Lord, *Men and Power, 1917–1918* (London, 1956)
Bell, Lady (ed.), *The Letters of Gertrude Bell*, 2 vols (London, 1927).
Bérenger, V. H., *Le Pétrole et la France* (Paris, 1921).
Bérenger, V. H., *La Politique du Pétrole* (Paris, 1920).
Bertie, Lord F., *The Diary of Lord Bertie of Thame* ed. Lady Algernon Gordon Lennox (London, 1924).
Birkenhead, Lord F. E., *Contemporary Personalities* (London, 1924).
Blaisdell, D. C., *European Financial Control of the Ottoman Empire* (New York, 1929).
Borchard, E., and Wynne, W. H., *State Insolvency and Foreign Bondholders* (New Haven, 1951).
Brodie, B., 'Foreign Oil and American Security', mimeographed pamphlet by Yale Institute of International Studies (New Haven, 1947).
Brooks, M., *Oil and Foreign Policy* (London, 1949).
Buchanan, Sir G. C., *The Tragedy of Mesopotamia* (Edinburgh, 1938).
Buchanan, Sir G. W., *My Mission to Russia and Other Diplomatic Memories*, 2 vols, (London, 1923).
Bullard, Sir R., *The Middle East: a Political and Economic Survey*, 3rd ed., RIIA (London, 1958).
Bullard, Sir R., *Britain and the Middle East: from the Earliest Times to 1950* (London, 1951).
Burgoyne, E., *Gertrude Bell: from her Personal Papers, 1914–1926* (London, 1961).
Busch, B., *Britain and the Persian Gulf, 1895–1914* (Berkeley, 1967).
Busch, B., *Britain, India, and the Arabs, 1914–1921* (Berkeley, 1971).
Callwell, C. E., *Field Marshal Sir Henry Wilson. His Life and Diaries* (London, 1927), II.
Cambon, P., *Correspondence 1870–1924* (Paris, 1946), III.
Chapman, M. K., 'Great Britain and the Baghdad Railway 1888–1914', *Smith College Studies in History*, XXXI (Northampton, Mass., 1948).
Churchill, R., *Winston S. Churchill*, II (London, 1967).
Churchill, Sir W. S., *The World Crisis*, 6 vols (London, 1925–9).
Corrigan, H. S. W., 'British, French and German Interests in Asiatic Turkey 1881–1914', unpublished Ph.D. thesis (University of London, 1966).

Cumming, H. H., *Franco-British Rivalry in the Post-War Near East* (London, 1938).

Davenport, E. H., and Cooke, S. R., *The Oil Trusts and Anglo-American Relations* (London, 1923).

De Novo, J. A., *American Interests and Policies in the Middle East, 1900–1939* (Minneapolis, 1963).

Djemal Pasha, A., *Memoirs of a Turkish Statesman, 1913–1919* (New York, 1922).

Ducruet, J., *Les Capitaux Européens au Proche Orient* (Paris, 1964).

Dugdale, B. *Arthur James Balfour* (London, 1936) II.

Earle, E. M., *Turkey, the Great Powers and the Baghdad Railway* (New York), 1923).

Edmonds, C. J., *Kurds, Turks and Arabs* (London, 1957).

Ellis, C. H., *The Transcaspian Episode, 1918–19* (London, 1963).

Emin, A., *Turkey in the World War* (New Haven, Oxford, 1930).

Evans, L., *U.S. Policy and the Partition of Turkey, 1914–1924* (Baltimore, 1965).

Evans, R. A., *Brief Outline of the Campaign in Mesopotamia* (London, 1926).

Feis, H., *Europe the World's Banker, 1870–1914* (New Haven, 1930).

Feis, H., *The Diplomacy of the Dollar* (New York, 1950).

Fisher, Admiral J. (Lord Fisher of Kilverstone), *Oil and the Oil Engine* (London, 1919); also in *Records* (London, 1919).

Frank, H. J., *Crude Oil Prices in the Middle East. A Study in Oligopolistic Price Behaviour* (New York, 1966).

Frischwasser-Ra'an, F. H., *Frontiers of a Nation* (London, 1955).

Frye, R. N., *The Near East and the Great Powers* (Cambridge, Mass., 1951).

Frye, R. N., *Iran* (New York, 1953).

Garnett, L. *Turkey of the Ottomans* (London, 1911).

Gerig, B., *The Open Door and the Mandates System* (London, 1930).

Gerretson, F. C., *History of the Royal Dutch*, 2nd ed., 4 vols (Leiden, 1958).

Gibb, G. S., and Knowton, E. H., *The Resurgent Years. The History of the Standard Oil Company (New Jersey), 1911–1927* (New York, 1956).

Gilbert, M., *Winston S. Churchill*, III: 1914–16 (London, 1971).

Gooch, G. P., *Before the War: Studies in Diplomacy*, 2 vols (London, 1938).

Gordon, L. J., *American Relations with Turkey 1830–1930* (Philadelphia, 1932).

Gosses, F., *The Management of British Foreign Policy before the First World War, 1880–1914* (Leiden, 1948).

Gottlieb, W. W., *Studies in Secret Diplomacy during the First World War* (London 1956).

Graves, P., *The Life of Sir Percy Cox* (London, 1941).

Graves, P., *The Question of the Straits* (London, 1931).

Greaves, R. L., *Persia and the Defence of India, 1884–1892* (London, 1959).

Grey of Fallodon, Viscount, *Twenty-Five Years, 1892–1916*, 2 vols (London, 1925).

Guinn, P., *British Strategy and Politics, 1914–1918* (London, 1965).

Hamilton, C. W., *Americans and Oil in the Middle East* (Texas, 1962).

Hankey, Lord M., *The Supreme Command: 1914–1918,* 2 vols (London, 1961).

Hankey, Lord M., *The Supreme Control at the Paris Peace Conference 1919* (London, 1963).

Hankey, Lord M., *Government Control in War* (Cambridge, 1945).

Hartshorn, J. E., *Oil Companies and Governments*, 2nd revised ed. (London, 1967).

Hauser, H., *Germany's Commercial Grip on the World*, trs. M. Emanuel (London, 1918).

Henriques, R., *Marcus Samuel, First Viscount Bearsted and Founder of the 'Shell' Transport and Trading Company, 1853–1927* (London, 1960).

Henriques, R., *Sir Robert Waley Cohen, 1877–1952* (London, 1966).

Hershlag, Z. Y., *Introduction to the Modern Economic History of the Middle East* (Leiden, 1964).

Hewins, R., *Mr Five per cent* (London, 1957).

Hidy, R. W. and M. E., *Pioneering in Big Business. The History of the Standard Oil Company (New Jersey), 1882–1911* (New York, 1955).

Hoffman, R. J. S., *Great Britain and the German Trade Rivalry, 1875–1914* (Philadelphia, 1933).

Hoskins, H. L., *British Routes to India* (London, 1928).

Hoskins, H. L., *The Middle East: Problem Area* (London, 1954).

Hough, R., *First Sea Lord. An Authorised Biography of Admiral Lord Fisher* (London, 1969).

Howard, H. N., *The Partition of Turkey* (Oklahoma, 1931).

Hurewitz, J. C., *Middle East Dilemmas: the Background to U.S. Policy* (New York, 1953).

Ise, J., *The United States Oil Policy* (New Haven, 1926).

Issawi, C., and Yeganeh, M., *The Economics of Middle East Oil* (London, 1963).

Jellicoe, Lord J. R., *The Crisis of the Naval War* (London, 1920).

Jellicoe, Lord J. R., *The Submarine Peril. The Admiralty Policy in 1917* (London, 1934).

Jenkins, R., *Asquith* (London, 1964).

Johnson, F. A., *Defence by Committee: the British Committee of Imperial Defence, 1855–1959* (London, 1960).

Kazemzadeh, F., *The Struggle for Transcaucasia, 1917–1921* (Oxford, 1951).

Kazemzadeh, F., *Russia and Britain in Persia, 1864–1914: a Study in Imperialism* (New Haven, 1968).

Kedourie, E., *England and the Middle East. The Destruction of the Ottoman Empire 1914–1921* (London, 1956).

Knaplund, P. (ed.), *Speeches on Foreign Affairs, 1904–1914, by Sir Edward Grey* (London, 1931).

Kuisel, R. F., *Ernest Mercier, French Technocrat* (Berkeley, 1967).

Larcher, Commandant M., *La Guerre Turque dans la Guerre Mondiale* (Paris, 1926).

Lee, D. C., *The Mandate for Mesopotamia and the Principle of Trusteeship in English Law* (London, 1921).

Leeman, W. A., *The Price of Middle East Oil: An Essay in Political Economy* (New York and London, 1961).

Lenczowski, G., *Oil and State in the Middle East. Russia and the West in Iran* (New York, 1949).

Leslie, S., *Mark Sykes: his Life and Letters* (London, 1923).

Lewis, B., *The Emergence of Modern Turkey* (London, 1961).

Lewis, B., *The Middle East and the West* (London, 1964).

Lichnowsky, Prince K. M. von, *Heading for the Abyss. Reminiscences* (London, 1928).

Lichnowsky, Prince K. M. von, *My Mission to London, 1912–1914* (London, 1918).

Lloyd George, D., *The Truth about the Peace Treaties*, 2 vols (London, 1938).

Loder, J. de V., *The Truth about Mesopotamia, Palestine, and Syria* (London, 1923).

Longhurst, H., *Adventure in Oil. The Story of British Petroleum* (London, 1959).

Longrigg, S. H., *Oil in the Middle East: its Discovery and Development*, 3rd ed. RIIA (London, 1968).

Longrigg, S. H., *Iraq, 1900–1950* (London, 1953).

Ludendorff, F. W. E., *My War Memories, 1914–1918*, 2 vols (London, 1919).

Magnus, P., *Kitchener, Portrait of an Imperialist* (London, 1958).

Marder, A. J., *From the Dreadnought to Scapa Flow: the Royal Navy in the Fisher Era, 1904–1919*, 5 vols (London, 1961–70).

Marder, A. J. (ed.), *Fear God and Dread Nought. Correspondence of Lord Fisher* (London, 1956), II.

Marlowe, J., *Late Victorian. The Life of Sir Arnold Talbot Wilson* (London, 1967).

Marlowe, J., *The Persian Gulf in the Twentieth Century* (London, 1962).

Martet, J., *Clemenceau*, trs. M. Waldman, (London, 1930).

Mears, E. G. (ed.), *Modern Turkey* (New York, 1924).

Medlicott, W. N., *Contemporary England* (London, 1967).

Meinertzhagen, R. M., *Middle East Diary: 1917–1956* (London, 1959).

Middlemass, R. K., *The Master Builders* (London, 1963).

Mikdashi, Z., *A Financial Analysis of Middle Eastern Oil Concessions: 1901–65* (New York, 1966).

Miller, D. H., *My Diary at the Paris Peace Conference, 1918–1919* (New York, 1924).

Mineau, W., *The Go-Devils* (London, 1958).

Mohr, A., *The Oil War* (London, 1926).

Monger, G., *The End of Isolation, British Foreign Policy, 1900–1907* (London, 1963).

Monroe, E., *Britain's Moment in the Middle East, 1914–1956* (London, 1963).

Mukhtar, Pasha, *La Turquie, l'Allemagne, et l'Europe* (Paris, 1924).

Nevakivi, J., *Britain, France, and the Arab Middle East 1914–1920* (London, 1969).

Nicolson, H., *Peacemaking, 1919* (London, 1933).

Nicolson, H., *Curzon: The Last Phase* (London, 1934).

Patterson, A. Temple, *Jellicoe, a Biography* (London, 1969).

Payton-Smith, D. J., *Oil. A Study of War-time Policy and Administration*, (HMSO, 1971).

Pears, Sir E., *Forty Years in Constantinople 1873–1915* (London, 1916).

Penrose, E. T., *The Large International Firm in Developing Countries. The International Petroleum Industry* (London, 1968).

Pichon, J. M., *Le Partage du Proche-Orient* (Paris, 1938).

Platt, D. C. M., *Finance, Trade and Politics. British Foreign Policy 1815–1914* Oxford, 1968).

Reisser, J., *The German Great Banks and their Concentration in Connection with the*

Economic Development of Germany (Government Printing Office: Washington, 1911).
Roberts G., *The Most Powerful Man in the World. The Life of Sir Henri Deterding* (New York, 1938).
Rohrbach, P., *Die Bagdadbahn* (Berlin, 1902).
Rohrbach, P., *German World Policies*, trs. Dr E. von Mach (New York, 1915).
Rohrbach, P., *Germany's Isolation*, trs. Dr P. H. Phillipson (Chicago, 1915).
Ronaldshay, Lord, *Life of Lord Curzon* (London, 1928), III.
Rondot, J., *La Compagnie Française des Pétroles du Franc-Or au Pétrole-Franc* (Paris, 1962).
Rowland, J., and Cadman, B. (Second Baron), *Ambassador for Oil. The Life of John, First Baron Cadman* (London, 1960).
Ryan, Sir A., *The last of the Dragomans* (London, 1951).
Salter, J. A., *Allied Shipping Control: an Experiment in International Administration* (*Economic and Social History of the World War*, British Series) (Oxford, 1921).
Sanders, L. von, *Five Years in Turkey* (translation) (London, 1927).
Sazonov, S., *Fateful Years. 1909–1916* (London, 1928).
Scott, J. B., *Official Statements of War Aims and Peace Proposals, December 1916–November 1918* (Washington, 1921).
Seton, Sir M., *The India Office* (London, 1926).
Seymour, C. (ed.), *Intimate Papers of E. M. House*, 2 vols (London, 1926).
Shotwell, J. T. and Deak, F., *Turkey at the Straits, a Short History* (New York, 1940).
Shwadran, B., *The Middle East, Oil and the Great Powers*, 3rd ed. (New York, 1973).
Singh, S. N., *The Secretary of State for India and his Council, 1858–1919* (Delhi, 1962).
Sousa, N., *The Capitulatory Régime of Turkey* (Baltimore, 1933).
Spender, J. A., *Men and Things*, 2nd ed. (London, 1937).
Spender, J. A., *Weetman Pearson, First Viscount Cowdray, 1856–1927* (London, 1930).
Spender, J. A., and Asquith, C., *Life of Herbert Henry Asquith, Lord Oxford and Asquith* (London, 1932).
Sprout, H. and M., *Towards a New Order of Sea Power: American Naval Policy and the World Scene, 1918–1922* (Princeton, N.J., 1940).
Stein, L., *The Balfour Declaration* (London, 1961).
Steiner, Zara, S., *The Foreign Office and Foreign Policy, 1898–1914* (London, 1969).
Storrs, Sir R., *Orientations* (London, 1937).
Sykes, C., *Two Studies in Virtue* (London, 1954).
Sykes, C., *Wassmuss, the German Lawrence* (London, 1936).
Temperley, H. W. V., *A History of the Peace Conference of Paris*, 6 vols (London, 1920–4).
Toynbee, Sir A., *Acquaintances* (London, 1967).
Tramerye, P. L'E. de la, *La Lutte Mondiale pour le Pétrole* (Paris, 1921), translated as *The World Struggle for Oil*, 3rd ed. (London, 1923).
Trevelyan, G. M., *Grey of Fallodon: Being the Life of Sir Edward Grey, afterwards Viscount Grey of Fallodon* (London, 1937).

Trumpener, U., *Germany and the Ottoman Empire, 1914–1918* (Princeton, N.J., 1968).

Ward, Sir A. W., and Gooch, G. P. (eds.), *The Cambridge History of British Foreign Policy, 1783–1919* (Cambridge, 1923), III.

Waugh, Sir T., *Turkey Yesterday, Today and Tomorrow* (London, 1930).

Williamson, H. E., *et al.*, *The American Petroleum Industry: the Age of Energy 1899–1959*, 2 vols (Evanston, 1963).

Wilson, Sir A. T., *Loyalties: Mesopotamia, 1914–1917* (London, 1930).

Wilson, Sir A. T., *Mesopotamia 1917–1920: a Clash of Loyalties* (London, 1931).

Wilson, Sir A. T., *South West Persia. A Political Officer's Diary, 1907–1914* (London, 1941).

Wilson, Sir A. T., *The Persian Gulf* (London, 1928).

Wolf, J. B., 'The Diplomatic History of the Baghdad Railway', *University of Missouri Studies*, XI (1 Apr. 1936).

Wolff, Sir H. D., *Rambling Reflections* (London, 1908), II.

Young, Sir H., *The Independent Arab* (London, 1933).

Young, K., *Arthur James Balfour* (London, 1963).

Zeine, Z. N., *The Struggle for Arab Independence 1914–1920* (Beirut, 1960).

(b) Articles, pamphlets and essays

Acworth, B., 'Oil and Policy', in *The English Review*, LVI (Feb 1933), pp. 119–28.

Barrère, C., 'La Conférence de San Remo', in *Revue des Deux Mondes*, CVIII (Aug 1938), p. 150.

Buell, R. L., 'Oil Interests in the Fight for Mosul', in *Current History*, XVIII (1923).

Cadman, J., 'Great Britain and Petroleum', *American Petroleum Institute Bulletin*, no. 20 (21 Dec 1921).

Cadman, J., 'The World's Unexpected Resources', in *The Petroleum Times*, VIII (30 Dec 1922), pp. 953–4.

Carter, J., 'The Bitter Conflict over Turkish Oilfields', in *Current History*, XXXIII (Jan 1926).

Challener, R. D., 'The French Foreign Office: the Era of Philippe Berthelot', in *The Diplomats, 1919–1939*, ed. G. A. Craig and F. Gilbert (Princeton, N.J., 1953).

Chase, A. J., and Thorpe, W. A. C., 'Oil Fuel Trials on the North-Western Railway of India, 1913–1916'; *Railways Department Technical Paper no. 193* (unofficial) (Simla, 12 May 1918).

Corrigan, H. S. W., 'German-Turkish Relations and the Outbreak of War in 1914: a Reassessment', *Past and Present*, 36 (1967), pp. 144–52.

Craig, G. A., 'The British Foreign Office from Grey to Austen Chamberlain', in *The Diplomats, 1919–1939*, ed. G. A. Craig and F. Gilbert (Princeton, N.J., 1953).

Cunningham, A., 'The Wrong Horse? A study of Anglo-Turkish Relations before the First World War, *St Antony's Papers no. 17*, Middle East Affairs no. 4 (London, 1965).

Dennis, A., 'The United States and the New Turkey', in *The North American Review*, CCXVII (June 1923), pp. 721–31.

De Novo, J. A., 'The Movement for an Aggressive American Oil Policy Abroad, 1918–1920', in *American Historical Review*, LXI (1955–6).

Duce, J., 'The History of Oil Concessions in the Middle East, in *Bulletin of the Near East Society*, VI, 7 (Sep 1953).

Earle, E. M., 'The Secret Anglo-German Convention of 1914 regarding Asiatic Turkey', in *Political Science Quarterly*, XXXVIII (Jan 1923), pp. 24–44.

Earle, E. M., 'The Turkish Petroleum Company – a Study in Oleaginous Diplomacy', in *Political Science Quarterly*, XXXIX (June 1924), pp. 265–79.

Feis, H., 'Petroleum and American Foreign Policy', *Commodity Policy Studies*, pamphlet no. 3 (Food Research Institute of Stanford University, California: March 1944).

'Fifty Years of British Oil Development', in *The Petroleum Times*, LIII, 1353 (17 June, 1949).

Jack, M., (now Kent), 'The Purchase of the British Government's Shares in the British Petroleum Company, 1912–1914', in *Past and Present*, 39 (Apr 1968).

Kazemzadeh, F., 'Russia and the Middle East', in *Russian Foreign Policy*, ed. Lederer (New Haven, 1962).

Kedourie, E., 'Cairo and Khartoum on the Arab Question, 1915–18', in *The Historical Journal*, VII, 2 (1964), pp. 280–97.

Kelly, J. B., 'The Legal and Historical Basis of the British Position in the Persian Gulf', in *St Antony's Papers no. 4*, Middle East Affairs no. 1 (OUP: London, 1958).

Kent, (see also under 'Jack'), 'Agent of Empire? The National Bank of Turkey and British Foreign Policy', in *The Historical Journal*, XVIII, 2 1975.

King, J. E., 'The New Broad Arrow: Origins of British Oil Policy', in *Mariners' Mirror*, XXXIX (1953).

Kurat, Y. T., 'How Turkey Drifted into World War I', in *Studies in International History (Essays Presented to W. N. Medlicott)*, ed. K. Bourne and D. C. Watt (London, 1967).

Laves, W. H. C., 'German Governmental Influence on Foreign Investments, 1871–1915, in *Political Science Quarterly* (Dec 1928).

Lewis, B., 'Some Reflections on the Decline of the Ottoman Empire', in *Studia Islamica* IX (1958), pp. 111–27.

Manning, V. H., 'International Aspects of the Petroleum Industry', in *Mining and Metallurgy*, Feb 1920, pp. 1–10.

Martin, L., 'The Chester Concession', in *Annals of the American Academy of Political and Social Science*, CXII (Mar 1924), pp. 186–8.

Maunsell, F., 'The Mesopotamian Petroleum Field', in *Geographical Journal*, IX (1897), pp. 523–32.

Minorsky, V. F., *The Mosul Question*, Bulletins 9 and 10 of the Reference Service on International Affairs of the American Library in Paris (15 Apr 1926).

Monroe, E., 'British Interests in the Middle East', in *The Middle East Journal*, II (Apr 1948), pp. 129–46.

Murray, J. A., 'Foreign Policy Debated: Sir Edward Grey and his Critics, 1911–1912', in *Power, Public Opinion and Diplomacy: Essays in Honour of Eber Malcolm Carroll by his Former Students*, ed. L. P. Wallace and W. P. Askew (Durham, N.C., 1959).

Nevakivi, J., 'Lord Kitchener and the Partition of the Ottoman Empire 1915–1916', in *Studies in International History (Essays Presented to W. N. Medlicott)*, ed. K. Bourne and D. C. Watt (London, 1967).

Ormsby-Gore, W., 'Great Britain, Mesopotamia, and the Arabs', in *Nineteenth Century and After* (Aug 1920).

'Our special correspondent', 'The Mesopotamian Oilfields', in *Oil Engineering and Finance*, (17 Feb, 1923).

Parker, A., 'The Baghdad Railway Negotiations', *Quarterly Review* (Oct 1917).

Pingaud, A., 'Partage de l'Asie Mineure pendant la Grande Guerre, 1914–1917. Étude de Diplomatie Secrète', in *Revue d'Histoire de la Guerre Mondiale*, (Apr 1939).

Platt, D. C. M., 'Economic Factors in British Policy during the "New Imperialism,"' in *Past and Present*, 39 (Apr 1968).

'Review of Middle East Oil', in *The Petroleum Times* (June 1948).

Rothwell, V. H., 'Mesopotamia in British War Aims 1914–1918', in *The Historical Journal*, XIII, 2 (1970).

Smith, C. Jay, Jr, 'Great Britain and the 1914–1915 Straits Agreement with Russia', in *American Historical Review*, LXX (1965), pp. 1015–34.

Staley, E., 'Business and Politics in the Persian Gulf: the Story of the Wonckhaus Firm', in *Political Science Quarterly*, XLVIII (1933), pp. 367–85.

Sumner, B. H., 'Tsardom and Imperialism in the Middle and Far East, 1880–1914', in *Proceedings of the British Academy*, 27 (1940), pp. 3–43.

Tardieu, A., 'Mossoul et ses Pétroles', in *L'Illustration* (19 June 1920), p. 380.

Temperley, H. W. V., 'British Policy towards Parliamentary Rule and Constitutionalism in Turkey, 1830–1914', in *Cambridge Historical Journal*, IV (1932–34), pp. 156–91.

Temperley, H. W. V., 'British Secret Diplomacy from Canning to Grey', in *Cambridge Historical Journal*, VI, 1 (1938), pp. 1–32.

Trumpener, U., 'Liman von Sanders and the German–Ottoman Alliance', in *Journal of Contemporary History*, I, 4 (Oct 1966), pp. 179–92.

Woodhouse, H., 'American Oil Claims in Turkey', in *Current History*, XV (Mar 1922).

Index

Index